D0939837

Trademark Acknowledgements

Credits

Authors
Andrew Krowczyk
Vinod Kumar
Nauman Laghari
Ajit Mungale
Christian Nagel
Tim Parker
Srinivasa Sivakumar

Technical Reviewers
Natalia Bortniker
Cristian Darie
Slavomir Furman
Shawn Garrington
Thomas Restrepo
Morgan Skinner
Helmut Watson

Managing Editor
Louay Fatoohi

Commissioning Editor
Julian Skinner

Technical Editors
Richard Deeson
Mike Foster
Douglas Paterson
Julian Skinner

Project Manager
Charlotte Smith

Production Coordinator
Sarah Hall

Cover
Natalie O' Donnell

Indexer
Andrew Criddle

Proofreader
Keith Westmoreland

About the Authors

Andrew Krowczyk

Andrew Krowczyk is a software development consultant working in the Chicago area. He's currently spending most of his time deep in the trenches of .NET development. A hardcore fan of Web Services, Andrew spends much time writing and reviewing .NET books and articles for Wrox Press. Andrew is also an Adjunct Faculty member in the Elmhurst College (Elmhurst, IL) Computer Science department where he teaches night courses.

In his spare time (if there is such a thing), Andrew likes to spend time with his wife Eleanore and their dog Louie. He also enjoys working on his 1967 Mustang.

Andrew can be contacted at Krowczyk@i-netway.com.

Vinod Kumar

Vinod Kumar is an author, developer and technical reviewer. He specializes in web and mobile technologies using Microsoft solutions. He currently works at Chennai, India for Emerald Software Ltd. He is a lead author for the forthcoming book titled as "Mobile Application development with .NET" and has written many technical articles for such sites as ASPToday.com, and CSharpToday.com. He also runs a community site named http://www.dotnetforce.com, which is the first Indian site to provide resources on Mobile.NET. In his free time he likes to take a quiet stroll near the beach with his friends. Vinod can be reached at vinod@dotnetforce.com.

I would like to dedicate my contribution to this book to Shiridi Sathya Sai Baba, for he has always bestowed his blessings on me in every venture that I have taken up.

I would also like to thank Wrox Press for giving me an opportunity to write and especially Charlotte and Julian, who have made it possible for me. I also need to say a special thanks to Charlotte for her continuing support and patience with me from day one of my contributions to ASPToday.com.

Nauman Laghari

Nauman Laghari is a software team leader at Creative Chaos (pvt) Limited in Karachi, Pakistan. He is a veteran C/C++ programmer who has worked on some cutting edge technology projects like implementing a real time trading system connected to Electronic Crossing Networks (ECN) using the Financial Information eXchange (FIX) protocol for a Wall Street Brokerage. When he's not designing system architecture or juggling project deadlines Nauman likes to write white papers and articles on emerging trends especially using the Microsoft platform. Nauman is an avid reader and likes to keep himself fit by playing cricket.

Ajit Mungale

Ajit Mungale has been a Senior Software Developer with IBM GSI for the last 3 years. In his 6 years of experience he has worked with various technologies. He started his career in CPLD and FPGA programming along with device drivers. He has worked on almost all Microsoft languages and technologies. Other than that he also has experience in IBM products. He specializes in COM/DCOM/MTS using ATL/VB and expertise in VB, ASP, C++, XML, IBM MQ Series and the .NET Framework. His recent achievement is the submission of a patent while working on a project related to encryption and web security.

Other than computers he enjoys nature and has a collection of several cacti, bonsai, and other plants. He can be reached at ajit_mungale@hotmail.com.

I would like to dedicate this book to my parents who have been a source of inspiration for me. Special thanks go to the Nazar family for motivating me all the time and Julian for his support throughout this project.

Christian Nagel

Christian Nagel is working as a trainer and consultant for Global Knowledge, the largest independent information technology-training provider. Christian started his computing career with PDP 11 and VAX/VMS platforms, covering a variety of languages and platforms. Since July 2000 he has been working with .NET and C# since it was officially announced for the first time. With his profound knowledge of Microsoft technologies – he is certified as a Microsoft Certified Trainer (MCT), Solution Developer (MCSD), and Systems Engineer (MCSE) – he enjoys teaching others programming and architecting distributed solutions. Besides being a book author, developer, trainer, and consultant, he has some more roles in the IT business. He founded the .NET User Group Austria, is a MSDN Regional Director, speaker at international conferences, and leader of INTEA Europe (International .NET User Group Association). You'll find Christian's web site at http://christian.nagel.net.

I would like to thank Eileen Crain, Stacey Giard, and Eric Ewing for their support at Microsoft, and Christian Seidler for his role at Global Knowledge. My special thanks go to my wife Elisabeth for her love and support.

Tim Parker

Dr. Tim Parker has been a programmer, writer, and trainer for 25 years. He's written over 60 books and 3,500 magazine articles. He has worked on the Web since it's inception, and designed hundreds of web sites. In his spare time he dives, flies a plane, and manages a temperamental network of 30 machines in his home in Ottawa, Canada.

For Margaret Francis, a great friend and supporter, with thanks.

Srinivasa Sivakumar

Srinivasa Sivakumar is a software consultant, developer, and writer. He specializes in web and mobile technologies using Microsoft solutions. He currently works at Chicago for TransTech, LLC. He has co-authored Professional ASP.NET Web Services, Professional ASP.NET Web Services with VB.NET, ASP.NET Mobile Controls – Tutorial Guide, Early Adopter .NET Compact Framework, Beginning ASP.NET 1.0 with VB.NET, Visual Basic .NET Threading Handbook, Beginning ASP.NET 1.0 with C#.NET, Professional ASP.NET Security, and written technical articles for ASPToday.com, CSharpToday.com, .NET Developer, etc. In his free time he likes to watch Tamil movies and listen to Tamil sound tracks (especially those sung by Mr S.P. Balasubramaniyam).

Table of Contents

Table of Contents

Table of Contents

Table of Contents

Introduction

Network programming is one of the core tasks of enterprise-level development – the need for disparate computers to communicate efficiently and securely, whether within the same building, or across the world, remains fundamental to the success of many systems. With the .NET Framework comes a new set of classes for tackling networking tasks.

After reading this book, you will be a confident .NET network programmer, and understand the underlying protocols. The current set of protocols supported by .NET classes is limited to the transport-level protocols TCP and UDP, and the application-level protocols HTTP and SMTP. In this book, we provide not only full coverage of these classes, but also examples of implementing application-level protocols in .NET – thus this book will be vital reading for anyone who needs to use a protocol that isn't currently supported by .NET, as well as for anyone who wants to get-to-grips with the predefined protocols.

What Does This Book Cover?

We begin with an introduction to some of the basic concepts and protocols of networking in Chapter 1. Whatever your requirements from network programming – if you plan to develop server applications running as Windows Services offering data for clients using a custom protocol, if you want to write client applications that request data from web servers, or if you want to create multicasting applications, or applications using mailing functionality, this chapter is your first port of call. We begin with a look at the physical network, and the hardware used in local area networks Then, we look at such things as the OSI seven-layer model, and how the TCP/IP protocol suite fits into the OSI layers. After that we learn about the various network, Internet, and e-mail protocols.

Chapter 2 provides our background for working with streams – a stream is an abstract representation of a serial device for storing and retrieving data one byte at a time – the underlying device can be a file, a printer, or a network socket for example. Through this abstraction, different devices can be accessed with the same process, and similar code can be used to read data from a file input stream as can be used to read data from a network input stream for example. In this way, the programmer's need to worry about the actual physical mechanism of the device is removed. In this chapter we take a look at streams in .NET – the `Stream` class, and work with the concrete `FileStream` class. We also cover reading to and writing from binary and text files, and serializing objects into XML and binary format.

Chapter 3 sees us start getting to grips with network programming in .NET with classes from the `System.Net` namespace. We begin with a discussion of these classes – they play a fundamental role in all the remaining chapters of the book. Specifically, we'll see how to work with URIs, IP addresses, and DNS lookups. We see how to handle requests and responses through the `WebRequest` and `WebResponse` classes, and begin looking at authentication, authorization, and the permissions relevant to network programming.

Chapter 4 is about socket programming, and we cover the low-level programming for performing network-related tasks. A socket is one end of a two-way communication link between two programs running on a network. We'll look at the Socket support in .NET – the `System.Net.Sockets.Socket` class, and create both synchronous and asynchronous client-server applications.

In Chapter 5, we begin our tour of the higher-level network classes in the .NET Framework, beginning with those for dealing with the Transmission Control Protocol (TCP). We start with a general introduction to TCP, and its architecture and data structures, before moving on to explore the `TcpClient` and `TcpListener` classes for working with TCP. We build client-server applications built with the `TcpClient` and `TcpListener` classes, we build a fully functional e-mail client to demonstrate the power of `TcpClient`, and also create a multithreaded echo server with the support of the .NET multithreading classes. We end the chapter with a quick look at the .NET Remoting Framework, and particularly the `TcpChannel` transport channel provided with the .NET Framework.

Chapter 6 is about the `UdpClient` class, through which we implement the User Datagram Protocol (UDP). We look at the basics of the UDP protocol, and then see how to use the `UdpClient` class. While TCP is a more reliable protocol than UDP, it also adds a lot of overhead. Accordingly, UDP is faster, and is well suited for multi-media transmissions such as video streams, where the precise order that packets arrive in may not be critical. In the chapter, we also take a look at higher-level UDP-based protocols.

Chapter 7 is about multicasting. This is the technology that made possible the transmission of a live Rolling Stones concert in 1994 over the Internet, and allows us to watch astronauts in space, or to hold meetings over the Internet, among others. With multicasting, a server only has to send messages once, and they will be distributed to a whole group of clients. We begin the chapter by comparing unicasts, broadcasts, and multicasts, and look at the architecture of multicasting, and how to implement multicast sockets in .NET. We create two Windows applications using multicasting features – one application makes it possible to chat with multiple systems, where everyone is both a sender and a receiver. The second application – in the form of a picture show – demonstrates how large data packets can be sent to multiple clients without using a large percentage of the network bandwidth.

Chapter 8 covers the HTTP protocol, and its robust implementation exposed by .NET. The HTTP protocol's importance as an application protocol is significant, since a large share of web traffic today uses this protocol. In this chapter we begin with an overview of the HTTP protocol – HTTP headers, and the format of HTTP requests and responses. We look at the classes in .NET for working with HTTP, and see how to read and write cookies. We then create an HTTP server with ASP.NET support, before continuing our look at .NET Remoting with a look at the HTTP transport channel.

We get to e-mail in Chapter 9. In this chapter, we begin with a high-level overview of the various e-mail protocols and how they are accessed and used in a .NET environment. We'll cover the basics of the SMTP, POP3, IMAP, and NNTP protocols, and see how these protocols work together to send and receive e-mail messages over the Internet. We'll also take a look at sending e-mails with the .NET Framework's classes for sending e-mails via SMTP, as well as developing some grassroots protocol implementation classes for POP3 and SMTP.

Chapter 10 is about securing network communications. The `System.Security.Cryptography` namespace of the .NET Framework provides programmatic access to the variety of cryptographic services that we can incorporate into our applications to encrypt and decrypt data, ensure data integrity, and handle digital signatures and certificates. In this chapter, we'll explore this namespace, but also provide an introduction to cryptography and all of its key concepts, if you'll excuse the pun. We'll also take a look at securing a chat application created earlier in Chapter 6.

Who Is This Book For?

Prior knowledge of network programming is not assumed, so basic and more advanced networking concepts are appropriately covered. The reader already familiar with network programming from another environment will find the pace quick enough for the book to still prove valuable.

> **All the code examples in this book are in C#, and a working knowledge of the language is assumed.**

What You Need to Use This Book

A prerequisite to running the samples in this book is that you have a machine with the .NET Framework installed upon it. This means that you'll need to be running either:

❑   Windows 2000 Professional (or better)

❑   Windows XP

It is also recommended that you use a version of Visual Studio .NET with this book.

Conventions

We've used a number of different styles of text and layout in this book to help differentiate between different kinds of information. Here are examples of the styles we used and an explanation of what they mean.

Code has several fonts. If it's a word that we're talking about in the text – for example, when discussing a for (...) loop, it's in this font. If it's a block of code that can be typed as a program and run, then it's also in a gray box:

```
IPHostEntry ipHost = Dns.Resolve("127.0.0.1");
```

Sometimes we'll see code in a mixture of styles, like this:

```
IPHostEntry ipHost = Dns.Resolve("127.0.0.1");
IPAddress ipAddr = ipHost.AddressList[0];
IPEndPoint ipEndPoint = new IPEndPoint(ipAddr, 11002);
Socket sender = new Socket(AddressFamily.InterNetwork,
                            SocketType.Stream, ProtocolType.Tcp);
sender.Connect(ipEndPoint);
```

In cases like this, the code with a white background is code we are already familiar with; the line highlighted in gray is a new addition to the code since we last looked at it.

Advice, hints, and background information come in this type of font.

> **Important pieces of information come in boxes like this.**

Bullets appear indented, with each new bullet marked as follows:

❑ **Important Words** are in a bold type font.

❑ Words that appear on the screen, or in menus like the Open or Close, are in a similar font to the one you would see on a Windows desktop.

❑ Keys that you press on the keyboard, like *Ctrl* and *Enter*, are in italics.

Customer Support

We always value hearing from our readers, and we want to know what you think about this book: what you liked, what you didn't like, and what you think we can do better next time. You can send us your comments, either by returning the reply card in the back of the book, or by e-mail to feedback@wrox.com. Please be sure to mention the book title in your message.

How to Download the Sample Code for the Book

When you visit the Wrox web site, www.wrox.com, locate the title through our Search facility or by using one of the title lists. Click Download Code on the book's detail page, or on the Download item in the Code column for title lists.

The files that are available for download from our site have been archived using WinZip. When you've saved the archives to a folder on your hard drive, you need to extract the files using a decompression program such as WinZip or PKUnzip. When you extract the files, the code will be extracted into separate folders for each chapter of this book, so ensure your extraction utility is set to use folder names.

Errata

We've made every effort to make sure that there are no errors in the text or in the code. However, no one is perfect and mistakes do occur. If you find an error in one of our books, such as a spelling mistake or a faulty piece of code, we would be very grateful to hear about it. By sending in errata you may save another reader hours of frustration, and, of course, you will be helping us to provide even higher quality information. Simply e-mail the information to support@wrox.com – your information will be checked and, if correct, posted to the errata page for that title, and used in reprints of the book.

To find errata on the web site, go to www.wrox.com, and simply locate the title through our Advanced Search or title list. Click the Book Errata link below the cover graphic on the book's detail page.

E-Mail Support

If you wish to query a problem in the book with an expert who knows the book in detail, then e-mail support@wrox.com with the title of the book and the last four numbers of the ISBN in the subject field of the e-mail. A typical e-mail should include the following things:

❑ The **title of the book**, the **last four digits of the ISBN** (7353), and the **page number** of the problem.

❑ Your **name**, **contact information**, and the **problem** in the body of the message.

We need the above details to save your time and ours – we *never* send unsolicited junk mail. When you send an e-mail message, it will go through the following chain of support:

❑ Customer Support – Your message is delivered to our customer support staff, who are the first people to read it. They have files on most frequently asked questions and will answer anything general about the book or the web site immediately.

❑ Editorial – Deeper queries are forwarded to the technical editor responsible for that book. They have experience with the programming language or particular product, and are able to answer detailed technical questions on the subject.

❑ The Authors – Finally, in the unlikely event that the editor cannot answer your problem, they will forward the request to the author. Wrox authors are glad to help support their books. They will e-mail the customer and the editor with their response, and again all readers should benefit.

The Wrox support process can only offer support for issues that are directly pertinent to the content of our published title. Support for questions that fall outside the scope of normal book support is provided via the community lists of our http://p2p.wrox.com/ forum.

p2p.wrox.com

For author and peer discussion, join the P2P mailing lists. Our unique system provides **programmer to programmer™** contact on mailing lists, forums, and newsgroups, all in addition to our one-to-one e-mail support system. If you post a query to P2P, you can be confident that the many Wrox authors and other industry experts who are present on our mailing lists are examining it. At p2p.wrox.com, you will find a number of different lists that will help you not only while you read this book, but also as you develop your own applications. Particularly appropriate to this book are the aspx and the aspx_professional lists.

To subscribe to a mailing list, just follow these steps:

1. Go to http://p2p.wrox.com/.

2. Choose the appropriate category from the left menu bar.

3. Click on the mailing list you wish to join.

4. Follow the instructions to subscribe, and fill in your e-mail address and password.

5. Reply to the confirmation e-mail you receive.

6. Use the subscription manager to join more lists and set your e-mail preferences.

Why This System Offers the Best Support

You can choose to join the mailing lists, or you can receive them as a weekly digest. If you don't have the time (or the facility) to receive the mailing lists, then you can search our online archives. Junk and spam mails are deleted, and your own e-mail address is protected by the Lyris system. Queries about joining or leaving lists, and any other general queries about lists, should be sent to listsupport@p2p.wrox.com.

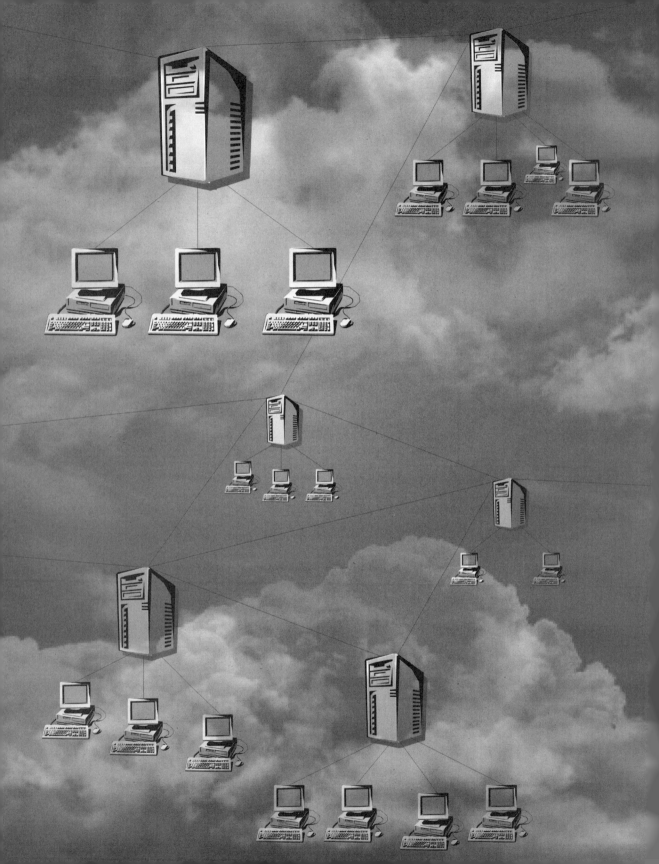

1

Networking Concepts and Protocols

In this chapter we will introduce some basic networking concepts and protocols. The chapter serves as a foundation to networking that will allow us to tackle programming in the rest of the book. It doesn't matter if you plan to develop server applications running as Windows Services that offer some data for clients using a custom protocol, if you write client applications that request data from web servers, or if you create multicasting applications, or applications using mailing functionality – you should start by reading this chapter. If you don't already know what a router or a network switch is, if you are not sure about the functionality of the seven layers in the OSI protocol, or if you just want a refresher or an overview of the different network protocols and their uses, this chapter is for you.

We will start with an introduction to the hardware used in local area networks, such as routers, hubs, and bridges. Then we will have a look at the seven layers of the OSI model and their functionality, and how the TCP/IP protocol suite fits into the OSI layers. After that, we will learn about the functionality of various network protocols.

In particular, we will look at:

❑   The Physical Network

❑   The OSI Seven-Layer Model

❑   Basic Network Protocols

❑   Internet Protocols

❑   E-mail Protocols

❏ Sockets

❏ Name Lookups

❏ The Internet

❏ Remoting

❏ Messaging

The Physical Network

In essence, a network is a **group of computers or devices** connected together by **communication links**. In networking terms, every computer or device (printers, routers, switches, and so on) connected to the network is called a **node**. Nodes are connected by links, which could be cables or wireless links (such as infrared or radio signals), and they can interact with any other node by transmitting **messages** over the network.

We can differentiate networks according to their size:

❏ A **LAN**, or **Local Area Network**, connects nodes over a limited area. This area can be as large as the site of a big company, or as small as connected computers in someone's home. The most commonly used LAN technology is the Ethernet network (see next section).

❏ **WAN** is the acronym for **Wide Area Network**. Multiple LAN sites are connected together by a WAN. WAN technologies that you might know of include Frame Relays, T1 lines, ISDN (Integrated Services Digital Network), X.25, and ATM (Asynchronous Transfer Monitor). In the next section, we'll further discuss the means of connecting to a WAN.

❏ A **MAN**, or **Metropolitan Area Network**, is very similar to a WAN in that it connects multiple LANs. However, a MAN restricts the area of the network to a city or suburb. MANs use high-speed networks to connect the LANs of schools, governments, companies, and so on, by using fast connections to each site, such as fiber optics.

*When talking about networks, the term **backbone** is often used. A backbone is a high-speed network that connects slower networks. A company can use a backbone to connect slower LAN segments. The **Internet backbone** is built up of high-speed networks that carry WAN traffic. Your Internet provider either connects directly to the Internet backbone, or to a larger provider that connects directly to the Internet backbone.*

WAN Lines

To connect to a WAN, there are several options available:

❏ Where a specific customer requires a dedicated network capacity, we can use **leased lines**. Such lines are usually charged at a flat rate, no matter how much traffic is sent.

Examples of leased lines are Digital Data Service (DDS, running at 2.4 Kbps and 56 Kbps), T1 (1.544 Mbps), and T3 (equivalent to 28 T1 lines).

❏ **Switched lines** are used by the regular telephone service. A circuit is established between transmitter and receiver for the duration of a call, or data exchange. When the line is no longer needed, it is freed for use by another customer of the network provider.

Examples of switched lines are POTS (Plain Old Telephony Service – standard analog lines that support speeds up to 56 Kbps), ISDN, and DSL (Digital Subscriber Line).

❑ A **packet-switching** network is where the service provider supplies switching technology to interface with the backbone network. This solution provides increased performance and shares resources between customers, so that bandwidth is available on demand.

Protocols used for switching networks include X.25 (up to 64 Kbps), Frame Relay (up to 44.736 Mbps), and ATM (up to 9.953 Gbps).

Ethernet Protocol

To get a better understanding of how physical networks work, we'll look at the most common LAN protocol, **Ethernet**. Ninety percent of devices attached to a LAN use the Ethernet protocol, originally developed by Xerox, Digital Equipment, and Intel in 1972. In 1980, the IEEE 802.3, CSMA/CD standard specified a 10 Mbps Ethernet.

Nowadays, Ethernets can support 100Mbps and 1Gbps lines. Many cabling technologies can be employed with an Ethernet. There is a standard naming which indicates the speed of the Ethernet network and the properties of the cable technology in use. Such names start with a number indicating the maximum data transfer speed, followed by a word indicating the transmission technology supported, and finally a number indicating the maximum distance between nodes. For instance, 10Base2 denotes an Ethernet that operates at 10Mbps using baseband transmission, with cables that have a maximum length of 200 meters. Some other common configurations are:

Ethernet Standard	Speed	Typical Cable Type	Description
10Base5	10 Mbps	Coaxial copper	This was the original standard for Ethernet, a so-called thick-net cabling technology.
10BaseT	10 Mbps	Copper	10BaseT is a 10 Mbps network with twisted pair cabling. A twisted pair is simply that – a pair of wires twisted around each other.
100BaseTX	100 Mbps	Copper	100 Mbps with twisted pair cabling and full-duplex (X) capability. Full-duplex means that data can pass in both directions simultaneously.
1000BaseSX	1000 Mbps	Multimode Fiber	1000 Mbps network with fiber optic cables. The S indicates the short wavelength (850 nm) of the laser.

CSMA/CD

Ethernet is a **CSMA/CD** (Carrier Sense Multiple Access / Collision Detect) network. Multiple devices are connected to the same network, and all have simultaneous access. When a message is sent, it is transported across the complete network as shown in the figure below. The receiver is identified by its unique address, and only this node reads the message; all other nodes ignore it.

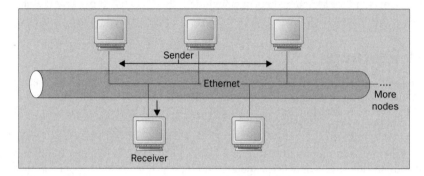

There is a potential problem because more than one node could attempt to send a message at the same time, which could result in the packets becoming corrupted. The solution used by Ethernet is that every node monitors the network and is thus aware if traffic is circulating. A node can only start sending data if no data is already being sent over the network. In short, this is the CSMA part of CSMA/CD.

There is still however the possibility that two nodes, after checking that the network is not already in use, start sending a packet at exactly the same time on the same network cable. This would cause a collision between the two packets, resulting in corrupted data. Both senders are aware of the corrupted packet because they still listen to the network while sending data, and thus detect the collision. This is the CD in CSMA/CD. Both nodes then halt their transmissions immediately, and wait a random time before checking the network again to see if it is free to resend the packet.

Every node on the local network uses a MAC (Media Access Control) address for unique identification. This address is defined by the network interface card. A network packet is sent across the network, but if the network card does not identify its host as a receiver, it ignores the packet and passes it on. Incidentally, if the packet is intended for it, it still passes it on, but this time flags it as received. The packet then continues around the network until it gets back to the sender, which can now be sure that the intended recipient received the data.

Other Protocols

IBM developed the Token Ring (IEEE 802.5) network, where nodes are connected in a ring as can be seen in the next picture. With Ethernet, any node can send a message as long as there's no traffic already on the network. With Token Ring, every node has a guaranteed access to the network in a predefined order. A token circulates around the network ring, and only the node that holds the token can send a message. Nowadays, Ethernet is gradually replacing Token Ring networks because Token Ring is more expensive and more difficult to implement.

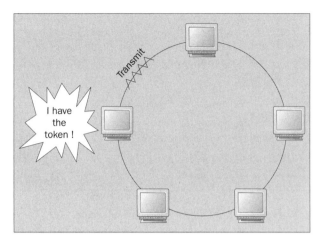

AppleTalk is a LAN protocol developed by Apple that has been quite popular in schools, factories, and so on.

Asynchronous Transfer Mode (ATM) is another protocol that can be found in LANs. It supports fast network switching and has a guaranteed Quality of Service (QOS), but because the cost of ATM network cards is very high, ATM is a niche player in the LAN market. ATM is only used for LANs in installations that require extremely high performance, for example to transmit medical images such as X-rays between hospitals. In the backbone that drives WAN networks, ATM plays a more important role.

Physical Components

An important aspect of understanding the network is knowing the hardware components. We are going to have a look at the major components of a LAN:

- ❑ Network Interface Card (NIC)
- ❑ Hub
- ❑ Switch
- ❑ Router

Network Interface Card

The NIC is the adapter card used to connect a device to the LAN. It allows us to send and receive messages to and from the network. A NIC has a unique **MAC (media access control)** address that provides a unique identification of each device.

The MAC address is a 12-byte hexadecimal number uniquely assigned to an Ethernet network card. This address can be changed by a network driver dynamically (as is the case with DECnet systems, a network developed by Digital Equipment), but usually the MAC address is not changed.

You can find the MAC address of a Windows machine using the command-line utility `ipconfig` in a DOS box with the `/all` switch. The next screenshot shows the output produced on my system, where the MAC address is 00-50-DA-E2-2C-97. The first part of this number, 00-50-DA, is assigned to the manufacturer of the network card; the manufacturer uses the remainder to create a unique MAC address:

```
C:\WINNT\System32\cmd.exe                                        _|□|×|

C:\>ipconfig /all

Windows 2000 IP Configuration

        Host Name . . . . . . . . . . . . : celticrain
        Primary DNS Suffix  . . . . . . . : eichkogelstrasse.local
        Node Type . . . . . . . . . . . . : Hybrid
        IP Routing Enabled. . . . . . . . : Yes
        WINS Proxy Enabled. . . . . . . . : No
        DNS Suffix Search List. . . . . . : eichkogelstrasse.local

Ethernet adapter Local Area Connection:

        Connection-specific DNS Suffix  . :
        Description . . . . . . . . . . . : 3Com EtherLink 10/100 PCI For Comple
te PC Management NIC (3C905C-TX)
        Physical Address. . . . . . . . . : 00-50-DA-E2-2C-97
        DHCP Enabled. . . . . . . . . . . : No
        IP Address. . . . . . . . . . . . : 192.168.0.1
        Subnet Mask . . . . . . . . . . . : 255.255.255.0
        Default Gateway . . . . . . . . . :
        DNS Servers . . . . . . . . . . . : 195.3.96.68
                                            195.3.96.67
```

Hub

Multiple devices can easily be connected with the help of a **hub**. A hub is a connectivity device that attaches multiple devices to a LAN. Each device typically connects via a UTP (Unshielded Twisted Pair) cable to a port on the hub. You may have already heard about the RJ-45 (Registered Jack-45) connector. This is one of the possible port types on a hub, but a hub can also support other cable types. A hub can have anything from four ports to 24. In a large network, multiple hubs are mounted in a cabinet and support hundreds of connections.

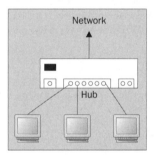

The hub acts as a **repeater** as it forwards every message from each port to every other port, and to the network. A hub is a fairly simple element of a network, operating at the physical network layer to retransmit data without any processing. This makes hubs easy to install and manage, as they don't require any special configuration.

Switch

Switches separate networks into segments. Compared to a hub, a switch is a more intelligent device. The switch stores the MAC addresses of devices that are connected to its ports in lookup tables. These lookup tables allow the switch to filter network messages, and, unlike the hub, avoid forwarding messages to every port. This eliminates possible collisions, and a better performing network can be achieved. Switching functionality is performed using hardware (through ASIC chips, which stands for Application Specific Integrated Circuit).

As seen in the next picture, switches can be used to connect hubs at a site. If Node A sends a message to Node B, the switch doesn't forward the message to segment 2 because the switch knows that Node B is on the same portion of the network as Node A. However, if Node A sends a message to Node C, the message is forwarded from segment 1 to segment 2.

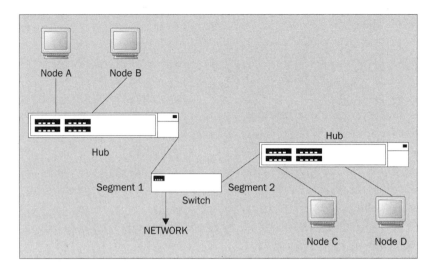

This sort of arrangement was popular in the early days, when hubs were much cheaper than switches, but it is less common now, as the price of a switch has dropped to pretty much the same as that of a hub. Because of the enhanced network performance from collision reduction, new networks often use switches in place of hubs, and end-users are connected directly to a switch.

Router

A router is an intermediary network device that connects multiple physical networks. With many hosts it can be useful to split a LAN into separate portions, or **subnets**. The advantages of subnets are:

❏ Performance is improved by reducing **broadcasts**, which is when a message is sent to all nodes in a network. With subnets, a message is only sent to the nodes in the appropriate subnet.

❏ The capability of restricting users to particular subnets offers security benefits.

❏ Smaller subnets are easier to manage than one large network.

❏ Subnets allow a single network to span several locations.

The next diagram shows how routers might connect several subnets.

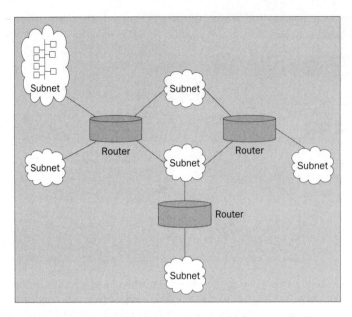

If using a router in a LAN, be aware that a router is not as fast as a switch. The router must apply more processing to messages than a switch needs to, and consequently takes a little more time before passing on packets.

Routers are not only used within LANs, they have an important place in WANs where they connect different network lines. The router receives a message and forwards it to the destination using the last known best path to that destination:

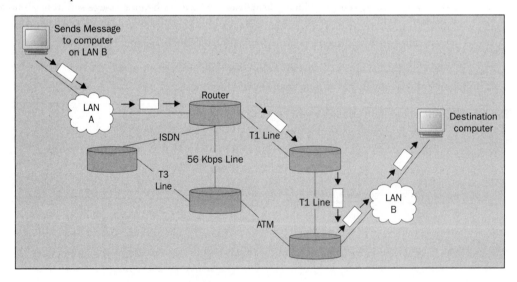

A router holds a routing table that lists the ways that particular networks can be reached. There will often be several different routes from one network to another, but one of these will be the best, and it is that one that is described in the routing table. Routers communicate using routing protocols that discover other routers on the network, and support the exchange of information about networks attached to each router.

The information that a router collates about the paths between networks is known as **router metrics**, and may include information such as packet loss and transmission time. The information used to produce the metrics depends on the routing protocol:

❑ Distance Vector Routing Protocols

RIP (Routing Information Protocol) and IGRP (Interior Gateway Routing Protocol) routing protocols use a **hop count**, which indicates the number of routers that are passed through on the way to the target network. These protocols prefer paths with fewer routers, regardless of its speed and reliability.

❑ Link State Routing Protocols

The best path calculation of the OSPF (Open Shortest Path First) and BGP (Border Gateway Protocol) routing protocols takes into account multiple factors such as the speed, reliability, and even cost of a path.

❑ Hybrid Routing Protocols

Hybrid routing protocols use a combination of distance vector and link state calculation.

Finding the Route

With TCP/IP configuration, a **default gateway** can be set up. This is the IP address of the router port that the machine's subnet is connected to. This router is used when a host outside the subnet needs to be contacted.

You can see the local routing table on a Windows system by entering ROUTE PRINT on the command-line. This command displays the gateways that will be used for each network connection. The picture below shows the output for a machine with an IP address of 192.168.0.1 with two network interfaces (one LAN NIC card and one WAN connection). If a host with the address 192.168.0.x is accessed, the local IP address 192.168.0.1 is used as a gateway – we can connect to these hosts directly. For other network destinations, the router 212.183.100.220 is used:

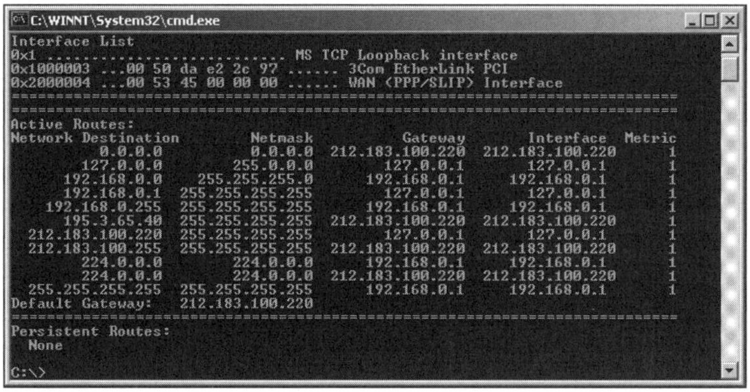

The ROUTE command has an option (ROUTE ADD) to specify the IP address of a router (gateway) and the network address to use with that router. This router will then be used to connect to hosts on the specified network.

Another useful command I want to look at is TRACERT. This allows us to examine the path used to reach a destination. Simply specify the host name or IP address after the TRACERT command – TRACERT www.globalknowledge.com in the example below – shows all routers that were used to reach the specified host. As you can see in the picture below, the command also displays the time needed to reach the next hop. This command is very helpful if a host cannot be reached, which could indicate that some network in between is down or not available.

The Layered OSI Model

With OSI (Open System Interconnection) the International Organization for Standardization (ISO) defined a model for a standardized network that would replace TCP/IP, DECNet, and other protocols, as the primary network protocol used in the Internet. However, because of the complexity of the OSI protocol, not many implementations were built and put to use. TCP/IP was much simpler, and thus can now be found everywhere. But many new ideas from the OSI protocol can be found in the next version of IP, IPv6.

While the OSI protocol didn't catch on, the OSI seven layer model was very successful, and it is now used as a reference model to describe different network protocols and their functionality.

The layers of the OSI model separate out the basic tasks that network protocols must accomplish, and describe how network applications can communicate. Each layer has a specific purpose and is connected to the layers immediately above and below it. The seven layers defined by OSI are shown here:

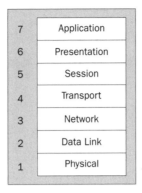

❑ The **application** layer defines a programming interface to the network for user applications.

❑ The **presentation** layer is responsible for encoding data from the application layer ready for transmission over the network, and vice versa.

❑ The **session** layer creates a virtual connection between applications.

❑ The **transport** layer allows reliable communication of data.

❑ The **network** layer makes it possible to access nodes in a LAN using logical addressing.

❑ The **data link** layer accesses the physical network with physical addresses.

❑ Finally, the **physical** layer includes the connectors, cables, and so on.

The next picture shows communication between two machines, and how data passes down through the **protocol stack** on the sender, and up through it on receipt. The D sent from the application on the first machine is shown in the figure as the box containing the letter D. The application layer (layer 7) adds a header to the message (called H7 in the figure), and passes the message to the presentation layer (layer 6), which adds H6 to the message before passing it to the session layer (layer 5). This continues until the message, with all its headers, arrives at the physical network (layer 1) and is transmitted to the receiver. At the receiving side, every layer performs any necessary processing, and removes the relevant header passing the message up to the next layer. At the end of all this, the receiving application accesses the original data sent by the application on the first computer:

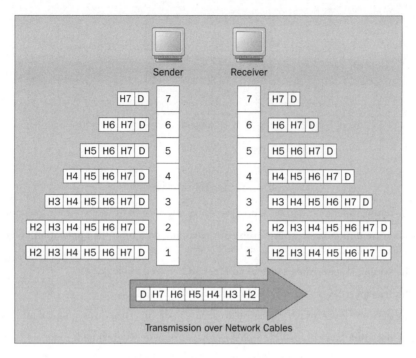

Transmission over Network Cables

Now we understand the concept of these seven layers, we can look at the functionality of each layer in more detail. We'll start at the bottom, and work our way up.

Layer 1: Physical Layer

The physical layer includes the physical environment such as cable requirements, connectors, interface specifications, hub and repeater specifications, and the like. This layer specifies exactly what physical network signal will be used to send a "1", and what will represent a "0".

Layer 2: Data Link Layer

The MAC address that we've already talked about is a layer 2 address. Nodes on the LAN send messages to each other using IP addresses, and these must be translated to the corresponding MAC addresses by the data layer.

The **Address Resolution Protocol** (ARP) translates IP addresses to MAC addresses. A cache of known MAC addresses speeds this process, and it can be examined with the **arp** utility, arp -a, which shows MAC addresses of all recently used nodes in the ARP cache:

```
C:\WINNT\System32\cmd.exe                                          _ □ X

C:\>arp -a

Interface: 192.168.0.1 on Interface 0x1000003
  Internet Address      Physical Address      Type
  192.168.0.44          00-10-5a-12-1d-b9     dynamic
  192.168.0.251         00-d0-59-0e-0d-2b     dynamic

C:\>_
```

The `arp` utility also allows us to map IP addresses to MAC addresses so that ARP queries for MAC addresses are no longer needed. However, the mapping would break if the network card were replaced, so it should be used with care.

Other responsibilities of the data layer include sending and receiving messages and error detection. With Ethernet, we also have collision detection, as discussed already.

A network switch operates at the data link layer by filtering messages according to their recipients' MAC addresses.

Layer 3: Network Layer

One layer above the data link layer is the network layer. Within layer 3, logical addressing is used to connect to other nodes. MAC addresses of layer 2 can only be used inside a LAN, and we have to use layer 3 addressing when accessing nodes in a WAN.

The Internet Protocol (IP) is a layer 3 protocol; it uses IP addresses to identify nodes on the network.

Routers work at layer 3 to route traffic between networks.

Layer 4: Transport Layer

The network layer identifies hosts by logical addresses. The transport layer identifies an application by what is known as an **endpoint**. With the TCP protocol, an endpoint is given by a **port number** and IP address combination.

The transport layer is differentiated according to whether or not we are using **reliable** or **unreliable** communication. Reliable communication is when an error is produced if a message was sent but not received correctly, while unreliable communication sends messages without checking if it is received at all. In reliable communication, the transport layer is responsible for sending acknowledgements of data packets, for retransmitting messages if data was corrupted or missing, for discarding duplicate messages, and so on.

Another way network communication can be differentiated at the transport layer is as either **connection-oriented** or **connection-less**:

❑ With connection-oriented communication, a connection must be made before messages can be sent or received.

❑ With a connection-less communication, setting up individual connections is not necessary, and messages are sent immediately.

The TCP protocol uses a connection-oriented communication mechanism, while UDP (User Datagram Protocol) uses a connection-less communication mechanism. Connection-oriented communication is reliable as acknowledgements are sent, and retransmitted if data is not received or has become corrupted for any reason. Connection-less communication can be useful with broadcasts where messages are sent to multiple nodes. Here message arrival is not guaranteed. If reliable messaging is needed, reliability can be enforced by a higher-level protocol on top of the connection-less mechanism.

Layer 5: Session Layer

With the OSI model, the session layer defines services for an application, such as logging in and out of an application. The session represents a virtual (logical) connection between applications. The session layer connection is independent of the underlying physical connection at the transport layer, and the virtual connection can exist for a longer time than the connection at the transport layer. Multiple transport layer connections may be required for a single session layer connection.

We can compare this functionality with the functionality offered by ASP.NET session objects. The session objects exist until a session times out (usually 20 minutes), independent of the underlying TCP connection.

Layer 6: Presentation Layer

The presentation layer is used to format the data according to application requirements. Encryption, decryption, and compression typically happen in this layer.

Layer 7: Application Layer

The application layer is the highest layer of the OSI model. This layer contains applications using networking features. These applications can perform tasks such as file transfer, printing, e-mail, web browsing, and more. The example applications that we will create in this book reside in this layer.

Network Protocols

The OSI layers define a model of protocol layers, their purpose, and how they work together. Let us compare the OSI layers with a concrete implementation: that of the TCP/IP protocol stack. The TCP/IP protocol stack is a simple form of the OSI model, which can be viewed by 4 layers as opposed to 7. The IP protocol corresponds to OSI layer 3; TCP and UDP are OSI layer 4 protocols. HTTP, FTP, and SMTP don't fit one layer of the OSI model, and the tasks they accomplish encompass the session, presentation, and application layers:

OSI 7 Layers		TCP/IP Protocol Stack	
7	Application	HTTP FTP SMTP RIP DNS	
6	Presentation		
5	Session		
4	Transport	TCP	UDP
3	Network	ICMP IP IGMP	
2	Data Link	Ethernet, ATM, Frame Relay, etc.	
1	Physical		

In the next section, we shall look into the functionality and purpose of the protocols of the TCP/IP suite in the following order:

❑ Basic Protocols

❑ Internet Protocols

❑ E-mail Protocols

❑ Other Protocols

Basic Protocols

As we can see, the TCP/IP protocol suite has a much simpler layered structure than the seven layers of the OSI model. The **Transmission Control Protocol** (TCP) and **User Datagram Protocol** (UDP) protocols are transport protocols corresponding to OSI layer 4. Both protocols make use of the Internet Protocol (IP), an OSI layer 3 protocol (the network layer). As well as these three protocols, there are two more basic protocols in the TCP/IP suite that extend the IP protocol: ICMP and IGMP. The functionality of these protocols must be implemented in the layer housing the IP protocol, hence they are shown in that layer in the preceding figure.

IP – Internet Protocol

The Internet Protocol connects two nodes. Each node is identified by a 32-bit address, called its IP address. When sending a message, the IP protocol receives the message from upper level protocols such as TCP or UDP and adds the IP header which contains information about the destination host.

The best way to understand the IP protocol is by examining this IP header in detail. The information it contains is listed in the following table:

Field	Length	Description
IP Version	4 bits	The IP version that created the header. The current IP protocol version is 4.
IP Header Length	4 bits	The length of the header. The minimum value is 5, in units of 32 bits – 4 bytes – so the minimum length is 20 bytes.
Type of Service	1 byte	The service type allows a message to be set as normal or high throughput, normal or high delay, and normal or high reliability. This is useful for datagram packets sent to the network. Several kinds of network use this information to prioritize certain traffic. Also, Network Control messages have a higher precedence and reliability than normal messages.
Total Length	2 bytes	These two bytes specify the total length of the message – header and data – in octets. The maximum size of an IP packet is 65,535 bytes, but that is impractical for most networks. The largest size that must be accepted by all hosts is 576 bytes. Large messages can be split into fragments – a process called fragmentation.
Identification	2 bytes	If the message is fragmented, the identification field helps to assemble the fragments of a message. If a message is split into multiple fragments, all fragments of a message have the same identification number.
Flags	3 bits	These flags indicate if the message is fragmented or not, and if the current packet is the last fragment of a message.
Fragment Offset	13 bits	These 13 bits specify the **offset** of a fragmented message. Fragments may arrive in a different order than when sent, so the offset is necessary to rebuild the original data. The first fragment of a message has an offset of 0, and other fragments give the offset where the fragment should be appended. The offset unit is 8 bytes, so a fragment offset value of 64 means that the second fragment should be appended after 512 bytes of the first packet.
Time to Live	1 byte	The time to live (TTL) value specifies the number of seconds a message can live before it is discarded. This value doesn't necessarily specify the number of seconds, as every router that the message crosses must decrement the TTL value by 1 no matter if the handling of the message took less than 1 second. So in practice, this value gives the number of hops to live.

Field	Length	Description
Protocol	1 byte	This byte indicates the protocol used at the next level in the protocol stack for this message. The protocol numbers are defined in an online database at the Internet Assigned Number Authority (IANA): http://www.iana.org/assignments/protocol-numbers. Some examples: ICMP has the value 1, IGMP 2, TCP 6, UDP 17.
Header Checksum	2 bytes	This is a checksum of the header only. Because the header changes with every message that is forwarded, the checksum changes also.
Source Address	4 bytes	This field gives the 32 bit IP address of the sender.
Destination Address	4 bytes	This is the 32-bit IP address where the message is to be sent.
Options	variable	Optional fields can appear here. We can specify that a message is confidential or top secret, and there is also room for future extensions.
Padding	variable	This field contains a variable number of zeros such that the header ends on a 32-bit boundary.

*The Internet Protocol (IP) is defined with RFC 791. The **RFC** (Request for Comments) documents contain technical information about many important Internet technologies. RFCs can be found at http://www.ietf.org/rfc.html.*

IP Addresses

Every node on a TCP/IP network can be identified by a 32-bit IP address. Usually the IP address is represented in a quad-notation with four decimal values, such as `192.168.0.1`. Each of these numbers represents one byte of the IP address, meaning that each falls in the range 0 to 255.

An IP address consists of two parts: the network part and the host part. Depending on the network class, the network part consists of the first one, two, or three bytes:

Class	Byte 1	Byte 2	Byte 3	Byte 4
A	Network (1–126)	Host (0–255)	Host (0–255)	Host (0–255)
B	Network (128–191)	Network (0–255)	Host (0–255)	Host (0–255)
C	Network (192–223)	Network (0–255)	Network (0–255)	Host (0–255)

The first bit of a Class A network address must be 0, so the first byte of a Class A network is in the binary range `00000001` (1) to `01111110` (126). The remaining three bytes serve to identify nodes on the network, allowing us to connect more than 16 million devices on a Class A network.

Note that the networks in the above table make no mention of addresses with 127 as the first byte – this is a reserved address range. The address 127.0.0.1 is always the address of the local host, and 127.0.0.0 is a local loopback. Loopbacks are used to test the network protocol stack on a machine without going through the network interface card.

Class B networks always have the first two bits of the IP address set to 10, giving a range of 10000000 (128) to 10111111 (191). The second byte further identifies the network with a value of 0 to 255, leaving the remaining two bytes to identify nodes on the network; a total of 65,534 devices.

Class C networks are denoted by an IP address where the first three bits are set to 110, allowing a range of the first byte from 11000000 (192) to 11011111 (223). With this network type, only one byte is set aside for node identification, so only 254 devices can be connected.

> *The number of devices that can be connected to each of these different network classes with a distinct IP address is inversely proportional to the number of networks of that type available. For instance, a Class A network, allowing 16 million hosts, only leaves part of the first byte for identifying the network. The result is that there are only 126 Class A networks available worldwide. Only big companies such as AT&T, IBM, Xerox, and HP have such a network address. When a company requests an IP network from a network authority, it will usually only be allocated a class C network. Should the company desire more hosts to be directly connected to the Internet, an additional Class C network can be sought. Another option applies if each network host doesn't need direct Internet access, when a private IP address can be used. We discuss private IP addresses in the next section.*

Class A, B, and C network addresses leave addresses that have a first byte of 224 to 255. Class D networks (224–239) are used for multicasting, as we will see in Chapter 7, and Class E (240–255) is reserved for testing purposes.

> *The IANA (Internet Assigned Numbers Authority) assigns network numbers, and lists them at http://www.iana.org/assignments/ipv4-address-space. Nearly every country has a regional registration authority to give network numbers to requestors. The regional authority receives a network range from IANA.*

Private IP Addresses

To avoid exhausting IP addresses, hosts that are not directly connected to the Internet can use an address in the private address ranges. Private addresses are not globally unique, and are just unique locally within the network. All network classes reserve certain ranges for use as private addresses for hosts that do not require direct two-way access to the Internet. Such hosts may well access the Internet through a gateway that doesn't forward private IP addresses.

Class	Private Address Range (Network Part of IP address)
A	10
B	172.16–172.31
C	192.168.0–192.168.255

Address allocation for private addresses is described with RFC 1918.

Subnets

Connecting two nodes of different networks requires a router. The host number is defined by 24 bits of a Class A IP address; while with a Class C network, just 8 bits are available. A router splits the host number into a subnet number and host number. Adding additional routers will reduce broadcasts in the network, which can reduce network load. The main reason for adding routers is to improve connectivity between sites in different buildings, cities, and so on.

Let's look at a subnetting example of a Class C network with an address 194.180.44. Such a network may have a **subnet mask** of 255.255.255.224 to filter addresses. The first three bytes (which consist of all ones) are the mask for the class C network. The last byte, 224, is the decimal value for the binary representation 11100000, so that 3 bits of the host number indicate the subnet, and the remaining 5 bits represent the host number on a particular subnet. These 3 subnet bits represent 128, 64, and 32, and thus support the subnet addresses shown below:

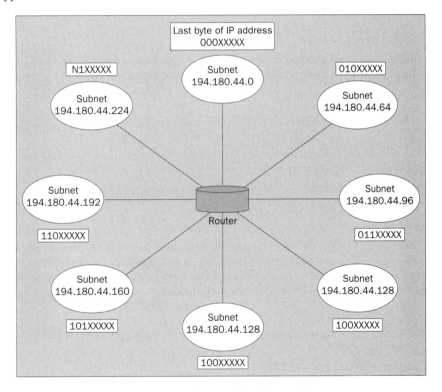

So the subnet 194.180.44.64 will contain hosts with addresses from 194.180.44.65 to 194.180.44.94, and the subnet 194.180.44.160 contains hosts from 194.180.44.161 to 194.180.44.190.

IPv6

The predecessor of the Internet Protocol was developed by the US Defense Department's Advanced Research Project Agency (DARPA) in the 1960s, and the TCP/IP protocol suite was not established until 1980. Because IP was based on the existing DARPA network protocols, it became version 4, now known as IPv4. At that time, when most people's idea of a mobile phone was one that could be taken off the wall and used on the couch, the number of hosts supported by IP seemed more than adequate. Now, however, everyone wants to connect their refrigerator and lawnmower to the Internet. To answer this demand, a new IP version has been under development by the IETF: IPv6. The most important change over IPv4 is the use of 128 bits to address nodes rather than 32 bits – which will allow every Tablet PC, Pocket PC, mobile phone, TV, car, lawnmower, coffee machine, and dustbin to become a fully-fledged Internet host.

As well as being able to allocate an address to just about every atom in the solar system, there are one or two other useful changes with IPv6:

❑   Extended Addressing Capabilities

Multicast routing information can be added to IPv6 addresses to define the scope of a multicast address. Also there's now an anycast address to send a message to any host or group of hosts.

❑   Header Format Simplification

Some of the header fields of IPv4 have been removed, and others are now optional. However, the complete header length of IPv6 is longer than IPv4 because of the 128-bit addresses for source and destination.

❑   Improved Extensibility Support

It should be easier to add extensions to the IPv6 protocol in the future. The length restriction for options has been removed.

❑   Flow Labeling

A new capability is added for particular traffic flows. A flow is a sequence of packets traveling from a source to a destination. With the new protocol, applications can offer both audio and video real-time capabilities over different flows. Each flow can request a real-time or specific quality-handling from routers that it travels through.

❑   Authentication and Privacy

IPv6 extensions to support authentication, privacy, and confidentially of data sent are added.

Transport Layer – Port Numbers

The IP protocol uses IP addresses to identify nodes on the network, while the transport layer (layer 4) uses endpoints to identify applications. TCP and UDP protocols use a **port number** together with an IP address to specify an application endpoint.

The server must supply a known endpoint for a client to connect to, although the port number can be created dynamically for the client.

TCP and UDP port numbers are 16 bits, and can be divided into three categories:

❑   System (Well-Known) Port Numbers

❑   User (Registered) Port Numbers

❑   Dynamic or Private Ports

The system port numbers are in the range 0 to 1023. System port numbers should only be used by system privileged processes. Well-known protocols have default port numbers in this range.

User port numbers fall in the range 1024 to 49151. Your server applications usually will take one of these ports, and you can also register the port number with the Internet Assigned Numbers Authority (IANA) if you wish to make it known to the Internet community.

Dynamic ports are in the range 49152 to 65535. When it is not necessary to know the port number before starting an application, a port in this range would be suitable. Client applications connecting to servers might use such a port.

If we run the `netstat` utility with the `-a` option, we'll see a list of all ports currently in use, and also an indication of the state of the connection – if it's in listening state, or if a connection has been already established:

The file `services` in the directory `<windir>\system32\drivers\etc` lists many predefined user and system port numbers. If a port is listed in this file, the `netstat` utility will display the name of the protocol instead of the port number.

IANA assigns system and user port numbers. You can find a list of defined port numbers at http://www.iana.org/assignments/port-numbers.

29

TCP – Transmission Control Protocol

Connection-oriented communication can use reliable communication where the layer 4 protocol sends acknowledgements of data receipts, and requests retransmission if data is not received or is corrupted. The TCP protocol uses such reliable communication.

Some of the application protocols that use TCP are HTTP, FTP, SMTP, and Telnet.

TCP requires that a connection must be opened before data can be sent. The server application must perform a so-called **passive open** to create a connection with a known port number, where rather than making a call to the network, the server listens and waits for incoming requests. The client application must perform an **active open** by sending a synchronize sequence number (SYN) to the server application to identify the connection. The client application can use a dynamic port number as a local port. The server must send an acknowledgement (ACK) to the client together with the sequence number (SYN) of the server. The client in turn answers with an ACK, and the connection is established.

Now sending and receiving can start. After receiving a message, an ACK messages is always returned. If the sender times out before receiving an ACK, the message is placed in the retransmit queue for sending again.

The TCP header fields are listed in the table below:

Field	Length	Description
Source port	2 bytes	Port number of the source.
Destination port	2 bytes	Port number of the destination.
Sequence number	4 bytes	The sequence number is generated by the source and is used by the destination to reorder packets to create the original message, and to send an acknowledgement to the source.
Acknowledgement number	4 bytes	If the ACK bit of the Control field is set, this field contains the next sequence number that can be expected.
Data offset	4 bits	Details where the packet data begins.
Reserved	6 bits	Reserved for future use.
Control	6 bits	The control bits contain flags that denote if the acknowledgement (ACK) or urgent pointer (URG) fields are valid, if the connection should be reset (RST), if a synchronize sequence number is sent (SYN), and so on.
Window Size	2 bytes	This field indicates the size of the receive buffer. The receiver can inform the sender of the maximum data size that can be sent using acknowledgement messages.
Checksum	2 bytes	A checksum for the header and data to determine if the packet has become corrupted.
Urgent Pointer	2 bytes	This field informs the target device of urgent data.
Options	*variable*	Again option values will only be specified when relevant.
Padding	*variable*	The padding field adds zeros so that the header ends on a 32-bit boundary.

The TCP protocol is complex and time consuming because of the handshaking mechanism, but this protocol takes care of guaranteeing delivery of packets, obviating the need to include that functionality in the application protocol.

> **The TCP protocol has a reliable delivery built-in. If a message isn't sent correctly, we will be informed by an error message.**

The TCP protocol is defined with RFC 793. Programming with the TCP protocol is covered in Chapter 5.

UDP – User Datagram Protocol

Contrary to TCP, UDP is a very fast protocol as it specifies just the minimum mechanism required for data transfer. Of course this has some disadvantages. Messages can be received in any order, and a message that was sent first could be received last. The delivery of UDP messages is not guaranteed at all, and messages can be lost, or even two copies of the same message might be received. This latter scenario can happen when two different routes are used to send the message to the same destination.

UDP does not require a connection to be opened, and data can be sent as soon as it is ready. UDP doesn't send acknowledgement messages, so the data can be received, or it can be lost. If reliable data transfer is needed over UDP, it must be implemented in a higher-level protocol.

So what are the advantages of UDP, why would we want to use an unreliable protocol such as this? To understand the most important reason for using UDP, we have to differentiate between unicast, broadcast, and multicast communications.

A **unicast** message is sent from one node to just one other. This is also called point-to-point communication. The TCP protocol only supports unicast communication. If a server wants to communicate with multiple clients using TCP, each client must make a connection, as messages can only be sent to single nodes. A **broadcast** means that a message is sent to all nodes in a network. **Multicast** is something in-between: messages are sent to selected groups of nodes.

UDP can be used with unicast communications if fast transfer is required, such as for multimedia delivery, but the major advantages of UDP apply to broadcasts and multicasts. Usually we don't want an acknowledgement from every node when sending a multicast or broadcast, as the server would be deluged, and the network load would be too great. An example of such a broadcast is the time service. A time server broadcasts a message containing the current time, and any host that wishes may synchronize the time with that in the broadcasted message.

The UDP header is a lot shorter and simpler than the TCP header:

Length	Field	Description
2 bytes	Source port	Specifying the source port is optional with UDP. If this field is used, the receiver of the message can send a reply to this port.
2 bytes	Destination port	Port number of the destination.
2 bytes	Length	The length of the message including header and data.
2 bytes	Checksum	A checksum for the header and data for verification.

> **UDP is a fast protocol, but delivery is not guaranteed. If message ordering and delivery is required, TCP should be used. UDP is primarily a protocol for broadcasts and multicasts.**

UDP is defined with RFC 786. You can read information on how to program applications using UDP in Chapter 6.

ICMP – Internet Control Message Protocol

ICMP is a control protocol used by IP devices to inform other IP devices of activity and errors in the network. Without TCP, IP is not a reliable protocol, and there are no acknowledgements, no error control for data (only a header checksum), and no retransmissions.

Errors detected may be reported with ICMP messages. The ICMP messages are used to send feedback about the status of the network. For example, a router sends an ICMP "destination unreachable" message if a suitable entry for a network cannot be found in a routing table. A router can also send an ICMP "redirect" message if a better path was found.

ICMP doesn't sit on top of the IP protocol as it may appear, rather ICMP messages are sent within the IP header. Hence, the ICMP protocol must be implemented by the IP module of the network stack. These ICMP message fields are prefixed to the IP header:

Length	Field	Description
1 byte	Type	This field specifies the ICMP message type. For example, a type value of 3 means that the destination is unreachable, 11 specifies that the time was exceeded, and 12 that incorrect header parameters were found.
1 byte	Code	The code provides more information about the message type. If the type is destination unreachable, the code specifies whether the network (0), host (1), protocol (2), or the port (3) is unreachable.
2 bytes	Checksum	A checksum of the ICMP message.
4 bytes	Depending on the type	The last 4 bytes of the ICMP header can supply additional information depending on the message type.
...	Regular IP Header	

Some of the types that can be sent using ICMP messages are:

❑   Echo, Echo reply

This ping command sends an ICMP Echo command to the destination device, and if all goes well an Echo reply is sent back.

❏ Destination unreachable, Redirect

A router returns the ICMP destination unreachable message if a target cannot be reached, or a redirect if a better path is found to a target.

❏ Time exceeded

The time to live (TTL) value was exceeded.

Ping Command

The Windows command line `ping` utility sends an ICMP Echo message to the target device specified by hostname or IP address in the `ping` command. If the device can be reached, an ICMP Echo Reply is sent back.

This command is very useful to check if a device can be reached, if there are intermediate problems (`PING -t` continues sending ping messages until it is stopped), and how long it takes to send a message to the device.

If you can't reach a host using the ping command it is not necessarily the case that the host cannot be reached by using other protocols. The ICMP echo messages may be blocked by routers or firewalls.

The picture below shows the output produced by `ping` for the host with IP address 212.183.100.193. By default, `ping` sends four ICMP messages to the target, and waits for the echo messages. The screenshot shows that 32 bytes of data were sent, and the time until the reply was received was less than 10 milliseconds. A summary appears after the four ICMP results, where we can see that 0% of the packets were lost. Intermediate failures would usually lose a certain percentage of the packets.

ICMP is defined with RFC 792.

IGMP – Internet Group Management Protocol

Similarly to ICMP, IGMP is an extension to the IP protocol and must be implemented by the IP module. IGMP is used by multicasting applications. When sending a broadcast message to a complete LAN, every node in the LAN analyzes the message up to the transport layer to verify if some application wants to receive messages from the port of the broadcast. If no application is listening, the message is destroyed and does not progress beyond the transport layer. This does mean that some CPU cycles are needed by every host no matter if the broadcast message is of interest or not.

Multicasts address this concern, by only sending messages to a group of nodes rather than every node in the LAN. The network interface card can detect if the system is interested in a particular message by analyzing the broadcast MAC address without needing the assistance of the CPU.

Registering interest in a multicast message is done by sending a group membership request for a multicast address with an IGMP message. Similarly, IGMP can be used to drop a membership.

You can read more about the use of IGMP in Chapter 7, where we create .NET multicasting applications. IGMP is defined by RFC 2236.

Internet Protocols

After discussing base protocols, we can now step up to a higher level. The HTTP and FTP protocols cover layers 5–7 of the OSI model.

FTP – File Transfer Protocol

FTP is used to copy files from and to a server, and to list files and directories on a server. It is an application level protocol based on TCP, where FTP commands are encapsulated within the TCP data block of a TCP message.

An application model with an FTP server and client is illustrated in the picture below. The client application presents a user interface and creates an FTP request according to the user's request and the FTP specification. The FTP command is sent to the server application over TCP/IP, and the FTP interpreter on the server interprets the FTP command accordingly. Depending on the FTP command, a list of files or a file from the server's file system is returned to the client in an FTP reply.

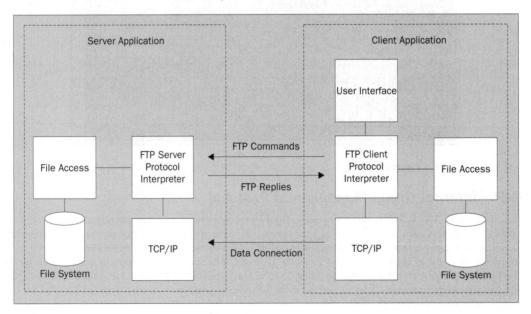

The FTP protocol has these characteristics:

❑ Reliable data transfer through TCP

❑ Anonymous access or user authentication with user name and password

❑ Files are sent as ASCII in a form supported by the target platform, or as unchanged binary data.

FTP commands can be grouped into these categories:

❑ Access Control Commands

FTP access control commands specify the user name (USER) and password (PASS), the settings can be reset (REIN), and the connection can be ended (QUIT).

❑ Transfer Parameter Commands

FTP transfer can be configured with transfer parameter commands. Changing the transfer from ASCII to binary, data compression, changing of ports to send data is supported by these commands.

❑ FTP Service Commands

Copying files from the server (RETR), copying files to the server (STOR), deleting files (DELE), renaming files (RNTO), creating directories (MKD), and asking for a list of files (LIST) are some of the FTP service commands.

FTP is defined by RFC 959.

FTP Clients

The best way to get to grips with the FTP protocol is by using the `ftp` command-line utility as shown below. The `ftp` program operates through the `ftp>` command prompt allowing us to enter commands. These commands are different from the commands of the FTP protocol – you can see them all by entering ?. Below, I enter the command `open ftp.microsoft.com` to create a connection to the host ftp.microsoft.com. Setting the username to `anonymous` indicates a guest user. The response `230` from the server indicates that a connection has been established, and we can list the files on the server using the `dir` command. On receiving the `dir` command, the `ftp` program sends an FTP LIST command to the server, `cd` can be used to change directories on the server, and the `get` command copies a file to the client by sending a RETR command. The `ftp` utility uses the `bye` command to close the connection:

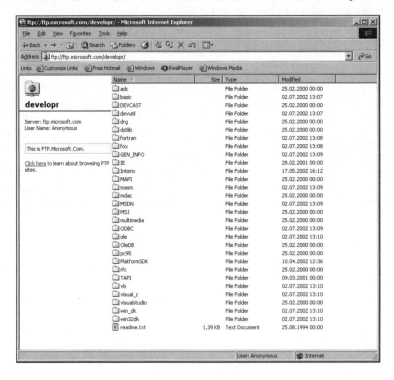

Another FTP client is Microsoft Internet Explorer. Instead of using a URL such as http://hostname, we start the FTP client with ftp:// as a schema identifier. This tool allows files to be copied with drag and drop:

HTTP – Hypertext Transfer Protocol

HTTP is the main protocol used by web applications. Similar to the FTP protocol, HTTP is a reliable protocol that is achieved by using TCP. Like FTP, HTTP is also used to transfer files across the network. Unlike FTP, it has features such as caching, identification of the client application, support for different attachments with a MIME format, and so on. These features are enabled within the HTTP header.

To demonstrate what an Internet browser is doing when it requests files from a web server, we can use the telnet application to simulate a browser. Start the telnet application by entering telnet in the Run dialog of the Start menu, and we see the Microsoft Telnet> prompt. Enter set local_echo (set localecho with Windows XP) to display the entered commands locally for demonstration purposes. If we don't set this option, commands we send to the server would not be displayed by the telnet application. Now we can connect to the web server with the open command. The command open msdn.microsoft.com 80 creates a TCP connection to port 80 of the server at msdn.microsoft.com. The telnet application uses port 23 by default, hence we have to specify a port for the HTTP request. The default port of a web server offering HTTP services is port 80.

```
C:\WINNT\System32\cmd.exe - telnet
Microsoft (R) Windows 2000 (TM) Version 5.00 (Build 2195)
Welcome to Microsoft Telnet Client
Telnet Client Build 5.00.99203.1

Escape Character is 'CTRL++'

Microsoft Telnet> set local_echo
Microsoft Telnet> open msdn.microsoft.com 80_
```

As soon as the connection is initiated we can send an HTTP request to the web server. A simple request consists of a request line followed by two returns (two CR-LF sequences). Such a request line can look like one we are using in the picture below: GET /default.asp HTTP/1.0. The server returns anHTTP response that consists of the status information (in this case 200 OK) followed by the HTML content:

```
Select C:\WINNT\System32\cmd.exe
GET /default.asp HTTP/1.0

HTTP/1.1 200 OK
Connection: close
Date: Thu, 25 Jul 2002 11:56:40 GMT
Server: Microsoft-IIS/6.0
P3P: policyref="http://www.microsoft.com/w3c/p3p.xml" CP="ALL IND DSP COR ADM CO
No CUR CUSo IVAo IVDo PSA PSD TAI TELo OUR SAMo CNT COM INT NAV ONL PHY PRE PUR
UNI"
Content-Length: 49279
Content-Type: text/html
Cache-control: private

<HTML>
        <HEAD>
                    <META HTTP-EQUIV="Content-Type" CONTENT="text/html; charset=UTF-8"/>
<TITLE>MSDN Home</TITLE>
                        <META NAME="Description" CONTENT="MSDN Home"/>
                                                        <META NAME
="Robots" CONTENT="all"/>
                        <META NAME="Keywords" CONTENT="MSDN, microsoft, develop
er, network, developer resources, microsoft developer resources"/>
                                                        <META NAME="MS
.LOCALE" CONTENT="en-us"/>
```

As we have seen, a basic HTTP request has only a single request line. A full HTTP request however will comprise a request line with additional headers and data.

HTTP commands such as GET, HEAD, and POST can be specified in the request line. Both GET and POST request data from the server. The GET command includes request parameters in the URL, while the POST request specifies that parameters follow in the data block. The HEAD command means that we just want to know when the requested file was changed so we can verify if the newest version is already in the cache.

General headers, request headers, and an entity header can follow the request line. This header information allows the client to tell the server about the browser in use, any preferred languages, to send a cookie, or to request files only if they have been changed. In the telnet example, we have already seen some header information returned by the server: the date, server version, content-length, content-type, and cache-control.

> *More information about the HTTP protocol and programming with the HTTP protocol can be found in Chapter 8. HTTP is defined by RFC 1945.*

HTTPS – HTTP over SSL (Secure Socket Layer)

If there is a requirement to exchange confidential data with a web server, HTTPS can be used. HTTPS is an extension to the HTTP protocol, and the principles discussed in the last section still apply. However, the underlying mechanism is different, as HTTPS uses SSL (Secure Socket Layer), originally developed by Netscape. SSL sits on top of TCP and secures network communication using a public/private key principle to exchange secret symmetric keys, and a symmetric key to encrypt the messages.

To support HTTPS, the web server must install a certificate so that it can be identified. The default port for HTTPS requests is 443.

> *For more information on SSL, go to the following page on the Netscape web site: http://wp.netscape.com/eng/ssl3/ssl-toc.html.*

E-Mail Protocols

There are quite a few protocols for use with e-mail. In this section, I'll try to provide an overview of the most important mail-related protocols. In Chapter 9, we will look into these more, and see how to create applications that use them.

SMTP – Simple Mail Transfer Protocol

SMTP is a protocol for sending and receiving e-mail messages. It can be used to send e-mail between a client and server that both use the same transport protocol, or to send e-mail between servers that use different transport protocols. SMTP has the capability to relay messages across transport service environments. SMTP does not allow us to read messages from a mail server, however, and for this activity POP3 or IMAP protocols should be used.

An SMTP service forms part of the Internet Information Server installation of Windows 2000 and XP.

> *The SMTP standard is defined with RFC 821; the SMTP message format is defined with RFC 822.*

POP3 - Post Office Protocol

The Post Office Protocol was designed for disconnected environments. In small environments it is not practical to maintain a persistent connection with the mail server, for instance, in environments where the connection time must be paid. With POP3 the client can access the server and retrieve the messages that the server is holding for it. When messages are retrieved from the client, they are typically deleted on the server, although this is not necessarily the case.

Windows .NET Server includes a POP3 server.

POP 3 is defined by RFC 1081.

IMAP - Internet Message Access Protocol

Like POP3, IMAP is designed to access mails on a mail server. Similar to POP3 clients, an IMAP client can have an offline mode where mails can be manipulated on the local machine. Unlike POP3 clients, IMAP clients have greater capabilities when in online mode, such as retrieving just the headers or bodies of specified mails, searching for particular messages on the server, and setting flags such as a replied flag. Essentially, IMAP allows the client to manipulate a remote mailbox as if it was local.

IMAP is defined with RFC 1730.

NNTP - Network News Transfer Protocol

Network News Transfer Protocol is an application layer protocol for submitting, relaying, and retrieving messages that form part of newsgroup discussions. This protocol provides client applications with access to a news server to retrieve selected messages, and also supports server to server transfer of messages.

NNTP is defined by the RFCs 850, 977, and 1036.

Other Application Protocols

There are two other interesting application protocols: SNMP and Telnet.

Simple Network Management Protocol (SNMP) aims to permit management of devices on the network. There is no lack of information such as performance counts from devices; instead there is too much information to manage it effectively. SNMP aims to manage devices effectively using alarms triggered by performance problems and faults, and allows devices to be configured.

An **SNMP agent** associated with a particular network device will have an MIB (Management Information Base) database that contains all manageable information for that device in an object-oriented manner (that is, consisting of objects, attributes, and instances). An SNMP client accesses the information in this database by sending SNMP GET requests. Conversely, SNMP SET requests are used to configure the MIB database.

In case of faults or performance problems, the SNMP agent sends trap messages to the SNMP client.

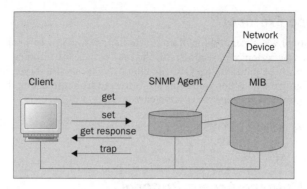

SNMP is defined with RFC 1157. The MIB database is defined with RFC 1155 and RFC 1156.

Earlier, we used the telnet application to simulate a browser as it carries out an HTTP request. However, the telnet application is primarily intended for connecting to a telnet server using the Telnet protocol. This protocol lets us connect to a remote system using user authentication, and to then invoke commands remotely from a console environment.

Sockets

The term **socket** doesn't define a protocol: it has two meanings, but neither of them relates to a protocol. One meaning is the socket programming API that was created initially by the University of Berkeley for BSD UNIX. BSD sockets were adapted as a programming interface for the Windows environment (and given the name WinSock). The WinSock API is wrapped in the .NET classes of the System.Net.Sockets namespace. Windows Sockets is a protocol independent programming interface for writing networking applications.

> *You will discover more about socket programming in Chapters 4 to 6. In later chapters where we show higher-level classes for Internet programming, sockets are used behind the scenes.*

The second usage of the term socket denotes an endpoint for communication between processes. In TCP/IP, an endpoint is bound to an IP address and a port number. We have to differentiate between **stream** and **datagram** socket types. A stream socket uses connection-oriented communication using the TCP/IP protocol; on the other hand the datagram socket uses connection-less communication using UDP/IP. We'll talk more about sockets in Chapter 4.

Domain Names

It is not easy to remember IP addresses with the quad-notation, and so more human-friendly names are given to hosts on the network. Because such names must be unique, the domain name system used supports hierarchical names. Examples of such hostnames are www.wrox.com, msdn.microsoft.com, and kerberos.vienna.globalknowledge.com. These names don't have to have three parts, but reading from right to the left, the name starts with the top-level domain. These top-level domains are country-specific (such as .com.tw) or generic (such as .org) and are defined by the IANA (Internet Assigned Numbers Authority). The name appearing directly to the left of the top-level domain is the domain name. To the left of that name, the person or organization holding the domain is responsible for maintaining uniqueness.

The generic top-level domains are listed in this table. In recent years, some new top-level domain names have been added:

Domain Name	Description
.aero	Air Industry
.biz	Business
.com	Commercial Organizations
.coop	Cooperative Associations
.info	No restriction on usage
.museum	Museums
.name	Individuals

Domain Name	Description
.net	Networks
.org	Nonprofit Organizations
.pro	Professionals
.gov	United States Government
.edu	Educational Institutions
.mil	United States Military
.int	Organizations established by international treaties between governments

A detailed description of these generic top-level domains, and of the sponsors and registrars of the domains, can be found at the following URL: http://www.iana.org/gtld/gtld.htm.

Additional to the generic top-level domains, there is a domain name for every country:

Domain Name	Description
.at	Austria
.cc	Cocos (Keeling) Islands
.de	Germany
.fr	France
.tv	Tuvalu
.uk	United Kingdom

The complete list of the country domains is at http://www.iana.org/cctld/cctld-whois.htm.

Whois Service

The whois service provides the means for querying a registration service to find the person or organization that registered a specific domain, their contact information, registration addresses, and so on. Such a whois service is available at the web site http://www.internic.net.

Domain Name Servers

Host names are resolved using DNS (Domain Name Service) servers. These servers have a database of hostnames and alias names mapping names to IP addresses. DNS servers also register information for Mail Servers, ISDN numbers, mailbox names, and services.

In Windows, it is the TCP/IP settings that specify which DNS server is to be used for queries, and the command ipconfig /all shows the DNS servers that have been set up, along with other configuration settings. When a hostname is used to connect to a remote system, the DNS server is queried for the IP address. The DNS server will first check its own database and cache, and if that fails to resolve the name, the DNS server asks a DNS root server. There are several root servers (named a.root-servers.net through to m.root-servers.net) worldwide which can access DNS servers of the top-level domains. The DNS server of the top-level domain knows the DNS server for a specific sub-domain, and will return the IP address corresponding to a particular hostname. DNS servers store information not found in their database in a cache to speed up subsequent requests.

Nslookup

The nslookup command-line utility provides IP addresses for hostnames by querying the default DNS server. In the case shown in the screenshot below, the DNS server is WS01IS02.highway.telekom.at. When I ask this server for the IP address of www.microsoft.com, it returns the real name of the server, www.microsoft.akadns.net, six IP addresses configured for this server, and its alias www.microsoft.com:

This is a non-authoritative answer, meaning that this server is not responsible for the domain that was queried, and reads the information of this domain from its cache. Incidentally, this caching is the cause of many hostname lookup problems. A name server will only clear its DNS cache infrequently, with the effect that different servers will hold inconsistent information. It can take whole days for a change of an address to filter through the Internet. The nslookup command-line utility lets us set up a different DNS server for querying, so we can compare information from different servers.

The Internet

In this chapter, we have covered many of the base technologies that underpin the Internet: hardware, protocols, and the domain name system. There remain some interesting topics for us to discuss:

❑ Intranets and Extranets

❑ Firewalls and Web Proxies

❑ XML Web Services

Intranets and Extranets

An **intranet** can use TCP/IP technologies in a very similar way to the Internet. The difference is of course that an intranet is a private network, where all users are known. The intranet is not intended for general public access, and some data, if not all, must be secured from outside access. Securing the intranet from the Internet at large is a task carried out by firewalls:

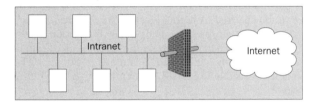

An **extranet** is a private network like an intranet, but extranets connect multiple intranet sites belonging to one company or partner companies over the Internet using a **tunnel**. Creating a VPN (Virtual Private Network) over the Internet in this way offers significant cost advantages over leasing private lines for the purpose.

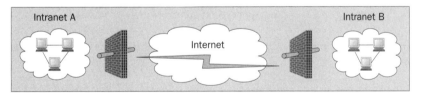

Firewalls

So, a firewall secures the intranet from the mayhem and disorder that is the Internet. Firewalls are also often used to secure a subnet inside a company from other subnets, to restrict access to the first subnet to only specified users and/or tasks.

In order to create a secure network with a firewall, that network must be configured so that all incoming and outgoing traffic has to pass through the firewall: naturally, there must be no alternative routes that bypass the firewall.

Firewalls can work at various layers of the OSI model. **Packet filters** check packets and filter them according to the IP addresses and port numbers of the network and transport layers. Packets from or to particular IP addresses can be granted permission to pass through the firewall, either into the network, or out to the world beyond. Port numbers can be used with packet filtering to specify what services can be used on each side of the firewall. For example, a firewall can be set so that the Internet side (known as the **red side** in firewall terminology) may access only web servers, at certain IP addresses behind the firewall, through HTTP. Such a configuration can be seen in the next picture, where a second firewall secures the internal company network that contains the mail server, file services, and user workstations. If applications running on the web server need access to data from the intranet, specific protocols and ports can be configured for the second firewall.

If security filters with a port number are defined, every packet sent through the firewall must be passed up to the transport layer to be checked. A higher level of checking is possible using **application filters**. An application filter must know about the commands of the application level protocol, such as FTP, HTTP, or SMTP, and can for instance permit certain files to be copied from the Internet to the intranet, but not the other way around, by allowing FTP GET commands, but not FTP PUT commands. SMTP application filters often deny mails that use DEBUG commands, as SMTP DEBUG mails can be used to break into local networks.

Web Proxies

A **web proxy** caches web requests from clients. Internet browsers on the intranet can be configured to use a web proxy that forwards the HTTP request to the web server on the Internet. The web proxy can cache web requests so that future client requests requesting the same page are not answered by the web server, but by the cached page stored by the web proxy.

Another function of the web proxy is to restrict access to specific web sites, and to log the web requests made by users.

> *The Microsoft Internet Security and Acceleration Server (ISA) acts both as a firewall and a web proxy to secure the network and increase performance.*

XML Web Services

An XML Web Service is an application that can be identified by a URI, and can be called remotely using Internet friendly protocols such as HTTP.

At the heart of XML Web Services lies SOAP (Simple Object Access Protocol). SOAP defines an XML format for calling remote methods regardless of the technologies used to implement those methods.

A typical process for invoking web services is shown in the following figure:

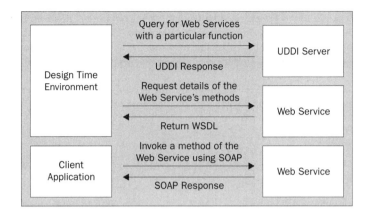

First we have to find a web service that meets our requirements, which we can do by querying a UDDI server using the UDDI (Universal Description, Discovery and Integration) protocol. Publicly available web services can be registered on a UDDI server, such as http://www.uddi.org or http://www.salcentral.com, which provides search functionality. The UDDI server returns certain information about web services that match specified requirements, such as a link to a WSDL (Web Service Description Language) document that details the methods exposed by the web service in a computer-readable XML format. If a web service is not to be made publicly available, its WSDL document can be exchanged in other ways, or by a private UDDI server. Microsoft offers a UDDI server that can be installed with Windows .NET Server.

The methods and parameters described by the WSDL document can be used to build SOAP requests to call the web service.

> *ASP.NET is an easy way to create a web service using the classes in the* `System.Web.Services` *namespace.*

> *The SOAP specification can be found at* http://www.w3.org/2000/xp/Group/.

.NET Remoting

The Remote Procedure Calls (RPC) protocol was the first widely recognized way to call functions across a network. RPC is a high-level protocol that does not require the client to create a message and send it to the receiving side, and to pick up the message on the server and analyze it to invoke the required function. Instead, the application programmer can invoke a function directly on the server. The RPC proxy running on the client marshals the remote method call (that is, transforms it to a network message) to send to the server, where the RPC stub unmarshals the message and invokes the method.

Because RPC was function-oriented, DCOM (Microsoft's Distributed Component Object Model) extended it to add object orientation.

.NET brings a new model for distributed applications, and a successor to DCOM – .NET Remoting. .NET Remoting offers far greater flexibility and extensibility over DCOM.

The picture below shows an architecture overview of .NET Remoting. The remote object exposes some methods for remote calls. A **proxy** is created on the client mirroring the remote object in that it exposes the same public methods. The client invokes these methods on the proxy class, and the proxy uses a **formatter** to format the messages so that they can be sent across the network.

The network transport is defined by the channel. On the server, another **formatter** unformats received messages, and passes them to the **dispatcher** which calls the methods on the remote object:

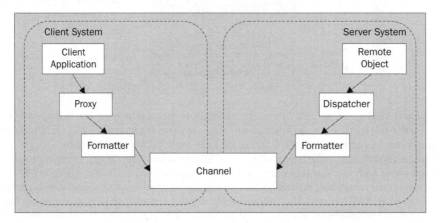

.NET Remoting permits interceptors, or **sinks**, to be placed at certain points in the flow on the client or server-side to add additional functionality, such as logging, duplicating calls for reliability reasons, or dynamically finding servers.

.NET Remoting supports a variety of channels and formatters. The .NET Framework v1.0 offers a TCP and an HTTP channel, and SOAP and binary formatters. If we choose the HTTP channel and the SOAP formatter, .NET Remoting becomes the same as XML Web Services. The TCP channel with binary formatters is a fast communication mechanism. If both the client and server use .NET technologies, .NET Remoting is a fast and easy to use communication mechanism.

> *You can read more about XML Web Services in the Wrox books* Professional XML Web Services *(ISBN 1-86100-509-1),* Professional ASP.NET Web Services *(ISBN 1-86100-775-2), and* C# Web Services *(ISBN 1-86100-439-7). The focus in* Professional XML Web Services *is independent of the underlying technology, while* Professional ASP.NET Web Services *concentrates on web services in ASP.NET, and* C# Web Services *is more technical, using both ASP.NET and .NET Remoting to implement web services.*

Messaging

Messaging is the process of sending messages from a client to a server. All networking protocols we have seen up to now require a connected environment. No matter if we use TCP or UDP sockets, the HTTP protocol, or .NET Remoting, the client and server must be running concurrently: that is, at the same time.

With message queuing, the client and server can be running at different times, and the client can send messages even when the connection to the server is not be available. The message will be queued, and will reach the server at a later time. Message queuing also gives us an easy way to set priorities for messages, which can be useful in a connected environment too, where we may wish to read higher priority messages first.

One scenario where message queuing can be particularly useful is when an application is run on a portable computer not connected to the company network, perhaps belonging to a sales person at a customer's site. Message queuing allows the application to send a message, but store it in the message queue of the client until connected back to the network. As far the application that sends the message is concerned, the message is sent immediately.

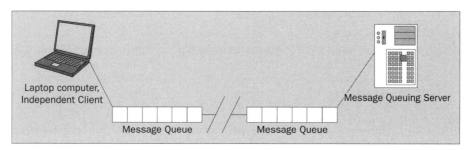

The `System.Messaging` *namespace houses the .NET classes that provide message queuing. For more about .NET Programming using Message Queuing, read* Data-Centric .NET Programming with C# *(Wrox Press, ISBN 1-86100-592-X).*

Other Ways to Access Network Objects

LDAP (Lightweight Directory Access Protocol) was designed for hierarchical object stores that hold long-lived objects. LDAP, or Active Directory, creates such stores for long-lived objects that are of interest in the enterprise, such as users, groups, computers, printers, network shares, services, or any custom object type. LDAP lets us read, write, and search for objects in the stores. Classes in the `System.DirectoryServices` namespace allow the .NET Framework to access objects in the Active Directory or other LDAP data stores.

The `System.Management` namespace offers classes to access WMI (Windows Management Instrumentation) classes. WMI enables management to be performed across the network, such as accessing hardware information, and configuring and administering services that offer WMI providers. WMI can be used to obtain information about hardware, such as free disk space, CPU utilization, performance data, DNS servers, and terminal services configuration.

For more on accessing objects in Active Directory, check out Wrox's 'Data-Centric .NET Programming with C#" (ISBN 1-86100-592-X).

Internet Organizations and Standards

There is a whole host of standards committees working on the development of networking specifications and standards. The table below lists the important groups in this area:

Standards Organization	Definition	Web Site	Technologies
ISO	International Organization for Standardization	http://www.iso.org	The International Standardization Organization defined the OSI network. The OSI Model is now commonly used.
IEEE	Institute of Electrical and Electronic Engineers	http://www.ieee.org	IEEE is responsible for LAN standards and hardware specifications: Ethernet, Token Ring, MAN, Wireless LAN, Broadband.
IAB	Internet Architecture Board	http://www.iab.org	The IAB is responsible for editorial management of RFCs and appoints the IETF chair.
IETF	Internet Engineering Task Force	http://www.ietf.org	Internet standards – RFCs can be found at the IETF.
IANA	Internet Assigned Numbers Authority	http://www.iana.org	As the name says – IANA is assigning Internet numbers like reserved IP address ranges, port numbers, protocol numbers, and so on.
W3C	World Wide Web Consortium	http://www.w3.org	The W3C is active developing Internet Technologies: HTTP, HTML, XML, SOAP, and so on

Summary

This chapter has worked through the basics of networking to provide an overview of important networking concepts and networking protocols. We started with a discussion of the physical network, looking at the purpose and function of the crucial components of a network: network interface cards, hubs, routers, and switches.

Another piece of fundamental knowledge that underpins much work in networking is that of the magic OSI seven-layer model. These seven layers are, from top to bottom, application, presentation, session, transport, network, data link, and physical.

We've also had a close look at the headers of the key IP, TCP, and UDP protocols, in order to gain an understanding of connection-oriented and connection-less communication.

We discussed the purpose of some important application protocols, namely HTTP, FTP, SMTP, and IMAP. These are only a few of the technologies found in use on the Internet and other networks.

We are now ready to move on to write some programs that perform stream manipulation in the next chapter, as this is very useful in network programming. We will start on network programming proper in Chapter 3.

2

Streams in .NET

A stream is an abstract representation of a serial device for storing and retrieving data one byte at a time – the underlying device can be a file, a printer, or a network socket for example. Through this abstraction, different devices can be accessed with the same process, and similar code can be used to read data from a file input stream as can be used to read data from a network input stream for example. Furthermore, the programmer's need to worry about the actual physical mechanism of the device is removed.

In this chapter we'll look at the following:

❑ Streams in .NET

❑ The `Stream` class and its members

❑ The `FileStream` class and other `Stream`-derived classes

❑ Reading to and writing from binary and text files

❑ Serialization

Streams in .NET

The .NET Framework provides a rich set of classes for performing operations on various types of streams. `Stream` is the main class, an abstract class from which all other stream-related classes derive.

Since a stream is an abstraction of data as a sequence of bytes, to manipulate these sequences of bytes you have to perform some basic operations such as reading, writing, or seeking. With the `Stream` class you can perform binary I/O operations on a stream. With `TextReader` and `TextWriter` you can perform character I/O operations, whereas with `BinaryReader` and `BinaryWriter` you can perform I/O operations on primitive types.

Synchronous and Asynchronous I/O

There are two ways to perform operations on a stream, synchronous or asynchronous – your choice will depend upon the requirements of your application. As we will see in a moment, the `Stream` class provides methods for both synchronous and asynchronous operations, but first let's discuss some of the advantages and disadvantages of each type of operation.

Synchronous I/O

By default, all operations on streams are performed synchronously – this is the simplest way to perform I/O operations. The disadvantage of synchronous I/O is that it blocks processing until the I/O operation is complete – then the application is allowed to continue processing.

Synchronous I/O is useful for performing operations on small sized files, but with large files the application may give poor performance as it blocks the current thread of execution. Synchronous I/O is not suitable for performing operations over a network where you have little control over the time required to complete the operation. Therefore, synchronous I/O is not a good choice for passing huge streams on a network with low bandwidth or speed. By threading synchronous methods, you can simulate asynchronous I/O.

Asynchronous I/O

In asynchronous I/O, other tasks can be performed while the I/O operation is being completed. When the I/O operation completes, the operating system notifies the caller. Therefore, a separate notification mechanism is required for asynchronous I/O.

This method is useful when an application needs to continue performing other tasks while processing large amounts of data from a stream, or needs to work with slow devices whose rate of access would otherwise slow down the application.

In asynchronous I/O a separate thread is created for each I/O request – this can lead to an extra overhead for the operating system.

The Stream Class

The `Stream` class in the `System.IO` namespace is the base class for all the other stream classes, and provides the functionality for performing fundamental operations on stream. If you understand the functionality of the `Stream` class, then you can easily understand the other derived classes too – the key thing is to learn how to create the different types of stream with each class. In short, all the `Stream`-derived classes represent various types of stream with common or derived methods from the `Stream` class, and some extra methods for performing operations on that specific type of stream.

The diagram below illustrates `Stream`, the derived classes, and various other classes provided for performing operations on stream.

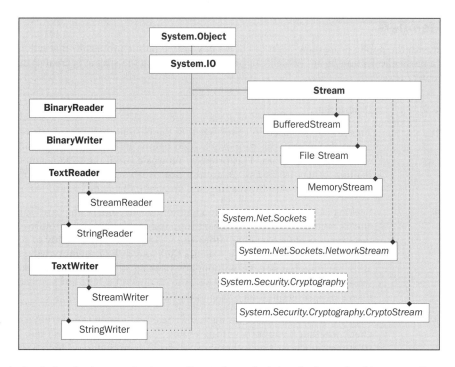

Each derived class is characterized according to its underlying device or backing store. For example, the FileStream class uses files as a backing store for streams, whereas the NetworkStream does not have any backing storage – this class is specially created for transferring streams across a network.

In the table below, some of the main classes derived from Stream are shown, along with a description of their purpose:

Class	Purpose
FileStream	Uses files as backing storage. The most widely used Stream class.
BufferedStream	Uses a buffer as backing storage. Used as intermediate storage for improving performance.
MemoryStream	Uses memory as backing storage and performs faster I/O operations when compared to other streams.
NetworkStream	Does not have any backing storage. Used with other streams for transferring data across a network.
CryptoStream	CryptoStream is used with other stream classes for performing encryption-decryption on streams.

Now let's have a look at the Stream class's members.

Stream Members

Let's start with the public properties – first of all, we have three public properties that tell us if a stream supports a particular feature or not, which can be determined when the stream is created through the relevant constructor:

Property	Description
CanRead	This property is used to check whether the current stream supports reading or not. In general, this property is used before performing any reading operation on a stream. This property returns true if the stream supports reading, otherwise false. A NotSupportedException is thrown if the stream does not support reading and an attempt is made to read from it.
CanSeek	Seeking is used to set the position within the current stream. CanSeek checks whether the current stream supports seeking or not. It returns true if the stream supports seeking, otherwise false. A stream's ability to seek depends on its backing store – media such as a disk or memory will generally allow seeking, but streams without any backing store such as network streams will always returns false. A NotSupportedException is thrown if seeking is attempted on a stream that does not support it.
CanWrite	CanWrite is used before doing any write operation on the current stream to check whether it supports writing or not. This property returns true if stream supports writing, otherwise false. Attempting to write to a stream that does not support writing throws a NotSupportedException.

There are two further properties to determine the size of the stream and the current position within the stream:

Property	Description
Length	This read-only property returns a long value representing the length of the stream in bytes. This property can be used for checking the end of the stream, or for determining the size of an array of bytes – a buffer used for storing the stream.
Position	Position can be used to set or to get the current position within the stream – used for moving around within a stream. To use this property, the stream must support seeking, which can be checked using the CanSeek property discussed above.

The Stream class has a number of methods for moving through the stream, reading and writing from the stream, and managing the stream.

Let's look first at the Seek() method for moving through the stream. Seek() is used for setting the position within stream. This method provides random access to the stream and is generally used while modifying or reading specific contents of stream. Seek() takes a long value and a value from the SeekOrigin enumeration. The long value specifies the offset from reference point specified by SeekOrigin value – this can be Begin, Current, or End, representing the beginning of the stream, the current position, or the end of the stream respectively. (Seek() is the method actually used when you set the Position property.)

The methods for reading to and writing from streams fall into two categories – there are corresponding sets of methods for synchronous and asynchronous operations.

Here are the synchronous methods:

Method	Description
Read() ReadByte()	Read() and ReadByte() are used for performing synchronous reading from a stream. Read() reads a specified number of bytes and advances the position within the stream by the number of bytes read, whereas ReadByte() reads a single byte from the stream and advances the current position within the stream by one byte. Note that Read() returns 0 at the end of stream whereas ReadByte() returns –1.
Write() WriteByte()	These methods are used to perform synchronous writing to a stream. Write() writes a sequences of bytes in a stream and advances the current position within the stream by the number of bytes written, whereas WriteByte() writes a single byte at the current position within a stream, advancing the position by a single byte.

and here are the asynchronous methods:

Method	Description
BeginRead() BeginWrite()	BeginRead() and BeginWrite() are the methods through which you can perform asynchronous I/O operations. Both methods take five parameters – a byte array buffer that data is read from or written to, an integer offset which indicates the starting position for reading or writing the data, and an integer count specifying the maximum number of bytes to read or write. The fourth parameter is an optional AsyncCallback delegate, called when the read or write operation is complete. The fifth and last parameter is a user-provided object to distinguish this particular read or write request from the other requests. Both methods return an IAsyncResult interface that represents the status of an asynchronous operation.
EndRead() EndWrite()	These methods are used for completing asynchronous I/O operations, waiting for the asynchronous operations to finish.

Finally, let's look at methods for managing a stream:

Method	Description
Flush()	Flush() clears all buffers and moves information to its destination depending upon the state of the Stream object.
Close()	This method is used to free resources such as file handlers and sockets associated with stream. This method automatically flushes any stored data so there is no need to call Flush() before a Close() method. The underlying mechanism for closing stream is different for each stream type – in FileStream it releases all file resources whereas in NetworkStream it closes the underlying socket. It's advisable to put a Close() method into a finally block to ensure that the stream is closed regardless of any exceptions thrown.
SetLength	This method is used to set the length of the current stream. Note that if the specified value is less than the current length of the stream then the stream is chopped down. If the specified value is greater than the current length of the stream the stream will expand.
	A stream must support both writing and seeking for SetLength() – this can be checked with the CanWrite and CanSeek properties.

When looking at the classes derived from Stream, we won't be discussing these methods any further unless they have meaning specific to that type of stream.

Our first Stream example will be the FileStream class. Once you've seen how to implement the members we've just looked at with the FileStream class, it's a short stretch to understand how to apply them to the other Stream-derived classes.

The FileStream Class

The FileStream class is useful for performing I/O operations on files, and as such, is one of the most important and widely used of all the Stream-derived classes.

With the FileStream class you can perform operations not only on files but also on operating system file handles such as standard input and output devices. You can use this class with other derived classes for creating temporary files – you can serialize objects to a binary file, for example, and then convert them back whenever required. While transferring the file across a network, you can stream the file contents using this class on the server-side and on the client-side you can recreate and store the retrieved stream back into the original file format.

The FileStream constructor allows several ways to create a FileStream object – but they all involve specifying either a string for the file path or a file handle that can be used for physical devices that support streaming.

Creating a FileStream Instance with a File Path

Various methods for creating a FileStream instance by specifying a path to a file are described below. A default buffer of 8192 bytes is allocated to the stream when it is created. This can be changed with one of the constructor overloads we'll meet in a moment.

Specifying the File Path and Mode

By specifying a string representing the path to a file and a value from the `FileMode` enumeration you can create a `FileStream` object. The `FileMode` parameter describes how to open a specified file, and its values are given below:

FileMode Value	Description
Append	Opens or creates a new file for appending data to – the file cannot be used for reading, and the file pointer is set to the end of the file.
Create	Creates a new file, overwriting if the file already exists.
CreateNew	Creates a new file, throwing an exception if the file already exists.
Open	Opens an already existing file, throwing an exception if the file does not exist.
OpenOrCreate	If the file specified exists it is opened, or else a new file is created.
Truncate	Opens a file and deletes its contents, setting the file pointer to the beginning of the file.

Thus to create a `FileStream` object that creates a new file called `C:\Networking\MyStream.txt` you would use the following:

```
// Using file path and file mode
FileStream inF = new FileStream("C:\\Networking\\MyStream.txt",
                                FileMode.CreateNew);
```

Specifying File Access

You can create an instance of `FileStream` by providing additional file access parameters from the `FileAccess` enumeration. This enumeration allows you to restrict the user to specific operations on the stream.

FileAccess Value	Description
Read	Allow read-only access to the file
Write	Allow write-only access to the file
ReadWrite	Allow both read and write access to the file

The `CanRead` and `CanWrite` properties discussed earlier can be used to check the `FileAccess` permission given to the file.

Thus to create a `FileStream` object that creates a new file called `C:\Networking\MyStream.txt` with write-only access you would use the following:

```
// Using file path, file mode and file access
FileStream inF = new FileStream("C:\\Networking\\MyStream.txt",
                        FileMode.Open, FileAccess.Write);
```

Specifying Sharing Permissions

With the addition of sharing permissions you can control access to other stream objects. This is useful when a file is shared between two or more processes. The sharing permissions are determined by a value from the `FileShare` enumeration that represents various access modes.

FileShare Value	Description
Inheritable	Child process can inherit the file handle. Not supported by Win32.
None	No process (including the current one) can access the file – thus the file cannot be shared.
Read	Gives read-only permission to the current process and other processes.
Write	Gives write-only permission to the current process and other processes.
ReadWrite	Grants read and write permission to the current process and other processes.

```
// Using file path, file mode, file access and sharing permission
// Open file for writing, other processes will get read-only access
FileStream inF = new FileStream("C:\\Networking\\MyStream.txt ",
                        FileMode.Open, FileAccess.Write, FileShare.Read);
```

Specifying Buffer Size

You can also create a `FileStream` instance by specifying the size of the buffer in addition to the parameters discussed above. Here we set the size of the buffer to 1000 bytes:

```
//Using path, mode, access, sharing permission and buffer size.
FileStream outF = new FileStream("C:\\Networking\\MyStream.txt",
                        FileMode.Open, FileAccess.Write,
                        FileShare.Read, 1000);
```

Specifying Synchronous or Asynchronous State

With a further Boolean value we can specify whether to use asynchronous or synchronous I/O operations on the stream – a value of `true` indicates asynchronous.

```
//Using path, mode, access, sharing permission, buffer size and
// specifying asynchronous operations
FileStream outF = new FileStream("C:\\Networking\\MyStream.txt",
                        FileMode.Open, FileAccess.Write,
                        FileShare.Read, 1000, true);
```

It's also possible to create a `FileStream` object using a file handle rather than passing a path to a file. A file handle is a unique identifier that the operating system assigns to a file when the file is opened or created. A file handle is represented using the `IntPtr` structure, which represents an integer of platform-specific length.

Creating a `FileStream` object with a file handle requires you to specify at least the file handle and the `FileAccess`. A further overload allows you to define the ownership of the stream – a value of `true` means the `FileStream` instance gets exclusive control. With further parameters you can specify the size of the buffer (the default size is still 8192 bytes).

You can obtain a file handle from a `FileStream` object by using its `Handle` property:

```
//Create FileStream instance
FileStream inF = new FileStream("C:\\Networking\\MyStream.txt", FileMode.Open);

//Get the file handle
IntPtr fHandle = inF.Handle;
```

Reading and Writing with the FileStream

We've spent enough time talking about the methods and properties of the `Stream`-derived classes that we can use, so let's actually get on with reading from and writing to a `FileStream`. We'll take a look at both synchronous and asynchronous modes of operation.

Synchronous I/O

`Stream` provides `Read()` and `Write()` methods for performing synchronous read/write operations on a stream.

The following example performs synchronous I/O operations on a file. It also uses the `Seek()` method to set the position within the stream.

We begin by adding the `System.IO` namespace for I/O operations, and the `System.Text` namespace for the methods to convert strings to byte arrays – we'll look more at these later in the chapter.

```
using System;
using System.IO;
using System.Text ;

class SyncIO
{
    public static void Main(string[] args)
    {
```

We create a `FileStream` instance, specifying its `FileMode` as `OpenOrCreate`. This will open our file if it exists, otherwise a new file is created. When you first run this example, a file `SyncDemo.txt` is created in the same folder as the executable.

```
// Create FileStream instance
FileStream syncF = new FileStream("SyncDemo.txt",FileMode.OpenOrCreate);
```

Now we are ready to examine various synchronous methods. Let's start with `WriteByte()`. In the example a character is converted to a byte and then written to a file by using the `WriteByte()` method. After writing a byte the file position is automatically incremented by one.

```
syncF.WriteByte(Convert.ToByte('A'));
```

By using the `Write()` method we can write more than one character to the file. Here we convert a string to a byte array (with the `GetBytes()` method of the `Encoding` class in the `System.Text` namespace), and this byte array is then written to the file with the `Write()` method. `Write()` takes three parameters, the first being the byte array to write, the position or offset in the array from where to start writing, and the length of data to be written – in this case we write the entire byte array from the start:

```
Console.WriteLine("--Write method demo--");
byte[] writeBytes = Encoding.ASCII.GetBytes(" is a first character.");
syncF.Write(writeBytes, 0, writeBytes.Length);
```

Thus we have written a single byte with the `WriteByte()` method, and an entire string (converted to a byte array) with the `Write()` method. Now we'll read this information back with the corresponding `Read()` methods.

When you perform read or write operations on a `FileStream`, the current position (or pointer) of the file automatically increases by the number of bytes read or written. We want to read the bytes just written, so we'll use the `Seek()` method to set the current position in the stream, in this case back to the beginning of the stream:

```
// Set pointer at origin
syncF.Seek (0,SeekOrigin.Begin);
```

Now we can read – we'll read a single byte with the `ReadByte()` method first of all. A `byte` is read from the stream (with the position automatically increased by one) and converted back into a `char`:

```
Console.WriteLine ("--Readbyte method demo--");

// Read byte and display
Console.WriteLine("First character is ->" +
    Convert.ToChar(syncF.ReadByte()));
```

Now we read the remainder of the file with the `Read()` method. This method takes three parameters – a byte array which will store the data read, the position or offset in array from where to start reading, and the number of bytes to read. Here we'll read in all the remaining bytes in the file – we're at position 1 in the file, so we want to read in `syncF.Length - 1` bytes:

```
// Use of Read method
Console.WriteLine("----Read method demo----");

// Allocate buffer
byte[] readBuf = new byte[syncF.Length-1];

// Read file
syncF.Read(readBuf,0,(Convert.ToInt32(syncF.Length))-1);
```

The byte array of data just read in is converted to a string with the `GetString()` method of the `Encoding` class and displayed:

```
        // Display contents
        Console.WriteLine("The rest of the file is : " +
                        Encoding.ASCII.GetString(readBuf));

    }
}
```

The output of this code is the following:

Asynchronous I/O

One of the overloads for the `FileStream` constructor provides the `IsAsync` flag that defines synchronous or asynchronous state. The `FileStream` opens asynchronously when you pass `true` to this flag. Note that the operating system must support asynchronous I/O operation or else it works as synchronous I/O – Windows NT, 2000, and XP support both synchronous and asynchronous I/O.

Asynchronous I/O is a little bit more complex than synchronous I/O. We'll only sketch out the basics of how to implement asynchronous operations here – we'll look at them in more depth in Chapter 4.

A special callback mechanism is needed to implement asynchronous I/O, and an `AsyncCallback` delegate provides a way for client applications to implement this callback mechanism. This callback delegate is supplied to the `BeginRead()` or `BeginWrite()` method.

We'll look at an example for asynchronous reading. We begin with the usual namespaces, and some static fields to hold a `FileStream` object and `byte` array:

```
using System;
using System.IO;
using System.Text;
using System.Threading;

public class AsyncDemo
{
    // Stream object for reading
    static FileStream fileStm;

    // Buffer to read
    static byte[] readBuf;
```

We declare an `AsyncCallback` delegate field for the callback function:

```
       // Async-Call-back delegate
       static AsyncCallback Callback;
```

In the `Main()` method, we initialize our callback delegate to point to the `CallBackFunction()` method – this is the method that will be called when the end of the asynchronous read operation is signaled. We'll see more about this process in Chapter 4.

```
       public static void Main(String[] args)
       {
           Callback = new AsyncCallback(CallBackFunction);
```

Now we can initialize our `FileStream` object, specifying asynchronous operations with the final `true` value:

```
           fileStm = new FileStream(@"C:\Networking\Streams\Test.txt",
                                   FileMode.Open, FileAccess.Read,
                                   FileShare.Read, 64, true);
           readBuf= new byte[fileStm.Length];
```

Now we can use the `BeginRead()` method to initiate asynchronous read operations on the stream. The callback delegate is passed to the `BeginRead()` method as its penultimate parameter.

```
           // Call async read
           fileStm.BeginRead(readBuf, 0, readBuf.Length, Callback, null);
```

Data will be read from our `FileStream` while we continue with other activities – here we'll simply give the appearance of doing some other work by looping, and every so often putting the main thread to sleep. Once the loop has finished, the `FileStream` is closed.

```
           // Simulation of main execution
           for (long i = 0; i < 5000; i++)
           {
             if (i % 1000 == 0)
             {
                 Console.WriteLine("Executing in Main - " + i.ToString());
                 Thread.Sleep(10);
             }
           }
           fileStm.Close();
       }
```

Note that if your loop completes before reading has finished then the `FileStream` is closed anyway – the main thread of our program isn't waiting for `BeginRead()` to finish. In Chapter 4 we'll look at an example that waits for an asynchronous operation to finish before continuing with the next activity – this can be very important if you need to perform asynchronous operations in a particular order or rely upon one operation completing before you can start the next one.

The callback function, suitably named `CallBackFunction()` here, is called when the buffer is full. `EndRead()` is called to complete the asynchronous read. If the end of the file hasn't been reached, `BeginRead()` is called again, to continue reading, and the contents of our current read are displayed:

```
static void CallBackFunction(IAsyncResult asyncResult)
{
    // Gets called when the buffer is full.
    int readB = fileStm.EndRead(asyncResult);
    if (readB > 0)
    {
        fileStm.BeginRead(readBuf, 0, readBuf.Length, Callback, null);
        Console.WriteLine(Encoding.ASCII.GetString(readBuf, 0, readB));
    }
}
```

And here is the typical output of this example – note that your processor speed, file and buffer size may give you different results:

The BufferedStream Class

A buffer is a reserved area of memory used for storing temporary data, and its main purpose is to improve I/O performance, and it is often used to synchronize data transfer between devices of different speeds. Many online media applications use buffers as intermediate storage. Devices such as printers have their own buffers for storing the data.

In .NET you can implement buffering through the `BufferedStream` class. A `BufferedStream` objects wraps another `Stream` object. The `BufferedStream` is generally used with `NetworkStream` to store data in memory. The `FileStream` already has its own internal buffer and a `MemoryStream` doesn't require buffering.

A default buffer of 4096 bytes is allocated when you create a buffer with `BufferedStream`, but you can also specify a custom size for buffer through one of the many constructor overloads.

The following example shows a method for reading a buffered stream. This method takes a `Stream` object parameter, wraps it in a `BufferedStream` and performs a read operation. In the same way you can perform other operations on `BufferedStream`.

```
// Reading BufferedStream
public static void readBufStream(Stream st)
{
    // Compose BufferedStream
    BufferedStream bf = new BufferedStream(st);
```

```
    byte[] inData = new Byte[st.Length];

    // Read and display buffered data
    bf.Read(inData, 0, Convert.ToInt32(st.Length));

    Console.WriteLine(Encoding.ASCII.GetString(inData));
}
```

The MemoryStream Class

There are situations where an application needs data frequently, such as a lookup table for reference data. In such cases, storing the data in a file can cause delays and reduce the performance of the application. MemoryStream is the solution for such cases where data needs to be stored in memory.

MemoryStream is useful for fast temporary storage. A good example is transferring serialized objects within a process – you can use MemoryStream for temporarily storing serialized objects. This gives better performance than using the FileStream or BufferedStream classes.

Creating a MemoryStream object is quite different from FileStream or BufferedStream. An instance can be created in several ways.

The following example shows how to create and use a MemoryStream – we use the WriteTo() method to write the entire memory stream to a file.

```
using System;
using System.IO;
using System.Text ;

public class memStreamDemoClass
{
    public static void Main(String[] args)
    {
```

The MemoryStream instance is created without passing any parameter. Reading and writing data in the MemoryStream is the same as we saw in the FileStream example. Here we are using the Write() method for writing a simple string.

```
        // Create empty Memory stream
        MemoryStream mS = new MemoryStream();
        byte[] memData = Encoding.ASCII.GetBytes("This will go in Memory!!");

        // Write data
        mS.Write(memData,0,memData.Length);
```

After writing a string, we'll read it using the Read() method. Note that before reading we set the current position to zero.

```
                // Set pointer at origin
                mS.Position = 0;
                byte[] inData = new byte[100];

                // Read memory
                mS.Read(inData, 0, 100);
                Console.WriteLine(Encoding.ASCII.GetString(inData));
```

The `WriteTo()` method is used to write the entire contents of this memory stream to the file stream.

```
            Stream strm = new FileStream("C:\\Networking\Streams\MemOutput.txt",
                                    FileMode.OpenOrCreate, FileAccess.Write);
            mS.WriteTo(strm);
        }
    }
```

The NetworkStream Class

Across a network, the data transferred between locations is in the form of a continuous flow or stream. For handling such streams, .NET has a special class – NetworkStream in the `System.Net.Sockets` namespace, which is used for sending and receiving data through network sockets.

NetworkStream is an unbuffered stream and does not support random access to data – you cannot change the position within the stream and therefore the use of `Seek()` and `Position` throws an exception. The `CanSeek` property always returns `false` for a NetworkStream object.

As NetworkStream is unbuffered, `BufferedStream` is usually used along with this class as an intermediate storage medium.

Some of the important members of NetworkStream are described below:

Property	Description
DataAvailable	Returns a Boolean value indicating whether data is available in the stream for reading or not. A value of `true` indicates that data is available in the stream.
Readable	Used to get or set a Boolean value indicating whether read access is given to the stream or not. This property works in the same way as the `CanRead` property in other streams.
Socket	Returns the underlying `Socket`.
Writeable	Used for checking whether the stream can be written to or not. A value of `true` indicates that the stream is writeable. This property works in the same way as the `CanWrite` property in other streams.

Each NetworkStream constructor requires at least a `Socket` – in addition you can specify a Boolean value indicating ownership of a stream and/or a value from the `FileAccess` enumeration we saw earlier to control read and write permissions. Setting the ownership flag to `true` gives control of the socket to the NetworkStream object, and by using the `Close()` method you can close the underlying socket.

A `NetworkStream` can also be retrieved from a `TcpClient` – we'll spend a whole chapter on TCP in Chapter 5, but we'll make use of it here to illustrate NetworkStream in a client-server scenario. The `TcpClient.GetStream()` method creates a `NetworkStream` object, passing in its underlying `Socket` as the constructor parameter.

Let's look at the code for a simple TCP listener using a `NetworkStream` – the TCP classes are found in the `System.Net.Sockets` namespace.

```
using System;
using System.IO;
using System.Text;
using System.Net;
using System.Net.Sockets;

class TCPListenerDemo
{
    public static void Main()
    {
        try
        {
```

The first thing we do is create our `TcpListener` object to listen on port 5001 here, and start listening with the `Start()` method. `AcceptClient()` accepts a connection request, returning a `TcpClient`. We use its `GetStream()` method to create our `NetworkStream` object:

```
            // Create TCP listener
            TcpListener listener = new TcpListener(5001);
            listener.Start();
            TcpClient tc = listener.AcceptClient();
            NetworkStream stm = tc.GetStream();
```

Now we can read data as we have done with the other streams, using the `Read()` method:

```
            byte[] readBuf = new byte[100];
            stm.Read(readBuf,0,100);

            //Display Data
            Console.WriteLine(Encoding.ASCII.GetString(readBuf));

            stm.Close();
        }
        catch (Exception e )
        {
            Console.WriteLine(e.ToString());
        }
    }
}
```

To use this example you need a client application for sending some data. Remember to start the listener application before the client application!

Here's the code for the TCP client:

```
using System;
using System.IO;
using System.Text;
using System.Net;
using System.Net.Sockets;

class TcpClientExample
{
    static void Main(string[] args)
    {
        try
        {
```

We create our `TcpClient`, and connect to the `localhost` on port 5001. Once again, we use the `GetStream()` method to return the underlying `NetworkStream`:

```
            // Create TCP Client
            TcpClient client = new TcpClient();
            //Connect using hostname and port
            client.Connect ("localhost", 5001);
            //Get NetworkStream instance for sending data
            NetworkStream stm = client.GetStream();
```

Now we have our `NetworkStream`, sending the data is the same process as we have used with the other streams:

```
            byte[] sendBytes = Encoding.ASCII.GetBytes("This data has come from" +
                                                " another place!!!");
            stm.Write (sendBytes, 0, sendBytes.Length);
```

Finally, our `TcpClient` is closed:

```
            client.Close();
        }
        catch (Exception e )
        {
            Console.WriteLine(e.ToString());
            Console.WriteLine("The listener has probably not started");
        }

    }
}
```

We'll see many more examples of creating client-server applications of differing complexity over the coming chapters.

The CryptoStream Class

For certain types of data, the need to secure its contents is a major consideration when transforming or storing it – the need for securing data is increasing day by day. To make data secure it is generally encrypted with some secret key into an unreadable form. To get back the original contents it is decrypted with a secret key. The secret key used for decryption may be the same as that used for encryption or different depending on the encryption algorithm.

.NET provides the `CryptoStream` class that links streams to cryptographic transformations. `CryptoStream` is not actually in the `System.IO` namespace, but does indeed derive from `Stream`. The `CryptoStream` class can be used to perform cryptographic operations on a `Stream` object.

The `CryptoStream` constructor takes three parameters – the first is the stream to be used, the second is the cryptographic transformation, and the third parameter specifies read or write access to the cryptographic stream.

We have a variety of cryptographic transformations at our disposal – any cryptographic service provider that implements the `ICryptoTransform` interface can be used. The following example demonstrates the use of various cryptographic providers – these reside in the `System.Security.Cryptography` namespace.

```
using System;
using System.IO;
using System.Text ;
using System.Security.Cryptography;

public class crypt
{
    public static void Main()
    {
```

First of all, we'll ask the user to choose a service provider. All service providers are derived from the `SymmetricAlgorithm` class that has a single secret key that is used for both encryption and decryption.

```
        Console.WriteLine("Select Service Provider for CryptoStream");
        Console.WriteLine("1 = DESCryptoServiceProvider");
        Console.WriteLine("2 = RC2CryptoServiceProvider");
        Console.WriteLine("3 = RijndaelManaged");
        Console.WriteLine("4 = TripleDESCryptoServiceProvider");
        Console.WriteLine("5 = SymmetricAlgorithm");

        // Create des object
        SymmetricAlgorithm des = null;

        switch (Console.ReadLine())
        {
            case "1":
                des = new DESCryptoServiceProvider();
                break;
            case "2":
                des  = new RC2CryptoServiceProvider();
                break;
```

```
        case "3":
            des  = new RijndaelManaged();
            break;
        case "4":
            des  = new TripleDESCryptoServiceProvider();
            break;
        case "5":
            des= SymmetricAlgorithm.Create(); //uses default algorithm
            break;
        default:
            Console.WriteLine ("Wrong selection");
            return;
    }
```

A `FileStream` object is created to save the encrypted data, around which we will wrap our `CryptoStream` object. The `ICryptoTransform` interface helps to define the basic operations of the cryptographic transformation that is created using the `CreateEncryptor` method of the `SymmetricAlgorithm` class.

```
    FileStream fs  = new FileStream("SecretFile.dat", FileMode.Create,
                                    FileAccess.Write);
    ICryptoTransform desencrypt = des.CreateEncryptor();

    CryptoStream cryptostream = new CryptoStream(fs, desencrypt,
                                        CryptoStreamMode.Write);
```

Now we encrypt our message. We'll use a simple string, which we convert to a byte array with the `GetBytes()` method of the `Encoding` class of the `System.Text` namespace – we'll talk more about this class later in the chapter. Once we have our byte array, it is written to the `CryptoStream` with its `Write()` method.

```
    string theMessage = "A top secret message";
    byte[] bytearrayinput = Encoding.Unicode.GetBytes(theMessage);

    Console.WriteLine("Original Message : {0}",theMessage);

    cryptostream.Write(bytearrayinput, 0, bytearrayinput.Length);

    cryptostream.Close();
    fs.Close();
```

After closing our streams, we can proceed to decrypt our message – in the second part of our code the encrypted message is read from the file and then converted back into the original.

```
    /***********Time to Decrypt...***********/

    // Create file stream to read encrypted file back
    FileStream fsread = new FileStream("SecretFile.dat", FileMode.Open,
                              FileAccess.ReadWrite);

    byte[] encByte = new byte[fsread.Length ];
    fsread.Read(encByte,0,encByte.Length );
```

Here we have defined the size of our byte array by using the Length property of the FileStream to determine the length of the data written to our file. We read the data into this byte array with the Read() method. Before we decrypt, we display the encrypted message to the console, and then set the Position within the FileStream back to zero before continuing.

```
Console.WriteLine ("Encrypted Message :" +
                        Encoding.ASCII.GetString(encByte));
fsread.Position =0;
```

Decrypting the data uses a similar procedure to that of encrypting the data. A main difference is the CreateDecryptor() method, which is used to create the specified decryptor object. We create a new byte array into which we read from the CryptoStream, and then use the GetString() method of the Encoding class to turn the byte array into a string for displaying.

```
// Create DES Decryptor from our des instance
ICryptoTransform desdecrypt = des.CreateDecryptor();

CryptoStream cryptostreamDecr = new CryptoStream(fsread, desdecrypt,
                                            CryptoStreamMode.Read);

byte[] decrByte = new byte[fsread.Length];
cryptostreamDecr.Read(decrByte,0,(int)fsread.Length);

string output = Encoding.Unicode.GetString(decrByte);

Console.WriteLine("Decrypted Message : {0}" ,output);
cryptostreamDecr.Close();
fsread.Close();
    }
  }
```

The screenshot below shows the output of the above code when it is run twice with the Symmetric Algorithm encryption method:

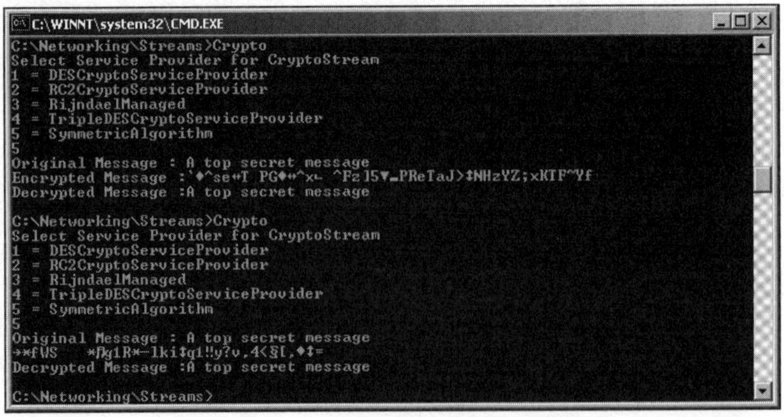

Stream Manipulation

We have looked at the different types of streams, how to create them, and how to read to and write from them. However, we've only been able to read and write byte arrays – this is a somewhat cumbersome way of reading data. For example, if we wanted to write some decimal values to a file, we'd have to break these down into bytes ourselves – there must be an easier way! Sure enough, the `System.IO` namespace provides classes and methods for manipulating different data types in streams.

We'll look at the following classes for stream manipulation in this section:

❑   Manipulating binary files with `BinaryReader` and `BinaryWriter`

❑   Manipulating text files with `StreamReader` and `StreamWriter`

Before we look at these classes, we need to consider encoding – this is something that we've alluded to earlier in the chapter when we were converting to and from byte arrays for transferring data from streams.

Encoding String Data

Although the data transported through streams is in byte form, without knowing what these bytes mean the information is meaningless. For example, if the byte is to be converted back into characters, then we need to know how these bytes map to characters – for example, a particular type of character may require more than one byte.

The `Encoding` class in the `System.Text` namespace is provided for performing such operations. The `Encoding` class handles sets of Unicode characters. Unicode is a worldwide character-encoding standard, which allows universal data exchange and improves multilingual text processing. Many languages cannot be represented without Unicode, such as Japanese. The wider range of characters supported by the Unicode format means that Unicode information typically requires 16-bit space instead of the standard 8-bit character strings.

The .NET Framework has several classes derived from the `Encoding` class for performing encoding between different formats.

Class	Use
`ASCIIEncoding`	Encodes Unicode characters as single 1-byte ASCII characters. This encoding has limitations because it supports 7-bit character values and is not a good choice for applications that support multilingual text processing.
`UnicodeEncoding`	Encodes each Unicode character in 2 bytes.
`UTF7Encoding`	Encodes in 7-bit Unicode encoding.
	UTF (Unicode Translation Format) 7 and 8 are commonly used formats to send Unicode-based data across networks.
`UTF8Encoding`	This class supports 8-bit UTF-8 encoding. This encoding is widely used with applications that support multilingual text processing.
	XML uses UTF-8 encoding by default.

Some of the principal methods of the Encoding class are given below – the general aim of these methods is to convert between byte arrays and character arrays or strings:

Methods	Purpose
GetCharCount()	This method takes an array of bytes and returns the calculated number of characters produced by decoding.
GetChars()	To decode a byte array into a character array.
	This method can be used in different ways depending upon the overload. Each overload takes a byte array and decodes it into an array of characters.
GetByteCount()	Number of bytes required for encoding a character array.
	Overloads of this method can take either a character array or string and returns the number of bytes required to encode.
GetBytes()	Encodes a string or character array into a byte array.
GetDecoder()	Gets a Decoder. Decoder is an abstract class used for converting bytes into Unicode characters.
	This method returns the Decoder object that can be used for decoding a sequence of bytes into characters.
GetEncoder()	Gets an Encoder. Encoder is an abstract class used for converting Unicode characters into a byte array.
	This method returns the Encoder object that can be used for encoding sequence of characters into bytes.

Let's have a look at a quick example which converts a string into a byte array using the different formats, and then displays the values in the byte array:

```
using System;
using System.IO;

using System.Text;

class EncodingTest
{
    public static void Main(string[] args)
    {
        string test = "This is our test string.";

        byte[] ascb;
        byte[] unicb;
        byte[] utfb;
```

We've created three byte arrays – now we'll convert our test string into these byte arrays using ASCII, Unicode, and UTF7 encoding. After each conversion, our DisplayArray() method will simply output all the bytes in the byte array:

```
        ascb = Encoding.ASCII.GetBytes(test);
        Console.WriteLine("ASCII Encoding : {0} bytes",ascb.Length);

        DisplayArray(ascb);

        unicb = Encoding.Unicode.GetBytes(test);
        Console.WriteLine("Unicode Encoding : {0} bytes",unicb.Length);
        DisplayArray(unicb);

        utfb = Encoding.UTF7.GetBytes(test);
        Console.WriteLine("UTF Encoding : {0} bytes",utfb.Length);
        DisplayArray(utfb);
```

Now that the bytes in the byte arrays have been displayed, let's see the effect of converting back from the byte array into a string – for these conversions we'll specify an encoding different from that originally used:

```
        string unics = Encoding.Unicode.GetString(ascb);
        Console.WriteLine(unics);

        string ascs = Encoding.ASCII.GetString(unicb);
        Console.WriteLine(ascs);

    }

    static void DisplayArray(byte[] b)
    {
    for (int i=0;i<b.Length;i++)
      Console.Write(b[i]+" ");

      Console.WriteLine();

    }

}
```

The output of this is the following – note the use of the two bytes in the Unicode encoded byte array for each character in the string. Note also that the reconverted strings illustrate the importance of using the correct encoding at each stage:

Binary Files

The `BinaryReader` and `BinaryWriter` classes of the `System.IO` namespace are used for working with primitive data types from streams. Each class is created around an existing `Stream`.

BinaryReader

`BinaryReader` is used to read primitive data types. By default it uses UTF-8 encoding to read the stream. You can specify custom encoding when creating an instance.

`BinaryReader` has various methods for reading primitive data types. The `Read()` method reads bytes from the stream, and advances the position in the stream, returning –1 if the end of the stream is reached. Two other overloads allow you to read into a byte array or character array, specifying the start position in the stream and then the number of bytes to read in. To read without advancing the position in the stream, the `PeekChar()` method returns the next character from the stream, or –1 if the end of the stream is reached or if the stream does not support seeking.

For each primitive data type, there is a method to read data of that type from the stream, and advance the position of the stream according to the length of the data type.

Method	Bytes Read From Stream
`bool ReadBoolean()`	1
`byte ReadByte()`	1
`byte[] ReadBytes(int count)`	count
`char ReadChar()`	Depends on encoding used.
`decimal ReadDecimal()`	16
`double ReadDouble()`	8
`short ReadInt16()`	2
`int ReadInt32()`	4
`long ReadInt64()`	4
`float ReadSingle()`	4
`string ReadString()`	Depends on length of string.

When reading from the stream, the end of the stream can be detected with the `PeekChar()` method – this reads the next character from the stream without advancing the position. A value of –1 is returned if no more characters are available.

The `Close()` method closes the reader. The underlying stream can be returned from the `BaseStream` property of the `BinaryReader`.

You can create a `BinaryReader` instance by providing a stream with or without encoding type.

```
//Create Stream instance
Stream strm = new FileStream("C:\\Networking\\Streams\\MyStream.txt",
                             FileMode.Open, FileAccess.Read);

//Use Stream instance for creating binary reader
BinaryReader br = new BinaryReader(strm);
```

You can also specify the encoding type when you create a `BinaryReader` object:

```
// Create Stream instance
Stream strm = new FileStream(@"C:\Networking\Streams\Book.txt", FileMode.Open,
                             FileAccess.Read);

// Use stream instance for creating binary reader
BinaryReader br = new BinaryReader(strm,Encoding.ASCII);
```

BinaryWriter

The `BinaryWriter` class is used for writing primitive types in a binary format to a stream.

Writing to the stream is achieved with the `Write()` method. There is an overload for writing each primitive data type to the stream, advancing the position in the stream according to the length of the data type. To move around the stream, the `Seek()` method sets the position in the stream as with the `Seek()` method of `Stream`. In fact, `BinaryWriter.Seek()` simply calls the `Seek()` method on the underlying `Stream` object (which can also be returned from the `BaseStream` property).

There are also `Close()` and `Flush()` methods for the standard management of the writer's resources.

Binary Reading and Writing Example

In the following example a `FileStream` is created for performing binary read and write operations. In the first part of the code data is written to a file, and in the second part this data is read in and displayed.

```
using System;
using System.IO;

class BinaryGetting
{
    static void Main(string[] args)
    {

        double angle, sinAngle

        FileStream fStream = new FileStream(@"C:\Networking\Streams\Sines.dat",
                                    FileMode.Create, FileAccess.Write);

        BinaryWriter bw = new BinaryWriter(fStream);
```

First we create our `FileStream` object – a file called `Sines.dat` in the `C:\Networking\Streams` folder is created, and we specify write access, since we'll be writing some data to the stream. Then we create our `BinaryWriter` object around this `FileStream`. We'll calculate the sine of angles between 0 and 90 degrees at 5 degree intervals (we have to convert the angle in degrees to radians before we can calculate the sine), and then use `Write()` to output these values to the stream.

```
        for (int i=0;i<=90;i+=5)
        {
            double angleRads = Math.PI*i/180;
            sinAngle = Math.Sin(angleRads);
            bw.Write((double)i);
            bw.Write(sinAngle);
        }

        bw.Close();
        fStream.Close();
```

The `BinaryWriter` and `FileStream` objects are closed, and we can begin the process of retrieving the data with the `BinaryReader`. First, we create new `FileStream` and `BinaryReader` objects.

```
        FileStream frStream = new FileStream(@"C:\Networking\Streams\Sines.dat",
                                    FileMode.Open, FileAccess.Read);

        BinaryReader br = new BinaryReader(frStream);

        int endOfFile;
```

We'll be using the `ReadDouble()` method to read the data back in – if this method tries to read beyond the end of the stream an exception will be thrown, so we use the `PeekChar()` method to detect the end of the file without advancing the position:

```
        do
        {
            endOfFile = br.PeekChar();
            if(endOfFile != -1)
            {
                angle = br.ReadDouble();
                sinAngle = br.ReadDouble();
                Console.WriteLine("{0} : {1}",angle,sinAngle);
            }

        }
        while(endOfFile!= -1);
```

Finally, we close the `BinaryReader` and the underlying stream.

```
        br.Close();
        frStream.Close();
    }
}
```

The output of this is the following:

TextReader

TextReader is used for reading text or characters in a stream – it's an abstract class from which StreamReader and StringReader derive. The text read in by a StringReader is stored as a StringBuilder, rather than a plain string.

Some of the important methods of TextReader are shown in the table below:

Method	Description
Peek()	Returns the next character from the stream/string, without advancing the position.
Read()	To read the characters/bytes from stream/string.
ReadBlock()	Reads a specified number of characters from the current stream from a given starting point.
ReadLine()	Read entire characters up to the end of the line (signified by a carriage return or line feed).
ReadToEnd()	To read all characters up to the end of the stream/string.
Synchronized()	To create a thread-safe wrapper so that more than one thread can use the TextReader.
Close()	Closes the current reader.

Working with StreamReader

It comes as no surprise to learn that StreamReader is used to read characters from a byte stream. The StreamReader uses encoding (specified in the constructor), or if no encoding is specified, then UTF-8 encoding is used. More than that, it essentially provides forward-only access to the stream, unlike the BinaryReader, which allows random access with its Seek() method. It is possible to change the position in the underlying stream by accessing it through the BaseStream property of the StreamReader – however, the current position in the stream and the current position of the reader may not be the same due to buffering reasons.

The following example demonstrates the use of StreamReader – it reads in text from a file called TextOut.txt – we actually create this file in the forthcoming StreamWriter example, but for now any text file will do.

```
using System;
using System.IO;

class TextReadingExample
{
    static void Main(string[] args)
    {
        Stream fS = new FileStream("TextOut.txt", FileMode.Open, FileAccess.Read);

        // Using Stream Object
        StreamReader sReader = new StreamReader(fS);

        string data;
        int line=0;
```

Now begins the central loop to read in each line. We use the ReadLine() method to read a line from the stream – if there are no lines available, null is returned. Thus we test for this in our while loop:

```
        while ((data = sReader.ReadLine()) != null)
```

We'll display more information than just the line read in – we'll display a line count that we increment ourselves, then the line read in, and then the position in the stream:

```
        {
            Console.WriteLine("Line {0} : {1} : Position = {2}",
                        ++line, data,  sReader.BaseStream.Position);
        }
```

Now we'll reset the position to the start of the stream, and read the entire contents in with the ReadToEnd() method:

```
        // Set position using seek property of underlying stream
        sReader.BaseStream.Seek(0, SeekOrigin.Begin);
        Console.WriteLine("* Reading entire file using ReadToEnd \n" +
                                sReader.ReadToEnd());
```

```
        sReader.Close();

        fS.Close();
    }
}
```

When you run the above code with the `TextOut.txt` file created next, you'll see output like the following:

The interesting thing to note here is the Position – this doesn't change between any of the lines, and is fixed at the value **267**. This value is the length of the entire file, and is a good illustration of how the `Stream` position and the reader position often don't agree. The contents of the file have been buffered – you can see this by adding the following line in the `while` loop:

```
    {
        Console.WriteLine("Line {0} : {1} : Position = {2}",
                          ++line, data,  sReader.BaseStream.Position);
        sReader.DiscardBufferedData();
    }
```

The `DiscardBufferedData()`method discards the reader's data. If you add this line then running the above code with the same file as above will display only one line, since the remaining lines are all jettisoned following the `DiscardBufferedData()` call.

TextWriter

`TextWriter` is an abstract class used for writing text and it outputs a sequential series of characters. `StreamWriter` and `StringWriter` are derived from `TextWriter`. Like `StringReader`, `StringWriter` deals with `StringBuilder` objects rather than plain strings.

The `TextWriter` methods allow management of the writer, and perform the actual writing:

Method	Purpose
Close()	To close current writer.
Flush()	Clears the buffers and writes to underlying device.
Synchronized()	To create a thread-safe wrapper.
Write()	To write given data.
WriteLine()	Similar to the Console.WriteLine() method, this method writes data with a line terminator. The WriteLine() method can be used in a number of ways depending on the parameters passed.

Working with StreamWriter

StreamWriter is used for writing characters in a stream. By default it uses UTF-8 character encoding.

There are several ways to create an instance of a StreamWriter class depending on overloading parameters, one way allows you to pass a Stream object. If you are using a FileStream object, this means that you have more control over the file's accessibility than is possible through the other StreamWriter constructors.

The following example demonstrates the use of various StreamWriter properties – it should make their use a lot clearer.

```
using System;
using System.IO;

class TextWritingExample
{
    static void Main(string[] args)
    {
        Stream fS = new FileStream("TextOut.txt", FileMode.Open, FileAccess.Write);

        // Using Stream Object
        StreamWriter sWriter = new StreamWriter(fS);
```

We start by displaying some properties of the StreamWriter, namely the Encoding type (we haven't specified any so the default will be UTF-8), and the format provider:

```
        // Display the encoding type
        Console.WriteLine("Encoding type : " + sWriter.Encoding.ToString());

        //Display Format Provider
        Console.WriteLine("Format Provider : " +
        sWriter.FormatProvider.ToString());
```

Now we will write to the file – we use the WriteLine() method first of all. As you can see, its use is similar to the Console.WriteLine() method in that it allows us to easily write out the values of variables or properties.

```
        sWriter.WriteLine("Today is {0}." ,DateTime.Today.DayOfWeek);

        sWriter.WriteLine("Today we will mostly be using StreamWriter.");

        for (int i=0;i<5;i++)
          sWriter.WriteLine("Value {0}, its square is {1}",i,i*i);
```

Now we'll use the `Write()` method to write out character arrays, and parts of character arrays. Since `Write()` doesn't attach a new line to the end of the output, we can use the escape sequence \r\n at the start of a line to ensure a new line before the text is written:

```
        sWriter.Write("Arrays can be written : ");
        char[] myarray = new char[]{'a','r','r','a','y'};

        sWriter.Write(myarray);
        sWriter.WriteLine("\r\nAnd parts of arrays can be written");
        sWriter.Write(myarray,0,3);

        sWriter.Close();
        fS.Close()
      }
    }
```

When viewed in NotePad, we can see that the following is written to the output file:

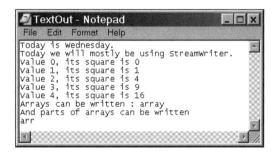

Serialization

Serialization is the process of taking objects and converting their state information into a form that can be stored or transported. The stored or transported object can then be deserialized to recreate the original state of the object. Thus you can serialize an object, transmit this information across a network and then restore the object and its original state from another application or system.

Here are some key areas where serialization is a benefit:

❑ Availability – a component can be saved in a file and can be made available whenever required.

❑ Lifetime – saving the object with its state increases its life. In normal practice, when you close an application all associated objects are destroyed automatically.

❑ Use within networked applications – the complex form of the object has been transformed to a format that is suitable for transferring across a network, and possibly through firewalls.

❑ Reliability – the saved object can be recreated "as-it-is".

In this section we'll be looking at two ways of serializing objects:

❑ Serializing into XML format

❑ Serializing with formatter objects into binary

Serializing into XML Format

Serializing an object to XML format has certain advantages – for one, you have transformed system-specific state information into text, which can easily be sent across a network, and through firewalls. However, the XML produced does not preserve the type of the various fields involved, instead it serializes properties/fields or return values of an object in XML format. This feature is useful when you want to pass values instead of the details of the actual object itself.

The `XmlSerializer` class in the `System.Xml.Serialization` namespace provides the functionality for serializing and deserializing objects in XML format.

There are two simple rules for serializing a class:

❑ The class must support a default public constructor with no parameters. This is required because when the object is recreated through the deserialization process, the object is first instantiated with the default constructor, and then the public properties are set from the incoming data stream. If there is no default constructor, the .NET Framework will not know how to create the object.

❑ Only public properties that support both `get` and `set` operations and public data members are persisted. This is because the serialization process cannot access the private and read-only data members. There are ways to serialize this data, but it involves changes to the class itself.

To save all the public properties and data members of an object, nothing extra needs to be done to the class itself.

In the following example a `Customer` class, with fields for storing data about a customer, is serialized using XML format. Note the presence of the private field:

```
using System;
using System.IO;
using System.Text ;
using System.Xml.Serialization;

public class XmlSerialExample
{
    public class Customer
    {
        public int CustomerID;
        public string CustomerName;
        public DateTime SignUpDate;
        private decimal currentCredit;
```

```
        public void SetCurrentCredit(decimal c)
        {
            currentCredit = c;
        }
        public decimal GetCurrentCredit()
        {
            return currentCredit;
        }
    }
```

Our `Customer` class is defined, and so we create a new instance, and set some of the fields.

```
    public static void Main()
    {
        // Prepare object for serialization
        Customer cm = new Customer();

        cm.CustomerID = 12;
        cm.CustomerName = "Ward Littell";
        cm.SignUpDate = DateTime.Now;
        cm.SetCurrentCredit(76.23M);
```

Now we begin the serialization process. We create a `StreamWriter` to output the produced XML to a file, `Customer.xml`. Then, we create the `XmlSerializer` object, passing in the type of the object we want serialized. All that remains is to call the `Serialize()` method of the `XmlSerializer`, passing in the `StreamWriter` and the object whose state we wish to persist:

```
        Console.WriteLine("Now Serializing....");

        // Create stream writer object
        StreamWriter writer = new StreamWriter("Customer.xml");

        // Create serializer
        XmlSerializer serializer = new XmlSerializer(typeof(Customer));

        // Serialize the object
        serializer.Serialize(writer, cm);
        writer.Close();
```

Our serialization process is now complete. To test, we'll deserialize from the `Customer.xml` file and create a new object with the same state as our current `Customer` object.

```
        Console.WriteLine("Now Deserializing....");

        // Open and create stream
        Stream streamOut = new FileStream("Customer.xml", FileMode.Open,
                                            FileAccess.Read);
```

Our stream for reading the data from the `Customer.xml` file has been created – all we need to do now is to call the `Deserialize()` method of our `XmlSerializer` object. For purposes of illustration, we create a new `XmlSerializer` called `deserializer`. The `Deserialize()` method returns an `object` – this needs a cast to `Customer` and we have our recreated `Customer`:

```
        XmlSerializer deserializer = new XmlSerializer(typeof(Customer));

        // Deserialize the stored stream.
        Customer recm = (Customer)deserializer.Deserialize(streamOut);

        streamOut.Close();
```

Finally, we display the state of our newly created object:

```
        // Display state of object
        Console.WriteLine ("Customer ID = {0}", recm.CustomerID);
        Console.WriteLine ("Customer Name = {0}", recm.CustomerName);
        Console.WriteLine ("Sign up date = {0}", recm.SignUpDate);
        Console.WriteLine ("Current Credit = {0}", recm.GetCurrentCredit());
        Console.Read();
    }
}
```

The output of this program is as follows – note that the value for `CurrentCredit` is 0, and not `76.23` as we set it originally. We'll see why when we look at the XML output next:

The serialized `Customer.xml` file looks as shown in the following screenshot. Note that this shows that the exact type of each field is not preserved here – the XML contains only the values of the fields. Note also that the value of the private field `currentCredit` has not been serialized:

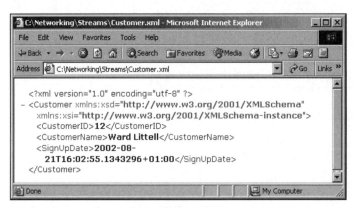

Serializing with Formatter Objects

Within the `System.Runtime.Serialization.Formatters` namespace lie the tools for serializing object state into formats such as binary or SOAP – the `BinaryFormatter` class provides functionality for serializing objects into binary format, and the `SoapFormatter` class serializes into SOAP format. We'll look at both of these here.

Binary format serializes object state and also assembly information, allowing exact reproduction of an object and its types. It also produces a compact format. The SOAP format is more verbose, but allows your object state to be passed to a Web Service for example.

The formatter objects allow the serialization of private fields, and the key to their use is the `[Serializable]` attribute, with which you mark a class to indicate that it can indeed be serialized.

Here are the steps for serializing an object:

1. Mark the class with `[Serializable]` attributes to make it serializable

2. Prepare the object's state for serialization

3. Create a new formatter object – `BinaryFormatter` for binary format, `SoapFormatter` for SOAP

4. Call the `Serialize()` method of the formatter object, passing in the stream to output the results to, and the object to be serialized

Deserializing is quite simple – you specify the format for deserializing the object with the relevant formatter object, call the `Deserialize()` method of this formatter object, and cast the `object` returned to the type you wish to recreate.

Before we look at serialization examples, here are a few points about serialization in general, and the use of the `[Serializable]` attribute.

For a class to be successfully serialized, each field must be serializable. Thus if our `Customer` class, marked as `[Serializable]`, had a field of type `Address`:

```
[Serializable]
public class Customer
{
    ...
    public Address HomeAddress;
}

public class Address
{
    public string StreetName;
    ...
}
```

then the `Address` class would itself have to be marked `[Serializable]`, or else serialization would fail.

Note also that the [Serializable] attribute is not inherited, thus derived types are not automatically serializable. To ensure that derived types can be serialized, they should also be marked as [Serializable].

In some situations you may not want to serialize certain fields of a class, for example if they are easily computed from other fields, or if they contain confidential data. You can use the [NonSerialized] attribute to mark any such *fields*, and they will not be serialized.

```
[Serializable]
   public class Customer
   {
      public string CustomerName;
      ...
      [NonSerialized]
      public string FirstName;
   }
```

Here's an example that uses a binary formatter object – we'll look at the SOAP formatter after that.

```
using System;
using System.IO;
using System.Text;
using System.Runtime.Serialization;
using System.Runtime.Serialization.Formatters.Binary;

public class BinSerialExample
{
   [Serializable]
   public class Customer
   {
      public int CustomerID;
      public string CustomerName;
      public DateTime SignUpDate;
      private decimal currentCredit;

      public void SetCurrentCredit(decimal c)
      {
         currentCredit = c;
      }
      public decimal GetCurrentCredit()
      {
         return currentCredit;
      }
   }

   public static void Main()
   {
      // Prepare object for serialization
      Customer cm = new Customer();

      cm.CustomerID = 12;
      cm.CustomerName = "Ward Littell";
      cm.SignUpDate=DateTime.Now;
      cm.SetCurrentCredit(76.23M);
```

```
        Console.WriteLine("Now Serializing....");

        // Create stream object for storage
        Stream stm = new FileStream("BinCustomer.bin", FileMode.Create,
                                    FileAccess.Write);
```

Our stream is created, and now we create our `BinaryFormatter` object and serialize:

```
        // Serialize object using Binary format
        BinaryFormatter inFormatter = new BinaryFormatter();
        inFormatter.Serialize(stm, cm);

        stm.Close();
        Console.WriteLine("Now Deserializing....");

        // Open and create stream
        Stream streamOut = new FileStream("BinCustomer.bin", FileMode.Open,
                                    FileAccess.Read);
```

To deserialize, we create our `BinaryFormatter` object, call the `Deserialize()` method and then cast the resulting object to our desired `Customer` type:

```
        // Perform deserialization on stored stream.
        BinaryFormatter outFormatter = new BinaryFormatter();

        Customer recm = (Customer)outFormatter.Deserialize(streamOut);

        streamOut.Close();

        // Display state of object
        Console.WriteLine ("Customer ID = {0}", recm.CustomerID);
        Console.WriteLine ("Customer Name = {0}", recm.CustomerName);
        Console.WriteLine ("Sign up date = {0}", recm.SignUpDate);
        Console.WriteLine ("Current Credit = {0}", recm.GetCurrentCredit());
    }
}
```

When you run this code, you'll see that the `currentCredit` field has now been serialized. The file produced is `BinCustomer.bin` – if you open it in Visual Studio .NET you should see the following:

```
Start Page   BinCustomer.bin
00000000  00 01 00 00  00 FF FF FF  FF 01 00 00  00 00 00 00   ...........CBinSerial
00000010  00 0C 02 00  00 00 43 42  69 6E 53 65  72 69 61 6C   ......CBinSerial
00000020  69 7A 65 2C  20 56 65 72  73 69 6F 6E  3D 30 2E 30   ize, Version=0.0
00000030  2E 30 2E 30  2C 20 43 75  6C 74 75 72  65 3D 6E 65   .0.0, Culture=ne
00000040  75 74 72 61  6C 2C 20 50  75 62 6C 69  63 4B 65 79   utral, PublicKey
00000050  54 6F 6B 65  6E 3D 6E 75  6C 6C 05 01  00 00 00 19   Token=null......
00000060  42 69 6E 53  65 72 69 61  6C 45 78 61  6D 70 6C 65   BinSerialExample
00000070  2B 43 75 73  74 6F 6D 65  72 04 00 00  00 0A 43 75   +Customer.....Cu
00000080  73 74 6F 6D  65 72 49 44  0C 43 75 73  74 6F 6D 65   stomerID.Custome
00000090  72 4E 61 6D  65 0A 53 69  67 6E 55 70  44 61 74 65   rName.SignUpDate
000000a0  0D 63 75 72  72 65 6E 74  43 72 65 64  69 74 00 01   .currentCredit..
000000b0  00 00 08 0D  05 02 00 00  00 0C 00 00  00 06 03 00   ................
000000c0  00 00 0C 57  61 72 64 20  4C 69 74 74  65 6C 6C 10   ...Ward Littell.
000000d0  DC A0 DF 39  17 C4 08 05  37 36 2E 32  33 0B         ...9....76.23.
```

All the contents of the file are stored in binary format. Note the assembly information, including the version information, for matching the correct version of the component to avoid any compatibility issues.

To use the SOAP formatter object, minor changes are required to the above code. First of all, we need to use the SOAP formatter namespace:

```
using System.Runtime.Serialization.Formatters.Soap;
```

The other changes to the previous code are the different formatter object – we use the `SoapFormatter` class for serializing into SOAP format, and the name of the file that we'll serialize to:

```
// Create stream object for storage
Stream stm = new FileStream("SoapCustomer.xml", FileMode.Create,
                            FileAccess.Write);


// Serialize object using SOAP format
SoapFormatter inFormatter = new SoapFormatter();
inFormatter.Serialize(stm, cm);

stm.Close();
Console.WriteLine("Now Deserializing....");

// Open and create stream
Stream streamOut = new FileStream("SoapCustomer.xml", FileMode.Open,
                                  FileAccess.Read);

// Perform deserialization on stored stream.
SoapFormatter outFormatter = new SoapFormatter();
Customer recm = (Customer)outFormatter.Deserialize(streamOut);

streamOut.Close();
```

Running this code produces the following file, `SoapCustomer.xml`. This is a valid SOAP message that can be passed to a Web Service for example.

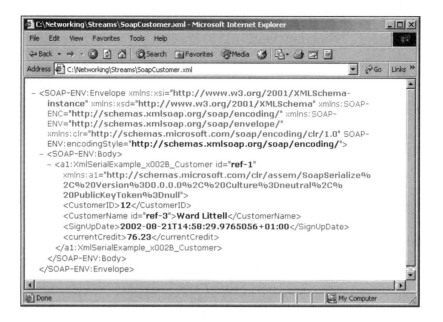

Summary

In this chapter we have looked at the `Stream` class in the `System.IO` namespace, and some of the classes derived from it that represent specific types of stream, characterized by their underlying device. We looked at the `FileStream` class, which allows access to a file on a disk, the `MemoryStream` class, and the `NetworkStream` class among others. We saw that the methods they each inherit from `Stream` makes stream manipulation reasonably straightforward.

.NET provides various other classes in the `System.IO` namespace for stream manipulation, and transferring data more complex than simple bytes. We looked at the `BinaryReader` and `BinaryWriter` classes for working with binary files, and the `StreamReader` and `StreamWriter` for working with text files.

Finally we saw how to serialize and deserialize objects into XML format, and using formatter objects to serialize into binary or SOAP format.

Network Programming in .NET

3

In Chapter 1 we saw an overview of networking and looked at the structure and usage of different network protocols such as TCP, UDP, IP, and DNS. In this chapter we will start with network programming using classes from the `System.Net` namespace.

First of all, we will briefly discuss all the classes from the `System.Net` namespace and then go into some of these classes in more detail. For the classes that are not covered here you will get a reference to the corresponding chapter, where they will be looked at more fully. The networking classes discussed in this chapter play a fundamental role in all the remaining chapters of this book.

In particular, we will look at:

❑   An overview of the `System.Net` classes

❑   Working with URIs

❑   IP Addresses

❑   DNS Lookups

❑   Request and Responses

❑   Authentication and Authorization

❑   Permissions

System.Net Classes – Overview

In the System.Net namespace we have networking classes for IP address lookups, network authentication, permissions, and classes for sending and receiving data.

Let us look at these classes by sorting them into some groups.

Name Lookup

To get an IP address from a DNS hostname, or to get a hostname from an IP address the Dns class can be used. The DnsPermission class represents the permission required for name lookups. DnsPermissionAttribute is an attribute class to mark assemblies, classes, or methods that need this privilege.

IP Addresses

IP addresses are handled within the class IPAddress. A single host can have multiple IP addresses and alias names. All this information is contained within the class IPHostEntry. The Dns class returns an object of type IPHostEntry when we do a name lookup.

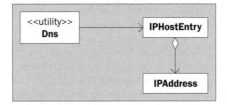

Authentication and Authorization

The AuthenticationManager class has static methods to authenticate the client user. This utility class uses modules that implement the IAuthenticationModule interface. The AuthenticationManager asks these modules to authenticate the user. The authentication modules get request information and the user credentials with the ICredentials interface, and return an Authorization object for authorized users that are allowed to use the resource.

The client application can pass credentials to the server with an instance of the NetworkCredential class. User credentials can be cached in the CredentialCache.

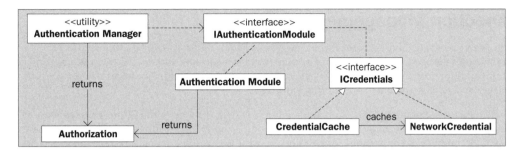

In this chapter we will cover an overview of the authentication and authorization mechanism, but we will look into it in detail in Chapter 11.

Requests and Responses

The abstract base classes for sending requests to a server and receiving a response are `WebRequest` and `WebResponse`. In the `System.Net` namespace we have some specific implementations of these classes for HTTP and file access: `HttpWebRequest`, `HttpWebResponse`, `FileWebRequest`, and `FileWebResponse`.

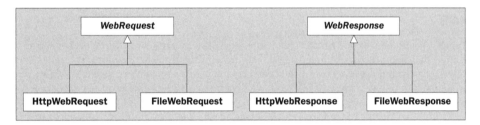

The `HttpXXX` classes also make use of another class in the `System.Net` namespace: the `HttpVersion` class is used to specify the HTTP version. `HttpWebRequest` and `HttpWebResponse` classes both have a `ProtocolVersion` property that defines the HTTP version – `HttpVersion.Version10` or `HttpVersion.Version11`. HTTP 1.0 was used in the early days of the Internet and is still used by some web servers, HTTP 1.1, the current version, has some more features such as keeping a connection open for multiple requests.

In this chapter we will discuss the functionality of the `WebRequest` and `WebResponse` classes, and the specific implementations `FileWebRequest` and `FileWebResponse`. The HTTP protocol and the related classes will be discussed in Chapter 8.

The permissions needed with the request and response classes are defined with the `WebPermission` class and the attribute class `WebPermissionAttribute`.

A component class that makes it easy to use `WebRequest` and `WebResponse` from the Visual Studio .NET designer is the `WebClient` class. This class derives from the `Component` class and so it can be used with drag and drop functionality from the Toolbox. However, it is not configured to the Toolbox by default. With the `WebClient` class it is easy to download files from and upload files to a server.

Connection Management

The `ServicePoint` and `ServicePointManager` classes play an important role for HTTP connections. An instance of the `ServicePoint` class is associated with a URI to a resource and can handle multiple connections. The utility class `ServicePointManager` manages `ServicePoint` objects by creating new objects or finding existing ones.

We can increase the throughput of an application that requests a lot of data from a server simultaneously by increasing the number of connections on an application base. By default, the maximum number of connections to the same server is two to limit network resources needed. Later in this chapter in the *Connection Pooling* section we will look at where the default value is specified, and how it can be changed.

Creating connection pools is useful for middle-tier applications that connect to Internet resources on behalf of a specific user. We can reuse connections in connection groups where each group is associated with user credentials.

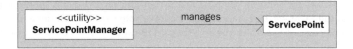

Cookies

Cookies are sets of data, stored on the client-side, and used by the server to remember some information between requests. When using a web browser like Internet Explorer to request some data from a web server, Internet Explorer itself manages the acceptance and storage of cookies, and sends the cookie back to the web server. If we create a custom application that requests data from a web server that sends cookies, we can read these in an object of the class `CookieCollection` that is returned from the `Cookies` property of an `HttpWebResponse`. We can pass cookies to the server with the help of the `CookieContainer` class. A cookie itself is represented in the `Cookie` class.

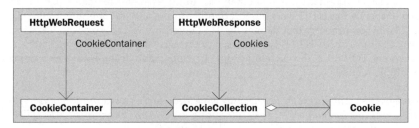

Cookies are sent within the header of the HTTP protocol, so cookies will be covered again when we look at the HTTP protocol in Chapter 8.

Proxy Server

A proxy server is used in a network environment to direct a connection to the Internet through a single system (or multiple systems depending on the network size). The proxy server can cache pages that are requested by users, so if the same page is requested several times a request to the web server is not needed anymore because the web proxy can answer the request itself.

The `WebProxy` class is used to define the proxy server that should be consulted for Internet requests. With the `GlobalProxySelection` class we can define a default proxy server that should be used for all requests if not specified otherwise for a specific request.

Sockets

Instead of using the web classes we can get more features and flexibility, but also more complexity with socket classes. Most of the classes that are used with socket programming can be found in the namespace `System.Net.Sockets`.

With socket programming not only can we do connection-oriented programming as it is used with HTTP, we can also do connection-less programming as is used with UDP broadcasts and multicasts. Socket programming is extremely flexible and allows the use of different protocols such as GGP, ICMP, IGMP, IPX, and SPX.

In the following chapters, we discuss socket programming with both the TCP and the UDP protocol, with connection-oriented data transfer and connection-less data transfer for broadcasts and multicasts.

Now that we have an overview of the most important classes in the `System.Net` namespace, let's take a more detailed look at some of these classes, as they are the foundation for the rest of the book.

Working with URIs

We use **Uniform Resource Identifiers (URIs)** every day browsing the Web. We need such URIs to identify and request different kind of resources. With a URI, not only can a web page be accessed, but also an FTP server, a web service, or local files.

> *For URIs the term **URL (Uniform Resource Locator)** is often used. URI is a generic term that is used to refer to resources. A URL is a URI that is associated with popular URI schemes such as http, ftp, or mailto. In technical documentations the term URL is no longer used.*
>
> *Another term that you may know already is **URN (Uniform Resource Name)**. A URN is a standardized URI and is used to specify a resource independent of its network location.*
>
> *The URI is defined with RFC 2396 (`http://www.ietf.org/rfc/rfc2396.txt`), the RFC for URN is RFC 2142 (`http://www.ietf.org/rfc/rfc2141.txt`).*

An example of a URI is shown here:

```
http://www.wrox.com
```

This URI uses the http scheme to reference a web site.

```
mailto:christian@nagel.net
```

The mailto scheme is used for electronic e-mail addresses.

```
news:msnews.microsoft.com
```

With the news scheme USENET news groups can be accessed.

Let's analyze the parts of a URI referencing a page at the Global Knowledge web site:

```
http://www.globalknowledge.net:80/training/generic.asp?pageid=1078&country=DACH
```

❑ The first part of the URI is the **scheme**. The scheme defines the namespace of the URI, and may restrict the syntax that follows. Many schemes are named like the protocol (such as http, ftp) they are using, but this is not a requirement. In our example http is the scheme identifier. The scheme delimiter (:// in the example) separates the scheme from the remaining URI.

❑ After the scheme delimiter (:// for the http scheme) the name of the server or the IP address in dotted quad-notation follows, for example, www.globalknowledge.at.

❑ After the server name or IP address is the port number for connecting to a specific application on the server. If the port number is not specified, the default port number of a protocol is used (for example port number 80 for HTTP).

❑ The **path** defines a page (and directory) of the requested resource. This is not necessarily a physical file on the server, but can be created dynamically. Here the path is /training/generic.asp.

❑ Separated from the path with a ? character is the last part of this URI, which is the **query**. In our example the query is defined with pageid=1078&country=DACH. A query string can have multiple query components each specifying a variable and a value connected with the = character. Multiple query components can be combined with the character &. Thus in our example the first component is pageid=1078, with the variable pageid and the value 1078, and the second component is country=DACH.

❑ Sections inside a resource can be identified with fragments. Fragments are used to reference a section within an HTML page. With web page developments fragments are also known as **bookmarks**. The # character separates fragment identifier from the path. With the URL http://www.microsoft.com/net/basics/glossary.asp#.NETFramework, the fragment is #.NETFramework.

If a # character is added to a query string, then it is not a fragment, but instead belongs to the query string. With a URL we can have a query string or a fragment, but not both.

The use of some characters is reserved in a URI – these characters may not be contained within hostnames or a path because these are some special separator characters. Reserved characters in a URI are:
; / ? : @ & = + $,

Uri Class

The Uri class in the System namespace encapsulates a uniform resource identifier. It has properties and methods for parsing, comparing, and combining URIs.

Constructing Uri Objects

We can create a `Uri` object by passing a URI string to the constructor:

```
Uri uri = new Uri("http://msdn.microsoft.com/code/default.asp");
```

If we already have a base `Uri` object we can create a new URI by combining the base URI with a relative URI:

```
Uri baseUri = new Uri("http://msdn.microsoft.com");
Uri newUri = new Uri(baseUri, "code/default.asp");
```

If the base URI already contains a path, this is ignored. Only the scheme, port, and server name are taken as a base for the new URI.

Commonly Used Schemes

The `Uri` class has some read-only static fields to get some commonly used schemes.

❑ `Uri.UriSchemeFile`

The **file** scheme is used to access files locally or on network shares where UNC (Universal Naming Convention) names can be used.

❑ `Uri.UriSchemeFtp`

With the **ftp** scheme, the FTP protocol is used to get and put files from and to an ftp server.

❑ `Uri.UriSchemeGopher`

The **gopher** protocol is a predecessor of the HTTP protocol. It offered some hierarchical browsing with text information about the content that was an advantage to the FTP protocol, but was soon replaced by HTTP.

❑ `Uri.UriSchemeHttp, Uri.UriSchemeHttps`

These two schemes are well known: **http** and **https**. The https scheme is used for secure communication. We discuss the HTTP protocol in Chapter 8.

❑ `Uri.UriSchemeMailto`

The mailto scheme is used for sending mails.

❑ `Uri.UriSchemeNews, Uri.UriSchemeNntp`

Both the news and nntp schemes are used for news group discussions using the NNTP protocol.

Checking for a Valid Host Name and Scheme

The `Uri` class has static methods to check for a valid scheme and hostname: `Uri.CheckSchemeName()` returns `true` if the scheme name is valid, and `Uri.CheckHostName()` not only checks the hostname, but also returns the type of the host with a value of the `UriHostNameType` enumeration.

Possible values of `UriHostNameType` are listed here:

UriHostNameType value	Description
Basic	The hostname is set, but the type cannot be determined.
Dns	This will be the type returned most often. Passing a string either with or without domain extensions will return this type value.
IPv4	If a string passed contains the dotted quad-notation, for example, 204.148.170.161, IPv4 is returned.
IPv6	Passing an IPv6 string for the hostname, IPv6 is returned. IPv6 has 128 bits for the host identification, whereas IPv4 has only 32 bits. An IPv6 address string looks like this: 1080:0:0:0:8:800:200C:417A
Unknown	If the hostname contains invalid characters, Unknown is returned.

You can use Uri.CheckHostName() to check if the user entered a valid string for a host name, but this method doesn't check if the host name exists or can be reached. We can verify if a host name really exists by translating the hostname to an IP address with the Dns class as shown later in this chapter.

Properties of the Uri Class

The Uri class has a lot of read-only properties to access all the parts of a URI.

In the following table we use the following URI as an example to show the results of the properties:

```
http://www.globalknowledge.net:80/training/generic.asp?pageid=1078&country=DACH
```

Property	Description
AbsoluteUri	The absolute URI shows the complete URI. If the port number specified is the default port number for the protocol, the Uri constructor automatically removes it. With our example the value of the AbsoluteUri property looks like this: `http://www.globalknowledge.net/training/generic.asp?pageid=1078&country=DACH` If a file name is passed to the constructor of the Uri class, the AbsoluteUri automatically prefixes the filename with the schema file://.
Scheme	The scheme can be seen first in the URI. Here it is http.
Host	The Host shows the hostname of the URI: www.globalknowledge.net
Authority	The Authority shows the same as the Host property if the port number used is the default for the protocol. If a different port number is used, the Authority shows the port number as well.

Property	Description
HostNameType	The type of the hostname depends on the name that is used. Here we get the same value of the enumeration UriHostNameType that we discussed above. In this case it is UriHostNameType.Dns.
Port	With the property Port we can get the port number – 80.
AbsolutePath	The absolute path starts after the port number of the URI and excludes the query string. Here it is /training/generic.asp.
LocalPath	The local path is /training/generic.asp. As you can see with an HTTP request there is no difference between AbsolutePath and LocalPath. A difference can be seen if the URI references a network share. With a URI such as file:\\server\share\directory\file.txt the LocalPath property just returns the directory and file name, whereas the AbsolutePath property includes the server and share names.
Query	The Query shows the string that follows the path: ?pageid=1078&country=DACH
PathAndQuery	PathAndQuery is a combination of both the path and the query string: /training/generic.asp?pageid=1078&country=DACH
Fragment	If a fragment follows the path, it is returned with the Fragment property. Only a query string or a fragment can follow the path. The fragment is identified by the # character.
Segments	The Segments property returns a string array formed from the path. Here we have three segments: /, training/, and generic.asp.
UserInfo	If a username is set in the URI it can be read with the UserInfo property. Passing usernames is common with the FTP protocol, if the anonymous user is not used, such as ftp://myuser@ftp.myserver.com, then the UserInfo property returns myuser.

In addition to the properties we have seen in this list there are some properties that return a Boolean value if the URI represents a file, a UNC path, a loopback address, or if the default port number for a specific protocol is used – IsFile, IsUnc, IsLoopback, and IsDefaultPort.

Modifying URIs with the UriBuilder Class

After creating an instance of the Uri class with the constructor it cannot be modified anymore. The properties of the Uri class are read-only. To change values in a URI dynamically the UriBuilder class can be used. It has similar properties to the Uri class, but here the properties are read/write. For read-only access the Uri class is a lot faster than the UriBuilder class. You are probably familiar with such a concept from the String and StringBuilder classes.

In the example below an instance of UriBuilder is constructed by passing the scheme, hostname, port number, and path. Then, we change the path by setting the Path property. The Uri property of the UriBuilder returns a read-only Uri instance.

```
UriBuilder uri1 = new UriBuilder("http", "www.gotdotnet", 80,
                               "team/codewise/default.aspx");


uri1.Path = "team/codewise/association.aspx";
Uri uri2 = uri1.Uri;
```

Absolute and Relative URIs

URIs can be absolute or relative. An absolute URI starts with the scheme, followed by the hostname and the optional port number. The absolute URI can have a path, but the path is ignored if it is used together with a relative URI. A relative URI is defined only with a path, so it requires an absolute URI as its base to know the exact resource location. If we have one URI in use, a relative URI is sufficient to access another resource from the same host. Relative URIs are shorter, so we need fewer characters.

If we read a link from an HTML page that is represented in an anchor tag <A>, the link can include an absolute or a relative URI. If it includes a relative URI that we want to use with a query, we have to create an absolute URI from it because the Uri class only stores absolute URIs.

In the code example below a base URI is created with the string http://www.gotdotnet.com and stored in the variable baseUri. The second object of type Uri that is created uses the variable baseUri as a base. The path /team/libraries is appended in the constructor. If the base URI were to include a path as well, that path would be ignored. The third URI in this example uses resource1 as a base URI and appends /userarea/default.aspx. The Uri resource1 already includes a path, but because it is used as a base URI the path is ignored.

```
Uri baseUri = new Uri("http://www.gotdotnet.com");
Uri resource1 = new Uri(baseUri, "team/libraries");
Uri resource2 = new Uri(resource1, "/userarea/default.aspx");
Console.WriteLine(resource1.AbsoluteUri);
Console.WriteLine(resource2.AbsoluteUri);
```

The screenshot below shows the output of the demo application with the resultant absolute URIs that are stored in the Uri objects. As you can see a missing / between a base URI and a path is added automatically, and the path in a base URI is ignored.

The Uri class not only supports creating absolute URIs by using a relative one, it also has a method, MakeRelative(), that creates a relative URI out of an absolute one.

The code example below shows the creation of a relative URI from two absolute ones: resource1.MakeRelative(resource2) returns a string that shows how we can go from the URI of resource1 to the URI of resource2.

```
Uri resource1 =
        new Uri("http://www.gotdotnet.com/userarea/default.aspx");
Uri resource2 =
        new Uri("http://www.gotdotnet.com/team/libraries/");
Console.WriteLine(resource1.MakeRelative(resource2));
Console.WriteLine(resource2.MakeRelative(resource1));

Uri resource3 =
        new Uri("http://msdn.microsoft.com/vstudio/default.asp");
Console.WriteLine(resource2.MakeRelative(resource3));
```

The result is shown below. If we want to go from the absolute URI
http://www.gotdotnet.com/userarea/default.aspx to the URI
http://www.gotdotnet.com/team/libraries the resultant relative URI is
../team/libraries. For the way back the relative URI ../../userarea/default.aspx is
needed. As when working with the local file system, .. references the parent directory. With the third
string we see that if a completely different URI is passed to the method MakeRelative(), the absolute
URI is returned because the absolute URI is needed to access the resource.

IP Addresses

In a TCP/IP network a computer can be uniquely identified with an IP address. IPv4 addresses are
contained within 32 bits – for easier reading of an IP address it is usually represented by dotted quad-
notation, such as 204.148.170.161, making it easier to differentiate between networks and sub-
networks as we have seen in Chapter 1.

The IPAddress class encapsulates an IP address to use it with many other classes from the
System.Net namespace, and supports conversion functionality from network to host byte order, and
the other way round.

To create an IPAddress object with the dotted quad-notation we can use the static method Parse():

```
IPAddress address = IPAddress.Parse("204.148.170.161");
```

The IPAddress class itself stores the IP address within an integer that can be accessed with the
Address property. The ToString() method returns the dotted quad-notation.

Predefined Addresses

The IPAddress class has some public read-only fields that return predefined IP addresses.

❑   `IPAddress.None` returns an address indicating that no network interface should be used. This is used by the `Socket` class to indicate that the server should not listen for client activity.

❑   `IPAddress.Loopback` returns the predefined loopback address 127.0.0.1. This loopback address is used not to connect to the network, but to stay locally on a machine.

❑   `IPAddress.Broadcast` returns the IP broadcast address. With broadcast messages we can send a message to every PC in the local network.

❑   A computer can have multiple network cards with multiple IP addresses. `IPAddress.Any` is used by a socket to listen to any network interface.

Host or Network Byte Order

Networking is about connecting computers together – computers that can use different CPUs and operating systems. Depending on the CPU used the ordering of bytes inside a short, an integer, or a long can be different between the systems. Here the terms **little endian** and **big endian** are used.

With little endian, the least significant byte is stored at a lower memory address, but with big endian it is the other way around – the most significant byte is stored at a lower memory address. Motorola CPUs use big endian, Intel compatible CPUs use little endian.

Defining the order of the bytes is an important issue when these different systems are connected together. Fortunately, there is a standard for the byte representation on the network – the network byte order – and it's the same as big endian.

Using IP addresses that are stored within integers, and port numbers that are stored within shorts we have to convert the little endian version of the Intel system to the network byte order. The `IPAddress` class offers some static methods to convert short, int, and long data types from the host byte order (which is little endian in the case of Intel CPUs) to the network byte order, and the other way around.

`IPAddress.NetworkToHostOrder()` converts a multi-byte integer value from network byte order to host byte order; `IPAddress.HostToNetworkOrder()` converts a multi-byte integer value from host byte order to network byte order.

> *For IP addresses and port numbers that are used with sockets, network byte order is needed. The .NET* `Socket` *class itself deals with the correct byte order. However, the byte order used for the data we send across the network is entirely our own concern. If we don't plan to communicate with systems of a different CPU architecture there's no need to check for the byte order – if we do communicate with different systems we have to deal with it somehow.*

> *One example how this can be done is by looking at Unicode text files as this is an issue for 2-byte characters. A Unicode text file has a beginning marker* FFFE. *With this marker it can be easily detected if the file arrives in the wrong order as the marker would show* FEFF. *Seeing the marker* FEFF, *all pairs of bytes must be reversed. A Unicode editor can reverse the order of the bytes, so there's no need to convert the data before sending.*

Dns Class

To connect to a server the IP address of the server is needed. Because IP addresses are not easy to remember and can change, we use DNS names. In Chapter 1 we saw the functionality of DNS, and how a DNS server resolves names to IP addresses.

For .NET applications the Dns class can be used to resolve domain names to IP addresses. This class not only uses DNS servers to resolve names to IP addresses, but we will see that there are other mechanisms too.

Resolve a Name to an IP Address

To get an IP address from a hostname we can use the static method Dns.Resolve(). For a single hostname multiple IP addresses can be configured. So Resolve() not only returns an IPAddress, but an IPHostEntry object. IPHostEntry holds an array of addresses, alias names, and the hostname itself.

In the example below, we resolve the IP addresses of the hostname www.microsoft.com with Dns.Resolve(). The IP addresses are written to the console by accessing the AddressList property that returns an array of IPAddress objects. Next we loop through all registered names with the Aliases property, and finally we write the real hostname to the console.

```
string hostname = "www.microsoft.com";
IPHostEntry entry = Dns.Resolve(hostname);

Console.WriteLine("IP Addresses for {0}: ", hostname);
foreach (IPAddress address in entry.AddressList)
   Console.WriteLine(address.ToString());

Console.WriteLine("\nAlias names:");
foreach (string aliasName in entry.Aliases)
   Console.WriteLine(aliasName);

Console.WriteLine("\nAnd the real hostname:");
Console.WriteLine(entry.HostName);
```

The output of this sample program shows that the hostname www.microsoft.com is only an alias for www.microsoft.akadns.com, and it has six IP addresses:

The `Dns` class has more static methods that return `IPHostEntry` objects. They differentiate mainly in the way the hostname can be passed:

Dns Static Method	Description
Resolve()	Accepts a DNS hostname or IP address in dotted quad-notation to resolve IP addresses.
GetHostByName()	This method only accepts the DNS hostname, but not an IP address.
GetHostByAddress()	This method returns an `IPHostEntry` object by passing either an IP address as a string in dotted quad-notation, or as an `IPAddress` object.

To get the hostname of the local computer, we can use the method `Dns.GetHostName()`.

How is the IP Address Resolved?

There are many ways that an IP address can be resolved. You may have already wondered why a name was resolved although it was never configured with a DNS server – let's look at the ways in which IP addresses can be resolved.

With early versions of the TCP/IP network, hostnames were resolved only by a `HOSTS` file. A `HOSTS` file has a mapping from an IP address to the name of the host with optional additional alias names. Such a host file named `hosts` can also be found on a Windows 2000 PC in the directory `<windir>\system32\drivers\etc`.

Later the domain name system was introduced with DNS servers that know about the mapping of hostnames to IP addresses, and also the other way around – getting the hostname from an IP address is known as reverse lookup. Instead of changing every `HOSTS` file when a new IP address should be added, the new IP address need only be added to the DNS server. The client systems only need to be aware of the DNS server, and therefore the IP addresses can be resolved by asking the DNS server. The DNS server can be configured with the TCP/IP properties of the network configuration.

In order to free network administrators from the tiresome task of manually assigning IP addresses to every client on the network, a DHCP (Dynamic Host Configuration Protocol) server can be used. DHCP introduced dynamic IP addresses for PC clients. With DHCP, a client PC no longer has a fixed IP address. This introduced a new challenge for DNS servers and was the reason why Dynamic DNS was introduced with Windows 2000. Using Dynamic DNS, the IP address and hostname of a client PC can be set automatically in the DNS server as soon as the DHCP address is received.

To summarize, IP addresses are resolved with `HOSTS` files and DNS servers – but there are other ways. In a local network, in addition to a DNS name a NetBIOS hostname is used. If the DNS lookup fails, some NetBIOS naming mechanisms are used to get an IP address. Let us look at how this works.

NetBIOS Hostnames

In a Microsoft network, PCs not only have DNS hostnames, but also **NetBIOS** hostnames. NetBIOS functionality can also be used with TCP/IP; here it is called NBT – NetBIOS over TCP/IP. Normally the NetBIOS name is the same as the DNS name without the domain name extension.

For NetBIOS name resolution an LMHOSTS file is used, similar to the HOSTS file– it's in the same directory as the HOSTS file in fact. The file LMHOSTS.SAM you may find on your PC is just a sample file that shows what the LMHOSTS file can look like. If the hostname cannot be resolved with the LMHOSTS file, the NetBIOS name resolution depends on the NetBIOS node type. We can differentiate between four different node types:

❑   B-Node (Broadcast)

With B-nodes a broadcast is used to resolve the NetBIOS hostname. If IP routers are used that don't forward name registration and name queries, the name cannot be resolved. B-nodes are a bad option for large networks because they load the network with broadcasts.

❑   P-Node (Point to Point)

Using P-nodes a WINS server is used to register the hostname. A WINS server is similar to a DNS server, except that it resolves NetBIOS names to IP addresses rather than DNS names to IP addresses. A client can ask the WINS server to get the IP address for a hostname. This method reduces the network traffic, but fails if the WINS server cannot be reached.

❑   M-Node (Mixed)

M-node configuration is a mixture of B-node and P-node. As a first try a broadcast is used; if the broadcast doesn't work because the target host is not in the same network, a WINS server is asked to resolve the hostname. This configuration is useful with many small sub-networks that communicate across slow links.

❑   H-Node (Hybrid)

An H-node is also a mixture of B-node and P-node, but here the P-node mechanism is used first, before the B-node mechanism. A broadcast is used as a last resort only if other mechanisms fail.

You can look at the node-type that is configured for your system with the command-line utility ipconfig /all. The default is the typically best performing node-type H-node.

If that naming resolution is not complex enough it is also possible to edit some entries in the Registry to change the order of DNS name lookup and NetBIOS name lookup – however, caution is advised with this, as it's a good idea not to mess up these Registry keys. The configuration of these values can be found in

HKLM\System\CurrentControlSet\Services\NetBT\Parameters.

If the variable DhcpNodeType is set to 4, this specifies an H-node.

Resolving the IP Address Asynchronously

Querying a DNS server can take some time; the methods we have seen so far are all synchronous. The Dns class has built-in support for asynchronous DNS lookups: the methods Resolve() and GetHostByName() have asynchronous versions. We will only discuss the asynchronous versions of the GetHostByName() method, but the Resolve() method is similar.

The asynchronous versions of the GetHostByName() method are BeginGetHostByName() and EndGetHostByName(). The BeginGetHostByName() method starts the name query but doesn't wait for a successful query or a timeout – it returns immediately. Besides passing the hostname (similar to GetHostByName()) this method accepts an AsyncCallback delegate that defines what method should be called as soon as the hostname is resolved, or the timeout happens. Here I'm using the class method DnsLookupCompleted() that has the return type and signature as it is defined by the AsyncCallback delegate.

```
using System;
using System.Net;

class AsyncDnsDemo
{
    private static string hostname = "www.wrox.com";

    static void Main(string[] args)
    {
        if (args.Length != 0)
            hostname = args[0];

        Dns.BeginGetHostByName(hostname,
            new AsyncCallback(DnsLookupCompleted), null);

        Console.WriteLine("Waiting for the results...");
        Console.ReadLine();
    }
```

As soon as the DNS lookup is finished, the DnsLookupCompleted() method gets called, and we get the result of the name lookup by calling Dns.EndGetHostByName(). Then we can access all IP addresses, alias names, and the real hostname as in the synchronous example:

```
    private static void DnsLookupCompleted(IAsyncResult ar)
    {
        IPHostEntry entry = Dns.EndGetHostByName(ar);

        Console.WriteLine("IP Addresses for {0}: ", hostname);
        foreach (IPAddress address in entry.AddressList)
            Console.WriteLine(address.ToString());

        Console.WriteLine("\nAlias names:");
        foreach (string aliasName in entry.Aliases)
            Console.WriteLine(aliasName);

        Console.WriteLine("\nAnd the real hostname:");
        Console.WriteLine(entry.HostName);
    }
}
```

As an alternative to passing a delegate to the BeginGetHostByName() method we can use a reference to the IAsyncResult interface that is returned to check for the completed DNS lookup using the IsCompleted property. As soon as the lookup is finished, we invoke the same method we have done previously to read the IP addresses and hostname: DnsLookupCompleted().

```
static void Main(string[] args)
{
    if (args.Length != 0)
        hostname = args[0];

    IAsyncResult ar = Dns.BeginGetHostByName(hostname, null, null);

    while (!ar.IsCompleted)
    {
        Console.WriteLine("Can do something else...");
        System.Threading.Thread.Sleep(100);
    }
    DnsLookupCompleted(ar);
}
```

Requests and Responses

After the name of the host is resolved the client and server can start communicating. The server creates a socket and listens for incoming clients, the client connects to a server, and then the client and server can send and receive data. In Chapter 4 when we discuss sockets you will see all the action that is behind the scenes. Here we use the WebRequest and WebResponse classes where all socket issues are handled in the implementation of these classes; consequently, these classes are very simple to use.

In this small code example we create a WebRequest object with the static method WebRequest.Create(). The Create() method accepts a Uri object, or a URI string. The GetResponse() method returns a WebResponse object and connects to the server to return some data. To read the data that is returned from the server we use a StreamReader to read line-by-line.

```
Uri uri = new Uri("http://www.wrox.com");
WebRequest request = WebRequest.Create(uri);
WebResponse response = request.GetResponse();
Stream stream = response.GetResponseStream();
StreamReader reader = new StreamReader(stream);

string line;
while ((line = reader.ReadLine()) != null)
{
    Console.WriteLine(line);
}
response.Close();
reader.Close();
```

Now that we've seen a simple application using WebRequest and WebResponse objects let's look at these classes in detail.

WebRequest and WebResponse

The base classes for requests and responses to servers are WebRequest and WebResponse.

First let's look at the WebRequest class.

WebRequest Static Methods	Description
Create() CreateDefault()	The WebRequest class has no public constructor. Instances can be created using the static methods Create() and CreateDefault() instead. These methods do not really create a new object of type WebRequest, but a new object of a class that derives from WebRequest, such as HttpWebRequest or FileWebRequest.
RegisterPrefix()	With RegisterPrefix() we can register a class to handle a specific protocol. Objects of this class will be created with the WebRequest.Create() method. This mechanism is called **pluggable protocols,** and is described later in this chapter.

WebRequest Instance Methods	Description
GetRequestStream()	GetRequestStream() returns a stream object that can be used to send some data to the server.
BeginGetRequestStream() EndGetRequestStream()	Getting access to the request stream in an asynchronous way is done with BeginGetRequestStream() and EndGetRequestStream().
GetResponse()	GetResponse() returns a WebResponse object that can be used to read the data that is received from the server.
BeginGetResponse() EndGetResponse()	Similar to the request stream we have asynchronous methods to get the response stream.
Abort()	If an asynchronous method is started with a BeginXX() method, it can be stopped prematurely with the Abort() method.

WebRequest Properties	Description
RequestUri	RequestUri is a read-only property that returns the URI that is associated with the WebRequest. The URI can be set in the static Create() method of this class.
Method	The Method property is used to get or set a method for a specific request. The HttpWebRequest supports the HTTP methods GET, POST, HEAD, and so on.
Headers	Depending on the protocol used, different header information can be passed to and received from the server. The protocol header information is contained within a WebHeaderCollection that can be accessed with the Header property.
ContentType ContentLength	The type of data sent to the server is defined with the ContentType property. We can have any different type of data as long as it can be represented in a byte array. The content type usually defines the MIME type of the data, such as image/jpeg, image/gif, text/html, or text/xml.

WebRequest Properties	Description
Credentials	If the server requires user authentication, the user credentials can be set with the Credentials property.
PreAuthenticate	For protocols that support preauthentication, the property PreAuthenticate can be set to true. By default, a web browser first tries to access the page of a web site without authentication. If the web site requires authentication, the server returns that access is denied for non-authenticated users. The next request done by the client is with authentication information. This additional round-trip can be avoided by setting the property PreAuthenticate to true.
Proxy	With the Proxy property we can set the web proxy that is used for this request.
ConnectionGroupName	With the ConnectionGroupName property we can define the connection pool that should be used with this WebRequest object.
Timeout	The Timeout property defines the time in milliseconds we wait for a response from the server. The default value is 100,000 milliseconds. If the server doesn't respond within the timeout value, a WebException is thrown.

The WebResponse class is used to read data from the server. An object of this class is returned with the GetResponse() method as we have seen with the WebRequest class.

WebResponse Methods	Description
GetResponseStream()	GetResponseStream() returns a stream object that is used to read the response from the server. We discussed stream objects in Chapter 2.
Close()	If the response object is no longer needed it should be closed with the Close() method.

WebResponse Properties	Description
ResponseUri	With the ResponseUri property we can read the URI that is associated with the response object. This can be the same as the URI of the WebRequest object, but can be different if the server redirected the request to another resource.
Headers	The Headers property returns a WebHeaderCollection that includes the protocol-specific header information returned from the server.
ContentType ContentLength	Similar to the WebRequest class, we have ContentType and ContentLength properties. Here these properties define the nature of the data that is returned from the server.

Now that we know the properties and methods of the WebRequest and WebResponse classes, let's look at some of the features of these classes.

Pluggable Protocols

The WebRequest class is abstract, so the WebRequest.Create() method cannot create an object of type WebRequest – an object of a class that is derived from WebRequest is created instead. Passing an HTTP request to the WebRequest.Create() method creates an HttpWebRequest object. We will discuss the HttpWebRequest class with detailed information about the HTTP protocol in Chapter 8. Passing a request with the file scheme creates a FileWebRequest object.

The http, https, and file schemes are predefined within the .NET configuration file machine.config as shown below. You can find this configuration file in the directory <windows>\Microsoft.NET\Framework\<version>\CONFIG.

```
<configuration>
  <system.net>
    <webRequestModules>
      <add prefix="http" type="System.Net.HttpRequestCreator" />
      <add prefix="https" type="System.Net.HttpRequestCreator" />
      <add prefix="file" type="System.Net.FileWebRequestCreator" />
    </webRequestModules>
  </system.net>
</configuration>
```

Adding a configuration file entry allows us to extend the protocols used by the WebRequest class, or we can extend them programmatically.

To support a different protocol from http, https, and the file scheme, a new class that derives from WebRequest must be created, such as FtpWebRequest for the FTP protocol. This class must override methods and properties of the base class to implement protocol-specific behavior. In addition to that, a factory class that creates objects of the FtpWebRequest class must be defined. Such a factory class that is used by WebRequest must implement the IWebRequestCreate interface. Let's call this class FtpWebRequestCreator. An instance of this class must be registered for the ftp scheme with the WebRequest class:

```
WebRequest.RegisterPrefix("ftp", new FtpWebRequestCreator());
```

If the ftp scheme is now used with the WebRequest.Create() method, a new instance of FtpWebRequest is created and returned:

```
FtpWebRequest request =
    (FtpWebRequest)WebRequest.Create("ftp://ftp.microsoft.com");
```

This request object can now be used to copy files from and to the FTP server similar to the request objects we are going to use in the next section. Here we are not going to implement the FtpWebRequest class, but you can do it yourself after reading Chapters 4 and 5. Programming an FTP client requires the use of socket classes with a TCP connection.

FileWebRequest and FileWebResponse

Reading and writing files locally or by using file shares is not very different from reading and writing files from web servers. To read and write files we can use the `FileWebRequest` and `FileWebResponse` classes. However, many methods and properties that are defined in the base classes `WebRequest` and `WebResponse` are not used with the derived classes, and the MSDN documentation just lists them as "reserved for future use".

To demonstrate how `FileWebRequest` and `FileWebResponse` can be used, I'm creating a simple Windows Forms application where the name of a file that should be opened can be entered in a text box, and then the file is opened and displayed in a multi-line text box (the big whitespace in the picture below). The file opened can then be saved with a different filename.

To make the code easier to read here are the controls that are used with this application.

Control Type	Name
TextBox	textFileOpen
TextBox	textFileSave
Button	buttonOpenFile
Button	buttonSaveFile
TextBox	textData

Reading from Files

The Click handler of the Open button opens the file and writes the content of the file to the multi-line text box. We pass the filename to the WebRequest.Create() method. It is not necessary to prefix the filename with the schema file://. The WebRequest class creates a Uri object and uses the AbsolutePath property of the Uri class. As we have seen earlier, the Uri class automatically prefixes the filename with the correct schema. So passing a filename the WebRequest class creates a FileWebRequest object, and we can successfully cast it. The GetResponse() method returns a FileWebResponse that we use immediately to get a Stream object with the method GetResponseStream(). The StreamReader class is used to read the stream with simple methods. We read the complete file data into a string and pass the string to the Text property of the multi-line textbox textData.

```csharp
private void buttonOpenFile_Click(object sender, System.EventArgs e)
{
    string fileName = textFileOpen.Text;
    FileWebRequest request =
        (FileWebRequest)WebRequest.Create(fileName);
    Stream stream = request.GetResponse().GetResponseStream();

    StreamReader reader = new StreamReader(stream);
    textData.Text = reader.ReadToEnd();
    reader.Close();
}
```

Starting the application we can enter a filename, and the file is opened and displayed in the multi-line text box:

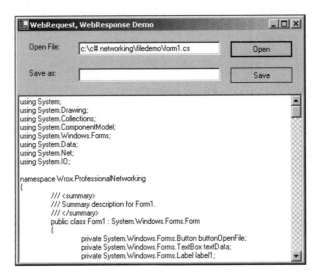

There's just a simple change necessary and we can read files from both the file system and the Web. If we enter an HTTP request into the current program, it will result in an invalid cast exception because we cast the object that is returned from WebRequest.Create() to the class FileWebRequest. Changing the program so that it does not cast to a FileWebRequest we can use any scheme:

```
        string fileName = textFileOpen.Text;
        WebRequest request = WebRequest.Create(fileName);
        Stream stream = request.GetResponse().GetResponseStream();
```

> **If we don't use specific methods or properties of the derived class, it is not necessary to cast the WebRequest object that is returned from the method WebRequest.Create() to the specific class!**

With .NET v1 the class FileWebRequest has no methods or properties that are specific to this class and they are not defined in the base class WebRequest. However, the HttpWebRequest class has some specific methods and properties as dealt with in Chapter 8.

Writing to Files

To write the data back to a file we implement a Click handler for the **Save** button. As before, we create a WebRequest object passing the filename. Now we use a StreamWriter instead of a StreamReader. There's one other important change. To make the stream writable, the Method property must be set to "PUT". The default method is "GET" specifying that the stream is read-only.

```
        private void OnFileSave(object sender, System.EventArgs e)
        {
            string fileName = textFileSave.Text;
            WebRequest request = WebRequest.Create(fileName);
            request.Method = "PUT";
            Stream stream = request.GetRequestStream();
            StreamWriter writer = new StreamWriter(stream);
            writer.Write(textData.Text);
            writer.Close();
        }
```

Now we have seen how the classes WebRequest and WebResponse can be used – but there are some further features of these classes that we will also take a look at.

Connection Pooling

The default number of connections that can be opened to the server at one time is defined in the configuration file machine.config, as can be seen below. With the default configuration we have a maximum of two simultaneous connections to the same host.

```
<configuration>
  <system.net>
    <connectionManagement>
      <add address="*" maxconnection="2" />
    </connectionManagement>
  </system.net>
</configuration>
```

We can override the settings not only by adding entries to the configuration file but also programmatically for specific requests using the `ServicePoint` and `ServicePointManager` classes. We can create multiple connection pools and use them by their name with the `ConnectionGroupName` property. This is useful if we do multiple requests to the same server simultaneously. These classes are discussed in Chapter 8.

Using a Web Proxy

In a local network a proxy server can be used to route Internet access to specific servers. A proxy server can reduce the transfer and network connections from the Internet, and increase the performance for local clients by caching resources.

The proxy server can do active and passive caching.

❑   With passive caching the web resources are stored in the cache of the proxy server as soon as a client requests a resource. If a second client requests the same resource, it is not necessary to get the resource from the web server in the Internet again as the web proxy can answer directly from the cache created by the first request.

❑   Using active caching the system administrator can configure specific web servers and directories that should be cached automatically following a specific schedule, such as during night hours. This way the network bandwidth needed for the Internet can be reduced during the daytime, and users will see a better performance for often used pages.

The default proxy server is set with the Internet Options in the Control Panel. You can also access this configuration from the Internet Explorer Tools | Internet Options | Connections | LAN Settings:

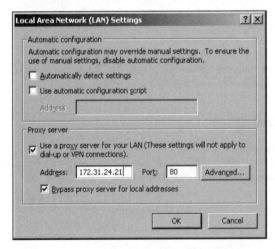

Here the web proxy server has the IP address 172.31.24.21 and listens to port 80. For web servers in an intranet, the proxy server should not be used. This is marked with the option Bypass proxy server for local addresses. With the Advanced... button it is possible to configure different proxy servers for different protocols (such as HTTP, HTTPS, or FTP), and it is possible to select specific web sites that should not be accessed by the proxy server.

WebProxy class

The WebProxy class is used to define a proxy server. This class has properties that are similar to the settings we have seen with the proxy server configuration:

WebProxy Properties	Description
Address	The Address is of type Uri and defines the URI to the proxy server, IP address, or name and port number.
BypassList	With the property BypassList, a string array can get and set URIs that should not use the proxy server.
BypassArrayList	BypassArrayList is a read-only property that returns an object of type ArrayList which represents the URIs that we set with the property BypassList.
BypassProxyOnLocal	BypassProxyOnLocal is a Boolean property that specifies if local addresses should be used with the proxy server or not.
Credentials	If the proxy server requires user authentication, we can pass the user credentials with the Credentials property.

Default Web Proxy

The default proxy server that is used for all connections is set with the GlobalProxySelection class. By default, the web proxy that is set with the Internet Options we have just seen is used. With the Select property we can set a different proxy for all uses of WebRequest.GetResponse().

In the program below we access the information from the default web proxy and write it to the console. The Select property of the GlobalProxySelection class returns an IWebProxy interface. To access the properties of the WebProxy class we have to cast this interface to the WebProxy class. Then we access the URI of the proxy server that is defined with the Address property. The BypassList property returns a string array that we write out inside the foreach loop. Finally, we use the BypassProxyOnLocal property to write a message to the console saying whether the proxy is used for local addresses or not.

```
WebProxy proxy = (WebProxy)GlobalProxySelection.Select;
Console.WriteLine("Address of the proxy server: {0}", proxy.Address);
foreach (string bypassAddress in proxy.BypassList)
{
    Console.WriteLine("Not using the proxy server for this " +
                    "address: {0}", bypassAddress);
}
Console.WriteLine ("For local addresses the proxy server is {0} used",
                proxy.BypassProxyOnLocal ? "not" : "");
```

In my case the output to the console is as follows:

```
C:\C# Networking\ShowDefaultProxy\bin\Debug\ShowDefaultProxy.exe        _ □ X
Address of the proxy server: http://172.31.24.21/
Not using the proxy server for this address: tubularbells\.globalknowledge\

For local addresses the proxy server is not used
Press any key to continue_
```

Changing the WebProxy for Specific Requests

Other than using the default web proxy for all requests we can use a different proxy for specific requests. In a network, multiple proxy servers can be used either to distribute the load, or because of security requirements. To select a different proxy we just have to set the Proxy property of the WebRequest class.

```
WebRequest request = WebRequest.Create("http://www.wrox.com");
request.Proxy = new WebProxy("172.31.24.28", 8080);
```

The Proxy property of the WebRequest class accepts an object that implements the IWebProxy interface. Of course, the WebProxy class implements the IWebProxy interface. The constructor of the WebProxy class is overloaded and accepts a URI to the proxy server, and also all the parameters to configure a WebProxy object that we know already, for example, the user credentials, and the list of URIs where the proxy server should be bypassed, among others.

Authentication

If the web server requires user authentication we can create user credentials and pass it to the web request. The interfaces and classes that are of use here are ICredentials, NetworkCredential, and CredentialCache.

For user authentication we can create an object of type NetworkCredential. This class provides credential information for basic, digest, NTLM, and Kerberos authentication.

In the constructor of the NetworkCredential class we can pass a username, password, and optionally a domain that authorizes the user.

```
NetworkCredential credentials =
    new NetworkCredential("UserName", "Password");
```

This credential information can be set with the Credentials property of the WebRequest class to authorize the user:

```
WebRequest request =
    WebRequest.Create("http://requireslogon.com/myfile.aspx");
request.Credentials = credentials;
```

If we want to use multiple credential information for different URIs, we can use the `CredentialCache` class as below. With this cache we can also define the authentication type for a specific connection. Here, I'm using basic authentication for the web site www.unsecure.com, and digest authentication for the web site www.moresecure.com where a hash is sent across the network instead of the password.

```
CredentialCache credentialCache = new CredentialCache();
credentialCache.Add(new Uri("http://www.unsecure.com"), "Basic",
                    new NetworkCredential("username", "password"));
credentialCache.Add(new Uri("http://www.moresecure.com"), "Digest",
                    new NetworkCredential("username", "password",
                                          "domain"));
```

To use the Windows logon credentials of the currently logged on user, we can use the default credentials that can be accessed with `CredentialCache.DefaultCredentials()`. For security reasons these credentials can only be used for the NTLM, Negotiate, and Kerberos authentication types, and it is not possible to read the username and domain from it.

Permissions

Whenever networking classes are used, permissions are required. For networking issues we have three permissions to consider:

❑   `DnsPermission`

❑   `WebPermission`

❑   `SocketPermission`

The `DnsPermission` is required to do DNS name lookups with the `Dns` class. The `WebPermission` is used by classes from the `System.Net` namespace that use URIs to send and receive data from the Internet; the `SocketPermission` is used to accept data on a local socket or to connect to a host using a transport protocol.

Applications that are installed locally on a system have full trust, so all permissions are available by default. .NET applications can also be started from a network share, or assemblies can be downloaded from the Internet – in these situations many permissions are not available by default. Therefore, we have to configure the security settings for these applications. First, we are going to discuss the programmatic aspects of the security, and after that we will look at how the permissions can be configured.

DnsPermission

Using the `Dns` class to make an IP address lookup, we need the `DnsPermission`. With this permission we only differentiate between allow and deny. Making DNS queries can be either completely unrestricted or not allowed at all.

WebPermission

The `WebPermission` is required for classes like `WebRequest` and `WebResponse` for sending data to and receiving data from the Internet.

Here we differentiate between **Accept** and **Connect** permissions. Accept is needed for URIs used inside classes and methods; client applications that use URIs to connect to a server need the Connect privilege. The WebPermission class also has a list for URIs that we can connect to, and a list for URIs that are accepted.

SocketPermission

SocketPermissions are needed for socket classes from the System.Net.Sockets namespace that we deal with in Chapter 4. This is the most flexible permission of the three network permission classes.

For server applications that wait for clients to be connected, we can pass the NetworkAccess.Accept enumeration value in the constructor; client applications that connect to servers use the value NetworkAccess.Connect. We can restrict the connection to specific host and port numbers, and also define a transport protocol used.

Using Permission Attributes

If a required permission is not available, the program fails with an exception of type SecurityException as soon as the privileged method is called. The user may have been using the application for some time when the exception is thrown, and may possibly lose some data if we don't handle the exception gracefully. A good way of avoiding this is to mark the assembly with the permissions that we need.

If we use the WebRequest class to get some data from the Internet, we need the WebPermission permission. We can mark classes and methods that require the permission with the WebPermission attribute (that's implemented in the class WebPermissionAttribute) as follows:

```
[WebPermission(SecurityAction.Demand,
               ConnectPattern="http://www.wrox.com")]
class PermissionDemo
{
```

In this case, the SecurityException happens as soon as the PermissionDemo class is instantiated. If we want this check at program startup we can apply the WebPermission attribute to the assembly scope:

```
[assembly: WebPermission(SecurityAction.RequestMinimum,
           ConnectPattern="http://www.wrox.com")]
```

If this WebPermission attribute is applied to the assembly, the runtime checks if the program has the required permission at program startup. If it doesn't have the required permission it stops immediately prior to the user entering (and losing) information.

Using the command-line utility permview that's part of the .NET Framework SDK, we can display the required assembly permissions:

```
Visual Studio .NET Command Prompt                                    _ □ x
C:\C# Networking>permview permissionclient.exe

Microsoft (R) .NET Framework Permission Request Viewer.  Version 1.0.3512.0
Copyright (C) Microsoft Corporation 1998-2001. All rights reserved.

minimal permission set:
<PermissionSet class="System.Security.PermissionSet"
               version="1">
    <IPermission class="System.Net.WebPermission, System, Version=1.0.3300.0, Cul
ture=neutral, PublicKeyToken=b77a5c561934e089"
                 version="1">
        <ConnectAccess>
            <URI uri="http://www.wrox.com"/>
        </ConnectAccess>
    </IPermission>
</PermissionSet>

optional permission set:
    Not specified

refused permission set:
    Not specified

C:\C# Networking>_
```

Permission Attribute Parameters

With all permission attributes we can pass a value of the enumeration `SecurityAction` in the constructor. Here we only look at the most important enumeration values.

SecurityAction Enumeration Values	Description
Demand Deny	The enumeration values `SecurityAction.Demand` and `SecurityAction.Deny` can be used with classes and methods. With `Demand` we specify that the class or method needs the permission, `Deny` says that we don't want this permission.
RequestMinimum RequestOptional RequestRefuse	The `RequestXXX` enumeration value can only be used for assembly scope; it cannot be specified with classes and methods. `RequestMinimum` defines that this permission is mandatory for using the program. With `RequestOptional` we say that the program can do some useful work without this permission. Here we have to handle a `SecurityException` gracefully. `RequestRefuse` defines that we don't want to have this permission. This is used in cases when there can be some misuse of permissions, such as calling some assemblies when we don't have the sources and we don't trust them fully.

With the `WebPermission` attribute in addition to the `SecurityAction` we can set these properties:

WebPermissionAttribute properties	Description
Accept AcceptPattern	With the `Accept` property we can define a URI to a resource that can be used within a class, method, or assembly where this attribute applies. With the `AcceptPattern` property we can specify a regular expression to allow or deny access to URIs.
Connect ConnectPattern	The two `ConnectXX` properties are similar to the `AcceptXX` properties, with the difference that these properties are used for a URI connection string.

The class `SocketPermissionAttribute` defines these additional properties:

SocketPermissionAttribute properties	Description
Access	With this property we can define the allowed network access method. Just two string values are allowed: `Accept` and `Connect`. `Accept` is used for a server application that listens to and accepts client connections, and `Connect` is for a client connecting to a server.
Host	With the `Host` property we can set the host name with DNS syntax or an IP address where the permission applies.
Port	The `Port` is a string property to specify the port number where we need permission. This can be used to restrict client applications to some specific servers. This property is of type `string` because different protocols don't necessarily define the port number as an integer.
Transport	With the `Transport` property we can restrict the network connection to a specific transport protocol. Possible values are `All`, `ConnectionLess`, `ConnectionOriented`, `Tcp`, and `Udp`. `ConnectionLess` allows the use of all connection-less protocols such as UDP; `ConnectionOriented` allows the use of connection-oriented protocols such as TCP.

Strong Name Assemblies

If we start network applications from an intranet or the Internet, we have to assign the permissions we discussed. However, it wouldn't be a pleasant task if these permissions had to be assigned to all Internet or intranet applications – this would be a lot of work and add a tremendous complexity. It would be much better to identify the specific assembly or a group of assemblies to configure permissions only for it.

With .NET, strong names may be used to uniquely identify assemblies, and are also a way to prevent tampering with assemblies.

> We will not cover all features of strongly named assemblies in this book. You can read more about them in Professional C# 2nd Edition, Wrox Press (ISBN 1-86100-704-3).

To create a strong name we can create a public/private key pair with the `sn` utility:

```
>sn - k mykey.snk
```

Using the assembly attribute `AssemblyKeyFile` (the class `AssemblyKeyFileAttribute` is in the namespace `System.Reflection`) we add a public key and a signature to the assembly:

```
[assembly: AssemblyKeyFile("../../mykey.snk")]
```

This strongly named assembly can now be used for security configuration as we will see next.

Configuring Permissions

Applications that are installed locally have full trust by default; configuring these applications is not necessary. If an application is downloaded from the Internet, it has no permissions by default – we have to add the permissions explicitly. When starting applications from an intranet, we have Dns permissions by default, but we must configure the WebPermission and SocketPermission permissions explicitly.

For permission configurations we have the command-line utility caspol.exe, and the .NET Framework Configuration Tool Windows application in the Control Panel.

First, we have to create a new permission set that will be used by our networking application. If you are happy with an existing permission set that already has the required permissions included, it's not necessary to create a new one. With the .NET Framework Configuration Tool I'm creating a new permission set called Network Permissions:

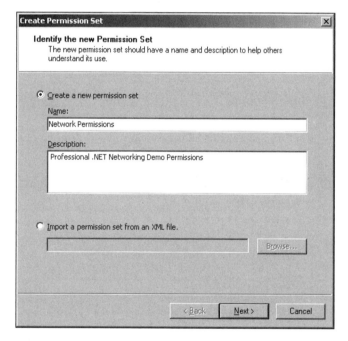

Clicking Next brings us on to a dialog for assigning the permissions to the permission set itself. This permission set includes the required permissions – DNS for name lookups, and Web Access for the WebXX classes. I'm configuring these permissions as unrestricted; you can also restrict the Web Access to a specific URI. The User Interface permission is needed for Windows applications.

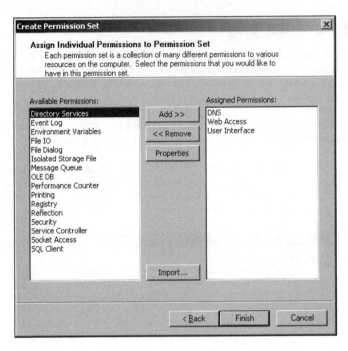

For the assembly that needs these permissions I'm creating a new code group, `Professional .NET Networking Zone`:

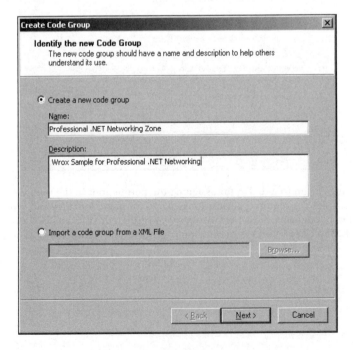

With this code group the condition type can be specified to define the assemblies that belong to this code group. The condition can be an application directory, a URI, or a site for example. Here I'm selecting the strong name condition and importing the strong name of the assembly created earlier. Selecting the check boxes for the name and version would restrict the code group to this specific assembly. Without selecting these options the code group includes all assemblies that use the same public key:

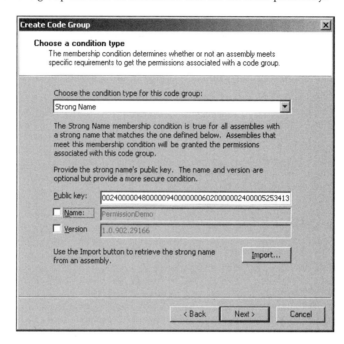

Pressing the **Next** key selects the previously created permission set for this code group.

With this configuration it is now possible to start the network application from a network share, or downloaded with a link from a web server.

> *You can read more about .NET permissions in* Professional C# 2nd Edition, *Wrox Press (ISBN 1-86100-704-3).*

Summary

In this chapter we have covered an overview of network programming with the .NET classes available within the System.Net namespace.

After the overview of the System.Net classes we discussed the Uri class for working with absolute and relative URIs, and split up a URI into its constituent parts.

After that we looked at the features of the IPAddress class that not only wraps IP addresses, but also has support to convert the network byte order.

Next, the Dns class was used to resolve hostnames to IP addresses. Because name lookups can take a while we looked at doing that asynchronously.

We met the major topics of requests and responses – these will be covered more fully in later chapters, particularly in Chapter 8. We discussed the base classes WebRequest and WebResponse, and also used them to read and write simple files.

Finally, we discussed two aspects of security: authentication to connect to web sites that require user logon, and the permissions needed by a networking application.

Thus the foundation is laid to continue with socket programming in subsequent chapters, and then onto Internet programming.

4

Working with Sockets

The preceding chapters talked generally about .NET support for network programming. They showed you how to manipulate streams in .NET applications, and the classes to work with IP addresses and DNS lookups. In this chapter we'll start programming with sockets.

In particular, we'll cover:

- ❑   What sockets are, and the different types of sockets
- ❑   Socket support in .NET – the `System.Net.Sockets.Socket` class
- ❑   Creating a TCP socket server application
- ❑   Setting socket options
- ❑   Creating an asynchronous TCP socket server application
- ❑   Socket permissions

Sockets

A socket is one end of a two-way communication link between two programs running on a network. By connecting the two sockets together, you can pass data between different processes (either local or remote). The socket implementation provides the encapsulation of the network and transport level protocols.

Sockets were originally developed for UNIX at the University of California at Berkeley. In UNIX, the input/output method for communication follows an open/read/write/close algorithm. Before a resource can be used, it needs to be opened, by specifying the relevant permissions and other parameters. Once the resource is opened, it can be read from or written to. After using the resource, the user can finally call the Close() method, signaling to the operating system that it has finished its tasks with the resource.

When Inter-Process Communication (IPC) and **Networking** facilities are added to the UNIX operating system, they adopt the familiar pattern of Input/Output. All the resources opened for communication are identified by a descriptor in UNIX and Windows. These descriptors (also called handles) can be a pointer to a file, memory, or any other channel, and actually point to an internal data structure primarily used by the operating system. A socket, being a resource, is also represented by a descriptor. Therefore, for sockets, a descriptor's life can be divided into three phases: open/create socket, receive and send to socket, and ultimately closing the socket.

The IPC interface for communicating between different processes is built on top of the I/O methods. They facilitate sockets to send and receive data. Each target is specified by a socket address; therefore this address can be specified in the client to connect with the target.

Socket Types

There are two basic types of sockets – **stream sockets** and **datagram sockets**.

Stream Sockets

A stream socket is a connection-oriented socket that consists of a stream of bytes that can be bi-directional, meaning that the application can both transmit and receive through the endpoint. A stream socket guarantees error correction, handles delivery, and preserves data sequence. It can be relied upon to deliver sequenced, unduplicated data. It is also suitable for transmitting large amounts of data because the overhead of establishing a separate connection for sending each message can be unacceptable for small amounts of data. Stream sockets achieve this level of quality through the use of the Transmission Control Protocol (TCP). TCP makes sure that your data arrives on the other side in sequence, and error free.

In these types of sockets, a path is formed before communicating messages. This ensures that both the sides taking part in the communication are alive and responding. If your application sends two messages to the recipient, then the messages are guaranteed to be received in sequence. However, individual messages can be broken up into several packets and there is no way to determine record boundaries. Under TCP, its up to the protocol to disassemble the transmission of data into packets of appropriate sizes, send them over and put them back together on the other side. An application only knows that it's sending a certain number of bytes to the TCP layer and that the other side gets those bytes. What TCP effectively does here is to break up that data into appropriately sized packets, receive the packets on the other side, unwrap the data and then put it back together.

Streams are based on explicit connections: socket A requests a connection to socket B, and socket B accepts or rejects the connection request.

Stream sockets are preferable to datagram sockets when the data must be guaranteed delivery on the other side, and when the data size is large. Therefore, if the reliability of the connection between two applications is paramount, use stream sockets. An e-mail server is one example of an application that must deliver content in the correct order, and without duplications or omissions. A stream socket depends on TCP to ensure the delivery of messages to their destinations – we'll talk more about TCP in the next chapter.

Datagram Sockets

Datagram sockets are sometimes called connection-less sockets, that is, no explicit connection is established – a message is sent to the specified socket that can be received appropriately from the specified socket. Using stream sockets is indeed a more reliable method than datagram sockets, but with some applications, the overhead incurred by establishing an explicit connection is unacceptable. An example application would be a day/time server, which is proving day/time synchronization to its clients. After all, it takes some time to establish a reliable connection with the server, which merely delays the service and ultimately the purpose of the server application is unseen. To reduce the overhead we would use datagram sockets.

The use of datagram sockets requires User Datagram Protocol (UDP) to pass the data from a client to the server. There are some limitations on the size of the message in this protocol, and unlike stream sockets, where a message can be reliably sent to the destination server, datagram sockets offer no such guarantee. There are no errors returned from the server if the data is lost in between. We'll talk more about UDP in Chapter 6.

Apart from the two types that are described above, there is also a generalized form of sockets, called raw sockets.

Raw Sockets

The main purpose of using raw sockets is to bypass the mechanism by which the computer handles TCP/IP. It works by providing a custom implementation of the TCP/IP stack replacing the mechanism provided by the TCP/IP stack on the kernel – the packet is passed directly to the application that needs it and therefore it is much more efficient than going through the client's main network stack.

A raw socket, by definition, is a socket that takes packets, bypasses the TCP and UDP layers in the TCP/IP stack and sends them directly to the application.

For such sockets, the packet is not passed through the TCP/IP filter, meaning that there is no processing on the packet, and it comes out in its raw form. This puts the responsibility of handling all the data appropriately, and dealing with such actions as stripping off the headers and parsing onto the receiving application – it's like making a small TCP/IP stack in the application. However, you rarely need to program with raw sockets. Unless you are writing system software, or a packet analyzer type program, you don't need to get into the details. They are mainly used when writing custom low-level protocol applications. For example, various TCP/IP utilities such as `traceroute`, `ping`, or `arp` use raw sockets.

Working with raw sockets requires substantial knowledge of the underlying TCP/UDP/IP protocol, and is beyond the scope of this book.

Ports

A port is defined to solve the problem of communicating with multiple applications simultaneously; it basically expands the notion of an IP address. A computer running simultaneous applications that receives a packet though the network can identify the target process using a unique port number that is determined when the connection is being made.

The socket is composed of the IP address of the machine and the port number used by the TCP application. Because the IP address is unique across the Internet and the port numbers are unique on the individual machine, the socket numbers are also unique across the entire Internet. This enables a process to talk to another process across the network, based entirely on the socket number.

Certain services have port numbers reserved for them; these are the **well-known port numbers**, such as FTP on port number 21. Your application can use any port number that hasn't been reserved or is already in use. The Internet Assigned Numbers Authority (IANA) prescribes the list of well-known port numbers.

Normally, a client-server application using sockets consists of two different applications – a client that initiates the connection with the target (the server), and the server, which waits for the connection from the client.

For example, on the client side, the client must know the target's address and the port number. To make the connection request, the client tries to establish the connection with the server:

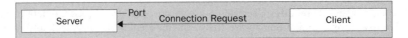

If everything goes well, provided that the server is already running before the client tries to connect to it, the server accepts the connection.

Upon acceptance, the server application creates a new socket to deal specifically with the connected client.

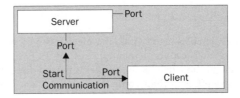

The client and server can now communicate with each other by reading from and writing to their respective sockets.

Working with Sockets in .NET

The classes in the `System.Net.Sockets` namespace provide sockets support in .NET – let's begin with a quick description of each of them.

Class	Description
MulticastOption	The `MulticastOption` class sets IP address values for joining or leaving an IP multicast group. This class is discussed further in Chapter 7.
NetworkStream	The `NetworkStream` implements the underlying stream class from which data is sent or received. It is a high-level abstraction representing a connection to a TCP/IP communication channel. We saw `NetworkStream` in Chapter 2.
TcpClient	The `TcpClient` builds upon the `Socket` class to provide TCP services at a higher level. `TcpClient` provides several methods for sending and receiving data over a network. Chapter 5 discusses `TcpClient` in more detail.

Class	Description
TcpListener	This class also builds upon the low level Socket class; its main purpose is in server applications. This class listens for the incoming client connections and notifies the application of any connections. We'll look into this class when we talk about TCP in Chapter 5.
UdpClient	UDP is a connectionless protocol, therefore a different type of functionality is required to implement UDP services in .NET. The UdpClient class serves the purpose of implementing UDP services – we'll look more at this in Chapter 6.
SocketException	This is the exception thrown when an error occurs in a socket. We'll look at this class later in this chapter.
Socket	Our last class in the System.Net.Sockets namespace is the Socket class itself. This class provides the basic functionality of a socket application.

System.Net.Sockets.Socket Class

The Socket class plays an important role in network programming, performing both client and server operations. Mostly, method calls to this class handle the necessary security checks, such as checking security permissions, and then are marshaled to counterparts in the Windows Sockets API.

Before we look at an example using the Socket class, let's first take a look at a list of some of the important System.Net.Sockets.Socket properties:

Property	Description
AddressFamily	Gets the address family of the socket – the value is from the Socket.AddressFamily enumeration
Available	Returns the amount of available data to read
Blocking	Gets or sets the value which indicates whether the socket is in blocking mode or not
Connected	Returns the value that informs whether the socket is still connected with the remote host
LocalEndPoint	Gets the local endpoint
ProtocolType	Get the protocol type of the socket
RemoteEndPoint	Gets the remote endpoint of a socket
SocketType	Gets the type of the socket

and some of the System.Net.Sockets.Socket methods:

Method	Description
Accept()	Creates a new socket to handle the incoming connection request.
Bind()	Associates a socket with the local endpoint for listening to incoming connections.
Close()	Forces the socket to close itself.
Connect()	Establishes a connection with the remote host.
GetSocketOption()	Returns the value of a SocketOption.
IOControl()	Sets low-level operating modes for the socket. This method provides low-level access to the underlying socket instance of the Socket class.
Listen()	Places the socket in listening mode. This method is exclusive to server applications.
Receive()	Receives data from a connected socket.
Poll()	Determines the status of the socket.
Select()	Checks the status of one or more sockets.
Send()	Sends data to the connected socket.
SetSocketOption()	Sets a SocketOption.
Shutdown()	Disables send and receive on a socket.

Creating a TCP Stream Socket Application

In the following example, we use TCP to provide sequenced, reliable two-way byte streams. Here we'll build a complete application involving both the client and the server. First we demonstrate how to construct a TCP stream-based socket server and then a client application to test our server. The following program creates a server that receives connection requests from clients. The server is built synchronously, therefore the execution of the thread is blocked until it accepts a connection from the client. The application demonstrates a simple server that replies to the client. The client ends its connection by sending <TheEnd> to the server.

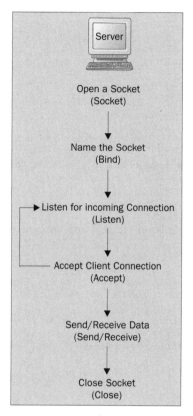

Here's the complete code for `SocketServer.cs`:

```csharp
using System;
using System.Net.Sockets;
using System.Net;
using System.Text;

public class SocketServer
{
    public static void Main(string [] args)
    {

        // establish the local end point for the socket
        IPHostEntry ipHost = Dns.Resolve("localhost");
        IPAddress ipAddr = ipHost.AddressList[0];
        IPEndPoint ipEndPoint = new IPEndPoint(ipAddr, 11000);

        // create a Tcp/Ip Socket
        Socket sListener = new Socket(AddressFamily.InterNetwork,
                            SocketType.Stream, ProtocolType.Tcp);

        // bind the socket to the local endpoint and
        // listen to the incoming sockets
```

```
    try
    {
        sListener.Bind(ipEndPoint);
        sListener.Listen(10);

        // Start listening for connections

        while (true)
        {
            Console.WriteLine("Waiting for a connection on port {0}",ipEndPoint);

            // program is suspended while waiting for an incoming connection
            Socket handler = sListener.Accept();

            string data = null;

            // we got the client attempting to connect
            while(true)
            {
                byte[] bytes = new byte[1024];

                int bytesRec = handler.Receive(bytes);

                data += Encoding.ASCII.GetString(bytes,0,bytesRec);

                if (data.IndexOf("<TheEnd>") > -1)
                {
                    break;
                }
            }

            // show the data on the console
            Console.WriteLine("Text Received: {0}",data);

            string theReply = "Thank you for those " + data.Length.ToString()
                            + " characters...";
            byte[] msg = Encoding.ASCII.GetBytes(theReply);

            handler.Send(msg);
            handler.Shutdown(SocketShutdown.Both);
            handler.Close();
        }
    }
    catch(Exception e)
    {
        Console.WriteLine(e.ToString());
    }

} // end of Main
}
```

The first step is to establish the local endpoint for the socket. Before opening a socket for listening, a socket must establish a local endpoint address. The unique address of a TCP/IP service is defined by combining the IP address of the host with the port number of the service to create an endpoint for the service. The Dns class provides methods that return information about the network addresses supported by the local network device. When the local network device has more than one network address, or if the local system supports more than one network device, the Dns class returns information about all network addresses, and the application must choose the proper address for the service from the array.

We create an IPEndPoint for a server by combining the first IP address returned by Dns.Resolve() for the host computer with a port number.

```
// establish the local end point for the socket
IPHostEntry ipHost = Dns.Resolve("localhost");
IPAddress ipAddr = ipHost.AddressList[0];
IPEndPoint ipEndPoint = new IPEndPoint(ipAddr, 11000);
```

The IPEndPoint class here represents the localhost on port number 11000.

Next, we create a stream socket with a new instance of the Socket class. Having established a local endpoint for listening, we can create the socket:

```
// create a TCP/IP Socket
Socket sListener = new Socket(AddressFamily.InterNetwork,
                             SocketType.Stream, ProtocolType.Tcp);
```

The AddressFamily enumeration indicates the addressing schemes that a Socket instance can use to resolve an address. Some important parameters are provided in the following table.

AddressFamily value	Description
InterNetwork	Address for IP Version 4.
InterNetworkV6	Address for IP Version 6.
Ipx	IPX or SPX Address.
NetBios	NetBios Address

The SocketType parameter distinguishes between a TCP and a UDP Socket. Other possible values are provided as follows:

SocketType value	Description
Dgram	Supports datagrams. Dgram requires the Udp ProtocolType and the InterNetwork AddressFamily.
Raw	Supports access to the underlying transport protocol.
Stream	Supports stream sockets. Stream requires the Tcp ProtocolType and the InterNetwork AddressFamily.

The third and the last parameter defines the protocol type that is the requested protocol for the socket. Some important values for the `ProtocolType` parameter are:

ProtocolType value	Description
Raw	Raw packet protocol.
Tcp	Transmission Control Protocol.
Udp	User Datagram Protocol.
Ip	Internet Protocol.

Our next step is to name the socket with the `Bind()` method. When the socket opens with the constructor, the socket has no name assigned to it. However, a descriptor is reserved for the socket created. To assign a name to the server socket, we call `Bind()`. To be identified by a client socket, a TCP stream socket server must name its socket.

```
try
{
    sListener.Bind(ipEndPoint);
```

The `Bind()` method associates a socket with a local endpoint. You must call `Bind()` before any attempt to call `Listen()` or `Accept()`.

Now that our socket is created and a name has been bound to it, we can listen for incoming connections with `Listen()`. In the listening state, the socket will poll for incoming connection attempts.

```
    sListener.Listen(10);
```

The parameter defines the `backlog`, which specifies the maximum number of *pending* connections in the queue. In the code above, the parameter allows a queue of 10 connections.

Now that we're listening, our next step is to accept the client connection with `Accept()`. `Accept()` is used to receive the client connection that completes the name association between client and server. The `Accept()` method blocks the caller thread until the connection is present.

The `Accept()` method extracts the first connection request from the queue of pending requests and creates a new socket to handle it. Although a new socket is created, the original socket continues to listen and can be used with multithreading to accept multiple client connections. Any server application must close the listening socket along with the incoming client sockets created by `Accept()`.

```
    while (true)
    {
        Console.WriteLine("Waiting for a connection on port {0}",ipEndPoint);

        // program is suspended while waiting for an incoming connection
        Socket handler = sListener.Accept();
```

Once the client and server are connected with each other, you can send and receive messages using the `Send()` and `Receive()` methods of the `Socket` class.

The Send() method writes outgoing data to the connected socket. The Receive() method reads the incoming data on a stream-based socket. When using a TCP-based system, the sockets must be connected before using Send() or Receive(). The exact protocol definition between the two communicating entities needs to be made clear beforehand, so that there will be no deadlocks between the client and server applications caused by not knowing who will send the data first.

```
string data = null;

// we got the client attempting to connect
while(true)
{
    byte[] bytes = new byte[1024];

    // the data received from the client
    int bytesRec = handler.Receive(bytes);
    // bytes are converted to string
    data += Encoding.ASCII.GetString(bytes,0,bytesRec);
    // checking the end of message
    if (data.IndexOf("<TheEnd>") > -1)
    {
        break;
    }
}

// show the data on the console
Console.WriteLine("Text Received: {0}",data);
```

The Receive() method receives the data from the socket and fills the byte array passed as an argument. The return value of the method actually determines the number of bytes read. In the code above, after receiving the data, we check for the end of message characters in the converted string. If the end of message characters are not found in the string, then the code again starts to listen for incoming data, otherwise we display the message to the console.

After exiting from the loop, we prepare a new byte array with our reply to pass back to the client. After conversion, the Send() method is used to send to it the client.

```
string theReply = "Thank you for those " + data.Length.ToString()
                        + " characters...";
byte[] msg = Encoding.ASCII.GetBytes(theReply);

handler.Send(msg);
```

When data exchange between the server and the client ends, close the socket with Close(). To ensure that there is no data left behind, always call Shutdown() before calling Close(). There should always be a corresponding Close() call to each successful socket instance.

```
        handler.Shutdown(SocketShutdown.Both);
        handler.Close();
    }
}
```

`SocketShutdown` is an enumeration, which can specify three different values for shutting down the socket:

SocketShutdown Value	Description
Both	Shuts down a socket for both sending and receiving
Receive	Shuts down a socket for receiving
Send	Shuts down a socket for sending

The socket is closed when the `Close()` method is called, which also sets the `Connected` property of the socket to `false`.

Building a TCP-based Client

The functions used to make a client application are more or less similar to the server application. Like the server, we employ the same methods for establishing the endpoint, creating a socket instance, sending and receiving data, and closing the socket.

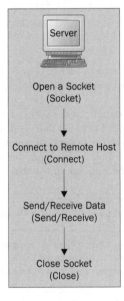

Here's the complete code for `SocketClient.cs` – we'll explain it in a moment.

```
using System;
using System.Net.Sockets;
using System.Net;
using System.Text;

public class SocketClient
{
    public static void Main(string [] args)
    {
```

```
            // data buffer for incoming data
            byte[] bytes = new byte[1024];

            // connect to a Remote device
            try
            {
               // Establish the remote end point for the socket
               IPHostEntry ipHost = Dns.Resolve("127.0.0.1");
               IPAddress ipAddr = ipHost.AddressList[0];
               IPEndPoint ipEndPoint = new IPEndPoint(ipAddr, 11000);

               Socket sender = new Socket(AddressFamily.InterNetwork,
                                       SocketType.Stream, ProtocolType.Tcp);

               // Connect the socket to the remote endpoint

                  sender.Connect(ipEndPoint);

                  Console.WriteLine("Socket connected to {0}",
                                 sender.RemoteEndPoint.ToString());
                  string theMessage = "This is a test";

                  byte[] msg = Encoding.ASCII.GetBytes(theMessage+"<TheEnd>");

                  // Send the data through the socket
                  int bytesSent = sender.Send(msg);

                  // Receive the response from the remote device
                  int bytesRec = sender.Receive(bytes);

                  Console.WriteLine("The Server says : {0}",
                                 Encoding.ASCII.GetString(bytes,0, bytesRec));

                  // Release the socket
                  sender.Shutdown(SocketShutdown.Both);
                  sender.Close();

            }
            catch(Exception e)
            {
               Console.WriteLine("Exception: {0}", e.ToString());
            }
         }
      }
```

The only new method used here is the Connect() method, which is used to connect to the remote server. Let's look at how it's used in the client. First, we need to establish the remote endpoint:

```
            // Establish the remote endpoint for the socket
            IPHostEntry ipHost = Dns.Resolve("127.0.0.1");
            IPAddress ipAddr = ipHost.AddressList[0];
```

```
IPEndPoint ipEndPoint = new IPEndPoint(ipAddr, 11000);

Socket sender = new Socket(AddressFamily.InterNetwork,
                           SocketType.Stream, ProtocolType.Tcp);
```

Now we can connect our socket to the remote endpoint:

```
sender.Connect(ipEndPoint);
```

Given the socket, the `Connect()` method establishes the connection between the socket and the remote host specified by the endpoint parameter. Once we're connected, we can send our data, and receive a response:

```
string theMessage = "This is a test";
byte[] msg = Encoding.ASCII.GetBytes(theMessage+"<TheEnd>");

// Send the data through the socket
int bytesSent = sender.Send(msg);

// Receive the response from the remote device
int bytesRec = sender.Receive(bytes);

Console.WriteLine("The Server says : {0}",
                  Encoding.ASCII.GetString(bytes,0, bytesRec));
```

Finally, we release the socket by calling `Shutdown()`, shutting it down for both sending and receiving, and then call `Close()`:

```
sender.Shutdown(SocketShutdown.Both);
sender.Close();
```

The screenshots below show our server and client in action:

Exception Management in System.Net.Sockets

The Socket class generally throws the SocketException when some error occurs in the network. SocketException is thrown by a variety of problems, we'll look at two cases here – problems in the Socket constructor, and problems when connecting to ports.

The Socket constructor takes three parameters; AddressFamily, SocketType, and the ProtocolType, throwing a SocketException if there is a mismatch or incompatibility between the three combinations.

For example, attempting to create a Socket instance with the following parameters throws a SocketException:

```
Socket sSocket = new Socket(AddressFamily.InterNetworkV6,
                            SocketType.Stream,
                            ProtocolType.Tcp);
```

When the exception is thrown, its Message property (inherited from Exception) is the following:

```
An address incompatible with the requested protocol was used
```

IP version 6 is not supported by TCP, so the AddressFamily parameter InterNetworkV6 is incompatible with a ProtocolType of Tcp.

Another method that is a good candidate for this exception handling mechanism is the Connect() method. This method throws an exception if it fails to establish a connection between the local and remote endpoints specified in the Connect() parameters. Let's put this to use.

A Port Scanner

We've looked at a simple client-server application – now let's make something more interesting here with the help of the SocketException.

In the following example, we make our own port scanner, which tries to connect to the localhost on each port specified in the loop – the scanner scans the first 1024 ports for our demonstration. We report successful connections, and if the connection fails, we catch the SocketException that is thrown.

This port scanner can be used to check out open ports on *your* computer; these open ports could be a potential weakness in your system, exploitable by "rogue" applications...

Here's the complete code for PortScanner.cs:

```
using System;
using System.Net.Sockets;
using System.Net;

public class SocketConn
{
    public static void Main(string [] args)
    {
```

```
            IPAddress address = IPAddress.Parse("127.0.0.1");


        for (int i=1; i < 1024; i++)
        {
            Console.WriteLine("Checking port {0}",i);

            try
            {
                IPEndPoint endPoint = new IPEndPoint(address,i);
                Socket sSocket = new Socket(AddressFamily.InterNetwork,
                                            SocketType.Stream,
                                            ProtocolType.Tcp);

                sSocket.Connect(endPoint);

                Console.WriteLine("Port {0} is listening",i);

            }
            catch(SocketException ignored)
            {
                if (ignored.ErrorCode != 10061)
                  Console.WriteLine(ignored.Message);
            }
        }
    }
}
```

The code works by making a connection with each port specified in the loop. If the port is opened, then the socket establishes a connection and prints out the line giving information about the port. If the port is closed, a SocketException will be thrown. When such an exception is thrown, its Message property would return the following:

```
No connection could be made because the target machine actively refused it
```

stating that a connection could not be made with the server. The SocketException has an ErrorCode property that holds an integer value that represents the last operating system error to occur. In the case of the exception thrown when an attempt is made to connect to a closed port, the ErrorCode value is 10061. In our catch block to handle the SocketException, we check if the ErrorCode is different from this value and display the actual error message – this is to advise the reader in case something other than a failure to connect to the specified port happens:

```
            catch(SocketException ignored)
            {
                if (ignored.ErrorCode != 10061)
                  Console.WriteLine(ignored.Message);
            }
```

The ErrorCode property actually calls the native method GetLastError() to get the error number. You can find the list of error codes in the WinError.h file in the following folder:

```
Microsoft Visual Studio .NET\Vc7\PlatformSDK\Include
```

Here's a summary of the output when I run this piece of code on my machine running Windows 2000 Server.

```
Checking port 1
Checking port 2
...
Port 21 is listening
...
Port 25 is listening
...
Port 80 is listening
```

Cleaning Up Connections

Code in a `finally` block will be executed regardless of whether an exception is thrown or not, making it an ideal candidate for `Shutdown()` and `Close()` methods. This will ensure that the socket is always closed before the program ends.

```
try
{
    ...
}
catch( .. )
{
    ...
}
finally
{
    if (socketOpened.Connected)
    {
        socketOpened.Shutdown(SocketShutdown.Both);
        socketOpened.Close();
    }
}
```

Here we use the `Connected` property to determine if the socket is still open. The `Connected` property returns the connection state of the socket, with a value of `true` indicating that the socket is open. If this is the case, then the socket is closed.

Socket Options

The .NET Framework provides `SetSocketOption()` and `GetSocketOption()` methods to set and retrieve socket options. The `SetSocketOption()` method calls through to the `setsockopt` function of the Windows Socket API.

The `SetSocketOption()` method requires a `SocketOptionLevel`, a `SocketOptionName`, and the value to set for the socket option – either a byte array, `int`, or `object`.

143

The `SocketOptionLevel` enumeration defines the option level for the socket – when we set or retrieve an option for a socket, this enumeration is used to specify what level in the OSI model the option is applied at (for example, whether the option is set at the TCP level, at the level of the individual socket, and so on):

SocketOptionLevel Value	Description
IP	Socket options apply to IP sockets
Socket	Socket options apply to the socket itself
Tcp	Socket options apply to TCP sockets
Udp	Socket options apply to UDP sockets

The second required parameter of `SetSocketOptions()` is `SocketOptionName`; it defines the parameter's name whose value is being set. The values for the `SocketOptionName` enumeration can be found in the .NET Framework SDK Documentation, we'll look at a few options here.

ReuseAddress

By default, only one socket may be bound to a local address that is already in use. However, you may want to bind more than one socket to a local address. Consider the following code that attempts to bind two sockets to the same local endpoint:

```
// Establish the local end point for the socket
IPEndPoint ipEndPoint = new
IPEndPoint(Dns.GetHostByName(Dns.GetHostName()).AddressList[0],    11000);

// Create a Tcp/ip Socket
Socket sListener = new Socket(AddressFamily.InterNetwork,
SocketType.Stream, ProtocolType.Tcp);

// Bind the socket to the local endpoint and
// Listen to the incoming sockets

sListener.Bind(ipEndPoint);

sListener.Listen(10);

// create a new Socket
Socket sListener2 = new Socket(AddressFamily.InterNetwork,
SocketType.Stream, ProtocolType.Tcp);

// Bind the socket to the local endpoint and
// Listen to the incoming sockets

sListener2.Bind(ipEndPoint);

sListener2.Listen(10);
```

Trying to bind two sockets to a single endpoint will throw a `SocketException` with the following `Message`:

```
Only one usage of each socket address (protocol/network address/port)
is normally permitted
```

The solution to this is the ReuseAddress option; by using this option and a non-zero integer value you can set the socket to allow multiple bindings:

```
sListener2.SetSocketOption(SocketOptionLevel.Socket,
                    SocketOptionName.ReuseAddress, 1);

sListener2.Bind(ipEndPoint);
```

Note the use of the non-zero integer – this will actually be interpreted as a Boolean value of true by the Windows Sockets API setsockopt function that is called by SetSocketOption().

Linger Time

Through the Linger value of SocketOptionName you can determine how the socket should behave when there is some data queued to be sent and the socket is closed. The LingerOption class contains information about the socket's linger time, and some of its important members are listed below:

Property	Description
Enabled	Determines whether to linger after the socket is closed or not
LingerTime	The time (in seconds) to linger if the Enabled property is true

If Enabled is false, then the socket will immediately close itself whenever a call to Close() method is executed. If Enabled is true, the remaining data will continue to be sent to the destination until the time specified by the LingerTime property has passed. The connection will then be closed when either of the two things occurs – either the time is over or all the data is sent. Note that if there is no data present in the queue then the socket is immediately closed, regardless of the Enabled property. The socket is also closed immediately if the LingerTime is specified as 0.

These two properties can also be set in the LingerOption class's constructor. The first parameter sets the Enabled property, and the second sets the LingerTime property. The value held by the LingerOption object is then passed to the SetSocketOption() method as below – note the explicit cast to object required to pass the LingerOption:

```
// Create a new LingerOption class and set properties in the constructor
LingerOption lingerOpts = new LingerOption(true,5);

mySocket.SetSocketOption(SocketOptionLevel.Socket, SocketOptionName.Linger,
                    (object)lingerOpts);
```

Let's demonstrate the GetSocketOption() method to retrieve the value for the LingerTime – GetSocketOption() has three overloads, each one returning a different data type – void, byte array, or object. The overload that returns the object requires only the SocketOptionLevel and SocketOptionName as parameters. The overload that has no return value fills a byte array that you specify as an extra parameter. The overload that returns the byte array requires you to specify the length of the information you expect returned with an extra int parameter.

We use the overload that returns an `object` – a cast to a `LingerOption` object allows us to retrieve the `LingerTime` property:

```
object o = mySocket.GetSocketOption(SocketOptionLevel.Socket,
                                    SocketOptionName.Linger);

Console.WriteLine(((LingerOption)o).LingerTime);
```

Asynchronous Programming

Most of the socket functions in the original Berkeley library take an indefinite amount of time to complete execution. In such situations, the function is said to be blocked; this means that calling the function would block the current thread of execution – if there is only one thread in the application then the whole application will have to wait for the function to return before continuing execution. For example, the send and receive functions are said to be blocked as they do not return immediately.

With asynchronous programming, a connection does not block an application while waiting for network processes to complete. Instead of blocking the current thread it uses the .NET asynchronous model to process the network connections on another thread while the application continues to run in the original thread. When the second thread has completed its execution, it sends an event object to the original thread to indicate the status of the task. Events can be either **signaled**, in which case methods that are waiting on the event will return immediately, or **non-signaled**. If the event is non-signaled, the waiting method will be blocked until the event is signaled.

There are two types of events – automatic events, which set themselves back to the non-signaled state whenever they are signaled, and manual reset events, which stay signaled until they are manually reset to the non-signaled state. .NET has a `ManualResetEvent` class that we can use to indicate to our program that we want to continue – by setting a `ManualResetEvent` object to the signaled state, it will stop blocking any waiting methods, and the program can continue. We will use this object to facilitate our asynchronous programming.

The asynchronous programming model is suitable for applications that cannot afford to hang around waiting for network operations to complete before moving ahead. In the world of .NET, there is a complete set of methods for asynchronous operations. For example, `BeginSend()` is used instead of the normal `Send()` method when doing asynchronous programming.

The asynchronous model uses the callback method to return the result of the operation. The .NET Framework has a set of methods responsible for initiating a task in an asynchronous manner but they require a callback function to end the operation. For example the `Connect()` method uses `BeginConnect()` to start a connection to the network device and the corresponding callback function is required to complete the connection.

The .NET Framework provides a delegate class for asynchronous operations. The class, which is called `AsyncCallback`, provides a way for applications to complete an asynchronous operation.

```
AsyncCallback aCallback = new AsyncCallback(AsyncCallback);
```

This delegate is supplied as an argument to the asynchronous function when the operation is initiated. The function pointer referenced by AsyncCallback contains program logic to finish processing the asynchronous task for the client.

This programming model uses multiple threads to process network connections. To facilitate synchronization between these different threads, we use the ManualResetEvent class to suspend execution of the main class and signal when execution can continue.

We begin by building an asynchronous client application, which will be tested with the socket server built earlier. After that we complete the asynchronous discussion by building an asynchronous server to plug with the client.

Asynchronous Client Application

The following diagram will help you to understand the flow of an asynchronous client application.

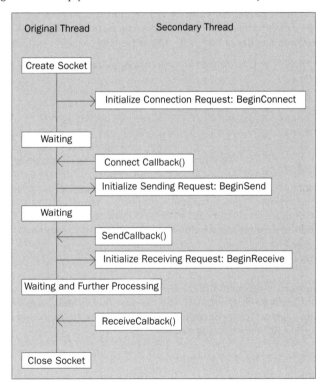

Thus we have three tasks to accomplish asynchronously here – connecting to the server, sending data to the server, and receiving data from the server.

First let's discuss how we're going to synchronize everything. The code will need to be synchronized because of its asynchronous nature – you couldn't work with the socket if you haven't finished connecting to the server, or a deadlock could result if we were to attempt to receive data when we should instead be sending. We will use the ManualEventReset class to synchronize the different threads that will be produced.

The complete code for this example can be found in the file ASyncClient.cs.

```
public class AsyncClient
{
    public static string theResponse = "";
    public static byte[] buffer = new byte[1024];

    public static ManualResetEvent ConnectDone = new ManualResetEvent(false);
    public static ManualResetEvent SendDone = new ManualResetEvent(false);
    public static ManualResetEvent ReceiveDone = new ManualResetEvent(false);
```

A ManualResetEvent object can have its state set and reset (that is, be set to the signaled or non-signaled state) with its Set() and Reset() methods. Each of three tasks, connecting, sending, and receiving, will have a ManualResetEvent object attached, and the main thread can wait for the relevant task to complete by calling the WaitOne() method of the relevant ManualResetEvent object – this method blocks the current thread until the object is signaled. When we create the ManualResetEvent objects above, the value of false indicates that the initial state is not set. Of course the main thread can continue with other processing, but before the next task begins we have to be certain that the previous one has completed – this is precisely where WaitOne() comes in.

Before we look at our first task, let's create and initialize the socket we're going to use.

```
IPHostEntry ipHost = Dns.Resolve("127.0.0.1");
IPAddress ipAddr = ipHost.AddressList[0];
IPEndPoint endPoint = new IPEndPoint(ipAddr, 11000);

Socket sClient = new Socket(AddressFamily.InterNetwork,
                            SocketType.Stream, ProtocolType.Tcp);
```

Our first task is to connect to the server. This is achieved with the BeginConnect() method. The BeginConnect() method starts an asynchronous connection request with the remote host. It requires a callback method that implements the AsyncCallback delegate. This callback method should call EndConnect() to end the pending connection request and return the connected socket.

```
sClient.BeginConnect(endPoint, new AsyncCallback(ConnectCallback), sClient);
```

There are three parameters to this method; the first represents the remote host using the IPEndPoint class, the second argument is the AsyncCallback delegate that is used for passing the function pointer, and the third argument is an object containing state information to be passed to the callback method specified. Here, the socket instance is being passed.

Let's look at the ConnectCallBack() method:

```
public static void ConnectCallback(IAsyncResult ar)
{
    Thread thr = Thread.CurrentThread;
    Console.WriteLine("ConnectCallback Thread State:" + thr.ThreadState);
```

First of all, we inspect the thread that our asynchronous method is running in. Thread information can be obtained from the CurrentThread property of the Thread object. This will show that the code in our asynchronous method runs in a background thread.

Next, let's see how to retrieve the `Socket` that we're actually working on. The `IAsyncResult` parameter contains information about the state of the asynchronous operation. Using the `AsyncState` property of the `IAsyncResult` interface we can retrieve the argument that we passed as the third parameter of the `BeginConnect()` method. The value retrieved needs to be cast to a `Socket`.

```
Socket sClient = (Socket) ar.AsyncState;
```

Next, the `EndConnect()` method is called to complete the asynchronous request. If some error occurred when accessing the socket, `EndConnect()` will throw a `SocketException`.

```
sClient.EndConnect(ar);

Console.WriteLine("Socket connected to {0}",
                   sClient.RemoteEndPoint.ToString());
```

Finally, we call the `Set()` method of the `ConnectDone ManualResetEvent` – this will indicate to the main thread that we've finished connecting.

```
ConnectDone.Set();
}
```

Now that we've connected to the server, the next step is to communicate with the server by sending and receiving data.

The `BeginSend()` method is used to send data asynchronously to the connected `Socket`.

```
sClient.BeginSend(byteData, 0 , byteData.Length, 0 ,
                  new AsyncCallback(SendCallback), sClient);
```

The first parameter is a byte array buffer containing the data to send, the second argument represents the position in the buffer from which to begin sending data, the third parameter is the buffer size, the fifth parameter is the `AsyncCallback` delegate, and the last parameter is used to store state information.

The `BeginSend()` method calls the callback function passed through the `AsyncCallback` delegate:

```
public static void SendCallback(IAsyncResult ar)
{
    Thread thr = Thread.CurrentThread;
    Console.WriteLine("SendCallback Thread State:" + thr.ThreadState);

    Socket sClient = (Socket) ar.AsyncState;

    int bytesSent = sClient.EndSend(ar);

    Console.WriteLine("Sent {0} bytes to server.", bytesSent);

    SendDone.Set();
}
```

The code is similar to the `ConnectCallback()` function, apart from the call to `EndSend()`, which ends the asynchronous send request, and the setting of the `SendDone ManualResetEvent`.

The `BeginReceive()` method start asynchronously receiving data from a `Socket`:

```
sClient.BeginReceive(buffer, 0 , buffer.Length , 0,
                    new AsyncCallback(ReceiveCallback), sClient);
```

The arguments are similar to the `BeginSend()` method. The callback method should use the `EndReceive()` method to return the data read from the `Socket`.

```
public static void ReceiveCallback(IAsyncResult ar)
{
    Thread thr = Thread.CurrentThread;
    Console.WriteLine("ReceiveCallback Thread State:" + thr.ThreadState);

    Socket sClient = (Socket) ar.AsyncState;

    int bytesRead = sClient.EndReceive(ar);

    if (bytesRead > 0)
    {
        theResponse += Encoding.ASCII.GetString(buffer, 0 , bytesRead);

        sClient.BeginReceive(buffer, 0 , buffer.Length ,0 ,
                        new AsyncCallback(ReceiveCallback), sClient);
    }
    else
    {
        ReceiveDone.Set();
    }
}
```

To ensure that we've received all of the data, `BeginReceive()` is called inside the callback. The `EndReceive()` method returns the number of bytes, so we can check if there is some data back in the queue. The returned data is then stored in a `string` field, `theResponse`.

Let's look at the `Main()` method that ties everything together – we've already seen some of this code. We start by displaying information about the current thread, to distinguish between the thread on which the socket is operating and the main thread. Then we create our socket as we've seen earlier:

```
public static void Main(string [] arg)
{
    try
    {

        Thread thr = Thread.CurrentThread;
        Console.WriteLine("Main Thread State:" + thr.ThreadState);

        IPHostEntry ipHost = Dns.Resolve("127.0.0.1");
        IPAddress ipAddr = ipHost.AddressList[0];
        IPEndPoint endPoint = new IPEndPoint(ipAddr, 11000);
```

```
Socket sClient = new Socket(AddressFamily.InterNetwork,
                        SocketType.Stream, ProtocolType.Tcp);
```

We can now begin establishing our connection. We call the `BeginConnect()` method, specifying the `ConnectCallBack()` method, and wait for the operation to be completed before sending a message to the connected socket. The main thread is blocked with `ConnectDone.WaitOne()` – this means that we will not move onto sending data before the connection has completed successfully. This is signaled with the `Set()` method of the `ConnectDone` object in `ConnectCallBack()`.

```
sClient.BeginConnect(endPoint, new AsyncCallback(ConnectCallback),
                    sClient);

ConnectDone.WaitOne();
```

Now we'll define the message to send to the server – we bloat it with some string concatenation to create a bigger message. This will give us more of an opportunity to see the asynchronous operations in action.

```
string data = "This is a test.";
for (int i=0;i<72;i++)
    data += i.ToString()+":" + (new string('=',i));

byte[] byteData = Encoding.ASCII.GetBytes(data+"<TheEnd>");
```

Now we can start the asynchronous send operation – we have our message and we know that connection has been established:

```
sClient.BeginSend(byteData, 0 , byteData.Length, 0 ,
                new AsyncCallback(SendCallback), sClient);
```

We "perform some other processing" to illustrate that our client is genuinely running asynchronously. Here we simply put the current `Thread` to sleep for a hundredth of a second while looping – this provides a convenient simulation of some processor-hungry computations.

```
for (int i=0;i<5;i++)
{
    // Perform some other processing....
    Console.WriteLine(i);
    Thread.Sleep(10);
}
```

Before we try to receive data from the server all the data needs to have been sent. Thus we use `SendDone.WaitOne()` to block the thread until `SendCallBack()` signals sending is finished with `SendDone.Set()`.

```
// Before we can receive we must have finished sending
SendDone.WaitOne();
sClient.BeginReceive(buffer, 0 , buffer.Length, 0,
                    new AsyncCallback(ReceiveCallback), sClient);
```

Finally, we wait for the data to be received before displaying it, and then shutdown and close our socket.

```
        ReceiveDone.WaitOne();

        Console.WriteLine("Response received: {0} ", theResponse);

        sClient.Shutdown(SocketShutdown.Both);
        sClient.Close();
    }
    catch(Exception e)
    {
        Console.WriteLine(e.ToString());
    }
}
```

The output of our asynchronous client when running with the (synchronous) socket server we developed earlier is:

```
C:\WINNT\system32\CMD.EXE

C:\Networking\Sockets>ASyncClient
Main Thread State:Running
ConnectCallback Thread State:Background
Socket connected to 127.0.0.1:11000
0
1
SendCallback Thread State:Background
Sent 2785 bytes to server.
2
3
4
ReceiveCallback Thread State:Background
ReceiveCallback Thread State:Background
Response received: Thank you for those 2785 characters...
```

Asynchronous Server Application

The flow for our asynchronous server application is demonstrated in the following diagram:

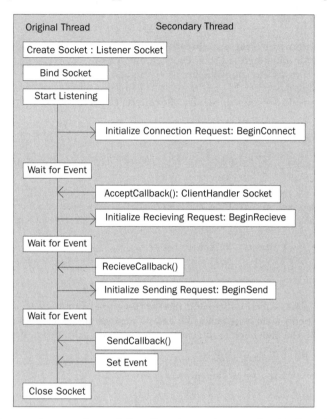

The server starts by creating a socket and then listening to the port that it is bound to. The asynchronous server application requires BeginAccept() to accept connections asynchronously, and after the connection is established, it uses the BeginReceive() and BeginSend() methods to send data to and receive it from the client socket.

After BeginAccept() is called, we set an event in the waiting state, so that a different thread in the application continues to execute when a client tries to connect to it. If we don't do this, the application finishes before the client because of the asynchronous nature of the server. The ManualResetEvent class is used here to set and wait for events:

```
AsyncCallback aCallback = new AsyncCallback(AcceptCallback);

// sListener is an instance of the Socket class
sListener.BeginAccept(aCallback, sListener);

// assume that socketEvent is an instance of ManualResetEvent() class
socketEvent.WaitOne();
```

The `BeginAccept()` method takes two parameters: an asynchronous delegate which references the callback method and a parameter which is used to pass data to the callback function (in this case, the listener socket itself). The `BeginAccept()` method calls the `AcceptCallback()` function when a new connection is received on the socket. This callback function calls the `EndAccept()` method to return the new socket for the client.

Asynchronous sockets programming uses threads for different asynchronous operations. The main thread is responsible for initiating the listener socket, one thread is responsible for accepting incoming requests, and another thread is responsible for receiving and sending data. We can get the thread ID of the current thread using the `GetCurrentThreadID()` function of the `AppDomain` class; we display this number in the console, so you can see that the different operations are running on different threads:

```
Console.WriteLine("Main Thread ID: " + AppDomain.GetCurrentThreadId());
```

Notice that we don't need to start the separate threads explicitly – this is done for us by the .NET Framework.

After accepting the connection by calling `EndAccept()`, the new socket can communicate with the client by calling the asynchronous `BeginReceive()` and the `BeginSend()` methods:

```
Socket handler = listener.EndAccept(ar);

handler.BeginReceive(buffer, 0, buffer.Length, 0, new
        AsyncCallback(ReceiveCallback), handler);
```

The `ReceiveCallback()` function first calls the `EndReceive()` function to complete the pending asynchronous task. Then we check whether the end-of-message character is found. If so, we use `BeginSend()` to send the data back to the client; otherwise, we call `BeginReceive()` to receive any data left:

```
int bytesRead = handler.EndReceive(ar);

if (bytesRead > 0)
{
    content += Encoding.ASCII.GetString(buffer, 0, bytesRead);

    if (content.IndexOf(".") > -1)
    {
        Console.WriteLine("Read {0} bytes from socket. \n Data: {1}",
                        content.Length, content);
        byte[] byteData = Encoding.ASCII.GetBytes(content);

        handler.BeginSend(byteData, 0 , byteData.Length, 0 ,
                        new AsyncCallback(SendCallback), handler);
    }
    else
    {
        handler.BeginReceive(buffer, 0 , buffer.Length, 0,
                        new AsyncCallback(ReceiveCallback), handler);
    }
}
```

The `SendCallback()` method completes the operation by calling `EndSend()`, closes the handler socket, and sets the `ManualResetEvent` on the main thread so that the application can proceed:

```
        int bytesSent = handler.EndSend(ar);

        Console.WriteLine("Sent {0} bytes to Client.", bytesSent);

        handler.Shutdown(SocketShutdown.Both);
        handler.Close();

        socketEvent.Set();
```

Here's the complete source for the `AsyncServer.cs`:

```csharp
using System;
using System.Net.Sockets;
using System.Net;
using System.Text;
using System.Threading;

public class AsyncServer
{
    // buffer to receive and send data
    public static byte[] buffer = new byte[1024];

    // the event class to support synchronization
    public static ManualResetEvent socketEvent = new ManualResetEvent(false);

    public static void Main(string [] args)
    {

        Console.WriteLine("Main Thread ID:" + AppDomain.GetCurrentThreadId());

        byte[] bytes = new byte[1024];

        IPHostEntry ipHost = Dns.Resolve(Dns.GetHostName());
        IPAddress ipAddr = ipHost.AddressList[0];

        IPEndPoint localEnd = new IPEndPoint(ipAddr, 11000);

        Socket sListener = new Socket(AddressFamily.InterNetwork,
                                      SocketType.Stream,
                                      ProtocolType.Tcp);

        // binding a socket
        sListener.Bind(localEnd);

        // start listening
        sListener.Listen(10);

        Console.WriteLine("Waiting for a connection...");

        AsyncCallback aCallback = new AsyncCallback(AcceptCallback);

        // asychronous funtion for accepting connections
        sListener.BeginAccept(aCallback,sListener);
```

```
    // waiting for the other threads to finish
    socketEvent.WaitOne();
}

public static void AcceptCallback(IAsyncResult ar)
{
    Console.WriteLine("AcceptCallback Thread ID:" +
                        AppDomain.GetCurrentThreadId());
    // retrieved the socket
    Socket listener = (Socket)ar.AsyncState;

    // new socket
    Socket handler = listener.EndAccept(ar);

    handler.BeginReceive(buffer, 0 , buffer.Length, 0,
                        new AsyncCallback(ReceiveCallback), handler);
}

public static void ReceiveCallback(IAsyncResult ar)
{
    Console.WriteLine("ReceiveCallback Thread ID:" +
                    AppDomain.GetCurrentThreadId());

    string content = String.Empty;

    Socket handler = (Socket) ar.AsyncState;

    int bytesRead = handler.EndReceive(ar);

    // if there is some data ..
    if (bytesRead > 0)
    {
        // append it to the main string
        content += Encoding.ASCII.GetString(buffer, 0, bytesRead);

        // if we encounter the end of message character ...
        if (content.IndexOf(".") > -1)
        {
            Console.WriteLine("Read {0} bytes from socket. \n Data: {1}",
                            content.Length, content);
            byte[] byteData = Encoding.ASCII.GetBytes(content);

            // send the data back to the client
            handler.BeginSend(byteData, 0 , byteData.Length, 0 ,
                            new AsyncCallback(SendCallback), handler);
        }
        else
        {
            // otherwise receive the remaining data
            handler.BeginReceive(buffer, 0 , buffer.Length, 0,
                                new AsyncCallback(ReceiveCallback), handler);
        }
    }
}
```

```
    public static void SendCallback(IAsyncResult ar)
    {
        Console.WriteLine("SendCallback Thread ID:" +
                        AppDomain.GetCurrentThreadId());

        Socket handler = (Socket) ar.AsyncState;

        // send data back to the client
        int bytesSent = handler.EndSend(ar);

        Console.WriteLine("Sent {0} bytes to Client.", bytesSent);

        // close down socket
        handler.Shutdown(SocketShutdown.Both);
        handler.Close();

        // set the main thread's event
        socketEvent.Set();
    }

}
```

Socket Permissions

The .NET Framework provides many classes that help us to develop secure code within our applications. Many of these classes offer role-based security and cryptography. The .NET Framework also brings code access permission objects, which are the building blocks for protecting against unauthorized code access. They are fundamental for enforcing security on managed code – only code that has permission to run in the current context can be executed.

Each code access permission demonstrates one of the following rights:

❑   The right to access protected resources such as files

❑   The right to perform a protected operation such as accessing managed code

For the Internet world, particularly for network applications, the System.Net classes provide built-in support for authentication and code access permissions. The .NET Framework provides the SocketPermission class for enforcing code access permissions.

The SocketPermission class is used to control rights to make or accept connections, controlling access to a network via sockets. A SocketPermission consists of a host specification and a set of "actions" specifying ways to connect to that host. It enforces secure code by monitoring the values of the hostname, IP address, and transport protocol.

There are two ways to enforce security permission in C# sockets

❑   Imperatively, using the SocketPermission class

❑   Declaratively, using the SocketPermissionAttribute

Imperative security syntax implements permissions by creating a new instance of the SocketPermission class to demand a particular permission when the code is executed, such as the right to make a TCP connection. It is generally used when the security settings are changed at runtime. Declarative syntax uses attributes to place security information into the metadata of our code, so that the client that calls our code can use reflection to see what permissions are required by the code.

Imperative Security

This type of security syntax creates a new instance of the SocketPermission class to enforce security. You can use imperative security syntax to perform demands and overrides, but not requests. Before calling the corresponding security measure, it is necessary to initialize the state of the SocketPermission class through the constructor so that it represents the particular form of permission that you are looking for. This kind of security syntax is useful only when you have some information needed for security that is only available at runtime, for example, if you want to secure some host over a port but don't know the host name and port number until the program executes.

The following application demonstrates the basic use of the SocketPermission class. As this code behaves as a client, the SocketServer.cs application created earlier in the chapter must be running before executing this program. Otherwise, it will throw a SocketException when the connect method is called. The program takes an optional command-line parameter that can be either assert (the default if no option is specified), or deny. We use this option to either grant or deny permission to the program to make a connection to the server:

```
using System;
using System.Net.Sockets;
using System.Net;
using System.Text;
using System.Security;
using System.Security.Permissions;

public class ImpSecurity
{
    public static void Main(String [] arg)
    {
        // option could be either assert or deny passed on the command line
        // if option is assert then the program executes successfully
        // otherwise it triggers a securityexception
        String option = null;

        if (arg.Length > 0)
        {
            option = arg[0];
        }
        else
        {
            option = "assert";
        }

        Console.WriteLine("option:" + option);

        MethodA(option);
    }
```

```
public static void MethodA(String option)
{
    Console.WriteLine("MethodA");

    IPHostEntry ipHost = Dns.Resolve("127.0.0.1");
    IPAddress ipAddr = ipHost.AddressList[0];
    IPEndPoint ipEndPoint = new IPEndPoint(ipAddr, 11000);

    Socket sender = new Socket(AddressFamily.InterNetwork, SocketType.Stream,
                               ProtocolType.Tcp);

    SocketPermission permitSocket = new SocketPermission(NetworkAccess.Connect,
                    TransportType.Tcp, "127.0.0.1", SocketPermission.AllPorts);

    // Select Assert or Deny on the basis of parameter passed
    if (option.Equals("deny"))
    {
        permitSocket.Deny();
    }
    else
    {
        permitSocket.Assert();
    }

    try
    {
        // Connect the socket to the remote endPoint. Catch any errors
        sender.Connect(ipEndPoint);
        Console.WriteLine("Socket connected to {0}",
                          sender.RemoteEndPoint.ToString());

        byte[] bytes = new byte[1024];

        byte[] msg = Encoding.ASCII.GetBytes("This is a test<EOF>");

        // Send the data through the socket
        int bytesSent = sender.Send(msg);

        // Receive the response from the remote device
        int bytesRec = sender.Receive(bytes);

        Console.WriteLine("Echoed Test = {0}", Encoding.ASCII.GetString(bytes,
                          0, bytesRec));

    }
    catch(SocketException se)
    {
        Console.WriteLine("Socket Exception:" + se.ToString());
    }
    catch(SecurityException sece)
    {
        Console.WriteLine("Socket Exception:" + sece.ToString());
    }
    finally
```

```
        {
            if (sender.Connected)
            {
                // Release the socket
                sender.Shutdown(SocketShutdown.Both);
                sender.Close();
            }
        }

        Console.WriteLine("Closing MethodA");
    }
}
```

The above code shows how to implement code access security using the imperative syntax. The important part of the code is a single method call, to either the Assert() or Deny() method of the SocketPermission. The program basically follows two different paths of execution, depending on the command-line argument passed in.

One path demonstrates a successful connection, and the other illustrates a failed connection request due to the security implications of the code. In the program just shown, we restrict the code from making a TCP connection to a server. This restriction is performed by calling the Deny() method of the SocketPermission class. But before calling any methods of that class, we first have to initialize the SocketPermission object. This initialization is performed in the constructor:

```
SocketPermission permitSocket = new SocketPermission(NetworkAccess.Connect,
                TransportType.Tcp, "127.0.0.1", SocketPermission.AllPorts);
```

The constructor creates a new instance of the SocketPermission class and initializes it for the given transport address with the specified permission. The parameters denote the network access for which we want to grant/deny permissions (here, connecting to a server), the transport type (TCP), the hostname, and the port number. The NetworkAccess value can be one of the following:

Member name	Description
Accept	Indicates that the application is allowed to accept connections from the Internet on a local resource.
Connect	Indicates that the application is allowed to connect to specific Internet resources.

The TranportType parameter represents the transport protocol, it can be All, Tcp, Udp, etc. The third parameter is the hostname, with the port number as the last parameter.

After the above line is executed, a new SocketPermission object is created that controls access to the specified hostname and port using the specified TransportType.

Once we have initialized the SocketPermission in this way, we can call Assert() or Deny() to allow or prevent the code from performing the specified NetworkAccess.

Passing "deny" as a parameter to this application (that is, running the application by entering ImpSecurity deny at the command line) produces the following output:

```
C:\Networking\Sockets>ImpPermissions deny
option:deny
MethodA
Socket Exception:System.Security.SecurityException: Request for the permission
of type System.Net.SocketPermission, System, Version=1.0.3300.0, Culture=neutral,
  PublicKeyToken=b77a5c561934e089 failed.
    at System.Security.SecurityRuntime.FrameDescHelper(FrameSecurityDescriptor
secDesc, IPermission demand, PermissionToken permToken)
    at System.Security.CodeAccessSecurityEngine.Check(PermissionToken permToken,
CodeAccessPermission demand, StackCrawlMark& stackMark, Int32 checkFrames, Int32
  unrestrictedOverride)
    at System.Security.CodeAccessSecurityEngine.Check(CodeAccessPermission cap,
StackCrawlMark& stackMark)
    at System.Security.CodeAccessPermission.Demand()
    at System.Net.Sockets.Socket.CheckCacheRemote(SocketAddress socketAddress,
EndPoint remoteEP, Boolean isOverwrite)
    at System.Net.Sockets.Socket.Connect(EndPoint remoteEP)
    at ImpSecurity.MethodA(String option)

The state of the failed permission was:
<IPermission class="System.Net.SocketPermission, System, Version=1.0.3300.0,
            Culture=neutral, PublicKeyToken=b77a5c561934e089"
            version="1">
  <ConnectAccess>
    <ENDPOINT host="127.0.0.1"
            transport="Tcp"
            port="11000"/>
  </ConnectAccess>
</IPermission>

Closing MethodA
```

Declarative Security

Declarative security uses .NET attributes to place security information inside the metadata of the code. Attributes can be placed at the assembly, class, or member level to indicate the type of request, demand, or override that is needed. In order to use this security syntax, the state data must be initialized first for the SocketPermissionAttribute object through the declarative syntax so that it represents the form of permission that is being enforced on the code.

The following example demonstrates how to enforce permissions using SocketPermissionAttribute. We define two methods, called LegalMethod() and IllegalMethod(), which both attempt to connect to a server via TCP. On the first method we place a SocketPermissionAttribute that grants the necessary permission to the method; on the second, we place an attribute to deny connect permission:

```
using System;
using System.Net.Sockets;
using System.Net;
using System.Text;
using System.Security;
using System.Security.Permissions;
```

```
public class DecSecurity
{
    public static void Main(String [] arg)
    {
        LegalMethod();
        IllegalMethod();
    }

    [SocketPermission(SecurityAction.Assert, Access = "Connect",
                      Host = "127.0.0.1", Port = "All", Transport = "Tcp")]
    public static void LegalMethod()
    {
        Console.WriteLine("LegalMethod");

        IPHostEntry ipHost = Dns.Resolve("127.0.0.1");
        IPAddress ipAddr = ipHost.AddressList[0];
        IPEndPoint ipEndPoint = new IPEndPoint(ipAddr, 11000);

        Socket sender = new Socket(AddressFamily.InterNetwork, SocketType.Stream,
                                   ProtocolType.Tcp);

        try
        {
            // Connect the socket to the remote endPoint. Catch any errors
            sender.Connect(ipEndPoint);
            Console.WriteLine("Socket connected to {0}",
                              sender.RemoteEndPoint.ToString());
        }
        catch(SecurityException se)
        {
            Console.WriteLine("Security Exception:" + se);
        }
        catch(SocketException se)
        {
            Console.WriteLine("Socket Exception:"  + se);
        }
        finally
        {
            if (sender.Connected)
            {
                // Release the socket
                sender.Shutdown(SocketShutdown.Both);
                sender.Close();
            }
        }
    }

    [SocketPermission(SecurityAction.Deny, Access = "Connect",
                      Host = "127.0.0.1", Port = "All", Transport = "Tcp")]
    public static void IllegalMethod()
    {
        Console.WriteLine("IllegalMethod");

        IPHostEntry ipHost = Dns.Resolve("127.0.0.1");
```

```
        IPAddress ipAddr = ipHost.AddressList[0];
        IPEndPoint ipEndPoint = new IPEndPoint(ipAddr, 11000);

        Socket sender = new Socket(AddressFamily.InterNetwork,
                                SocketType.Stream, ProtocolType.Tcp);

        try
        {
            // Connect the socket to the remote endPoint. Catch any errors
            sender.Connect(ipEndPoint);
            Console.WriteLine("Socket connected to {0}",
                            sender.RemoteEndPoint.ToString());
        }
        catch(SocketException se)
        {
            Console.WriteLine("Socket Exception:" + se );
        }
        catch(SecurityException se)
        {
            Console.WriteLine("Security Exception:" + se );
        }
            finally
        {
            if (sender.Connected)
            {
                // Release the socket
                sender.Shutdown(SocketShutdown.Both);
                sender.Close();
            }
        }
    }
}
```

The above program is similar in functionality to the previous one. This program, however, uses the declarative security syntax instead of the imperative security demonstrated earlier. The code contains two different methods for connecting to the server, because the attributes couldn't be dynamically manipulated. The SocketPermissionAttribute declaration is placed on each method that we need to secure:

```
[SocketPermission(SecurityAction.Deny, Access = "Connect",
                Host = "127.0.0.1", Port = "All", Transport = "Tcp")]
```

The above code declares and initializes the SocketPermissionAttribute, very much as we did in the SocketPermission's constructor. The properties of the SocketPermissionAttribute must have values that are not a null reference or invalid. Also, once set, these properties cannot be changed. The properties' values are the same as in the SocketPermission class. The declarative code, once compiled, is stored inside the metadata of the application code, so calling code can use reflection to see what permissions the code requires to run.

Summary

In this chapter, we looked at developing client and server applications with the `Socket` class. The important points we have discussed include:

- What a socket is, and how sockets are introduced into the operating system.

- The two main types of sockets are stream sockets and datagram sockets.

- There is another type of socket, used for custom lower-level programming, which is known as a raw socket.

- We learned that all the socket support is provided through the `System.Net.Sockets.Socket` class.

- Exception management for network applications is provided by the `SocketException` class.

- The `Close()` and `Shutdown()` methods should generally be placed inside the `finally` block.

- We covered the basic socket options and outlined how to set and get them using `SetSocketOption()` and `GetSocketOption()`.

- We covered .NET's asynchronous programming model, and applied it to build an asynchronous socket-based client-server application.

- We used the `AsyncCallback` delegate for providing callback functions for asynchronous processing.

- The `ManualResetEvent` class is used for synchronizing different threads inside an asychronous application.

- We looked at the declarative and imperative security syntax for providing code-level security in networking applications.

- The imperative syntax should be used when the permissions needed are only known at runtime; if the permissions needed are known at compile time, declarative security should be used.

In the next chapter, we'll cover TCP and see how this important concept in covered in the .NET Framework.

TCP

In the previous chapter, we looked at low-level sockets programming for performing network-related tasks. In this chapter, we will look in detail at the higher-level network classes provided in the .NET Framework. We'll start with a general introduction to TCP, and its architecture and data structures. Next, we'll explore the `TcpClient` and `TcpListener` classes provided in the .NET Framework for working with TCP. Finally, we'll discuss using the TCP channel with .NET Remoting.

Overview of TCP

TCP, or Transmission Control Protocol, is used as a reliable protocol to communicate across an interconnected network of computers. TCP verifies that the data is properly delivered to the destination in the correct sequence. We'll look briefly at how TCP achieves this in a moment.

TCP is a connection-oriented protocol designed to provide reliable transmission of data from one process to another process running on the same or different computers. The term "connection-oriented" means that the two processes or applications must establish a TCP connection prior to exchanging any data. This is in contrast to UDP (which we'll look at in the next chapter), which is a "connection-less" protocol, allowing data to be broadcast to an unknown number of clients.

Encapsulation

When an application sends data using TCP, it travels down the protocol stack. The data is passed through each of the layers and finally transferred across the network as stream of bits.

Each layer in the TCP/IP protocol suite adds some information in the form of headers and/or trailers:

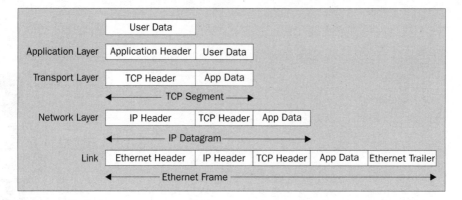

When the packet arrives on the other side of the network, it is again passed through each layer from bottom to top. Each layer strips out its header/trailer information to verify the data and finally it reaches the server application in the same form as it left the client application.

TCP Terminology

Before looking at how TCP establishes a connection with another TCP host, there are a number of terms that we need to define:

Segment

The unit of data that TCP sends to IP is called a TCP segment.

Datagram

The unit of data that IP sends to the Network Interface Layer is called an IP datagram.

Sequence Number

Every TCP segment sent over a connection has a number assigned to it, which is called the "Sequence Number". This is used to ensure that the data arrives in the correct order.

TCP Headers

To understand how TCP works, we also need to look quickly at the structure of a TCP header:

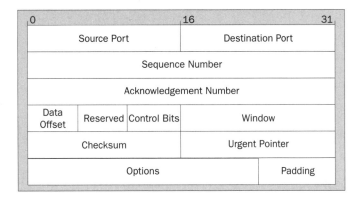

The sequence and acknowledgement numbers are used by TCP to ensure that all the data arrives in the correct order, and the control bits contain various flags to indicate the status of the data. There are six of these control bits (usually represented by three-letter abbreviations):

- ❑   URG – indicates that the segment contains urgent data
- ❑   ACK – indicates that the segment contains an acknowledgement number
- ❑   PSH – indicates the data is to be pushed through to the receiving user
- ❑   RST – resets the connection
- ❑   SYN – used to synchronize sequence numbers
- ❑   FIN – indicates the end of data

TCP Connections

TCP uses a process called a "Three-Phase Handshake" to establish a connection. As the name suggests, this process consists of three steps:

1.   The client initiates communication with the server by sending a segment to the server with the SYN control bit set. This segment contains the client's initial sequence number.

2.   The server responds by sending a segment with both the SYN and ACK bits set. This segment contains the server's initial sequence number (unrelated to that of the client), and the acknowledgement number, which will be equal to the client's sequence number plus one (that is, it is the next sequence number expected from the client).

3.   The client must acknowledge this segment by sending back a segment with the ACK bit set. The acknowledgement number will be the server's sequence number plus one, and the sequence number will be the same as the server's acknowledgement number (that is, the client's original sequence number plus one).

169

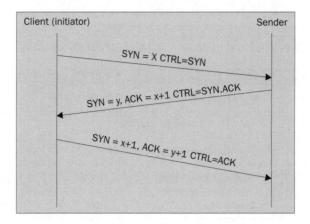

TCP Operations

Now that we've seen the basics of how TCP establishes connections, let's look in a bit more detail at a few TCP operations, to see how TCP transfers data.

Basic Stream Data Transfer

As we've seen, TCP transfers data in byte chunks known as segments. In order to ensure that segments are received correctly and in the correct order, a sequence number is assigned to each segment. The receiver sends an acknowledgement that the segment has been received. If the acknowledgement is not received before the timeout interval expires, the data is resent.

Each octet (eight bits) of data is assigned a sequence number. The sequence number of the segment is the sequence number of the first octet of data within the segment, and this number is sent in the TCP header for the segment. Segments can also have an acknowledgement number, which is the sequence number for the next expected data segment:

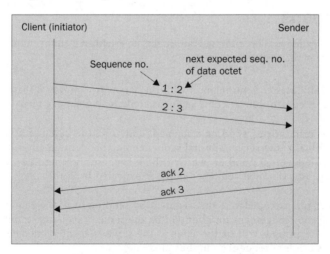

TCP uses the sequence numbers to ensure that duplicate data isn't passed on to the receiving application, and that the data is delivered in the correct order. The TCP header contains a checksum which is used to ensure that the data hasn't been corrupted in transit. If a segment with an invalid checksum is received, it is simply discarded, and no acknowledgement is sent. This means that the sender will resend the segment when the timeout value expires.

Flow Control

TCP governs the amount of data sent to it by returning a "window size" with every acknowledgement. A "window" is the amount of data that the receiver can accept. A data buffer is placed between the application program and the network data flow. The "window size" is actually the difference between the size of the buffer and the amount of data stored in it. This number is sent to inform the remote host about the current window size. This is called a "Sliding Window". The Sliding Window algorithms control the flow for network data transfers:

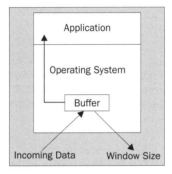

The data received is stored in this buffer, and the application can access and read the data from the buffer at its own speed. As the application reads data, the buffer empties itself to accept more input from the network.

If the application is too slow reading the data from the buffer, the window size will drop to zero and the remote host will be told to stop sending the data. As soon as the local application processes the data in the buffer, the window size increases and can start receiving data from the network again.

If the size of the window is greater than the packet size, the sender knows that the receiver can hold multiple packets at once, improving the performance.

Multiplexing

TCP allows many processes on a single machine to use a TCP socket simultaneously. A TCP socket consists of a host address and a unique port number, and a TCP connection comprises two sockets on different ends of a network. A port may be used for simultaneous multiple connections – a single socket on one end may be used for several connections with different sockets on the other end. An example of this is a web server listening on port 80 answering requests from more than one computer.

Introduction to TCP in .NET

.NET support for TCP sockets is a great improvement on the previous programming model. Previously, most developers using Visual C++ have either employed the CSocket and CAsyncSocket classes for manipulating all types of socket communication, or used third-party programming libraries. There was almost no built-in support for higher-level TCP programming. In .NET, there is a separate namespace provided for working with sockets – the System.Net.Sockets namespace (as discussed in the previous chapter). This namespace contains low-level classes such as Socket as well as higher-level classes such as TcpClient and TcpListener to offer simple interfaces to TCP communication.

The TcpClient and TcpListener classes follow the stream model for sending and receiving data, as opposed to the Socket class, which employs the byte-level approach. In these classes, all communication between the client and the socket is based on a stream, using the NetworkStream class. However, we can also work with bytes where necessary.

The TcpClient Class

The TcpClient class provides client-side connections for TCP services. It is built upon the Socket class to provide TCP Services at a higher level – TcpClient has a private data member called m_ClientSocket, which is used to communicate with the TCP server. The TcpClient class provides simple methods for connecting to another socket application over the network, and for sending and receiving data to it. The important class members of TcpClient class are listed below:

Public Properties

Name	Type	Description
LingerState	LingerOption	Sets or returns a LingerOption object that holds information about whether the connection will remain open after the socket is closed, and if so for how long.
NoDelay	bool	Specifies whether the socket will delay sending or receiving data if the send or receive buffer isn't full. If set to false, TCP will delay sending the packet until there is sufficient data in order to avoid the inefficiency of sending very small packets over the network.
ReceiveBufferSize	int	Specifies the size of the buffer for incoming data (in bytes). This property is used when reading data from a socket.

Name	Type	Description
ReceiveTimeout	int	Specifies the length of time in milliseconds that the TcpClient will wait to receive data once initiated. A SocketException will be thrown after this time has elapsed if no data is received.
SendBufferSize	int	Specifies the size of the buffer for outgoing data.
SendTimeout	int	Specifies the length of time in milliseconds that the TcpClient will wait to receive confirmation of the number of bytes sent to the remote host from the underlying Socket after a send is initiated. A SocketException will be thrown if the SendTimeOut expires.

Public Methods

Name	Description
Close()	Closes the TCP connection.
Connect()	Connects to a remote TCP host.
GetStream()	Returns the NetworkStream used for transferring data between the client and the remote host.

Protected Properties

Name	Type	Description
Active	bool	Specifies whether there is an active connection to a remote host.
Client	Socket	Specifies the underlying Socket used by the TcpClient. Because this property is protected, the underlying socket can only be accessed if you derive your own class from TcpClient.

Instantiating a TcpClient

The constructor for the TcpClient class has three overloads:

```
public TcpClient();
public TcpClient(IPEndPoint ipEnd);
public TcpClient(string hostname, int port);
```

The default constructor initializes a TcpClient instance:

```
TcpClient newClient = new TcpClient();
```

If a TcpClient is instantiated in this way, we must call the Connect() method with an IPEndPoint to establish a connection to a remote host.

The second overload takes a single parameter of type IPEndPoint. This initializes a new instance of the TcpClient class bound to the specified endpoint. Notice that this IPEndPoint is the local endpoint, not the remote endpoint. If we try to pass a remote endpoint to the constructor, an exception will be thrown, stating that the IP address isn't valid in this context.

If we use this constructor, we still have to call the Connect() method with the remote endpoint after creating the TcpClient object:

```
// Create a local end point
IPAddress ipAddr = IPAddress.Parse("192.168.1.51");
IPEndPoint endPoint = new IPEndPoint(ipAddr, 11100);

TcpClient newClient = new TcpClient(endPoint);

// You must call connect() to make a connection with the server
newClient.Connect("192.168.1.52", 11000);
```

The parameter passed to TcpClient constructor is the local endpoint, whereas the Connect() method actually connects the client with the server, so takes the remote endpoint as a parameter.

The last overload creates a new instance of the TcpClient class and establishes a remote connection using a DNS name and port number parameters passed in as arguments:

```
TcpClient newClient = new TcpClient("localhost", 80);
```

This is the most convenient method, as it allows us to initialize the TcpClient, resolve the DNS name, and connect with the host in one easy step. However, notice that we can't specify the local port to which we want to bind using this overload.

Establishing a Connection with the Host

Once we've instantiated a TcpClient, the next step is to establish a connection with the remote host. The Connect() method is provided to connect the client with the TCP host. We only need to call this method if we used the default constructor or a local endpoint to instantiate the TcpClient; otherwise, if we pass a hostname and port number into the constructor, attempting to call Connect() will cause an exception.

There are three overloads for the Connect() method:

```
public void Connect(IPEndPoint endPoint);
public void Connect(IPAddress ipAddr, int port);
public void Connect(string hostname, int port);
```

These are fairly self-explanatory, but we'll quickly demonstrate examples of using each overload:

1. Passing in an IPEndPoint object representing the remote endpoint we want to connect to:

```
// Create a new instance of the TcpClient class
TcpClient newClient = new TcpClient();
```

```
// Establish a connection with the IPEndPoint
IPAddress ipAddr = IPAddress.Parse("127.0.0.1");
IPEndPoint endPoint = new IPEndPoint(ipAddr, 80);

// Connect with the host using IPEndPoint
newClient.Connect(endPoint);
```

2. Passing in an `IPAddress` object and a port number:

```
// Create a new instance of the TcpClient class
TcpClient newClient = new TcpClient();

// Establish a connection with the IPEndPoint
IPAddress ipAddr = IPAddress.Parse("127.0.0.1");

// Connect with the host using IPAddress and port number
newClient.Connect(ipAddr, 80);
```

3. Passing in a hostname and port number:

```
// Create a new instance of the TcpClient class
TcpClient newClient = new TcpClient();

// Connect with the host using hostname as string and port
newClient.Connect("127.0.0.1", 80);
```

If there is a connection failure or other problem, a `SocketException` will be thrown:

```
try
{
    TcpClient newClient = new TcpClient();

    // Connect to the server
    newClient.Connect("192.168.0.1", 80); // Socket raises exception here
                                           // if there is some problem with the
                                           // connection
}
catch(SocketException se)
{
    Console.WriteLine("Exception: " + se);
}
```

Sending and Receiving Messages

The `NetworkStream` class is used for stream-level processing as a communication channel between two connected applications. This class has already been discussed in Chapter 2, so here we'll just look at using it with a `TcpClient`.

Before sending and receiving any data, we need to get the underlying stream. TcpClient provides a GetStream() method exclusively for this purpose. GetStream() creates an instance of the NetworkStream class using the underlying socket and returns it to the caller. The following code sample demonstrates how to get a network stream using the GetStream() method.

We assume that newClient is an instance of the TcpClient, and that a connection with the host has already been established. Otherwise, an InvalidOperation exception would be thrown.

```
NetworkStream tcpStream = newClient.GetStream();
```

After getting the stream, we can use the Read() and Write() methods of NetworkStream to actually read from the host application and write to it.

The Write() method takes three parameters – a byte array containing the data we want to send to the host, the position in the stream where we want to start writing, and the length of the data:

```
byte[] sendBytes = Encoding.ASCII.GetBytes("This is a Test<EOF>");
tcpStream.Write(sendBytes, 0, sendBytes.Length);
```

The Read() method has exactly the same set of parameters – a byte array to store the data that we read from the stream, the position to start reading, and the number of bytes to read:

```
byte[] bytes = new byte[newClient.ReceiveBufferSize];
int bytesRead = tcpStream.Read(bytes, 0, newClient.ReceiveBufferSize);

// Convert from bytes to string
// returnData will contain the incoming data from socket
string returnData = Encoding.ASCII.GetString(bytes);
```

The TcpClient's ReceiveBufferSize property allows us to get or set the size of the receive buffer (in bytes), so we use it as the size of the byte array. Note that setting this property doesn't restrict the number of bytes we can read in each operation, as the buffer will be dynamically resized if necessary, but it does reduce overhead if we specify a buffer size.

Closing a TCP Socket

After communicating with the client, the Close() method should be called to free all resources:

```
// Close client socket
newClient.Close();
```

That is all that is required to use the TcpClient class to communicate with the server.

Apart from this basic functionality, if we need to access the socket instance underlying the `TcpClient` object, for example to set options by calling `SetSocketOption()`, we can call the `Client` property to access the members of the underlying `Socket`. We can also use the `Client` property to set the `TcpClient`'s underlying socket to an existing `Socket` object. But since this is a protected member of the `TcpClient` class, we must inherit from `TcpClient` before using it. The `Client` property allows protected access to the private `m_ClientSocket` member we mentioned earlier. The `TcpClient` class passes calls made on it to the `Socket` class's parallel method after checking the validity of parameters and initializing the socket instance. The `m_ClientSocket` object is instantiated in the constructor. The constructor calls the private `initialize()` method that constructs the new `Socket` object and then calls the `set_Client()` method to assign it to the `Client` property. The method also sets the `m_Active` Boolean value, which is used to track the state of the `Socket` instance. It also checks for redundant `Socket` connections and for any operation that requires the connection. A separate protected property, `Active`, is provided for setting and getting the value of the private `m_Active` member.

There are a lot of socket options that the `TcpClient` class does not cover. If we want to set or get any of these properties that are not exposed by the `TcpClient` (such as `Broadcast` or `KeepAlive`), we need to derive a class from `TcpClient` and use its `Client` member.

The following code demonstrates how to use these protected properties, and specifically the `Active` member of the `TcpClient` class:

```
using System;
using System.Net;
using System.Net.Sockets;
using System.IO;
using System.Text;

public class PSocket : TcpClient
{
    public PSocket() : base()
    {
    }

    public PSocket(string ipaddress, int port) : base(ipaddress, port)
    {
    }

    public static void Main()
    {
        // Creating a TcpClient object but not connecting
        PSocket ps2 = new PSocket();

        // Showing the state of the socket
        Console.WriteLine("trackActive: " + ps2.Active);

        // Connecting with the client
        ps2.Connect("127.0.0.1", 11000);

        // Checking the state of the socket
        Console.WriteLine("trackActive: " + ps2.Active);
```

```
        // Creating another TcpClient class, this time connecting
        // within the constructor
        PSocket newClient = new PSocket("127.0.0.1", 11000);

        // Checking the state of the other socket
        Console.WriteLine("trackActive: " + newClient.Active);

        // Getting the internal protected socket member
        Socket s = newClient.Client;

        // Use the socket to set an option
        s.SetSocketOption(SocketOptionLevel.Socket, SocketOptionName.KeepAlive, 1);
    }
}
```

Building a Real World Socket Application

To demonstrate the use of the TcpClient class, we'll build a simple e-mail client implementing two of the most common protocols in the Internet world. These are SMTP and POP3 protocols. We won't show the POP3 implementation in this chapter, as another implementation is provided in Chapter 9, but it is available as part of the code download for the book. So, let's start with some theory behind the SMTP protocol, and then we'll move on to see how the application works. We won't cover everything about SMTP here – just enough to understand the application – as we will look at it in more detail in Chapter 9. .NET does provide classes for sending e-mails over SMTP (we cover these in Chapter 9), but it's important to see how to implement application-level protocols such as this, and SMTP provides a useful example because of its simplicity.

Simple Mail Transfer Protocol (SMTP)

The following figure shows the basic model behind the SMTP protocol involved in completing a mail transaction:

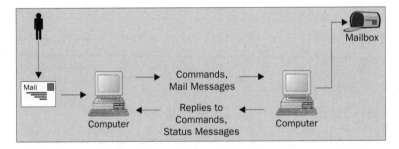

The process starts when the user sends the mail. The sending system contacts the receiving system on TCP port 25 to establish a communication link. The receiving system, which may be the final destination or an intermediate system, replies back with status messages to inform the sender that it's ready to receive the message. These responses consist of a three-digit status code and a human-readable message. The receiving system continues by sending commands followed by the original e-mail. The receiving system responds appropriately with status messages and commands. The link is terminated when the sender has finished sending the message and disconnects itself from the receiving system.

SMTP Commands

The command syntax for the SMTP protocol isn't very difficult, and contains very few commands:

❑   HELO. The HELO command is used to initiate communications between the sending and receiving hosts. This command is accompanied by a parameter identifying the sending host. The receiving host then identifies itself back to the sending host; this places both the machines into the ready state to begin communications. If successful, this command should be met with the reply code 250, which indicates that the command completed without error.

An example HELO command and the host's response would be:

```
Sending System:     HELO wrox.com
Receiving System:   250 gg.mail.com
```

❑   MAIL. This command lets the receiving system know who is sending the mail message so that any error in delivering the mail message can be directed back to the original e-mail sender. Since mail can be intercepted en route by more than one host, it is used to identify the final destination of the e-mail. Most e-mail servers put some restriction on this parameter, such as ensuring that the user's domain name is the same as the e-mail server's domain, to prevent anonymous e-mails and spamming.

An example MAIL command and response would be:

```
Sending System:     MAIL FROM:<noman@csquareonline.com>
Receiving System:   250 OK
```

❑   RCPT. This command is used to send the mailbox names of the users to whom the mail is being sent. It's possible to have more than one recipient for a particular mail message.

Identifying the Recipient of the Mail Message

```
Sending System:     RCPT TO:<noman@csquareonline.com>
Receiving System:   250 OK
```

❑   DATA. This command indicates that the information that follows contains the body of the message file. The message end is indicated by the sending system's transmission of a line containing only a period (.). The following listing shows the transaction between the sending and the receiving system. Note that the subject of the mail is specified within this data by adding a SUBJECT: line just after sending the DATA command. The text between SUBJECT: and the carriage return/line feed characters construct the subject of the message:

```
Sending System:     DATA
Receiving System:   354 Ready to receive data...
Sending System:     SUBJECT:Subject of the message<CR><LF>This is a test
message. <CR><LF>.<CR><LF>
Receiving System:   250 OK
```

After the receiving system gets the end of message line, it replies to the sender about the status of the message.

❑   QUIT. This command indicates that the sending system is ready to close down the communication link between the sender and the receiver:

```
Sending System:     QUIT
Receiving System:   221 web.akros.net closing connection.
```

SMTP Communication Sample

Below you can find an example of a successful SMTP session between a sending and the receiving system. For each command and response, CLIENT represents the system that will be initiating and sending the mail, and SERVER represents the system to which the mail is sent:

```
[Establish Connection with SMTP Server]
Connection Established with xyz.com
SERVER: 220 web1.xyz.com ESMTP SendMail
CLIENT: HELO xyz.com
SERVER: 250 OK
CLIENT: MAIL FROM: <noman@csquareonline.com><CR><LF>
SERVER: 250 <noman@csquareonline.com>... Sender OK
CLIENT: RCPT TO: <noman@csquareonline.com><CR><LF>
SERVER: 250 <noman@csquareonline.com>... Recepient OK
CLIENT: DATA<CR><LF>
SERVER: 354 Enter mail, end with "." on a line by itself
CLIENT: SUBJECT: test<CR><LF>
test<CR><LF>
.<CR><LF>
SERVER: 250 asdkauy83 Message accepted for delivery
CLIENT: QUIT<CR><LF>
SERVER: 221 web.xyz.com Closing Connection
```

To test this, you can use a Telnet application and connect to your local SMTP server on port 25. Then you can manually type the client portion of the example into the Telnet application to get a more "hands on" feel for the process. We look at a sample SMTP Telnet session in Chapter 9, and discussed the Microsoft Telnet client in Chapter 1.

SMTP Client in .NET

Our e-mail client application will be a Windows Application, but we'll keep the user interface as simple as possible. There will be single-line textboxes to specify the SMTP server we want to connect to, the From and To fields for the e-mail, and the subject of the e-mail. We'll also have a multi-line textbox for the body of the e-mail and a listbox where we'll display status messages:

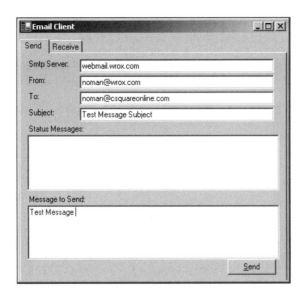

There are two tabs on the form, one for sending e-mails via SMTP, and the other for retrieving them from an inbox via POP. The SMTP tab contains the following controls (we show the text of the labels associated with the controls, so that they can be identified in the screenshot above):

Name	Type	Associated Label Text
txtSmtpServer	text box	Smtp Server:
txtFrom	text box	From:
txtTo	text box	To:
txtSubject	text box	Subject:
lstLog	list box	Status Messages:
txtMessage	text box	Message to Send:
btnSend	button	–

All the code for connecting to the server and sending the message is implemented in the Click event handler for the **Send** button. We start by making a connection to the SMTP server:

```
private void btnSend_Click(object sender, System.EventArgs e)
{
    // Create an instance of the TcpClient class
    TcpClient smtpServer = new TcpClient(txtSmtpServer.Text, 25);
    lstLog.Items.Add("Connection Established with smtpserver.com");
```

The next step is to build the `Stream` classes to communicate with the SMTP server. We have used a `NetworkStream` for writing a stream to the server, but a `StreamReader` for reading from the server. This provides a `ReadLine()` method that is much easier to use than calling the `NetworkStream`'s `Read()` method, which reads the stream into bytes that we then have to convert into a string using the `Encoding` class. The `StreamReader`'s `ReadLine()` method returns a string.

```
// Create the stream classes for communication
NetworkStream writeStream = smtpServer.GetStream();
StreamReader readStream = new StreamReader(smtpServer.GetStream());
```

Once we've connected to the server, it will send us a message back to tell us that the connection has been made. We read this message using the `StreamReader.ReadLine()` method, and display it in the list box:

```
// Retrieve connection success message
receiveData = readStream.ReadLine();

// Add it to the listbox
lstLog.Items.Add(receiveData);
```

Next, we send the user's e-mail address to the server by writing an SMTP `MAIL FROM` command to our `NetworkStream` object. Again, the server will send a response message, which we retrieve from the `StreamReader` and add to the listbox:

```
// Send 'From' E-mail Address
sendString = "MAIL FROM: " + "<" + txtFrom.Text + ">\r\n";
dataToSend = Encoding.ASCII.GetBytes(sendString);
writeStream.Write(dataToSend, 0, dataToSend.Length);

// Display response message
receiveData = readStream.ReadLine();
lstLog.Items.Add(receiveData);
```

Then we send the destination e-mail address in a `RCPT TO` command, and again display the server's response:

```
// Sending 'To' E-mail Address
sendString = "RCPT TO: " + "<" + txtTo.Text + ">\r\n";
dataToSend = Encoding.ASCII.GetBytes(sendString);
writeStream.Write(dataToSend, 0, dataToSend.Length);

// Display response message
receiveData = readStream.ReadLine();
lstLog.Items.Add(receiveData);
```

Now, after both the e-mail addresses have been authenticated, the actual data (including the e-mail's subject) is sent following the DATA SMTP command:

```
    // Send data
    sendString = "DATA " + "\r\n";
    dataToSend = Encoding.ASCII.GetBytes(sendString);
    writeStream.Write(dataToSend, 0, dataToSend.Length);

    // Display response message
    receiveData = readStream.ReadLine();
    lstLog.Items.Add(receiveData);

    // Sending Message Subject and Text
    sendString = "SUBJECT: " + txtSubject.Text + "\r\n" + txtMessage.Text +
                "\r\n" + "." + "\r\n";
    dataToSend = Encoding.ASCII.GetBytes(sendString);
    writeStream.Write(dataToSend, 0, dataToSend.Length);

    receiveData = readStream.ReadLine();
    lstLog.Items.Add(receiveData);
```

The last step is to send the QUIT command to the server and free any resources used by the application:

```
    // Send Disconnect Message to Server
    sendString = "QUIT " + "\r\n";
    dataToSend = Encoding.ASCII.GetBytes(sendString);
    writeStream.Write(dataToSend,0,dataToSend.Length);
    receiveData = readStream.ReadLine();
    lstLog.Items.Add(receiveData);

    // Close all open resources
    writeStream.Close();
    readStream.Close();
    smtpServer.Close();
}
```

Post Office Protocol (POP)

The second tab of our e-mail client application allows us to read e-mails from an inbox using the POP3 protocol:

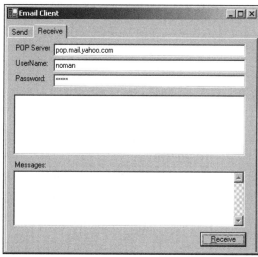

The complete code for this application is available in the code download for the book, but since we present a very similar example in Chapter 9, we won't show the code here.

Implementing an FtpWebRequest Class

The second example we'll look at is a bit more complicated – we'll implement `FtpWebRequest` and `FtpWebResponse` classes that will allow us to download files from or upload them to an FTP server in much the same way that we can access files using the `FileWebRequest` and `FileWebResponse` classes that we saw in Chapter 3.

Overview of FTP

File Transfer Protocol (FTP) is, as we saw in Chapter 1, an application-level protocol built on top of a transport-level protocol, usually TCP. It is used for uploading and downloading files on a remote server. In many ways, implementing an FTP client is very similar to our implementation of the SMTP client in the previous section – we open up a TCP connection to the server, send text commands to perform actions such as retrieving a file from the server, and the server returns a three-digit code (along with a human-readable message) to indicate the status of the requested action.

Where FTP differs from SMTP, however, is that two different connections are used – the control connection, on which we send the commands and receive the server's responses; and the data connection, which is used for the actual transfer of the files to be downloaded or uploaded. By default, the server listens on port 21 for commands from the client, and when it needs to send data will open a second connection to port 20 of the client.

Active and Passive Modes

The data connection is opened only when a command has been sent to upload or download a file. In active mode (the default), the client must listen for connections. When data needs to be sent, the FTP server will open up a connection to this socket, and transfer the data over to the client.

The problem with this approach is that most firewall configurations won't permit connections from outside to machines behind the firewall – they will only allow connections that were initialized from behind the firewall. FTP's answer to this is passive mode. In this case, the client sends a command to indicate that passive mode is to be used, and the server will respond with the port number that the server is listening on. When the data needs to be sent, the client can now open up a connection to the specified port, instead of having to listen for the server's request. Our implementation will use passive mode.

FTP Commands

The FTP specification defines a number of commands for authentication, uploading and downloading files, and changing the directory on the server. We won't use all of these commands in our code, so we'll only look at those that we do use:

Command	Description
USER <username>	The username to be authenticated on the server
PASS <password>	The password associated with the username
RETR <filename>	Download the specified file
STOR <filename>	Upload a file and store it in the specified location

Command	Description
TYPE <*type indicator*>	The format for the data. This can be one of: A – ASCII E – EBCDIC I – Image (binary data) L <*byte size*> – Local byte size
PASV	Use passive mode
STAT	Cause the server to send a status message to the client. This can be used while data is being transferred, to indicate the status of the operation
QUIT	Close the connection to the server

FTP Status Codes

As with SMTP reply codes, the three digit FTP codes are ordered according to the granularity of detail provided by the digit – the first digit gives a general indication of the status of the command; the second digit indicates the general type of error that occurred; and the third digit gives more specific information. The possible first digits are:

Digit	Description
1	Positive preliminary response – the requested action is being initiated, and another response will be sent before the client should send a new command
2	Positive completion response – the requested action has been completed
3	Positive intermediate response – the command has been accepted, but the server requires more information before proceeding
4	Temporary negative response – the command was rejected, but the error is temporary, and the command can be resent
5	Permanent negative response – the command was rejected

Some of the specific responses that we will handle are:

Code	Description
125	Data connection open – starting transfer
150	About to open data connection
200	Command accepted
220	Service ready for new user
227	Entering passive mode
230	User logged in
331	Username accepted – send password

Coding an FTP Client

Now that we've had a quick overview of the FTP protocol, we can start to implement a client in .NET. As we mentioned above, to make this class as intuitive as possible for developers using it, we'll do this by implementing an `FtpWebRequest` class that inherits from `WebRequest` and can be used in the same way. This is implemented as a Class Library project, and consists of five classes:

❑ `FtpRequestCreator` – Used when we register the `"ftp"` prefix with `WebRequest`

❑ `FtpWebRequest` – Represents a request to download or upload a file on an FTP server

❑ `FtpWebResponse` – Represents the response from the server

❑ `FtpWebStream` – Represents the stream between the client and server

❑ `FtpClient` – The utility class which we use for connecting to the server and executing the FTP commands

The FtpRequestCreator Class

The first thing we need to do is create an implementation of the `IWebRequestCreate` interface. This interface has one method, `Create()`, which is called by the `WebRequest.Create()` static method. In this method, we simply return a new instance of our `FtpWebRequest` class:

```
using System;
using System.Net;

namespace Wrox.Networking.TCP.FtpUtil
{
    public class FtpRequestCreator : IWebRequestCreate
    {
        public FtpRequestCreator()
        {
        }

        public System.Net.WebRequest Create(System.Uri uri)
        {
            return new FtpWebRequest(uri);
        }
    }
}
```

When we want to create an `FtpWebRequest` object, we need to register the `"ftp"` prefix, and pass in an `FtpRequestCreator` object, so that the `WebRequest` class knows that it must use this class to handle any web requests beginning with `"ftp"` (we'll see how to do this later on).

The FtpWebRequest Class

Next, we can define the `FtpWebRequest` class itself. This will have five data members, to store the username and password of the user we will connect as, the URI we want to connect to, a Boolean value indicating whether the data is to be in binary rather than ASCII format, and a string representing the "method" for the request. This last field represents the command we want to execute against the server; to make this more accessible to users who aren't familiar with the FTP protocol, we will allow this to be set to `"GET"` instead of `"RETR"`, and `"PUT"` instead of `"STOR"`. These values are also exposed as public properties of the class. The constructor of the class simply sets the `uri` field to the `Uri` passed in. The only other method in the class is the `GetResponse()` method, which simply instantiates and returns a new `FtpWebResponse` object, passing the current `FtpWebRequest` as a parameter:

```csharp
using System;
using System.Net;

namespace Wrox.Networking.TCP.FtpUtil
{
    public class FtpWebRequest : WebRequest
    {
        private string username = "anonymous";
        internal string password = "someuser@somemail.com";
        private Uri uri;
        private bool binaryMode = true;
        private string method = "GET";

        internal FtpWebRequest(Uri uri)
        {
            this.uri = uri;
        }

        public string Username
        {
            get { return username; }
            set { username = value; }
        }

        public string Password
        {
            set { password = value; }
        }

        public bool BinaryMode
        {
            get { return binaryMode; }
            set { binaryMode = value; }
        }

        public override System.Uri RequestUri
        {
            get { return uri; }
        }

        public override string Method
        {
            get { return method; }
            set { method = value; }
        }

        public override System.Net.WebResponse GetResponse()
        {
            FtpWebResponse response = new FtpWebResponse(this);
            return response;
        }
    }
}
```

The FtpWebResponse Class

Next, we define the `FtpWebResponse` class. This has two private data members – the `FtpWebRequest` object with which it is associated, and an instance of a class called `FtpClient`, where we will implement most of the actual code for communicating with the FTP server. The class's constructor simply sets the `request` field to the `FtpWebRequest` object that is passed in:

```
using System;
using System.IO;
using System.Net;
using System.Net.Sockets;

namespace Wrox.Networking.TCP.FtpUtil
{
    public class FtpWebResponse : WebResponse
    {
        private FtpWebRequest request;
        private FtpClient client;

        internal FtpWebResponse(FtpWebRequest request)
        {
            this.request = request;
        }
```

The `GetResponseStream()` method is where we actually connect to the server and download/upload the data. This method first separates the URI we want to connect to into its component parts – the name of the server, and the path and name of the file we want to download or save to the server. Next, we create an instance of the `FtpClient` class, passing in the username and password from the `FtpWebRequest` object, and we use this object to connect to the server. Next, we execute the command represented by the `FtpWebRequest` object. This could be either GET/RETR to download a file, or PUT/STOR to upload a file. In either case, we retrieve a `NetworkStream` object that is used to represent the stream between the client and the server. If the method isn't one of these, we throw an exception to state that the method isn't supported. Finally, we create a new `FtpWebStream` object from this `NetworkStream`, and return it to the caller:

```
public override System.IO.Stream GetResponseStream()
{
    // Split up URI to get hostname and filename
    string hostname;
    string filename;
    GetUriComponents(request.RequestUri.ToString(), out hostname,
                     out filename);

    // Connect to the FTP server and get a stream
    client = new FtpClient(request.Username, request.password);
    client.Connect(hostname);

    NetworkStream dataStream = null;
    switch (request.Method)
    {
        case "GET":
        case "RETR":
```

```
                dataStream = client.GetReadStream(filename,
                                           request.BinaryMode);
            break;
        case "PUT":
        case "STOR":
            dataStream = client.GetWriteStream(filename,
                                           request.BinaryMode);
            break;
        default:
            throw new WebException("Method " + request.Method +
                                " not supported");
    }

    // Create and return an FtpWebStream
    // (to close the underlying objects)
    FtpWebStream ftpStream = new FtpWebStream(dataStream, this);
    return ftpStream;
}
```

The GetUriComponents() method parses a URI in string format and populates two output parameters with the hostname and the filename components from this:

```
private void GetUriComponents(string uri, out string hostname,
                          out string fileName)
{
    // Check that URI has at least 7 characters, or we'll get an error
    uri = uri.ToLower();
    if (uri.Length < 7)
        throw new UriFormatException("Invalid URI");

    // Check that URI starts "ftp://", and remove that from the start
    if (uri.Substring(0, 6) != "ftp://")
        throw new NotSupportedException(
                                "Only FTP requests are supported");
    else
        uri = uri.Substring(6, uri.Length - 6);

    // Divide the rest of the URI into the hostname and the filename
    string[] uriParts = uri.Split(new char[] { '/' }, 2);
    if (uriParts.Length != 2)
        throw new UriFormatException("Invalid URI");

    hostname = uriParts[0];
    fileName = uriParts[1];
}
```

Finally, the Close() method simply calls Close() on the FtpClient object:

```
public override void Close()
{
    client.Close();
}
```

The FtpWebStream Class

The `FtpWebStream` class inherits from `Stream`. It has two private fields – the `FtpWebResponse` object that returns it to the client application, and the underlying `NetworkStream` between the client and the FTP server. Again, the constructor just populates these fields:

```
using System;
using System.IO;
using System.Net.Sockets;

namespace Wrox.Networking.TCP.FtpUtil
{
    internal class FtpWebStream : Stream
    {
        private FtpWebResponse response;
        private NetworkStream dataStream;

        public FtpWebStream(NetworkStream dataStream, FtpWebResponse response)
        {
            this.dataStream = dataStream;
            this.response = response;
        }
```

The remaining methods and properties simply pass on the call to the underlying `NetworkStream`, or (if the functionality isn't supported), throw a `NotSupportedException`:

```
        public override void Close()
        {
            response.Close();
            base.Close();
        }

        public override void Flush()
        {
            dataStream.Flush();
        }

        public override int Read(byte[] buffer, int offset, int count)
        {
            return dataStream.Read(buffer, offset, count);
        }

        public override long Seek(long offset, System.IO.SeekOrigin origin)
        {
            throw new NotSupportedException("Seek not supported");
        }

        public override void SetLength(long value)
        {
            throw new NotSupportedException("SetLength not supported");
        }
```

```
public override void Write(byte[] buffer, int offset, int count)
{
   dataStream.Write(buffer, offset, count);
}

public override bool CanRead
{
   get { return dataStream.CanRead; }
}

public override bool CanSeek
{
   get { return false; }
}

public override bool CanWrite
{
   get { return dataStream.CanWrite; }
}

public override long Length
{
   get { throw new NotSupportedException("Length not supported"); }
}

public override long Position
{
   get { throw new NotSupportedException("Position not supported"); }
   set { throw new NotSupportedException("Position not supported"); }
}
   }
}
```

The FtpClient Class

The final class in our project, FtpClient, is where most of the actual work is done. This class is only intended to be called from within our application, so we've set its accessibility to internal, and also made the class sealed. The class has seven private fields:

❏ bufferSize – A constant representing the size of the buffer we'll use for reading from and writing to the NetworkStream

❏ controlStream – The NetworkStream that is used to send commands and receive responses from the FTP server

❏ dataStream – The NetworkStream that is used to send data to and receive it from the FTP server

❏ username – A string representing the name of the user, for authenticating against the FTP server

❏ password – The password associated with the username

❏ client – A TcpClient object used to make the control connection to the FTP server

❏ dataClient – A TcpClient object used to make the data connection to the FTP server

```
using System;
using System.Net;
using System.Net.Sockets;
using System.IO;
using System.Text;

namespace Wrox.Networking.TCP.FtpUtil
{
    internal sealed class FtpClient
    {
        private const int bufferSize = 65536;
        private NetworkStream controlStream;
        private NetworkStream dataStream;
        private TcpClient client;
        private string username;
        private string password;
        private TcpClient dataClient = null;
```

The constructor takes the username and password as parameters, and stores these in the data members:

```
public FtpClient(string username, string password)
{
    this.username = username;
    this.password = password;
}
```

The `Connect()` method makes the initial connection with the FTP server. It opens a connection to port 21 (the default port for the control connection to an FTP server) using the `TcpClient` class, and retrieves the `NetworkStream` for this connection. We then call the `GetResponse()` method, which retrieves the status code and message from the stream. If all is well, this should be a `220` "service ready for new user" response, so we log on using the username and password. If any other status code is returned, something has gone wrong, so we throw an exception:

```
public void Connect(string hostname)
{
    // Set the private fields representing the TCP control connection to
    // the server and the NetworkStream used to communicate with the
    // server
    client = new TcpClient(hostname, 21);
    controlStream = client.GetStream();

    string responseMessage;
    if (GetResponse(out responseMessage) != 220)
    {
        throw new WebException(responseMessage);
    }

    Logon(username, password);
}
```

The `GetResponse()` method is used to read a response from the FTP server on the control connection. It returns the three-digit status code as an integer and populates an output parameter with the response message:

```
public int GetResponse(out string responseMessage)
{
    // Read the response from the server, trim any nulls, and return it.
    byte[] response = new byte[client.ReceiveBufferSize];
    controlStream.Read(response, 0, response.Length);
    responseMessage = Encoding.ASCII.GetString(response).Replace(
                                                       "\0", "");

    return int.Parse(responseMessage.Substring(0, 3));
}
```

The Logon() method sends a USER command to the server. If the server requires a password, it will respond with a 331 response, in which case we send a PASS command with the user's password. Otherwise, it should return a 230 response to say that the user has logged in successfully. If any other response is returned, we throw an UnauthorizedAccessException.

> Note that FTP has no built-in security features for protecting passwords, so passwords must be sent in plain text format. For this reason, sensitive passwords should not be sent.

```
private void Logon(string username, string password)
{
    // Send a USER FTP command. The server should respond with a 331
    // message to ask for the user's password.
    string respMessage;
    int resp = SendCommand("USER " + username, out respMessage);

    if (resp != 331 && resp != 230)
        throw new UnauthorizedAccessException(
                              "Unable to login to the FTP server");

    if (resp != 230)
    {
        // Send a PASS FTP command. The server should respond with a 230
        // message to say that the user is now logged in.
        resp = SendCommand("PASS " + password, out respMessage);
        if (resp != 230)
            throw new UnauthorizedAccessException(
                              "FTP server can't authenticate username");
    }
}
```

The next two methods simply return a NetworkStream for downloading or uploading a file via the data connection, by calling the DownloadFile() or UploadFile() method (we'll look at these next):

```
public NetworkStream GetReadStream(string filename, bool binaryMode)
{
    return DownloadFile(filename, binaryMode);
}

public NetworkStream GetWriteStream(string filename, bool binaryMode)
{
    return UploadFile(filename, binaryMode);
}
```

The DownloadFile() method opens the data connection to the FTP server, and then sets the binaryMode to specify whether we're expecting binary or ASCII data. Next, we send a RETR command to tell the server we want to download a file. This should be met with a 125 or 150 response to signal that the data connection either is already open or is about to be opened. If it isn't, we throw a WebException; otherwise, we return the NetworkStream from our dataClient TcpClient:

```
private NetworkStream DownloadFile(string filename, bool binaryMode)
{
    if (dataClient == null)
        dataClient = CreateDataSocket();

    SetBinaryMode(binaryMode);

    string respMessage;
    int resp = SendCommand("RETR " + filename, out respMessage);

    if(resp != 150 && resp != 125)
        throw new WebException(respMessage);

    dataStream = dataClient.GetStream();

    return dataStream;
}
```

The UploadFile() method is almost identical, except that a STOR command is sent instead of a RETR command:

```
private NetworkStream UploadFile(string filename, bool binaryMode)
{
    if (dataClient == null)
        dataClient = this.CreateDataSocket();

    // Set binary or ASCII mode
    SetBinaryMode(binaryMode);

    // Send a STOR command to say we want to upload a file.
    string respMessage;
    int resp = SendCommand("STOR " + filename, out respMessage);

    // We should get a 150 response to say that the server is
    // opening the data connection.
    if (resp != 150 && resp != 125)
        throw new WebException("Cannot upload files to the server");

    dataStream = dataClient.GetStream();
    return dataStream;
}
```

The SetBinaryMode() method allows us to specify whether we want to retrieve binary or text (ASCII) data. We do this by sending a TYPE command to the FTP server with the parameter A for ASCII data or I for image (binary) data. We should receive a 200 response code if all went well:

```
private void SetBinaryMode(bool binaryMode)
{
    int resp;
    string respMessage;
    if(binaryMode)
        resp = SendCommand("TYPE I", out respMessage);
    else
        resp = SendCommand("TYPE A", out respMessage);

    if (resp != 200)
        throw new WebException(respMessage);
}
```

The CreateDataSocket() method is the most complicated of our methods. First, we send a PASV command to the server to say that we want to use passive mode; the server responds with a message similar to the following:

```
227 Entering Passive Mode (192,168,0,1,177,147).
```

The first four values in the parentheses represent the IP address, and the last two the port number the server is listening on. We use these values to retrieve the IP address and port number used by the server for data connections. These are returned as 8-bit values, so we calculate the IP address by concatenating the values (separated by period signs) into a string in the normal quad format (for example, "192.168.0.1"), and the port number by shifting the fifth value left by eight bits, and adding the sixth value. Once we've done this, we can create and return a TcpClient object to open up the data connection to the specified IP address and port number:

```
private TcpClient CreateDataSocket()
{
    // request server to listen on a data port (not the default data
    // port) and wait for a connection
    string respMessage;
    int resp = SendCommand("PASV", out respMessage);
    if (resp != 227)
        throw new WebException(respMessage);

    // The response includes the host address and port number
    // IP address and port number separated with ','
    // Create the IP address and port number
    int[] parts = new int[6];
    try
    {
        int index1 = respMessage.IndexOf('(');
        int index2 = respMessage.IndexOf(')');
        string endPointData = respMessage.Substring(index1 + 1,
                                            index2 - index1 - 1);
        string[] endPointParts = endPointData.Split(',');
        for (int i = 0; i < 6; i++)
        {
            parts[i] = int.Parse(endPointParts[i]);
        }
    }
```

```
        catch
        {
            throw new WebException("Malformed PASV reply: " + respMessage);
        }

        string ipAddress = parts[0] + "." + parts[1] + "." + parts[2] +
                           "." + parts[3];
        int port = (parts[4] << 8) + parts[5];

        // Create a client socket
        TcpClient dataClient = new TcpClient();

        // Connect to the data port of the server
        try
        {
            IPEndPoint remoteEP = new IPEndPoint(IPAddress.Parse(ipAddress),
                                                 port);
            dataClient.Connect(remoteEP);
        }
        catch(Exception)
        {
            throw new WebException("Can't connect to remote server");
        }
        return dataClient;
    }
```

The Close() method simply reads any outstanding responses from the server, logs off, and cleans up the resources we've opened:

```
    public void Close()
    {
        if (dataStream != null)
        {
            dataStream.Close();
            dataStream = null;
        }

        string respMessage;
        GetResponse(out respMessage);

        Logoff();

        // Close the control TcpClient and NetworkStream
        controlStream.Close();
        client.Close();
    }
```

The Logoff() method simply sends a STAT command to the server for debugging purposes, and then sends a QUIT command. There will be two responses to the STAT command, so we need to call GetResponse() to read the second:

```
        public void Logoff()
        {
            // Send the QUIT command to log off from the server
            string respMessage;
            SendCommand("STAT", out respMessage);   // Test only
            GetResponse(out respMessage);            // STAT has 2 response lines!

            SendCommand("QUIT", out respMessage);
        }
```

The last method, SendCommand(), is where we actually write the command to the control stream. We add the final CRLF combination to the command before sending it, so that we don't need to do this every time we call the method. Once we've sent the command, we call GetResponse() to read the server's response:

```
        internal int SendCommand(string command, out string respMessage)
        {
            // Convert the command string (terminated with a CRLF) into a
            // byte array, and write it to the control stream.
            byte[] request = Encoding.ASCII.GetBytes(command + "\r\n");
            controlStream.Write(request, 0, request.Length);

            return GetResponse(out respMessage);
        }
    }
}
```

That completes the code for the class library, so now let's write a simple console application to test it out.

A Client Console Application

The first thing we need to do in our Main() method is register the "ftp" prefix with WebRequest. We do this by calling the WebRequest.RegisterPrefix() static method, and passing in the prefix associated with our new WebRequest extension, and an IWebRequestCreate implementation that will create an instance of our FtpWebRequest. After this, we call two methods to demonstrate uploading and downloading files respectively:

```
using System;
using System.IO;
using System.Net;
using Wrox.Networking.TCP.FtpUtil;

namespace TestClient
{
    class Class1
    {
        const int bufferSize = 65536;

        static void Main(string[] args)
        {
            // Register the ftp schema.
            // Alternatively, a config file could be used
            WebRequest.RegisterPrefix("ftp", new FtpRequestCreator());
```

```
        UploadDemo();
        DownloadDemo();
}
```

The `UploadDemo()` method creates a new instance of our `FtpWebRequest` class, and sets its properties to specify the username and password used to make the connection, to specify the data format for the file (here, we want to use binary format, so we set the `BinaryMode` property to `true`), and the method to execute against the server. As we want to upload a file, this could be either `"PUT"` or `"STOR"`. Next, we call the `GetResponseStream()` method of the associated `FtpWebResponse` object to retrieve an `FtpWebStream` that we can use to write the file content to the FTP server. In order to do this, we open up a `FileStream` object pointing to the file we want to upload, and copy it in 65,536-byte chunks into the `FtpWebStream`. Finally, we close the `FtpWebStream` (which will close the associated response and log off from the server), and the `FileStream`:

```
// Upload a file using FtpWebRequest
public static void UploadDemo()
{
    FtpWebRequest req = (FtpWebRequest)WebRequest.Create(
                                "ftp://192.168.0.1/demofile.bmp");
    req.Username = "Administrator";
    req.Password = "secret";
    req.Method = "PUT"; // STOR or PUT
    req.BinaryMode = true;
    Stream writeStream = req.GetResponse().GetResponseStream();

    FileStream fs = new FileStream(@"c:\temp\cool.bmp", FileMode.Open);

    byte[] buffer = new byte[bufferSize];
    int read;
    while ((read = fs.Read(buffer, 0, bufferSize)) > 0)
    {
        writeStream.Write(buffer, 0, bufferSize);
    }
    writeStream.Close();
    fs.Close();
}
```

> Note that you will need the appropriate permissions on the FTP server to upload files. By default, uploading files to the server is not permitted.

The `DownloadDemo()` method is similar, but the way we use it depends on whether we're downloading binary or text data. If it's binary data, we copy the file data into a `FileStream` object in 65,536-byte chunks as in `UploadDemo()`. If it's a text file, we can use the far simpler `StreamReader`:

```
// Download a file using FtpWebRequest
public static void DownloadDemo()
{
    FtpWebRequest req = (FtpWebRequest)WebRequest.Create(
                                "ftp://192.168.0.1/sample.bmp");
```

```
            // defaults:
            /* req.Username = "anonymous";
               req.Password = "someuser@somemail.com";
               req.BinaryMode = true;
               req.Method = "GET";    */

            FtpWebResponse resp = (FtpWebResponse)req.GetResponse();
            Stream stream = resp.GetResponseStream();

            // Read a binary file
            FileStream fs = new FileStream(@"c:\temp\sample.bmp",
                                          FileMode.Create);
            byte[] buffer = new byte[bufferSize];
            int count;
            do
            {
                Array.Clear(buffer, 0, bufferSize);
                count = stream.Read(buffer, 0, bufferSize);
                fs.Write(buffer, 0, count);
            } while (count > 0);

            stream.Close();
            fs.Close();

            /* read a text file
                StreamReader reader = new StreamReader(stream);
                string line;
                while ((line = reader.ReadLine()) != null)
                {
                    Console.WriteLine(line);
                }
                reader.Close(); */
        }
    }
}
```

And that completes the project! This isn't the most robust possible implementation, and we haven't implemented every possible command, but it should give you a clear idea of what's involved in implementing an FTP client, and it provides an example of implementing an application-level protocol that is a bit more complex than SMTP. It also shows how we can integrate our classes with the existing WebRequest framework, so that it's very intuitive to call.

The TcpListener Class

Typically, a server-side application starts by binding to the local endpoint and listening to incoming requests from clients. As soon as a client is found knocking on the port, the application activates by accepting the request and then creating a channel that is then responsible for communicating with the client. The application continues to listen for more incoming client requests on the main thread. The TcpListener class does exactly that – it listens to the client's request, accepts it, and then creates a new instance of the Socket class or the TcpClient class that we can use to communicate with the client. Just like the TcpClient, the TcpListener also encapsulates a private Socket object, m_ServerSocket, available only to derived classes.

The following tables show the important properties and methods:

Public Properties

Name	Type	Description
LocalEndpoint	IPEndpoint	This property returns an IPEndpoint object that contains information about the local network interface and the port number which is being used to listen for incoming client requests

Public Methods

Name	Description
AcceptSocket()	Accepts a pending connection request and returns a Socket object to use to communicate with the client
AcceptTcpClient()	Accepts a pending connection request and returns a TcpClient object to use to communicate with the client
Pending()	Indicates whether there are any connection requests pending
Start()	Causes the TcpListener to start listening for connection requests
Stop()	Closes the listener

Protected Properties

Name	Type	Description
Active	bool	Indicates whether the TcpListener is currently listening for connection requests
Server	Socket	Returns the underlying Socket object used by the listener to listen for connection requests

Instantiating of TcpListener Class

The TcpListener constructor has three overloads:

```
public TcpListener(int port);
public TcpListener(IPEndPoint endPoint);
public TcpListener(IPAddress ipAddr, int port);
```

The first simply specifies which port we want to listen on. The IP address in this case is IPAddress.Any, which provides an address that the server should listen to for a client's activity on all network interfaces. This field is equivalent to 0.0.0.0:

```
int port = 11000;
TcpListener newListener = new TcpListener(port);
```

The second takes an `IPEndPoint` object that specifies the IP address and port we want to listen on:

```
IPAddress ipAddr = IPAddress.Parse("127.0.0.1");
IPEndPoint endPoint = new IPEndPoint(ipAddr, 11000);
TcpListener newListener = new TcpListener(endPoint);
```

The last overload takes an `IPAddress` object and a port number:

```
IPAddress ipAddr = IPAddress.Parse("127.0.0.1");
int port = 11000;
TcpListener newListener = new TcpListener(ipAddr, port);
```

Listening for Clients

The next step after creating a socket is to start listening for client requests. The `TcpListener` class has a `Start()` method that does two things. First, it actually binds a socket using the IP address and port provided as arguments in the `TcpListener` constructor. Next, it begins listening for client connections by calling the `Listen()` method on the underlying `Socket`:

```
TcpListener newListener = new TcpListener(ipAddr, port);
newListener.Start();
```

Once we've started listening to the socket, we can check whether there already are connections in the queue by calling the `Pending()` method. This allows us to check for any awaiting clients before the accept method is called, which will then block the running thread:

```
...
if (newListener.Pending())
{
    Console.WriteLine("There are connections pending in queue");
}
```

Accepting Connections from a Client

A typical server program uses two sockets, one that is used by the `TcpListener` class and the other that is returned when the listener accepts a client's connection and is used to communicate individually with that client. The `AcceptSocket()` or the simpler `AcceptTcpClient()` method can be used to accept any request that is currently pending in the queue. These methods return a `Socket` or `TcpClient` respectively to accept client requests.

```
Socket sAccepted = newListener.AcceptSocket();
```

```
TcpClient sAccepted = newListener.AcceptTcpClient();
```

Sending and Receiving Messages

The actual communication between the client and the server socket can be performed using the `Socket`'s `Send()` and `Receive()` methods or by writing to/reading from the `NetworkStream`, depending on the type of socket created when accepting the connection. This topic was covered in detail earlier in the section on the `TcpClient` class, so we will skip the code here.

Stopping the Server

After communicating with the client, the last step is to stop the listening socket. Calling the `Stop()` method of the `TcpListener` class performs this step:

```
newListener.Stop();
```

A Multithreaded Client-Server Application

In the following section, we'll build a simple multithreaded echo server that can serve multiple echo clients using threads. Before going into the code, we will have a short introduction to multithreading by presenting a small example on how to create and run a thread. As the topic is not directly connected with network programming, we won't attempt to cover multithreaded programming in detail, and we will assume familiarity with the basic concepts of threading.

The multithreading support in .NET is provided through the `System.Threading` namespace. The `Thread` class in this namespace represents an individual thread. The thread needs an entry point for running an alternative flow of code. This entry point is the method where the thread will begin execution. Naturally enough, this method is represented by a delegate, and specifically the `ThreadStart` delegate. Therefore, before creating an instance of the `Thread` class, we need to create an instance of the `ThreadStart` delegate, specifying the method name in the constructor.

After specifying the method using the delegate in the `Thread` constructor, the next step is to inform the operating system about the change in the thread state. The `Start()` method of the `Thread` class notifies the operating system that the thread is changing its state to running:

```
// Threading.cs
using System;
using System.Threading;

public class MultiThread
{
    public static void runThread()
    {
        Console.WriteLine("Thread is running");
    }

    public static void Main(string [] arg)
    {
        // The ThreadStart specifying the delegate function
        ThreadStart threadMethod = new ThreadStart(runThread);

        // Create a thread instance with the ThreadStart delegate
        Thread newThread = new Thread(threadMethod);
        Console.WriteLine("Starting Thread");

        // Start the thread, which calls the runThread method in a separate thread
        newThread.Start();
    }
}
```

This is all that we need to know about using threads in a basic multithreaded server, although you will need a more intensive usage of the `Thread` class to build a more robust server application, with support for synchronization techniques such as locking, and advanced thread manipulation such as thread pooling.

The client is a simple application, much as we saw in the previous section on the `TcpClient` class, so we don't need to look at it in too much detail here:

```
using System;
using System.Net;
using System.IO;
using System.Net.Sockets;
using System.Text;

public class EchoClient
{
    const int ECHO_PORT = 8080;

    public static void Main(string [] arg)
    {
        Console.Write("Your UserName:");
        string userName = Console.ReadLine();
        Console.WriteLine("-----Logged In----->");

        try
        {
            // Create a connection with the ChatServer
            TcpClient eClient = new TcpClient("127.0.0.1", ECHO_PORT);

            // Create the stream classes
            StreamReader readerStream = new StreamReader(eClient.GetStream());
            NetworkStream writerStream = eClient.GetStream();

            string dataToSend;

            dataToSend = userName;
            dataToSend += "\r\n";

            // Send username to the server
            byte[] data = Encoding.ASCII.GetBytes(dataToSend);

            writerStream.Write(data,0,data.Length);

            while(true)
            {
                Console.Write(userName + ":");

                // Read line from server
                dataToSend = Console.ReadLine();
                dataToSend += "\r\n";

                data = Encoding.ASCII.GetBytes(dataToSend);
                writerStream.Write(data, 0, data.Length);
```

```
            // If QUIT is sent, then quit application
            if (dataToSend.IndexOf("QUIT") > -1)
                break;

            string returnData;

            // Receive response from server
            returnData = readerStream.ReadLine();

            Console.WriteLine("Server: " + returnData);
        }

        // Close TcpClient
        eClient.Close();
    }
    catch(Exception exp)
    {
        Console.WriteLine("Exception: " + exp);
    }
}
}
```

The server application obviously has a change from the one we saw in the last chapter – it uses multiple threads for serving more than one client simultaneously. The following diagram shows the flow of the server application:

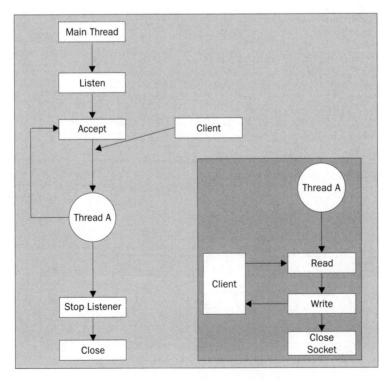

We start as usual by creating an instance of the `TcpListener` class and specifying the port number to bind the socket to. The listener socket then starts listening and accepting client requests. The change in the code appears when the listener accepts a client's request. In a single-user server model, which only serves a single client at a time, a `Stream` object is built to communicate directly with the client. After wrapping up the existing client, the server would be able to start listening for a new client. All the tasks performed in this type of application are executed on a single thread. In a multithreaded application, as soon as the listener accepts a client's socket, it starts a new thread, which is responsible for negotiating with the client. The main server thread continues to listen for further requests.

The method that executes on the secondary thread is implemented in a different class, called `ClientHandler`. We use a member variable to pass data between the main thread and this secondary thread. When the listener accepts a `TcpClient`, we instantiate a new object of the `ClientHandler` class, and assign the `TcpClient` object to its public field. We then execute the `RunClient()` method on a new thread. Since this is a member of the `ClientHandler` class, it can access the `TcpClient` object that we set from the main thread.

The `RunClient()` method in the `ClientHandler` class is completely responsible for negotiating with a single client. It performs the procedure of creating streams and then reading and writing messages to the socket.

This is the complete code listing for the server application:

```
// MEchoServer.cs

using System;
using System.Net;
using System.Net.Sockets;
using System.IO;
using System.Threading;
using System.Collections;
using System.Text;

public class ClientHandler
{
    public TcpClient clientSocket;

    public void RunClient()
    {
        // Create the stream classes
        StreamReader readerStream = new StreamReader(clientSocket.GetStream());
        NetworkStream writerStream = clientSocket.GetStream();

        string returnData = readerStream.ReadLine();
        string userName = returnData;

        Console.WriteLine("Welcome " + userName + " to the Server");

        while (true)
        {
            returnData = readerStream.ReadLine();

            if (returnData.IndexOf("QUIT") > -1)
            {
                Console.WriteLine("Bye Bye " + userName);
```

```
                break;
            }

            Console.WriteLine(userName + ": " + returnData);
            returnData += "\r\n";

            byte[] dataWrite = Encoding.ASCII.GetBytes(returnData);
            writerStream.Write(dataWrite,0,dataWrite.Length);
        }

        clientSocket.Close();
    }
}

public class EchoServer
{
    const int ECHO_PORT = 8080;
    public static int nClients = 0;

    public static void Main(string [] arg)
    {
        try
        {
            // Bind the server to the local port
            TcpListener clientListener = new TcpListener(ECHO_PORT);

            // Start to listen
            clientListener.Start();

            Console.WriteLine("Waiting for connections...");

            while (true)
            {
                // Accept the connection
                TcpClient client = clientListener.AcceptTcpClient();

                ClientHandler cHandler = new ClientHandler();

                // Pass value to the ClientHandler object
                cHandler.clientSocket = client;

                // Create a new thread for the client
                Thread clientThread = new Thread(new ThreadStart(cHandler.RunClient));
                clientThread.Start();
            }

            clientListener.Stop();
        }
        catch(Exception exp)
        {
            Console.WriteLine("Exception: " + exp);
        }
    }
}
```

You can test the application by running the server first and then running multiple instances of the client and logging on with different names. Although this is the simplest of servers, just built for demonstration purposes, it can be used as a framework for building a more robust server application.

.NET Remoting

Operating systems typically provide some level of protection for each application from the effects of other applications. These are necessary to save one application from the effects of failure of another application. Microsoft Windows followed this approach by implementing processes for each application. Each application is loaded in a separate process space. The code and memory running in a process could not access another code running in a different process, although there are well-defined methods regulated by the Operating System to achieve this. In the .NET Framework, Microsoft introduced the concept of **application domains**.

Application Domains

Application domains (AppDomains) are the units that the .NET Framework uses to provide isolation between two different applications. It is possible to run multiple application domains in a single process. This AppDomain-based isolation provides several overall advantages, specifically for a server-side application. The existence of different AppDomains within a single process means that if any piece of code in an AppDomain malfunctions for any reason, it won't harm the other AppDomains in the same process. We can also stop a piece of code included in an AppDomain. However, the most important factor is that the code running in an AppDomain cannot access another code in a different AppDomain. The process that is used to provide communication between different objects in different AppDomains is called **.NET Remoting**.

The Microsoft .NET Remoting framework can be used to enable communications between two different applications. These applications can be on the same computer, on a single LAN, on the Internet, or in any other geographically located area connected with some protocol.

One of the advantages of .NET Remoting comes from the fact that, unlike the proprietary protocols employed by Microsoft DCOM and Java RMI, Remoting is built on accepted industry standards, such as Simple Object Access Protocol (SOAP), HTTP, and TCP. This makes it possible for different applications on the Internet to communicate in the same way as if they were making the connection over a private network.

However, while Remoting *can* use the SOAP and HTTP protocols, it doesn't have to. In fact, it's probably worth thinking twice if you're using SOAP with Remoting, as you lose some of the performance benefits of Remoting over ASP.NET web services. If you're using Remoting rather than web services, efficiency is probably a significant factor, and for best performance use binary encoding with the TCP channel.

A complete, in-depth description of Microsoft .NET Remoting is outside the scope of this book. We'll cover the important concepts in building a Remoting application with a sample which shows you how to build your own application based on the Microsoft .NET Remoting Framework.

How Remoting Works

In order to use the Remoting framework, the hosting application must first be loaded, and we must register a channel and port to listen to connections. The client also needs to register the same channel. We'll discuss channels in more detail in the next section, but, for the time being, think of a channel as a transport medium between the server and the client. Channels use network protocols like TCP or HTTP to send data from one object to another. After the client has registered the channel, it creates a new instance of the remote class. If the client succeeds in instantiating a remote object, it then receives a reference to the server object, through which it can call methods on the remote object, as if it were part of the client process. The remoting system uses a proxy to implement this. When the client creates an instance of the remote object, the Remoting framework intercepts the call and creates a proxy object with the same public interface as the real object, and returns this proxy object to the client. The client then makes method calls on this proxy. These calls are intercepted by the Remoting framework, and routed to the server process. The server process then instantiates the object, calls the method, and sends the return value to the client application via the client proxy:

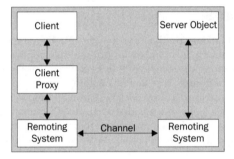

Channels

Channels are used to transport messages to and from the remote objects. When a client calls a method on the server object, the parameters and other details for the method are packed inside a message object and transported through the channel to the remote object. A client can select any channel type that is registered on the server to be used as the transport medium. This allows developers to choose the best channel for their needs. Although there are a couple of built-in transport channel types, it's possible to extend those, or even to create an altogether new channel type to be used in specialized environments or scenarios. The results are returned from the server in a similar way.

Channel Sinks

Channels route each message through a series of channel sinks. Each sink changes or filters the message, and then passes it on to the next sink in the chain, to the receiving application, or to the channel itself. There can be any number of sinks that process the messages sent over the channel, such as a security sink (for encrypting the message), or a logging sink (for tracking the remoting process).

On the client side, the first sink is the formatter sink; this passes the message onto any custom sinks implemented in the sink chain. Finally, the message reaches the transport sink, which writes it to the transport channel.

On the server side, the whole process is reversed. The transport sink retrieves the message from the channel, and forwards it to the channel sink chain. The last sink in the chain is the formatter sink, which routes the message to the Remoting infrastructure, so that it can be passed to the receiving application:

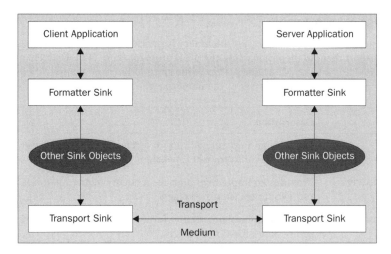

There are two types of channel provided by the .NET Framework:

❑ TcpChannel

❑ HttpChannel

The TcpChannel is discussed in the next section, while Chapter 8 provides a section on the HttpChannel.

Formatters

The formatter sinks are used for encoding and decoding of messages before the channel transports them. There are two formatters provided with the .NET Remoting framework:

1. **The Binary Formatter**. When binary formatting is used for messages, both the client and server require the .NET Framework to process messages. The type system maintains its state when transmission is performed using the binary formatter. Because the binary formatter depends on the .NET Framework, it can preserve the type system information by serializing or deserializing the object.

The binary formatter has better performance than the SOAP formatter because less data is sent over the network, and because it requires less time for serialization and deserialization.

2. **The SOAP XML-based Formatter**. The SOAP formatter follows the SOAP specifications outlined by the W3C (http://www.w3.org/TR/2002/WD-soap12-part1-20020626/). This allows interoperability with other clients or servers. As the SOAP formatter can include different implementations from different languages, it is not possible for it to preserve the type system information.

Because the SOAP formatter is designed for interoperability rather than performance, it generally has worse performance than the binary formatter.

The TCP Transport Channel

The TCP transport channel by default uses the binary formatter to serialize all messages to the binary stream and transport them to the target using the TCP protocol. The .NET Framework provides the `System.Runtime.Remoting.Channels.Tcp` namespace to be used in applications that use the TCP transport channel. There are three classes in the namespace:

Class	Description
TcpChannel	Provides an implementation for a sender-receiver channel that uses the TCP protocol to transmit messages.
TcpClientChannel	Provides an implementation for a client channel that uses the TCP protocol to transmit messages.
TcpServerChannel	Provides an implementation for a server channel that uses the TCP protocol to transmit messages.

The following example shows how to write a simple Remoting application. The client passes a string to the remote object, which echoes back the same string to the client.

There are three steps required to build a remoting application:

1. Create the remote object

2. Create the hosting application for the remote object

3. Create the client application

Creating the Remote Object

The remote object is a simple class instance. The only extension that it needs is that the class must inherit from the `MarshalByRefObject` class. We can convert all our existing classes to remote classes just by deriving them from `MarshalByRefObject`. There can be any number of methods and properties in the class. Here we define a simple class that can be used to instantiate a remote object.

The first step before starting any remoting application is to include all the namespaces required. The following namespaces are used for a TCP transport-based remoting application:

```
// ServerObj.cs

using System.Runtime.Remoting;
using System.Runtime.Remoting.Channels;
using System.Runtime.Remoting.Channels.Tcp;
```

The next step is to define the class for the remote object:

```
// Notice that the class is derived from MarshalByRefObject
public class ServerObj : MarshalByRefObject
{
    public string ServerMethod(string argument)
    {
        Console.WriteLine(argument);
        return argument;
    }
}
```

We must build this class as a DLL, so we use the following command to compile the remote object:

```
csc /target:library /out:ServerObj.dll ServerObj.cs
```

Creating the Hosting Application

After creating the remote object, the next thing to do is to create an application that hosts our remote object on the server. The application that we build here is a simple console-based application (although for production you might need to consider the idea of using Windows Services as a better alternative).

The first step is to include all the necessary using directives in the code as above. The next step is to create and register the TcpChannel. (You should close the server created in the previous section before doing this, because we use Remoting on the same port.)

```
TcpChannel tcpChannel = new TcpChannel(8080);
```

The TcpChannel constructor is used to specify the port number for listening for client connections.

Next, we register the TCP channel:

```
ChannelServices.RegisterChannel(tcpChannel);
```

The ChannelServices class provides static methods for registering channels, getting registered channels, unregistering channels, creating the channel sink chain, dispatching messages to the sink chain, and URL discovery. All the channels that are registered can be accessed through the RegisteredChannels property, which returns an array of IChannel objects. The most important member of this class is the RegisterChannel() method. It performs the registration of a channel with the channel services. It takes a single argument, which is the channel object we created earlier:

```
public static void RegisterChannel(IChannel channelObject);
```

It is important to note here that you cannot register two channels with the same name in the application domain. By default, the names of the HttpChannel and TcpChannel are "http" and "tcp" respectively. If you need to register two channels, then you must change the name of the respective channel by altering the ChannelName property of the channel object.

After creating and registering the channel, the RegisterWellKnownServiceType() method of the RemotingConfiguration class is called to register the class with the Remoting framework:

```
RemotingConfiguration.RegisterWellKnownServiceType(
    typeof(RemoteSample.ServerObj),
    "EchoMessage",
    WellKnownObjectMode.SingleCall);
```

The `RemotingConfiguration` class provides static methods for configuring the remoting options.

The `RegisterWellKnownServiceType()` method takes three parameters that indicate the type of the remoting class, the string to identify the remoting object (that is, its URI), and the object activation mode.

There are two types of activation for remote objects:

❑ **Server Activation**. Server-activated objects are created by the server only when they are needed, for instance when the client invokes the first method on that server. There are two activation modes for server-activated objects, `Singleton` and `SingleCall`. `Singleton` objects have only one instance, regardless of how many clients there are for that object. When an object is specified as `SingleCall`, a new instance is created every time for each client method invocation.

❑ **Client Activation**. Client-activated objects are created on the server when the client calls `new` or `Activator.CreateInstance()`.

In the code sample, we created a server-activated object with `SingleCall` mode.

Finally, we wait for the client to connect with the server by blocking the input stream through `Console.ReadLine()`:

```
Console.ReadLine();
```

The complete sourcecode is provided below for a quick reference:

```
// ServerApp.cs

using System;
using System.Runtime.Remoting;
using System.Runtime.Remoting.Channels;
using System.Runtime.Remoting.Channels.Tcp;

namespace RemoteSample
{
    public class ServerApp
    {
        public static void Main(string [] arg)
        {
            TcpChannel tcpChannel = new TcpChannel(8080);
            ChannelServices.RegisterChannel(tcpChannel);

            RemotingConfiguration.RegisterWellKnownServiceType(
                typeof(RemoteSample.ServerObj),
                "EchoMessage",
```

```
                WellKnownObjectMode.SingleCall);

            Console.WriteLine("Hit <enter> to continue...");
            Console.ReadLine();
        }
    }
}
```

Creating the Client Application

The last step in implementing the remoting sample is to create the client application. As with the server application, the client must also register the TCP channel with the channel services:

```
TcpChannel tcpChannel = new TcpChannel();
ChannelServices.RegisterChannel(tcpChannel);
```

Being a sharp reader, you may have noticed that the server IP address and port number have been omitted. Normally, a client requires two things to connect with the server – the server IP address and the port number. Here we don't specify either of those. You will see in the next step how the Remoting framework overcomes this.

The next step is the most important for the client; here the object is created on the server and a reference to that object is returned to the client:

```
ServerObj obj = (ServerObj)Activator.GetObject(typeof(RemoteSample.ServerObj),
                                "tcp://localhost:8080/EchoMessage");
```

The `Activator` class provides methods to create types of object remotely or locally, or to obtain references to existing remote objects. The `GetObject()` method creates a proxy for a currently running remote server-activated well-known object. The object type and the URL are passed as parameters. Notice the URL here, which is used to define the protocol, the port number, and the IP address for the remote object – all the things required to connect with a remote server that were missing from the `TcpChannel` constructor.

Here, we are trying out the sample on a single PC, so we specified `localhost`, but it can be replaced with any server IP address on which you want to host your remote object.

After creating the proxy and getting the reference to the remote object by means of the proxy, we can call any of the methods declared in our remote object:

```
obj.ServerMethod("Wrox Remoting Sample");
```

The complete client code is as follows:

```
// ClientApp.cs

using System;
using System.Runtime.Remoting;
using System.Runtime.Remoting.Channels;
using System.Runtime.Remoting.Channels.Tcp;
```

```
namespace RemoteSample
{
   public class ClientApp
   {
      public static void Main(string[] arg)
      {
         TcpChannel tcpChannel = new TcpChannel();

         ChannelServices.RegisterChannel(tcpChannel);

         ServerObj obj = (ServerObj)Activator.GetObject(
                           typeof(RemoteSample.ServerObj),
                           "tcp://localhost:8080/EchoMessage");

         Console.WriteLine(obj.ServerMethod("Wrox Remoting Sample"));
      }
   }
}
```

When compiling both the client and server applications, we need to include a reference to the server object DLL, or we will receive an error stating that "The type or namespace name `ServerObj` does not exist in the class". The server is compiled using:

csc /r:ServerObj.dll ServerApp.cs

And the client application using:

csc /r:ServerObj.dll ClientApp.cs

After compiling all the files, you must execute the server application first to start listening for the client request.

Creating a Client-Activated Remote Object

The above example demonstrates the remote instantiation of server-activated objects. For a client-activated object, although the remote object remains the same, there are some changes required in the server and client applications. In the server application, we call the `RegisterActivatedServiceType()` method instead of `RegisterWellknownServiceType()`. The `RegisterActivatedServiceType()` takes a single argument that represents the type of the remote object. The URI in this case is assigned using the `ApplicationName` property of the `RemotingConfiguration` class:

```
using System;
using System.Runtime.Remoting;
using System.Runtime.Remoting.Channels;
using System.Runtime.Remoting.Channels.Tcp;

namespace RemoteSample
{
   public class ServerApp
   {
```

```
       public static void Main(string [] arg)
       {
          TcpChannel tcpChannel = new TcpChannel(8080);
          ChannelServices.RegisterChannel(tcpChannel);

          RemotingConfiguration.ApplicationName = "EchoMessage";
          RemotingConfiguration.RegisterActivatedServiceType(
                                          typeof(RemoteSample.ServerObj));

          Console.WriteLine("Hit <enter> to continue...");
          Console.ReadLine();
       }
    }
  }
```

On the client side, we have two different methods to access the remote objects –
Activator.CreateInstance() and
RemotingConfiguration.RegisterActivatedClientType(). To create an instance of the
remote object using the new keyword, you must first register the object type on the client by calling the
RegisterActivatedClientType() method. Calling CreateInstance() gives us a new instance of
the server object, and requires the URL of the remote application as a parameter. The UrlAttribute
class is used to pass attributes to CreateInstance(). The CreateInstance() method returns an
ObjectHandle object that acts as a wrapper for the remote object; we can call this object's UnWrap()
method to get the remote object itself:

```
using System;
using System.Runtime.Remoting;
using System.Runtime.Remoting.Channels;
using System.Runtime.Remoting.Channels.Tcp;
using System.Runtime.Remoting.Activation;

namespace RemoteSample
{
   public class ClientApp
   {
      public static void Main(string [] arg)
      {
         TcpChannel tcpChannel = new TcpChannel();
         ChannelServices.RegisterChannel(tcpChannel);

         // Method 1
         object[] attrs = {new UrlAttribute("tcp://localhost:8080/EchoMessage")};
         ObjectHandle handle = Activator.CreateInstance("ServerObj",
                                          "RemoteSample.ServerObj", attrs);

         ServerObj obj = (ServerObj)handle.Unwrap();
         Console.WriteLine("Client:" + obj.ServerMethod("Wrox Remoting Sample"));

         // Method 2
         RemotingConfiguration.RegisterActivatedClientType(
            typeof(RemoteSample.ServerObj), "tcp://localhost:8080/EchoMessage");
```

```
            ServerObj obj2 = new ServerObj();
            Console.WriteLine("Client2:" + obj2.ServerMethod(
                                            "Wrox Remoting Sample"));
        }
    }
}
```

Although this sample application does perform all the basic steps involved in .NET Remoting, there is a lot to improve on this; you can see that there is no error checking performed in the code. There is an exception class called `RemotingException` provided specially for the Remoting framework, which can be used to help out with most of the hiccups involved in these types of application. As the TCP channel employs the `Socket` class to connect to the server, a `SocketException` will be thrown if the server is not listening to the port. If you forget to inherit the remote class from `MarshalByRefObject`, the client code will throw a `RemotingException` when calling `GetObject()` to create a proxy for the running remote object. A `RemotingException` is also thrown when you try to register a channel that is already registered. In this case, you can call the `ChannelServices.GetChannel()` method, which will return the channel interface if it is already registered; otherwise `null` is returned.

Summary

In this chapter, we looked into the TCP core architecture, and its data recovery and formation. We then covered client-server applications built using the higher level `TcpClient` and `TcpListener` classes. To demonstrate the power of `TcpClient`, we built a fully functional e-mail client. We also built a multithreaded echo server with the support of the .NET multithreading classes.

Next, we covered the .NET Remoting Framework, and particularly the `TcpChannel` transport channel provided with the .NET Framework. Finally, we demonstrated a simple Remoting application that instantiates an object on the server from a remote client.

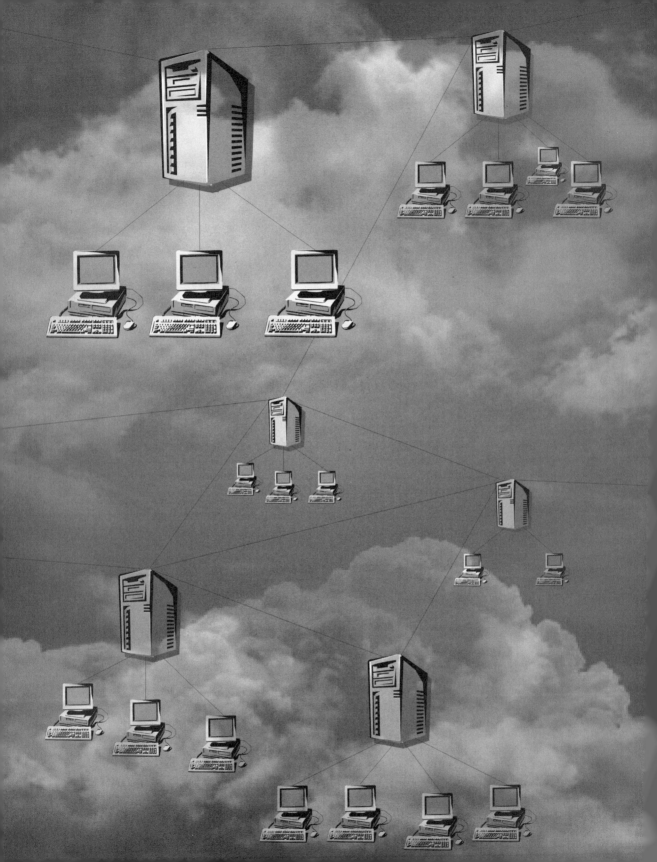

6

UDP

In Chapter 4, we looked at socket programming in .NET, and saw how we can use the `Socket` class to connect to remote hosts using different protocols. In the last chapter, we looked at the `TcpClient` and `TcpListener` classes, which provide a higher-level implementation for connecting over TCP. The Microsoft .NET Framework also provides a special class called `UdpClient` specifically for implementing the User Datagram Protocol (UDP). In this chapter we'll look at the basics of the UDP protocol, and then see how to use the `UdpClient` class.

In the previous chapter, we saw the "three-phase handshake" that TCP uses to ensure that data is transmitted correctly. While this does make TCP far more reliable, it also adds a lot of overhead. UDP has none of this overhead, so it's much faster. This makes it well suited for multi-media transmissions such as video streams, where the precise order that packets arrive in may not be critical.

In fact, UDP is an exceptionally simple protocol – the specification (RFC 768) is only three pages long! (This compares to 85 pages for the TCP specification, RFC 793.)

In this chapter we'll look at:

- ❑ A basic introduction to UDP
- ❑ The advantages and disadvantages of the UDP protocol
- ❑ Implementation of the UDP protocol in .NET using the `UdpClient` class
- ❑ Higher-level UDP-based protocols

Overview of the UDP Protocol

The User Datagram Protocol (UDP) is a simple, connection-less, datagram-oriented protocol and provides a fast but not necessarily reliable transport service. It supports and is often used for one-to-many communications, using broadcast or multicast IP datagrams.

Internet Protocol (IP) is the basic protocol of the Internet. Transmission Control Protocol (TCP) and UDP are both transport-level protocols built on top of the underlying IP protocol. The following figure shows how the OSI model maps to the TCP/IP architecture and the TCP/IP protocol suite:

	OSI 7 Layers	TCP/IP Protocol	TCP/IP Protocol Stack				
7	Application	Application	HTTP	FTP	SMTP	RIP	DNS
6	Presentation						
5	Session						
4	Transport	Transport	TCP			UDP	
3	Network	Internet	ICMP		IP		IGMP
2	Data Link	Network	Ethernet, ATM, Frame Relay, etc.				
1	Physical						

TCP/IP is a suite of protocols, also known as the Internet Protocol Suite, which consists of four layers. Remember TCP/IP is not a single protocol but actually a family or suite of protocols, and consists of other low-level protocols such as IP, TCP, and – the subject of this chapter – **UDP**. UDP is situated in the transport layer on top of IP (a network-layer protocol). The transport layer provides communications between networks through gateways. It uses IP addresses to send packets of data across the Internet or over a network through various device drivers.

TCP and UDP are part of the TCP/IP suite; each has its own advantages and disadvantages, which we will discuss later in this chapter.

Some UDP Terminology

Before we examine how UDP works, there is some basic terminology that we need to be familiar with. In the following section, we'll briefly define some of the major terms related to UDP.

Packets

In data communication, a packet is a sequence of binary digits, representing data and control signals, which is transmitted and switched across the host. Within the packet, this information is arranged in a specific format.

Datagrams

A datagram is a self-contained, independent packet of data, carrying sufficient data to be routed from source to destination without further information, so no exchanges between the source and destination computers and the transporting network are required.

MTU

MTU stands for **Maximum Transmission Unit**. The MTU is a characteristic of the link layer that describes the maximum number of bytes of data that can be transferred in a single packet. In other words, the MTU is the largest packet that a given network medium can carry. Ethernet, for example, has a fixed MTU of 1,500 bytes. In UDP, if the size of a datagram is larger than the MTU, IP performs fragmentation, breaking the datagram up into smaller pieces (fragments), so that each fragment is smaller than the MTU.

Ports

UDP uses ports to map incoming data to a particular process running on a computer. UDP routes the packet at the appropriate location using the port number specified in the UDP header of the datagram. Ports are represented by 16-bit numbers, and therefore range from 0 to 65,535. Ports are also referred to as the endpoints of logical connections, and are divided into three categories:

❑ **Well-Known Ports** – From 0 to 1,023

❑ **Registered Ports** – From 1,024 to 49,151

❑ **Dynamic/Private Ports** – 49,152 to 65,535

Note that UDP ports can receive more than one message at a time. In some cases, TCP and UDP services may use the same port numbers, such as port 7 (Echo) or port 23 (Telnet).

UDP has the following well-known ports:

UDP Port Number	Description
15	NETSTAT – Network Status
53	DNS – Domain Name Server
69	TFTP – Trivial File Transfer Protocol
137	NetBIOS Name Service
138	NetBIOS Datagram Service
161	SNMP

The list of UDP and TCP Ports is maintained by IANA (Internet Assigned Numbers Authority). For more information about the associated ports, see http://www.iana.org/assignments/port-numbers.

IP Addresses

The IP datagram consists of 32-bit source and destination IP addresses. The destination IP address specifies the endpoint for the UDP datagram, whereas the source IP address is used to check who sent the message. At the destination, packets are filtered, and those from restricted source IP addresses are discarded, without notifying the sender.

A unicast IP address uniquely identifies a host in a network, whereas a multicast IP address identifies a particular group of hosts in a network. Broadcast IP addresses are received and processed by all the hosts in the local network or in a particular subnet.

IP addresses are divided into five classes, as shown in the table below:

IP class	IP address range	Use
Class A	0.0.0.0 to 127.255.255.255	Networks with a large number of hosts, such as large international organizations
Class B	128.0.0.0 to 191.255.255.255	Networks with a medium number of hosts, such as universities
Class C	192.0.0.0 to 223.255.255.255	Networks with a smaller number of hosts, such as small businesses
Class D	224.0.0.0 to 239.255.255.255	Used for multicast networks, for example online news channels
Class E	240.0.0.0 to 247.255.255.255	Reserved for experimental purposes

A few IP addresses are restricted for special uses:

IP address	Use
0.0.0.0	Default IP address of host (listen on all available interfaces)
127.0.0.1	Local loopback IP address
255.255.255.255	Broadcast IP address for entire local network

TTL

The *time-to-live* or TTL value allows us to set an upper limit of routers through which a datagram can pass. The TTL value prevents packets from getting caught in routing loops forever. The TTL is initialized by the sender, and the value is decremented by every router that handles the datagram. When the TTL reaches zero, the datagram is discarded.

Multicasting

Multicasting is an open, standards-based method for simultaneously distributing identical information to multiple users. Multicasting is a major feature of the UDP protocol, and is not possible with the TCP protocol. Multicasting allows us to achieve one-to-many communication, for example sending news or mail to multiple recipients, Internet radio, or on-line demo programs. Multicasting is less bandwidth-intensive than broadcasting, because data for multiple users is sent at once:

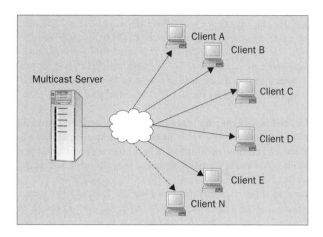

We'll look at multicasting in detail in the next chapter.

How UDP Works

When a UDP-based application sends data to another networked host, UDP adds an eight-byte header containing the destination and source port number, along with the total length of the data and a checksum. IP adds its own header on top of the UDP datagram to form an IP datagram:

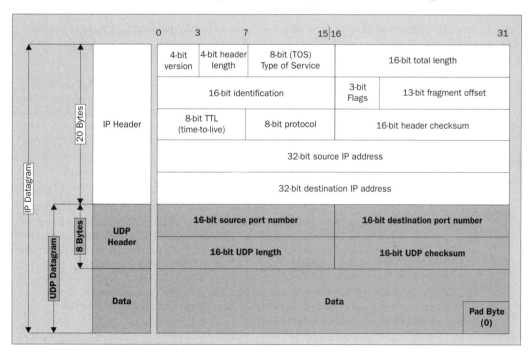

In the previous figure, the total length of the UDP header is specified as eight bytes. Theoretically, the maximum size of an IP datagram is 65,535 bytes. Allowing for an IP header of 20 bytes and a UDP header of 8 bytes, the maximum size for user data is 65,507 bytes. However, most programs use a smaller size than this maximum value. For example, the default size for most applications is around 8,192 bytes because that is the amount of user data that the Network File System (NFS) reads and writes by default. You can set the size of receive and send buffers.

The checksum is used to check whether the data has properly arrived at the destination without being corrupted. The checksum covers both the UDP header and data. A pad byte is used if the checksum of the datagram is odd. If the checksum transmitted is zero, the receiver detects a checksum error and the datagram is discarded. The checksum is optional, but it is recommended always to keep it enabled.

Note that the checksum can't be enabled or disabled using the UdpClient class. To do this, we need to use the low-level Socket class that we looked at in Chapter 4, and set the NoChecksum option by calling its SetSocketOption() method.

In the next step, the IP layer adds 20 bytes of header that include the TTL, the source and destination IP addresses, along with other information. This is known as IP encapsulation.

As we mentioned above, the maximum size of a packet is 65,507 bytes. If the size of the packet exceeds the default size or the maximum size of the MTU, the IP layer breaks it into segments. These segments are called **fragments**, and the process of breaking the data into segments is known as **fragmentation**. The IP header contains all the information about the fragments.

When the sender application 'throws' a datagram onto the network, the datagram is routed to the destination IP address specified in the IP header. While passing through the router, the TTL (time-to-live) value in the IP header is decreased by one.

When the datagram arrives at the correct destination and port, the IP layer checks whether the datagram is fragmented or not from the IP header. If it is fragmented, the datagram is reassembled using the information available in the header. Finally, the application layer retrieves the filtered data by removing the header.

Disadvantages of UDP

Compared to TCP, UDP has the following disadvantages:

❑ **Lack of handshaking signals**. Before sending a segment, UDP does not use handshaking signals between sending and receiving the transport layer. The sender therefore has no way of knowing whether the datagram reaches the end system. As a result, UDP cannot guarantee that the data will actually be delivered at the destination (for example, in cases where the end system is off or the network is down).

In contrast, TCP is a connection-oriented service and provides communication between a networked host using packets. TCP uses handshaking signals to check whether the transportation of data was successful.

❑ **Use of sessions**. To make TCP connection-oriented, sessions are maintained between hosts. TCP uses session IDs to keep track of connections between two hosts. UDP doesn't have any support for sessions due to its connection-less nature.

❑ **Reliability**. UDP does not guarantee that only one copy of the data will be delivered to the destination. To send large amounts of data to the end system, UDP breaks it into small segments. UDP does not guarantee that these segments will be delivered to the destination in the same order as they were created at the source. In contrast, TCP uses sequence numbers along with port numbers and frequent acknowledgement packets, which guarantee sequenced delivery of data.

❑ **Security**. TCP is more secure than UDP. In many organizations, firewalls and routers do not allow UDP packets. This is because hackers can use UDP ports, as explicit connections aren't required.

❑ **Flow control**. UDP doesn't have flow control; as a result, a poorly designed UDP application can tie up a big chunk of network bandwidth.

Advantages of UDP

❑ **No connection establishment**. UDP is a connection-less protocol, so the overhead of making connections can be avoided. As UDP does not use any handshaking signals, the delay in making connections can be avoided. This is why DNS prefers UDP over TCP – DNS would be much slower if it ran over TCP.

❑ **Speed**. UDP is fast compared to TCP. Because of this, many applications prefer UDP over TCP. The features that make TCP more robust than UDP (such as handshaking signals) also make it slower.

❑ **Topology support**. UDP supports both one-to-one and one-to-many connections, whereas TCP supports only one-to-one communication.

❑ **Overheads**. TCP has higher overhead requirements; UDP has comparatively low overhead requirements. TCP uses substantially more OS resources than UDP does, and as a result UDP is widely used in environments where servers handle many simultaneous clients.

❑ **Header size**. UDP has only eight-byte headers for every segment, whereas TCP has 20-byte headers, making UDP less consuming of network bandwidth.

The following table summarizes the differences between TCP and UDP:

Characteristics	UDP	TCP
Connection-oriented	N	Y
Use of session	N	Y
Reliability	N	Y
Acknowledgement	N	Y
Sequencing	N	Y
Flow control	N	Y
Secure	Less	More

Table continued on following page

Characteristics	UDP	TCP
Data checksum	Optionally	Y
Overhead	Less	More
Speed	Fast	Slower
Topology	One-to-one	One-to-one
	One-to-many	
Header	8 bytes	20 bytes

When to Use UDP

Many applications on the Internet use UDP. UDP is known as a "best effort service" protocol. Looking at the advantages and disadvantages of UDP we can conclude that UDP is beneficial:

❏   For broadcasting or multicasting purposes where the application wants to communicate with multiple hosts

❏   Where the datagram size is small and the sequence of fragments is not important

❏   Where connection setup is not required

❏   When the application doesn't want to send important bulk data (as UDP has no flow control)

❏   If retransmission of packets is not required

❏   Where low overhead on the operating system is required

❏   Where network bandwidth is crucial

UDP in .NET

In .NET, the UDP protocol can be implemented using:

❏   The UdpClient class

❏   The Socket class

❏   The Winsock control

❏   The Winsock unmanaged API

The last two of these rely on COM interoperability and P/Invoke respectively, and are not covered in this book. .NET's System.Net.Sockets namespace is essentially a wrapper for the Winsock API, so it is preferable to use the .NET classes. The Winsock control may be a good option for former Visual Basic programmers who want to keep their programming as visual as possible, but it adds the overhead of COM interop, so is better avoided.

We looked at using the Socket class in Chapter 4. Note that this class gives us access to more options than the higher-level UdpClient class (such as the ability to disable the checksum we mentioned earlier), but it does make the code slightly more complex. However, as we'll see shortly, the UdpClient class is built on top of the Socket class, and by inheriting from UdpClient, we can access the underlying Socket.

Therefore, in this chapter we will look at the UDP implementation using the UdpClient class. Before implementing UdpClient, the user must be familiar with some of the other primary classes in .NET, and understand the basics of working with sockets in .NET. These topics were covered in Chapters 3 and 4.

The .NET classes for working with UDP reside in the System.Net.Sockets namespace. This namespace provides managed classes for TCP, UDP, and generic sockets programming:

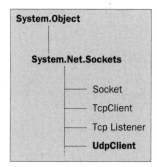

The UdpClient Class

The Microsoft .NET Framework provides the UdpClient class for implementing the UDP protocol on a network. As with the TcpClient and TcpListener classes, this class is built upon the Socket class but hides unnecessary members that aren't required for implementing a UDP-based application.

Using UdpClient is quite simple. First, create an instance of UdpClient. Next, connect to the remote host by calling its Connect() method. These two steps can be achieved in one line of code by specifying the remote IP address and remote port number in the UdpClient's constructor. We said earlier that UDP is a connection-less protocol; so, you might be wondering, why do we need to connect? In fact, the Connect() method does not actually establish a connection to the remote host prior to sending and receiving data. When you send a datagram, the destination needs to be known; the specified IP address and port number serve this purpose.

The third step is to send or receive the data using the Send() or Receive() method. Finally, the Close() method closes the UDP connection. All these steps are illustrated in the following figure:

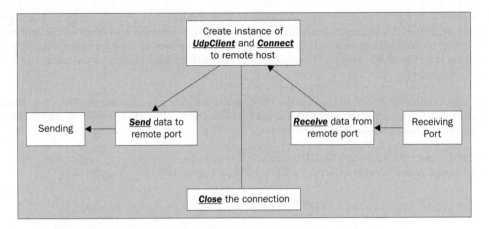

UdpClient Methods and Properties

The diagram below shows methods and properties of the UdpClient class. The methods and properties inherited from System.Object will not be discussed here. We'll look at these in detail as we discuss using the UdpClient class:

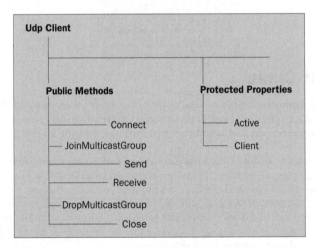

Instantiating a UdpClient

A UdpClient instance can be created in a number of different ways, depending on the parameters passed in. How we use the UdpClient object depends on how it was created.

The simplest way to create a UdpClient instance is to use the default constructor (passing in no parameters). When we use an instance created in this way, we have to either call the Connect() method to establish a connection or specify the connection information when we send data.

```
// Instantiate UdpClient using the default constructor
UdpClient udpClient = new UdpClient();
```

If we use this constructor, an arbitrary free port number will be chosen, and the IP address 0.0.0.0 will be used.

We can also create a UdpClient instance specifying a port number as a parameter. In this case, the UdpClient will listen on all local interfaces (that is, it will use the IP address 0.0.0.0). If the port number is not within the range specified by the MinPort and MaxPort fields of the IPEndPoint class, an ArgumentOutOfRangeException (derived from ArgumentException) is thrown. If the port is already in use, a SocketException will be thrown.

```
// Instantiate UdpClient using port number
try
{
    UdpClient udpClient = new UdpClient(5001);
}
catch (ArgumentOutOfRangeException e)
{
    Console.WriteLine("Invalid port number");
}
catch (SocketException e)
{
    Console.WriteLine("Port is already in use");
}
```

The next way is to use an IPEndPoint instance representing the local IP address and port number that we want to use for the connection. The first step here is to instantiate the IPEndPoint; the IPEndPoint instance can be created using a long IP address or an IPAddress object. The IP address must be one of the interfaces of the local machine, or a SocketException will be thrown with the error "The requested address is not valid in its context".

If a null instance of IPEndPoint is passed into the constructor, an ArgumentNullException is thrown.

```
// Creates an instance of IPEndPoint.
IPAddress ipAddress = IPAddress.Parse("127.0.0.1");
IPEndPoint ipLocalEndPoint = new IPEndPoint(ipAddress, 5001);
try
{
    // Use IPEndPoint instance to create the UdpClient instance
    UdpClient udpClient = new UdpClient(ipLocalEndPoint);
}
catch (Exception e)
{
    Console.WriteLine(e.ToString());
}
```

The final way is to pass both a host name and a port number into the constructor. In this case, the constructor is initialized using the host name and port number of the remote host. This allows us to eliminate the step of calling the Connect() method, as this method is called from within this constructor (as you can see if you use ILDasm to look at the IL code for this constructor).

```
// Instantiate UdpClient using remote host name and a port number.
try
{
    UdpClient udpClient = new UdpClient("remoteHostName", 5001);
}
catch (Exception e)
{
    Console.WriteLine(e.ToString());
}
```

Specifying the Connection Information

The second step, once we've created a `UdpClient` object, is to provide the connection information that is used if we want to send any data to a remote host. Remember that UDP is a connection-less protocol, so this information isn't needed if we only want to receive data – it's only used to indicate where we want to send data to.

This information can be specified in any of three places – we can specify it in the `UdpClient` constructor, as we've just seen; we can call the `UdpClient`'s `Connect()` method explicitly; or we can include it in our call to the `Send()` method, when we actually send the data.

The `Connect()` method has three overloads:

❑   Using an `IPEndPoint` instance

❑   Establishing a connection using the IP address and the port number of the remote host

❑   Using a DNS or machine name and the port number of the remote host

Using an IPEndPoint Object

The first overload for `Connect()` uses an instance of the `IPEndPoint` class to connect to the remote host, so you should create an `IPEndPoint` instance before calling the `Connect()` method. If any error occurs while connecting, a `SocketException` will be thrown.

```
// Create instance of UdpClient
UdpClient udpClient = new UdpClient();

// Get the IP address of the remote host
IPAddress ipAddress = IPAddress.Parse("224.56.0.1");

// Create instance of IPEndPoint using IPAddress and port number
IPEndPoint ipEndPoint = new IPEndPoint(ipAddress, 1234);

try
{
    // Connect using this IPEndPoint instance
    udpClient.Connect(ipEndPoint);
}
catch (Exception e)
{
    Console.WriteLine("Error while connecting: " + e.ToString());
}
```

Using an IPAddress and Port Number

The second overload takes an IPAddress object and the port number of the remote host. If you know the remote IP address and the remote UDP port, you can make the connection to the remote UDP host as shown in the example below:

```
// Create instance of UdpClient
UdpClient udpClient = new UdpClient();

// Get the IP address of remote host
IPAddress ipAddress = IPAddress.Parse("224.56.0.1");

try
{
    //Connect using created IPAddress instance and remote port
    udpClient.Connect(ipAddress, 1234);
}
catch (Exception e )
{
    Console.WriteLine("Error while connecting: " + e.ToString());
}
```

Using the Hostname and Port Number

The final overload uses the DNS or machine name and the port number of the remote host. This method is quite easy, as you do not need to create an IPAddress or IPEndPoint instance:

```
// Create instance of UdpClient
UdpClient udpClient = new UdpClient();

try
{
    udpClient.Connect("remoteMachineName", 1234);
}
catch (Exception e)
{
    Console.WriteLine("Error while connecting: " + e.ToString());
}
```

Sending Data Using the UdpClient

Once we've got a UdpClient instance and (optionally) supplied the connection details, we can start to send data. Unsurprisingly, we do this by calling the Send() method, which is used to send a datagram from the client to the remote host. One important point about the UDP protocol is that it does not receive any type of acknowledgement after sending data to a remote host. Like the Connect() method, Send() has several overloads. Send() returns the length of the data, which can be used to check whether the data was sent properly.

The basic procedure for sending data with the UdpClient class is shown in the following diagram:

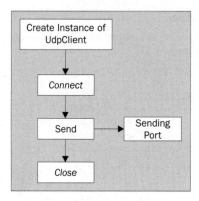

The four steps for sending data using UDP are:

1. Create a `UdpClient` instance

2. Connect to the remote host (optional)

3. Send the data

4. Close the connection

Before we look at the `Send()` method in detail, let's take a quick look at an example that shows this general process:

```
// Example: Sending Data.
private static void Send(string datagram)
{
    // Remote IP address
    IPAddress remoteAddress = IPAddress.Parse("127.0.0.1");

    // Port we want to connect to
    int remotePort = 5001;

    // ** STEP 1 ** Create the UdpClient instance
    UdpClient sender = new UdpClient();

    try
    {
        // ** STEP 2 ** Connect to remote host
        sender.Connect(remoteAddress, remotePort);

        Console.WriteLine("Sending datagram: {0}", datagram);
        byte[] bytes = Encoding.ASCII.GetBytes(datagram);

        // ** STEP 3 ** Send data to connected host
        sender.Send(bytes, bytes.Length);
```

```
        // ** STEP 4 ** Close the connection
        sender.Close();
    }
    catch (Exception e)
    {
        Console.WriteLine(e.ToString());
    }
}
```

The Send() Method

Although this example shows the general approach, the Send() method can be used in various ways, depending on how the UdpClient was connected to the remote port, and how the UdpClient instance was created. If no connection information has been specified before we call Send(), we need to include this information within the call.

The first overload takes three parameters: the data as an array of bytes, the length of the data as an int, and an IPEndPoint object. To use this overload of Send(), first create an IPEndPoint instance by specifying the end point we want to connect to – the remote IP address and port number. We then pass this IPEndPoint object into the Send() method. Note that we cannot call this overload if we called the Connect() method manually, or if we supplied connection information in the UdpClient constructor. The example below illustrates how to send data using an IPEndPoint:

```
// Create udpClient instance. Note how instance is created.
UdpClient udpClient = new UdpClient();

// Get the remote IPAddress
IPAddress ipAddress = IPAddress.Parse("148.182.27.1");

// Create instance of IPEndPoint by passing IP address and remote port
IPEndPoint ipEndPoint = new IPEndPoint(ipAddress, 5005);

// Create data in Byte[] format
byte[] sendBytes = Encoding.ASCII.GetBytes("Wrox UDP Send Example");
try
{
    // Send data using the IPEndPoint instance.
    udpClient.Send(sendBytes, sendBytes.Length, ipEndPoint);
}
catch (Exception e)
{
    Console.WriteLine("Error: " + e.ToString());
}
```

The second overload allows us to specify the hostname and port number of the remote endpoint, as well as the actual data and its length in bytes. Again, Send() assumes that the connection has not been established between the client and the remote host, so this overload cannot be called if we have already called the Connect() method, or if we specified connection information in the UdpClient constructor.

```
// Create udpClient instance. Note how instance is created.
UdpClient udpClient = new UdpClient();
```

```
   // Create data in byte[] format
   byte[] sendBytes = Encoding.ASCII.GetBytes("Wrox UDP Send Example");
   try
   {
      // Send data by specifying remote machine name and remote port
      udpClient.Send(sendBytes, sendBytes.Length, "remoteHostName", 5001);
   }
   catch (Exception e)
   {
      Console.WriteLine("Error: " + e.ToString());
   }
```

The final overload assumes that the UDP client is already connected to the remote host, so it only remains for us to send the data and an `int` representing the data length using the `Send()` method. This is the only overload that can be used in conjunction with the `Connect()` method.

```
   // Create udpClient instance. Note how instance is created.
   UdpClient udpClient = new UdpClient("remoteHostName", 5001);

   // Create data in Byte[] format
   byte[] sendBytes = Encoding.ASCII.GetBytes("WROX UDP Send Example");
   try
   {
      // Send data
      udpClient.Send(sendBytes, sendBytes.Length);
   }
   catch (Exception e)
   {
      Console.WriteLine("Error: " + e.ToString());
   }
```

Receiving Data Using the UdpClient

To receive data from a remote host via UDP, we naturally enough call the `Receive()` method. This method takes one reference parameter, an instance of `IPEndPoint`, and returns the received data as a `byte` array. It is generally advised to execute this method on a separate thread, since this method polls the underlying socket for incoming datagrams, and blocks until data is received. If this is run on the main thread, your program execution will halt until it receives the datagram packet.

If we've already specified connection information for the `UdpClient`, either in the constructor or by calling `Connect()`, only data from the specified remote endpoint will be accepted and returned to our application; connections from other sources will be rejected. If no connection information has been specified, all incoming connections to the local endpoint will be accepted.

After receiving a datagram, the method returns the sent data as a `byte` array (with the header information stripped off), and populates the `IPEndPoint` reference parameter with information about the remote host that sent the data.

The process for receiving data from a remote host is very similar to that for sending data:

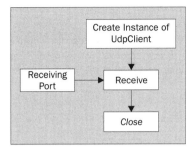

The general steps for creating a UDP receiver application are:

1. Create a UdpClient instance

2. Receive the data

3. Close the UdpClient

All three steps are shown in the following example. Step 2 occurs when the UdpClient wants to receive data:

```
// Example: Receiving Data
private static void Receive()
{
    // ** STEP 1 ** Create a UdpClient for reading incoming data.
    UdpClient receivingUdpClient = new UdpClient(5001);  // Listening on port 5001

    // Create IPEndPoint variable to pass into Receive() as ref parameter
    IPEndPoint RemoteIpEndPoint = null;
    try
    {
        Console.WriteLine("Listening on port 5001...");

        // ** STEP 2 ** Without thread, blocks until the socket finishes
        // receiving the data
        byte[] receiveBytes = receivingUdpClient.Receive(ref RemoteIpEndPoint);

        // Convert the data
        string returnData = Encoding.ASCII.GetString(receiveBytes);

        Console.WriteLine("{0} bytes received from {1}",
                    receiveBytes.Length, RemoteIpEndPoint.ToString());
        Console.WriteLine(returnData);

        // ** STEP 3 ** Close the UdpClient
        receivingUdpClient.Close();
    }
    catch (Exception e)
    {
        Console.WriteLine(e.ToString());
    }
}
```

Closing the Connection

The last step in working with the `UdpClient` is to close the connection. The `Close()` method is used to close an open UDP connection. If any error occurs while closing the connection, a `SocketException` is thrown. Closing a connection is very simple:

```
udpClient.Close();
```

Methods for Multicasting

We're not going to look at multicasting in depth in this chapter, as the next chapter is dedicated solely to that topic. However, for completeness' sake, we will mention here the two methods of the `UdpClient` class that are used for multicasting.

The JoinMulticastGroup() Method

This method is used to join a multicast group. With this method, the `UdpClient` can receive multicast datagrams broadcast to the specified IP address.

Multicasting allows data to be delivered to multiple destinations. Multicasting is a characteristic of the UDP protocol and widely used in the Internet world.

The `JoinMulticastGroup()` method allows us to join a multicast IP address. There are two overloads; the first just takes an `IPAddress` object representing the IP address of the multicast group we want to join. The `UdpClient` will receive any datagrams broadcast to this IP address:

```
// Create instance of UdpClient
UdpClient udpClient = new UdpClient();

// IPAddress with multicast ip
IPAddress multicastIP = IPAddress.Parse ("224.123.32.64");

try
{
    // Join multicast group
    udpClient.JoinMulticastGroup(multicastIP);
}
catch (Exception e)
{
    Console.WriteLine(e.ToString());
}
```

The second overload takes the multicast IP address with the TTL value as an `int`:

```
UdpClient udpClient = new UdpClient();

// Create an IPAddress to use to join
IPAddress multicastIP = Dns.Resolve("mutliCastHost").AddressList[0];

try
{
```

```
        // The life of packet is 30 router hops.
        UdpClient.JoinMulticastGroup(multicastIP, 30);
}
catch (Exception e)
{
    Console.WriteLine(e.ToString());
}
```

> **To send a multicast datagram, specify an IP multicast address within the range**
> `224.0.0.0` **to** `239.255.255.255`**.**

The DropMulticastGroup() Method

This method can be used to disconnect a `UdpClient` from a multicast group. This method takes one parameter – the IP address of the multicast group from which the client is to be dropped:

```
try
{
    // Drop multicast group by sending instance of IPAddress
    udpClient.DropMulticastGroup(multicastIP);
}
catch (Exception e)
{
    Console.WriteLine("Error while using DropMulticastGroup :" +
                    e.ToString());
}
```

Protected Properties

The `UdpClient` class has two protected properties, which are accessible from within the class in which it is declared, and from within a derived class. This means that we cannot directly use the `UdpClient` instance to access the protected properties.

The Active Property

The `Active` property is used to check the connection with the remote host. This property returns `true` if the connection is active.

The Client Property

This property is used for retrieving the underlying `Socket` object that is used by the `UdpClient`. As we mentioned earlier, the `UdpClient` class is built on the top of `Socket` class. The `Client` property allows us to access the underlying socket, and therefore all the members of the `Socket` class that are not available through the `UdpClient` class. This is the biggest advantage of this property. For example, the `Blocking` property of the `Socket` class can be used to specify whether the `Socket` is in blocking mode or not. This cannot be done with the available members of the `UdpClient` class.

The following example uses both the `Active` and the `Client` properties:

```
// Example: Use of Active and Client property
using System;
using System.Net;
using System.Net.Sockets;

class UdpDerived : UdpClient
{
    public void insideSocket()
    {
        // Uses the protected Active property belonging to the UdpClient base
        // class to determine if a connection is established.
        if (this.Active)
        {
            Console.WriteLine("Connection is Active!");

            // Retrieve underlying Socket instance to get rich set of all
            // methods and properties of Socket class
            Socket richSock = this.Client;

            // e.g. following Socket property returns socket type you used
            Console.WriteLine("Socket Type is: " + richSock.SocketType.ToString());
        }
    }

    [STAThread]
    static void Main(string[] args)
    {
        UdpDerived derivedInstance = new UdpDerived();

        // Connect to test Active property
        IPEndPoint endPoint = new IPEndPoint(IPAddress.Parse("127.0.0.1"), 5001);

        // Connect using instance of derived class
        derivedInstance.Connect(endPoint);

        // Call protected method
        derivedInstance.insideSocket();
    }
}
```

Creating a Chat Application Using UDP

In order to provide a more concrete illustration of how these processes tie together, we'll develop a simple chat application in C# using the UdpClient class. Once we've written the send and receive example above, creating a chat application is actually quite simple.

The chat application uses a separate thread to listen for messages from the remote hosts. The Thread class is in the System.Threading namespace, so we will add the following using directive to the project:

```
using System.Threading;
```

The application is divided into three logical parts. In the first part, the user is asked to enter information about the local and remote ports and the remote IP address to use. The diagram below shows a possible setup for the ports that allows the application to be tested on a single machine. Port 5001 is used as the sending port for host A, and the receiving port for client B, and vice versa for port 5002:

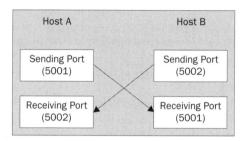

In the second part, the application listens for incoming data from the remote host. As we discussed earlier, the Receive() method polls for the incoming datagrams and blocks the execution of the thread until a message returns from a remote host. To separate out this process from main flow, a new thread is created. The ThreadStart delegate references the Receiver() method, which is invoked when the thread starts:

```
Thread tRec = new Thread(new ThreadStart(Receiver));
tRec.Start();
```

In the Receiver() method, the UdpClient instance is created using the specified localPort:

```
UdpClient receivingUdpClient = new UdpClient(localPort);
```

Next, we create a new instance of the IPEndPoint class, and assign it the value null, so that we can pass it into the Receive() method as a reference parameter:

```
IPEndPoint RemoteIpEndPoint = null;
```

We then start an infinite while loop in order to receive data using the Receive() method. The data is returned as a byte array, which we convert back into the original string using the Encoding.ASCII class:

```
while(true)
{
    // Wait for datagram
    byte[] receiveBytes = receivingUdpClient.Receive(ref RemoteIpEndPoint);

    // Convert and display data
    string returnData = Encoding.ASCII.GetString(receiveBytes);
    Console.WriteLine("-" + returnData);
}
```

The third logical block in the application accepts the data entered by the user and *sends* it to the specified remote port. This executes on the main thread while the worker thread continues to listen for incoming data. To send data to the remote port, the first step is to create the UdpClient instance:

```
UdpClient sender = new UdpClient();
```

Next, the `IPEndPoint` instance is created using the specified remote IP address and port:

```
IPEndPoint endPoint = new IPEndPoint(remoteIPAddress, remotePort);
```

The string data entered by the user is converted into a byte array using the `Encoding.ASCII` class:

```
byte[] bytes = Encoding.ASCII.GetBytes(datagram);
```

Finally, we call the `UdpClient`'s `Send()` method to send the converted bytes to the remote endpoint:

```
sender.Send(bytes, bytes.Length, endPoint);
```

The full code for the chat application is given below:

```csharp
using System;
using System.Net;
using System.Net.Sockets;
using System.Text;
using System.Threading;

namespace Wrox.Networking.UDP.ChatApp
{
    class Chat
    {
        private static IPAddress remoteIPAddress;
        private static int remotePort;
        private static int localPort;

        [STAThread]
        static void Main(string[] args)
        {
            try
            {
                // Get necessary data for connection
                Console.WriteLine("Enter Local Port");
                localPort = Convert.ToInt16(Console.ReadLine());

                Console.WriteLine("Enter Remote Port");
                remotePort = Convert.ToInt16(Console.ReadLine());

                Console.WriteLine("Enter Remote IP address");
                remoteIPAddress = IPAddress.Parse(Console.ReadLine());

                // Create thread for listening
                Thread tRec = new Thread(new ThreadStart(Receiver));
                tRec.Start();

                while(true)
                {
```

```
                    Send(Console.ReadLine());
            }
        }
        catch (Exception e)
        {
            Console.WriteLine(e.ToString());
        }
    }

    private static void Send(string datagram)
    {
        // Create UdpClient
        UdpClient sender = new UdpClient();

        // Create IPEndPoint with details of remote host
        IPEndPoint endPoint = new IPEndPoint(remoteIPAddress, remotePort);

        try
        {
            // Convert data to byte array
            byte[] bytes = Encoding.ASCII.GetBytes(datagram);

            // Send data
            sender.Send(bytes, bytes.Length, endPoint);
        }
        catch (Exception e)
        {
            Console.WriteLine(e.ToString());
        }
        finally
        {
            // Close connection
            sender.Close();
        }
    }

    public static void Receiver()
    {
        // Create a UdpClient for reading incoming data.
        UdpClient receivingUdpClient = new UdpClient(localPort);

        // IPEndPoint with remote host information
        IPEndPoint RemoteIpEndPoint = null;

        try
        {
            Console.WriteLine(
                    "-----------*******Ready for chat!!!*******-----------");

            while(true)
            {
                // Wait for datagram
                byte[] receiveBytes = receivingUdpClient.Receive(
                                            ref RemoteIpEndPoint);
```

```
                    // Convert and display data
                    string returnData = Encoding.ASCII.GetString(receiveBytes);
                    Console.WriteLine("-" + returnData.ToString());
                }
            }
            catch (Exception e)
            {
                Console.WriteLine(e.ToString ());
            }
        }
    }
}
```

And here's the result:

A File Transfer Application

We have seen how to use the `UdpClient` class to send and receive datagrams, and we created a chat application using the same principle. Next, we'll see how to transfer a file and serialized object using `UdpClient`. The sender and receiver programs are divided into two logical parts. In the first part, the sender sends file details (namely the file extension and file size) to the receiver(s) as a serialized object, and in the second part the actual file is sent to the destination. In the receiver, the first part accepts the serialized object with the associated information, and in the second part it creates the file on the destination machine. To make the application more interesting, we'll open the saved file using the associated program (for example, a `.doc` file might be opened with Microsoft Word, or an `.htm` file with Internet Explorer).

File Server

The file server is a simple console application implemented in a class named `FileSender`. This has a nested class called `FileDetails` that contains the information about the file – the file size and the file type. We start by importing the necessary namespaces, and declaring the fields for the class. The class has five private fields – an instance of our `FileDetails` class, a `UdpClient` object, plus information about the connection to the remote client, and a `FileStream` object for reading in the file we'll send to the client:

```
using System;
using System.IO;
using System.Net;
using System.Net.Sockets;
using System.Text;
using System.Xml.Serialization;
using System.Diagnostics;
using System.Threading;

public class FileSender
{
    private static FileDetails fileDet = new FileDetails();

    // UdpClient-related fields
    private static IPAddress remoteIPAddress;
    private const int remotePort = 5002;
    private static UdpClient sender = new UdpClient();
    private static IPEndPoint endPoint;

    // Filestream object
    private static FileStream fs;
```

Next we define the `FileDetails` class. Our `FileDetails` object will need to be serialized for sending over the network, so we add the `[Serializable]` attribute. As we've already intimated, the class just has two public fields, to store the type and the size of the file:

```
// File details (Req. for receiver)
[Serializable]
public class FileDetails
{
    public string FILETYPE = "";
    public long FILESIZE = 0;
}
```

Now we come to the `Main()` method for the server. In this method we invite the user to input a remote IP address to send the file to, and then to enter the path and filename of the file to send. We open up this file with the `FileStream` object, and check its length. If this is greater than the maximum permitted size of 8,192 bytes, we close the `UdpClient` and the `FileStream`, and exit the application. Otherwise, we send the file information, wait two seconds by calling the `Thread.Sleep()` method, and then send the file itself:

```
[STAThread]
static void Main(string[] args)
{
    try
    {
        // Get remote IP address and create IPEndPoint
        Console.WriteLine("Enter Remote IP address");
        remoteIPAddress = IPAddress.Parse(Console.ReadLine().ToString());
        endPoint = new IPEndPoint(remoteIPAddress, remotePort);

        // Get file path. (IMP: file size should be less than 8K)
        Console.WriteLine("Enter File path and name to send.");
        fs = new FileStream(@Console.ReadLine().ToString(), FileMode.Open,
                                                        FileAccess.Read);

        if (fs.Length > 8192)
        {
            Console.Write("This version transfers files with size < 8192 bytes");
            sender.Close();
            fs.Close();
            return;
        }

        SendFileInfo();         // Send file info to receiver
        Thread.Sleep(2000);     // Wait for 2 seconds
        SendFile();             // Send actual file
    }
    catch (Exception e)
    {
        Console.WriteLine(e.ToString());
    }
}
```

The `SendFileInfo()` method populates the fields of the `FileDetails` object, and then serializes this object into a `MemoryStream`, using an `XmlSerializer` object. This is then read into a byte array, which is passed into the `UdpClient`'s `Send()` method, to send the file information to the client:

```
public static void SendFileInfo()
{
    // Get file type or extension
    fileDet.FILETYPE = fs.Name.Substring((int)fs.Name.Length - 3, 3);

    // Get file length (Future purpose)
    fileDet.FILESIZE = fs.Length;

    XmlSerializer fileSerializer = new XmlSerializer(typeof(FileDetails));

    MemoryStream stream = new MemoryStream();

    // Serialize object
    fileSerializer.Serialize(stream, fileDet);
```

```
        // Stream to byte
        stream.Position = 0;
        byte[] bytes = new byte[stream.Length];
        stream.Read(bytes, 0, Convert.ToInt32(stream.Length));

        Console.WriteLine("Sending file details...");

        // Send file details
        sender.Send(bytes, bytes.Length, endPoint);
        stream.Close();
    }
```

The `SendFile()` method just reads the file content from the `FileStream` into a byte array, and then sends this to the client:

```
    private static void SendFile()
    {
        // Creating a file stream
        byte[] bytes = new byte[fs.Length];

        // Stream to bytes
        fs.Read(bytes, 0, bytes.Length);

        Console.WriteLine("Sending file...size = " + fs.Length + " bytes");

        try
        {
            sender.Send(bytes, bytes.Length, endPoint); // Send file
        }
        catch (Exception e)
        {
            Console.WriteLine(e.ToString());
        }
        finally
        {
            // Clean up
            fs.Close();
            sender.Close();
        }
        Console.Read();
        Console.WriteLine("File sent suceessfully.");
    }
}
```

File Receiver

The file receiver is again a console application, and is implemented in a class named `FileRecv`. Again, we start by importing the necessary namespaces and declaring the fields for the class:

```
using System;
using System.IO;
using System.Net;
```

```
using System.Diagnostics;
using System.Net.Sockets;
using System.Text;
using System.Xml.Serialization;

public class FileRecv
{
    private static FileDetails fileDet;

    // UdpClient vars
    private static int localPort = 5002 ;
    private static UdpClient receivingUdpClient = new UdpClient(localPort);
    private static IPEndPoint RemoteIpEndPoint = null ;

    private static FileStream fs;
    private static byte[] receiveBytes = new byte[0];
```

We will need to deserialize the file information sent from the server into a `FileDetails` object, so we need to define that class within the client application, too:

```
[Serializable]
public class FileDetails
{
    public string FILETYPE = "";
    public long FILESIZE = 0;
}
```

The `Main()` method for the application just calls two methods, to get respectively the file details and the file itself:

```
[STAThread]
static void Main(string[] args)
{
    // Get the file details
    GetFileDetails();

    // Receive file
    ReceiveFile();
}
```

The `GetFileDetails()` method calls the `Receive()` method of the `UdpClient` object. This receives the serialized `FileDetails` object from the server, which we save to a `MemoryStream`. We use an `XmlSerializer` object to deserialize this stream back into a `FileDetails` object, and display the retrieved information in the console:

```
private static void GetFileDetails()
{
    try
    {
        Console.WriteLine(
            "-----------*******Waiting to get File Details!!*******-----------");
```

```
        // Receive file info
        receiveBytes = receivingUdpClient.Receive(ref RemoteIpEndPoint);

        Console.WriteLine("----Received File Details!!");


        XmlSerializer fileSerializer = new XmlSerializer(typeof(FileDetails));
        MemoryStream stream1 = new MemoryStream();

        // Received byte to stream
        stream1.Write(receiveBytes, 0, receiveBytes.Length);
        stream1.Position = 0; // IMP

        // Call the Deserialize method and cast to the object type.
        fileDet = (FileDetails)fileSerializer.Deserialize(stream1);
        Console.WriteLine ("Received file of type ." + fileDet.FILETYPE +
                " whose size is " + fileDet.FILESIZE.ToString () + " bytes");
    }
    catch (Exception e)
    {
        Console.WriteLine (e.ToString ());
    }
}
```

The `ReceiveFile()` method retrieves the file from the server and saves it to disk with the filename `temp`, plus the extension retrieved from the `FileDetails` object. We then call the `Process.Start()` static method to open the document with the associated program:

```
public static void ReceiveFile()
{
    try
    {
        Console.WriteLine(
                "-----------*******Waiting to get File!!*******-----------");

        // Receive file
        receiveBytes = receivingUdpClient.Receive(ref RemoteIpEndPoint);

        // Convert and display data
        Console.WriteLine("----File received...Saving...");

        // Create temp file from received file extension
        fs = new FileStream("temp." + fileDet.FILETYPE, FileMode.Create,
                                    FileAccess.ReadWrite, FileShare.ReadWrite);
        fs.Write(receiveBytes, 0, receiveBytes.Length);

        Console.WriteLine("----File Saved...");
        Console.WriteLine("-------Opening file with associated program------");

        Process.Start(fs.Name);   // Opens file with associated program
    }
    catch (Exception e)
    {
```

```
        Console.WriteLine(e.ToString ());
    }
    finally
    {
        fs.Close();
        receivingUdpClient.Close();
    }
}
}
```

Here's the output on the client and server when we run this program:

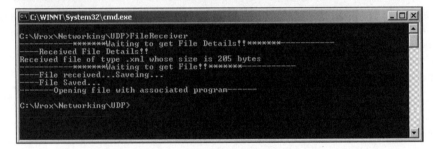

This application has some limitations; firstly, the size of the file depends upon the size of the internal message buffer or network limit. The default buffer size is 8,192 bytes, so we cannot send files larger than 8,192 bytes. This could be overcome by dividing the file into multiple segments, each with a buffer size of 8,192 bytes. By calling the Read() method with the required buffer size, we can divide the file into multiple segments.

As UDP does not use acknowledgement signals, we would have to implement a separate mechanism to check whether each segment was received correctly or not before sending the next segment. This can be achieved by creating another instance of UdpClient in both the sender and receiver, which will check for acknowledgement messages.

Broadcasts

When we run this application, we can specify an individual IP address to send the file to, but we can also specify a **broadcast address**, to send the file to all machines on the subnet, or on the entire network. A broadcast address consists of the subnet ID, with all remaining bits set to 1. For example, if we want to broadcast a message to all hosts with IP addresses in the range 192.168.0, we would use the broadcast address 192.168.0.255. To send a message to all machines on the network, regardless of the subnet mask, we can therefore use the address 255.255.255.255. With broadcasts, the message is sent to every machine on the network; it is for the client to decide whether or not it wants to process the data.

We'll discuss broadcasts in a bit more detail in the next chapter, where we look at multicasting. Unlike broadcasts, multicast connections can cross over a firewall. They are also less bandwidth-intensive, and are therefore generally recommended in preference to broadcasts. We will therefore concentrate on multicasting rather than broadcasts in the next chapter.

Higher-level UDP-based Protocols

UDP is useful where the order of delivery is not important and does not need to be guaranteed. As the sender does not know which destination is active, it uses a port number to specify the type of service required from the remote host.

In the Internet world of today, there are many applications that use UDP services, including Internet phone, Internet video conferencing, and real-time audio/video broadcasting. Most people don't know that DCOM's preferred transport protocol is UDP. The connection-less nature of UDP allows DCOM to perform several optimizations by merging many low-level acknowledgement packages with actual data and pinging messages. This minimizes network round trips as much as possible, and therefore improves speed and performance. Microsoft networking uses UDP for logon, browsing, and name resolution.

Some of the higher-level protocols based on UDP are:

Application-layer protocol	Description/Use
RTP (Real-time Protocol)	Real time media
NFS (Network File System)	Remote file server
SNMP (Simple Network Management Protocol)	Network management
RIP (Routing Information Protocol)	Routing protocol
DNS (Domain Name Service)	Hostname resolution
TFTP (Trivial File Transfer Protocol)	File transfer application
RPC (Remote Procedure Call)	Typical client-server model
LDAP (Lightweight Directory Access Protocol)	Directory services

Real-time Protocol (RTP)

RTP is an application-layer protocol designed for delivering real-time media such as audio/video over unicast or multicast private and public IP networks. One example is Microsoft NetMeeting, which uses RTP to send real-time information across the Internet.

The RTP-based application implements RTP by using UDP protocol and by adding some functionality. The added functionality provides sequence numbering, payload identification, source identification, and time-stamping.

Network File System (NFS)

Another popular application that uses UDP is Network File System, which provides transparent file access to files and file-systems across the network. The advantage of NFS over FTP (File Transfer Protocol) is that it provides transparent access to files. That is, NFS can access the portion of the file that is referenced by an application or process.

NFS is built using Sun RPC, and uses the reserved UDP port number 2049 to perform file operations.

Simple Network Management Protocol (SNMP)

As its name indicates, Simple Network Management Protocol (SNMP) is a network-management protocol widely used in networks. SNMP allows administrators to monitor and control remote hosts and gateways on a network. The SNMP service can handle one or more requests from the host. It communicates between a management program run by an administrator and the network management agent running on a host. SNMP uses ports 161 and 162 for the manager and agent respectively.

Domain Name Service (DNS)

The Domain Name Service is a distributed database used by TCP/IP applications to map hostnames to IP addresses. UDP is the preferred protocol for DNS applications, and it uses port 53 to send DNS queries to a name server.

Trivial File Transfer Protocol (TFTP)

TFTP is an application-layer protocol useful for transferring files between remote hosts. This protocol is intended to be used when bootstrapping diskless systems. It uses UDP port number 69 for its file transfer activity.

Summary

In this chapter, we discussed the basics of the UDP protocol and saw how it compares with the TCP protocol. We covered how to implement the UDP protocol in .NET using the UdpClient class. We looked at the members of the UdpClient class, and saw how to use them within our programs. We then looked at two longer applications – a chat application, which demonstrated the use of the UdpClient class for two-way communication; and a file server/receiver application that could be used to send files to a specific address, or that could broadcast a file to all addresses in the network/subnet. Lastly, we discussed some higher-level UDP-based protocols, which provide a demonstration of the sort of tasks that UDP is ideally suited to perform.

7

Multicast Sockets

In 1994, you may recall, the Rolling Stones transmitted a live concert over the Internet for free. This was made possible due to multicasting, the same technology that makes it possible to watch astronauts in space, to hold meetings over the Internet, and more.

Unicasting would be inappropriate for these applications, as for events attended by thousands of clients, the load on the server and the network would be excessive. Multicasting means that the server only has to send messages just once, and they will be distributed to a whole group of clients. Only systems that are members of the group participate in the network transfers.

In the last few chapters, we discussed socket programming using connection-oriented and connection-less protocols. Chapter 6 showed how we can send broadcasts with the UDP protocol. In this chapter, the UDP protocol again rears its head, but now we are using multicasts.

Multicasts can be used for group communications over the Internet, where every node participating in the multicast has to join the group set up for the purpose. Routers can forward messages to all interested nodes.

In this chapter, we will create two Windows applications using multicasting features. With one application it will be possible to chat with multiple systems, where everyone is both a sender and a receiver. The second application – in the form of a picture show – demonstrates how large data packets can be sent to multiple clients without using a large percentage of the network bandwidth.

In particular, we will:

❑   Compare unicasts, broadcasts, and multicasts

❑   Examine the architecture of multicasting

❑   Implement multicast sockets with .NET

❑   Create a multicast chat application

❑   Create a multicast picture show application

Unicasts, Broadcasts, and Multicasts

The Internet Protocol supports three kinds of IP addresses:

❑   **Unicast** – unicast network packets are sent to a single destination

❑   **Broadcast** – broadcast datagrams are sent to all nodes in a subnetwork

❑   **Multicast** – multicast datagrams are sent to all nodes, possibly on different subnets, that belong to a group

The TCP protocol provides a connection-oriented communication where two systems communicate with each other; with this protocol, we can only send unicast messages. If multiple clients connect to a single server, all clients maintain a separate connection on the server. The server needs resources for each of these simultaneous connections, and must communicate individually with every client. Don't forget that the UDP protocol can also be used to send unicast messages, where, unlike TCP, connection-less communication is used, making it is faster than TCP, although without TCP's reliability.

> *Sending unicast messages with TCP is covered in Chapter 5; using UDP for unicast is discussed in Chapter 6.*

Broadcast addresses are identified by IP addresses where all bits of the host are set to 1. For instance, to send messages to all hosts in a subnet with a mask of 255.255.255.0 in a network with the address 192.168.0, the broadcast address would be 192.168.0.255. Any host with an IP address beginning 192.168.0 will then receive the broadcast messages. **Broadcasts** are *always* performed with connection-less communication using the UDP protocol. The server sends the data regardless of whether any client is listening. Performance reasons mean it wouldn't be possible to set up a separate connection to every client. Connection-less communication means that the server does not have to allocate resources for every single client – no matter how many clients are listening, the same server resources will be consumed.

Of course, there are disadvantages to the connection-less mechanism. For one, there is no guarantee that the data is received by anyone. If we wanted to add reliability, we would have to add a handshaking mechanism of our own at a higher level than UDP.

Broadcasts introduce a performance issue for every system on the destination subnet, because each system on that subnet has to check whether the receiving packet is of interest. A broadcast can be of interest to any system in the network, and it passes all the way up to the transport layer in the protocol stack of each system before its relevancy can be determined. There is another issue with broadcasts: they don't cross subnets. Routers don't let broadcasts cross them – we would soon reach network saturation if routers forwarded broadcasts, so this is desired behavior. Thus, broadcasts can be only used inside a particular subnet.

> **Broadcast communication is useful if multiple nodes in the same subnet should get information simultaneously. NTP (Network Time Protocol) is an example where broadcasts are useful.**

Multicast addresses are identified by IP class D addresses (in the range 224.0.0.0 to 239.255.255.255). Multicast packets can pass across different networks through routers, so it is possible to use multicasts in an Internet scenario as long as your network provider supports multicasting. Hosts that want to receive particular multicast messages must register their interest using IGMP (Internet Group Management Protocol). Multicast messages are not then sent to networks where no host has joined the multicast group. Class D IP addresses are used for multicast groups, to differentiate them from normal host addresses, allowing nodes to easily detect if a message is of interest.

Application Models with Multicasts

There are many types of application where multicasts are of good use. One such scenario is when every system in a group wants to send data to every other system in the group (many-to-many). Multicasting means that each system doesn't need to create a connection to every other system, and a multicast address can be used instead. A peer-to-peer chat application, as seen in the picture below, would benefit from such behavior. The chat sender sends a message to every node of the group by sending a single message to the network:

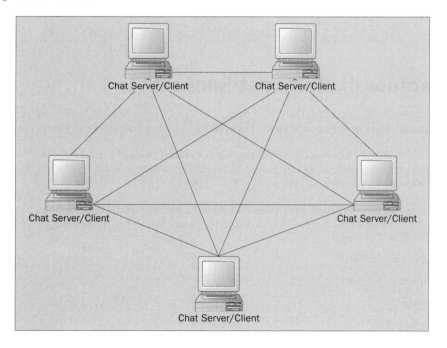

Another scenario where multicasts play an important role is if one system wants to send data to a group of systems (one-to-many). This can be useful for sending audio, video, or other large data types. The server only sends the data once, to the multicast address, and a large number of systems can listen. The Rolling Stones concert in November 1994 was the first time audio and video of a live rock concert was transmitted over the Internet using multicast. This was a big success, and it demonstrated the usefulness of multicasting. The same technology is used in a local network to install applications on hundreds of PCs simultaneously without the servers having to send a big installation package to every client system separately:

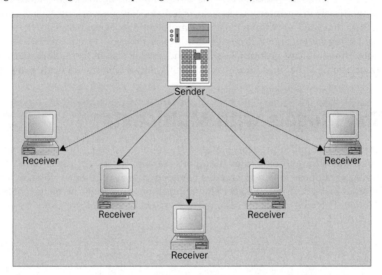

Architecture of Multicast Sockets

Multicast messages are sent using the UDP protocol to a group of systems identified by a class D subnet address. Certain class D address ranges are reserved for specific uses, as we will see soon.

In addition to UDP, the **Internet Group Management Protocol** (IGMP) is used to register clients that want to receive messages for a specific group. This protocol is built into the IP module, and allows clients to leave a group as well as join.

In this section, we'll cover foundation issues and other important factors of multicasting:

- ❑ The IGMP protocol
- ❑ Multicast addresses
- ❑ Routing
- ❑ Scoping
- ❑ Scalability
- ❑ Reliability
- ❑ Security

The IGMP Protocol

IGMP is used by IP hosts to report group memberships to any immediately neighboring routers that are multicast enabled. Similarly to the ICMP protocols, IGMP is implemented in the IP module as the picture below shows. IGMP messages are encapsulated in IP datagrams with the IP protocol number 2. In Chapter 1, we saw the protocol number listed in the IP header, where 2 denotes IGMP, 1 is for ICMP, 6 for TCP, and 17 for UDP.

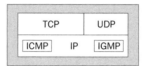

An IGMP v2 message consists of 64 bits, and contains the type of the message, a maximum response time (used only for membership queries), a checksum, and the group address:

8-bit Type	8-bit Max Response Time	16-bit Checksum
32-bit Group Address		

IGMP v2 is defined in RFC 2236 (http://www.ietf.org/rfc/rfc2236.txt).

The message types used for communication between a host and a router are defined by the first 8 bits of IGMP v2 message headers, and are described in the following table:

Hex Value	Message	Description
0x11	Membership Query	These are used by the router to see whether any group members exist. Two types of membership query can be differentiated by the group address in the 32-bit group address field. A **general query** has a group address in the IGMP header of all zeros, and asks which groups have members on an attached network. A **group-specific query** returns information on whether a particular group has members.
0x16	Version 2 Membership Report	When a host **joins a multicast group**, a membership report is sent to the router to inform the router that a system on the network is listening to multicast messages.

Table continued on following page

Hex Value	Message	Description
0x17	Leave Group	The last host of a multicast group inside a subnet must send a **leave group** message to all routers (224.0.0.2) when it leaves a group. A host may remember the hosts of the multicast group (received in membership reports in response to membership queries) so that it knows when it is the last one in the group, but this is not a requirement. If the group members are not remembered, every host leaving a group sends a leave group message. In any case the router checks if it was the last host in the group, and stops forwarding multicast messages if so.
0x12	Version 1 Membership Report	This report is used for compatibility reasons with IGMP v1.

IGMP Versions

Version 2 of IGMP added the leave group message so that a client can explicitly leave the group. Version 1 had to wait for a timeout that could take up to five minutes. During this time, unwanted multicast transmissions are sent to the network, and for large data such as audio or video streams, this can use up a substantial part of the available bandwidth. When leaving the group with IGMP v2, latency is reduced to just a few seconds.

IGMP v3 is still in draft stage, but it is already available with Windows XP and adds specific joins and leaves with the source address(es). This capability makes the Source-Specific Multicast (SSM) protocol possible. With an IGMP v2 multicast, every member of the group can send multicast messages to every other member. SSM makes it possible to restrict the sender (source) of the group to a specific host or multiple hosts, which is a great advantage in the one-to-many application scenario. IGMP v3 messages have a different layout to IGMP v2 messages, and the size of an IGMP v3 message depends on how many source addresses are used.

> At the time of writing, IGMP v3 is available as a draft version. With its release, a new RFC will update RFC 2236.

Multicast Addresses

A class D multicast address starts with the binary values 1110 in the first four bits, making the address range from 224.0.0.0 to 239.255.255.255.

However, not every address of this range is available for multicasting; for example, the multicast addresses 224.0.0.0–224.0.0.255 are special purpose, and routers do not pass them across networks. Unlike normal IP addresses, where every country has a local representation to assign IP addresses, only the Internet Assigned Names and Numbers Authority (IANA, http://www.iana.org) is responsible for assigning multicast addresses. RFC 3171 defines the use of specific ranges of IP multicast addresses and their purposes.

*RFC 3171 uses **CIDR** (Classless InterDomain Routing) addresses for a shorthand notation of a range of IP addresses. The CIDR notation 224.0.0/24 is similar to the address range with the dotted quad-notation 224.0.0.0–224.0.0.255. In the CIDR notation, the first part shows the fixed range of the dotted quad-notation followed by the number of fixed bits, so 232/8 is the shorthand CIDR notation for 232.0.0.0–232.255.255.255.*

As a quick overview of multicast addresses, let's look at the three main ways in which they can be allocated:

❑   Static

❑   Dynamic

❑   Scope-relative

Static Multicast Addresses

Static multicast addresses that are needed globally are assigned by IANA. A few examples are listed in the table below:

IP Address	Protocol	Description
224.0.0.1 224.0.0.2 224.0.0.12	All systems on this subnet All routers on this subnet DHCP Server	The addresses starting with 224.0.0 belong to the **Local Network Control Block**, and are never forwarded by a router. Examples of these are 224.0.0.1 to send a message to all systems on the subnet, or 224.0.0.2 to send a message to all routers on the subnet. The DHCP server answers messages on the IP address 224.0.0.12, but only on a subnet.
224.0.1.1 224.0.1.24	NTP, Network Time Protocol WINS Server	The addresses in the CIDR range 224.0.1/24 belong to the **Internetwork Control Block**. Messages sent to these addresses can be forwarded by a router. Examples are the Network Time Protocol and WINS requests.

A static address is one of global interest, used for protocols that need well-known addresses. These addresses may be hard-coded into applications and devices.

A complete list of actually reserved multicast addresses and their owners in the ranges defined by RFC 3171 can be found at the IANA web site at http://www.iana.org/assignments/multicast-addresses.

The IANA web site offers a form that allows us to request multicast addresses for applications that need a globally unique IP address; this can be found at http://www.iana.org/cgi-bin/multicast.pl.

Dynamic Multicast Addresses

Often, a dynamic multicast address would fit the purpose rather than a fixed static address. These requested-on-demand addresses have a specific lifetime. The concept of requesting dynamic multicast addresses is similar to DHCP (Dynamic Host Configuration Protocol) requests, and indeed in the first versions of MADCAP (Multicast Address Dynamic Client Allocation Protocol) was based on DHCP. Later MADCAP versions are completely independent of DHCP as they have quite different requirements.

With MADCAP, the client sends a unicast or a multicast message to a MADCAP server to request a multicast address. The server answers with a lease-based address.

> *The MADCAP protocol is defined by RFC 2730.*

> *A MADCAP server comes with Windows 2000 Server and can be configured as part of the DHCP Server services.*

Scope-Relative Multicast Addresses

Scope-relative multicast addresses are multicast addresses that are used only within a local group or organization. The address range `239.0.0.0` to `239.255.255.255` is reserved for administrative scope-relative addresses. These addresses can be reused with other local groups. Routers are typically configured with filters to prevent multicast traffic in this address range from flowing outside of the local network.

> *Administrative scope-relative addresses are defined in RFC 2365.*

Another way to define the scope of multicast addresses is by using a TTL. We will look at TTLs in the next section.

Routing

Adding multicast capabilities to the Internet was not a straightforward task. When the multicast protocol was defined, router manufacturers didn't implement multicasting functionality because they didn't know if multicasting had a real use. Instead, they preferred to wait until they knew whether their customers actually wanted multicasting technology, creating a problem in that the technology couldn't take off, as it wasn't possible to use it over the Internet. To resolve this dilemma, the Multicast Backbone (**MBone)** was created in 1992. The MBone started with 40 subnetworks in four different countries, and now spans 3400 subnets in 25 countries.

The MBone connects together islands of subnetworks capable of multicasting through **tunnels** as can be seen in the next figure. Multicast messages are forwarded using a unicast connection between both tunnel ends to connect multiple islands across the Internet where multicasting is not supported:

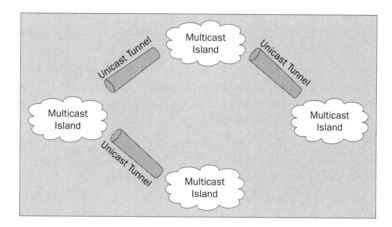

Today, routers are capable of routing multicast messages, but many Internet providers still don't support multicasts, and so the MBone is still a useful facility.

The web page reporting the actual status of multicast enabled networks in the Internet can be found at http://www.multicasttech.com/status.

Today, the MBone is used for audio and video multicasts, technical talks and seminars, NASA Space Shuttle missions, and so on. MBone tools (such as `sdr` or `multikit`) provide us with information about planned multicast events.

How is a multicast packet sent to a client? The next picture shows a server that sends multicast messages to a specific multicast group address. A client that wants to receive multicast packets for the defined multicast address must join the multicast group. Suppose client E joins the multicast group by sending an IGMP request to the routers on its local network. All routers of a subnet can be reached using the IP address `224.0.0.2`. In the picture, only router Z is in client E's subnet. The router registers the client as a member of the multicast group and informs other routers using a different protocol in order to pass information on multicast members across routers. We will discuss the multicast protocol used by routers shortly: MOSPF, PIM, or DVRMP. Multicast-enabled routers pass the information about the member in this group on to other routers. The server just needs to send a UDP message to the group address. Because router X now knows that a client wants to receive those messages, it forwards the multicast message to router Z that in turn forwards the message to the subnetwork of client E. Client E can read the multicast message. The message is never transmitted to the network of router Y because no client of that network joined the multicast group.

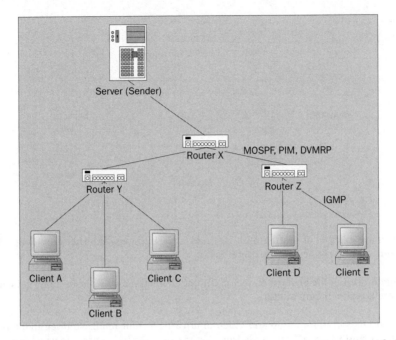

The scope of the multicast determines how many times multicast messages are forwarded by routers. Let's look at how the scope can be influenced.

Scoping

We have already discussed scoping when looking at administrative scope-relative multicast addresses belonging to a specific class D address range assigned by IANA, but there's another way to scope multicast messages.

When the client sends a multicast group report to join a multicast group, it defines a TTL (time to live) value that is sent in the IP packet. The TTL value defines by how many hops the membership report should be forwarded. A TTL value of 1 means that the group report never leaves the local network. Every router receiving the group report decrements the TTL value by 1 and discards the packet when the TTL reaches 0.

There's a problem defining the exact number of hops to a sender, as different routes may need a different number of hops, and administrative scope-relative multicast addresses have some advantages.

Routing Protocols

Different protocols can be used by routers to forward multicast membership reports and to find the best way from the sender to the client. When the MBone was created, the Distance Vector Multicast Routing Protocol (DVMRP) was the only protocol used. Now, Multicast Open Shortest Path First (MOSPF) and Protocol-Independent Multicast (PIM) are also widely used protocols for multicasting.

DVMRP uses a reverse path-flooding algorithm, where the router sends a copy of the network packet out to all paths except the one from where the packet originated. If no node in a router's network is a member of the multicast group, the router sends a prune message back to the sending router so that it knows it does not need to receive packets for that multicast group. DVMRP periodically refloods attached networks to reach new nodes that may be added to the multicast group. Now you can see why DVMRP doesn't scale too well!

MOSPF is an extension of the OSPF (Open Shortest Path First) protocol. With MOSPF, all routers must be aware of all available links to networks hosting members of multicast groups. MOSPF calculates routes when multicast traffic is received. This protocol can only be used in networks where OSPF is used as a unicast routing protocol because MOSPF routes are exchanged between routers using OSPF. Also, MOSPF won't scale well if many multicast groups are used, or if the groups change often, because this can gobble up a lot of the router's processing power.

PIM uses two different algorithms for sending messages to group members. When the members are widely distributed across different networks, PIM-SM (Sparse Mode) is employed, and when a group uses only a few networks, PIM-DM (Dense Mode) is used. PIM-DM uses a reverse path-flooding algorithm similar to DVMRP, except that any unicast routing protocol can be used. PIM-SM defines a registration point for proper routing of packets.

Scalability

A great advantage of multicasting is scalability. If, say, we send 123 bytes to 1000 clients using unicast, the network is loaded with 123,000 bytes because the message must be sent once for every client. With multicast, sending the same 123 bytes to 1000 clients only requires 123 bytes to be sent to the network, because all clients will receive the same message.

On the other hand, if we send the 123 bytes using a broadcast, the network load would be low with 123 bytes similar to multicast. But broadcast not only has the disadvantage that messages can't cross different networks, but also that all other clients not interested in the broadcast message need to handle the broadcast packet up to the transport layer before it can determine that no socket is listening to the message, and the packet is discarded.

Multicasting is the most efficient and scalable way to send messages to multiple clients.

Reliability

IP multicasting doesn't offer any compatible transport-level protocol that is both reliable and implements a flow mechanism. UDP on the other hand guarantees neither that messages arrive, nor that they arrive in the correct order. In many scenarios we don't have a problem if some messages are lost, and when listening to a live concert on the net, users expect to miss a few packets – and it is preferable to a faithful reproduction that pauses while data is resent. However, a high quality listening application that caches a lot of data in advance would probably prefer a reliable mechanism. If we want to use multicasting to install an application on multiple workstations simultaneously, a reliable mechanism is essential. If some messages were lost, the installed application may not run, or could even produce harmful effects.

If guaranteed delivery is needed for a multicast, we must add custom handshaking using a reliable protocol. One way this can be done is by adding packet numbers and a checksum to the data that is sent as part of the multicast. If the receiver detects a corrupted packet because of an incorrect checksum, or a packet is missing, it sends a NACK message to the sender, and the sender can resend the corrupted or missing packet. Note that the use of NACK messages in the event of errors is far more scalable than the alternative of sending acknowledgement messages for every packet correctly received.

Windows XP uses NACK messages in this way, as part of its reliable multicasting, provided through Message Queuing. If we use Windows XP (or Windows .NET Server) on both the client and server, we wouldn't need to implement a NACK mechanism ourselves.

Security

What about multicasting and security? We can differentiate multicasting security issues according to whether the Internet or an intranet is used, and whether we're securing multicast communication within a group.

A firewall acts as a security gateway between the Internet and an intranet. We'll assume that our Internet provider supports the MBone on the Internet side, and that multicasting is enabled in the intranet. Our firewall would stop multicast messages passing from the Internet to the intranet, and vice versa, and we must explicitly enable the multicast address and the port to pass through the firewall.

Regarding secure communication within a multicast group, the IETF's working group on Multicast Security (MSEC) has made a proposal for multicasting group key management that promises to establish a standard way for secure communication among authorized group members. This proposal would prevent anyone outside the group reading the group's messages. At the time of writing, the IETF already has a draft document describing secure group key management. The release of this document is planned for December 2002.

Using Multicast Sockets with .NET

Now that we've covered the basic principles and issues of multicasting, let's start playing with the .NET classes that support it. We'll start with a look at the code needed for a sender and a receiver.

Sender

The sending application has no special tasks that we haven't already talked about in previous chapters, and we can simply use the UdpClient class to send multicast messages. The only difference to what we've done in previous chapters is that we must now use a multicast address. The IPEndPoint object remoteEP will point to the group address and the port number that will be used by the group:

```
IPAddress groupAddress = IPAddress.Parse("234.5.6.11");
int remotePort = 7777;
int localPort = 7777;
IPEndPoint remoteEP = new IPEndPoint(groupAddress, remotePort);
UdpClient server = new UdpClient(localPort);
server.Send(data, data.Length, remoteEP);
```

The multicast group address must also be made known to clients joining the group. We can do this using a fixed address defined in a configuration file that clients can access, but we can also use a MADCAP server to get a multicast address dynamically. In that case, we have to implement a way to tell the client about the dynamically assigned addresses. We could do this using a stream socket that the client connects to, and sending the multicast address to the client. We will implement a stream socket to tell the client about the multicast address later on, when we come to the picture show application.

Receiver

Clients have to join the multicast group. The method `JoinMulticastGroup()` of the `UdpClient` class already implements this. This method sets the socket options `AddMembership` and `MulticastTimeToLive`, and sends an IGMP group report message to the router. The first parameter of `JoinMulticastGroup()` denotes the IP address of the multicast group, and the second parameter represents the TTL value (the number of routers that should forward the report message).

```
UdpClient udpClient = new UdpClient();
udpClient.JoinMulticastGroup(groupAddress, 50);
```

To drop a group membership, we call `UdpClient.DropMulticastGroup()`, which takes an IP address parameter specifying the same multicast group address as used with `JoinMulticastGroup()`:

```
udpClient.DropMulticastGroup(groupAddress);
```

Using the Socket Class

Instead of using the `UdpClient` class, we can also use the `Socket` class directly. The following code does practically the same as the `UdpClient` class above. A UDP socket is created with the constructor of the `Socket` class, and then the socket options `AddMembership` and `MulticastTimeToLive` are set with the method `SetSocketOption()`. We have already used this method in Chapter 4, now we'll use it with multicast options. The first argument we pass is `SocketOptionLevel.IP`, because the IGMP protocol is implemented in the IP module. The second argument specifies a value of the `SocketOptionName` enumeration. The `AddMembership` value is used to send an IGMP group membership report, and `MulticastTimeToLive` sets the number of hops by which the multicast report should be forwarded. For the group membership report, we also have to specify the IP address of the multicast group. The IP address can be specified with the helper class `MulticastOption`:

```
public void SetupMulticastClient(IPAddress groupAddress, int timeToLive)
{
    Socket socket = new Socket(AddressFamily.InterNetwork,
                               SocketType.Dgram, ProtocolType.Udp);

    MulticastOption multicastOption = new MulticastOption(groupAddress);
    socket.SetSocketOption(SocketOptionLevel.IP,
                           SocketOptionName.AddMembership,
                           multicastOption);

    socket.SetSocketOption(SocketOptionLevel.IP,
                           SocketOptionName.MulticastTimeToLive,
                           timeToLive);
}
```

Leaving the multicast group is done by calling SetSocketOption() with the enumeration value SocketOptionName.DropMembership:

```
public void StopMulticastClient(IPAddress groupAddress, int timeToLive)
{
    Socket socket = new Socket(AddressFamily.InterNetwork,
                        SocketType.Dgram, ProtocolType.Udp);

    MulticastOption multicastOption = new MulticastOption(groupAddress);
    socket.SetSocketOption(SocketOptionLevel.IP,
                    SocketOptionName.DropMembership,
                    multicastOption);
}
```

The advantage of the Socket class over UdpClient is that we have more options available for multicasting. In addition to the options we have seen for joining and dropping a group, Windows XP has the enumeration value SocketOptionName.AddSourceGroup to join a multicast source group using SSM.

Creating a Chat Application

Now we can start writing a full multicast application. The first of our sample applications is a simple chat application that multiple users can use to send messages to all other chat clients. In this application, every system acts as both client and server. Every user can enter a message that is sent to all multicast participants.

The chat application is created as a Windows Forms project called MulticastChat, creating an executable with the name MulticastChat.exe. The main form class in this application is ChatForm.cs.

User Interface

The user interface of the chat application allows the user to enter a chat name, and join the network communication by pressing the **Start** button. When this button is pressed, the multicast group is joined, and the application starts listening to the group address. Messages are entered in the text box below the **Message** label, and are sent to the group when the **Send** button is pressed:

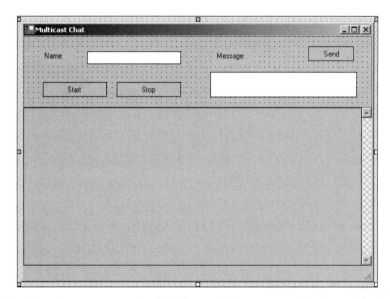

The table below shows the major controls of the form with their name and any non-default property values:

Control Type	Name	Properties
TextBox	textName	Text = ""
Button	buttonStart	Text = "Start"
Button	buttonStop	Enabled = false Text = "Stop"
Button	buttonSend	Enabled = false Text = "Send"
TextBox	textMessage	Multiline = true Text = ""
TextBox	textMessages	Multiline = true ReadOnly = true Scrollbars = Vertical Text = ""
StatusBar	statusBar	

ChatForm is the main class of the application as you can see in the code below. The code shows the .NET namespaces and private fields that will be used by all the methods that we'll add to the class as we progress:

```
using System;
using System.Configuration;
using System.Collections.Specialized;
using System.Net;
using System.Net.Sockets;
using System.Text;
using System.Threading;
using System.Windows.Forms;
```

```
namespace Wrox.Networking.Multicast
{
    public class ChatForm : System.Windows.Forms.Form
    {
        private bool done = true;         // Flag to stop listener thread
        private UdpClient client;         // Client socket
        private IPAddress groupAddress;   // Multicast group address
        private int localPort;            // Local port to receive messages
        private int remotePort;           // Remote port to send messages
        private int ttl;

        private IPEndPoint remoteEP;
        private UnicodeEncoding encoding = new UnicodeEncoding();

        private string name;              // user name in chat
        private string message;           // message to send

        //...
```

Configuration Settings

The multicast address and port numbers should be easily configurable, so we'll create an XML application configuration file called `MulticastChat.exe.config` with the following content. This configuration file must be placed in the same directory as the executable resides (which will be `Debug\bin` when running from Visual Studio .NET with debugging).

```
<?xml version="1.0" encoding="utf-8" ?>
<configuration>
    <appSettings>
        <add key="GroupAddress" value="234.5.6.11" />
        <add key="LocalPort" value="7777" />
        <add key="RemotePort" value="7777" />
        <add key="TTL" value="32" />
    </appSettings>
</configuration>
```

The value of the `GroupAddress` key must be a class D IP address as discussed earlier in the chapter. `LocalPort` and `RemotePort` use the same values to make the chat application both a receiver and a sender with the same port number.

> *To start this application twice on the same system for testing purposes, you will have to copy the application together with the configuration file into two different directories. Because two running applications on one system may not listen to the same port number, you will also have to change the port numbers for* LocalPort *and* RemotePort *in the configuration file to two different ports. Each application will need* RemotePort *to be set to the value of* LocalPort *in the second application.*

We've set the TTL value in this file to 32. If you don't want to forward group membership reports across routers in your multicast environment, change this value to 1.

This configuration file is read by the ChatForm class constructor using the class System.Configuration.ConfigurationSettings. If the configuration file doesn't exist, or it is incorrectly formatted, an exception is thrown that we catch to display an error message:

```
public ChatForm()
{
    //
    // Required for Windows Form Designer support
    //
    InitializeComponent();

    try
    {
        // Read the application configuration file
        NameValueCollection configuration =
                            ConfigurationSettings.AppSettings;
        groupAddress = IPAddress.Parse(configuration["GroupAddress"]);
        localPort = int.Parse(configuration["LocalPort"]);
        remotePort = int.Parse(configuration["RemotePort"]);
        ttl = int.Parse(configuration["TTL"]);
    }
    catch
    {
        MessageBox.Show(this,
                    "Error in application configuration file!",
                    "Error Multicast Chat", MessageBoxButtons.OK,
                    MessageBoxIcon.Error);
        buttonStart.Enabled = false;
    }
}
```

Joining the Multicast Group

In the Click handler of the Start button, we read the name that was entered in the text box textName and write it to the name field. Next, we create a UdpClient object and join the multicast group by calling the method JoinMulticastGroup(). Then we create a new IPEndPoint object referencing the multicast address and the remote port for use with the Send() method to send data to the group:

```
private void OnStart(object sender, System.EventArgs e)
{
    name = textName.Text;
    textName.ReadOnly = true;

    try
    {
        // Join the multicast group
        client = new UdpClient(localPort);
        client.JoinMulticastGroup(groupAddress, ttl);

        remoteEP = new IPEndPoint(groupAddress, remotePort);
```

In the next section of code, we create a new thread that will receive messages sent to the multicast address because the `UdpClient` class doesn't support asynchronous operations. An alternative way of achieving asynchronous operations would be to use the raw `Socket` class. The `IsBackground` property of the thread is set to `true` so that the thread will be stopped automatically when the main thread quits.

After starting the thread, we send an introduction message to the multicast group. To convert a string to the byte array that the `Send()` method requires, we call `UnicodeEncoding.GetBytes()`:

```
// Start the receiving thread
Thread receiver = new Thread(new ThreadStart(Listener));
receiver.IsBackground = true;
receiver.Start();

// Send the first message to the group
byte[] data = encoding.GetBytes(name + " has joined the chat");
client.Send(data, data.Length, remoteEP);
```

The last action performed by the `OnStart()` method is to enable the **Stop** and **Send** buttons, and disable the **Start** button. We also write a handler for the `SocketException` that could occur if the application is started twice listening on the same port:

```
        buttonStart.Enabled = false;
        buttonStop.Enabled = true;
        buttonSend.Enabled = true;
    }
    catch (SocketException ex)
    {
        MessageBox.Show(this, ex.Message, "Error MulticastChat",
                    MessageBoxButtons.OK, MessageBoxIcon.Error);
    }
}
```

Receiving Multicast Messages

In the method of the listener thread that we created earlier, we wait in the `client.Receive()` method until a message arrives. With the help of the class `UnicodeEncoding`, the received byte array is converted to a string.

The returned message should now be displayed in the user interface. There is an important issue to pay attention to when using threads and Windows controls. In native Windows programming, it is possible to create Windows controls from different threads, but only the thread that created the control may invoke methods on it, so all function calls on the Windows control must occur in the creation thread. In Windows Forms, the same model is mapped to the .NET Windows Forms classes. All methods of Windows Forms controls must be called on the creation thread – with the exception of the method `Invoke()` and its asynchronous variants, `BeginInvoke()` and `EndInvoke()`. These can be called from any thread, as it forwards the method that should be called to the creation thread of the Windows control. That creation thread then calls the method.

So instead of displaying the message in the text box directly, we call the `Invoke()` method of the Form class to forward the call to the creation thread of the Form class. Because this is the same thread that created the text box, this fulfills our requirements.

The `Invoke()` method requires an argument of type `Delegate`, and because any delegate derives from this class, every delegate can be passed to this method. We want to invoke a method that doesn't take parameters: `DisplayReceivedMessage()`, and there's already a predefined delegate in the .NET Framework to invoke a method without parameters: `System.Windows.Forms.MethodInvoker`. This delegate accepts methods without parameters, such as our method `DisplayReceivedMessage()`.

```
// Main method of the listener thread that receives the data
private void Listener()
{
   done = false;

   try
   {
      while (!done)
      {
         IPEndPoint ep = null;

         byte[] buffer = client.Receive(ref ep);
         message = encoding.GetString(buffer);

         this.Invoke(new MethodInvoker (DisplayReceivedMessage));
      }
   }
   catch (Exception ex)
   {
      MessageBox.Show(this, ex.Message, "Error MulticastChat",
                  MessageBoxButtons.OK, MessageBoxIcon.Error);

   }
}
```

In the `DisplayReceivedMessage()` implementation, we write the received message to the `textMessages` text box, and write some informational text to the status bar:

```
private void DisplayReceivedMessage()
{
   string time = DateTime.Now.ToString("t");
   textMessages.Text = time + "   " + message + "\r\n" +
                  textMessages.Text;
   statusBar.Text = "Received last message at " + time;
}
```

Sending Multicast Messages

Our next task is to implement the message sending functionality in the `Click` event handler of the **Send** button. As we have already seen, a string is converted to a byte array using the `UnicodeEncoding` class:

```
private void OnSend(object sender, System.EventArgs e)
{
   try
   {
      // Send a message to the group
      byte[] data = encoding.GetBytes(name + ": " + textMessage.Text);
      client.Send(data, data.Length, remoteEP);
      textMessage.Clear();
      textMessage.Focus();
   }
   catch (Exception ex)
   {
      MessageBox.Show(this, ex.Message, "Error MulticastChat",
                      MessageBoxButtons.OK, MessageBoxIcon.Error);
   }
}
```

Dropping the Multicast Membership

The Click event handler for the **Stop** button, the method OnStop(), stops the client listening to the multicast group by calling the DropMulticastGroup() method. Before the client stops receiving the multicast data, a final message is sent to the group saying that the user has left the conversation:

```
private void OnStop(object sender, System.EventArgs e)
{
   StopListener();
}

private void StopListener()
{
   // Send a leaving message to the group
   byte[] data = encoding.GetBytes(name + " has left the chat");
   client.Send(data, data.Length, remoteEP);

   // Leave the group
   client.DropMulticastGroup(groupAddress);
   client.Close();

   // Tell the receiving thread to stop
   done = true;

   buttonStart.Enabled = true;
   buttonStop.Enabled = false;
   buttonSend.Enabled = false;
}
```

Because the multicast group should be left not only when the user presses the **Stop** button, but also when they exit the application, we will handle the Closing event of the form in the OnClosing() method. If the server has not already been stopped, we again call the StopListener() method to stop listening to the group after sending a final message to the group:

```
          private void OnClosing(object sender,
                           System.ComponentModel.CancelEventArgs e)
          {
             if (!done)
                StopListener();
          }
```

Starting the Chat Application

Now we can start the chat application on multiple systems and start the conversation. Note that newer messages appear towards the top of the chat window:

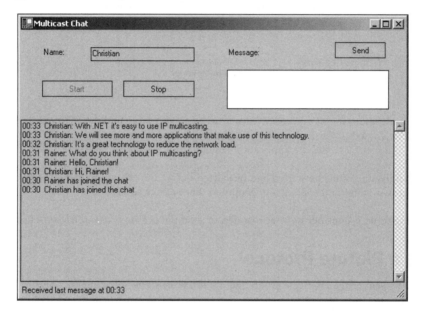

A Picture Show Application

The second application we are going to look at is a picture show application. This application illustrates a multicast scenario where a single application sends messages to multiple clients. This application is a little more challenging as the messages that can be sent are of larger sizes which don't necessarily fit into datagram packets.

The picture show server allows pictures on its file system to be selected for multicasting to all clients that have joined the multicast group.

The picture show is a large application, and so rather than try to cover it in its entirety, we'll focus on the most important aspects related to network communication. The complete working application is available for download from the Wrox web site.

The Picture Show Solution

The complete picture show application consists of three Visual Studio .NET projects:

❑ `PictureShowServer` – a Windows server application

❑ `PictureShowClient` – a Windows client application

❑ `PicturePackager` – a class library used by both client and server

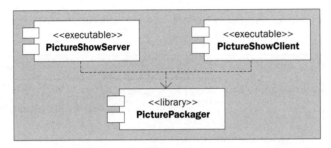

To run the application, the `PictureShowServer.exe` executable and the `PicturePackager.dll` library must be copied to the server. The client systems need `PictureShowClient.exe`, `PicturePackager.dll`, and the application configuration file `PictureShowClient.exe.config`.

The server application must be started and initialized before the client applications can run. You must also set the server name in the client application to that of your server.

The first thing to do is consider how we're going to send pictures to our application's users.

Creating a Picture Protocol

Pictures can be sent to the multicast group that are too large to fit in a datagram packet. We have to split the picture into multiple packages. Also, we want to send some more data in addition to the picture stream. So we need some layout of the data that are sent across the wire.

To make it easy to parse the data so that the format can easily be extended for future versions of the application, we'll use an XML format for the packages that contain the picture data, and make use of classes from the `System.Xml` namespace.

> *To save space, we could define a custom binary format for the data packet, but when sending a picture, the XML overhead is not large compared to the size of the picture. Using XML gives us the advantage of an existing parser, and this format allows us to easily add more elements in future versions.*

One of our XML packages will fit into a single IP datagram. The root element is `<PicturePackage>` with an attribute called `Number` that identifies the fragments that belong together. `<Name>` and `<Data>` are child elements of the `<PicturePackage>` element. The `<Name>` element is informational and can be used for a name of the picture; the `<Data>` element is the base-64 encoded binary data segment of the picture. The attribute `SegmentNumber` allows us to work out how to put the segments together to create a complete picture; `LastSegmentNumber` informs us how many segments are needed to do so:

```
<PicturePackage Number="4">
  <Name>hello.jpg</Name>
  <Data SegmentNumber="2" LastSegmentNumber="12" Size="2400">
    <!-- base-64 encoded picture data -->
  </Data>
</PicturePackage>
```

The PicturePackager assembly contains two classes: the PicturePackager utility class and the entity class PicturePackage. A single PicturePackage object corresponds to an XML <PicturePackage> file like that we see above. We can produce the XML representation for a single picture segment using the GetXml() method on the class.

The PicturePackage class offers two constructors. The first is for use on the server, creating a picture fragment from native data types (int, string, and byte[]).The second constructor is designed for use on the client, and creates a fragment from an XML source.

PicturePackager is a utility class that has static methods only. It splits up a complete picture into multiple segments with the GetPicturePackages() method, and recreates a complete picture by merging the constituent segments with the GetPicture() method.

Picture Packages

So, the PicturePackage class represents one segment of a complete picture, and here it is reproduced in full. It starts by defining read-only properties that map to XML elements of the above format:

```
using System;
using System.Xml;
using System.Text;

namespace Wrox.Networking.Multicast
{
    public class PicturePackage
    {
        private string name;
        private int id;
        private int segmentNumber;
        private int numberOfSegments;
        private byte[] segmentBuffer;

        public string Name
        {
            get
            {
                return name;
            }
        }

        public int Id
        {
            get
            {
                return id;
            }
        }
```

```
public int SegmentNumber
{
   get
   {
      return segmentNumber;
   }
}

public int NumberOfSegments
{
   get
   {
      return numberOfSegments;
   }
}

public byte[] SegmentBuffer
{
   get
   {
      return segmentBuffer;
   }
}
```

Next, we come to the two constructors. One takes multiple arguments to create a `PicturePackage` object by the sender, and the other takes XML data received from the network to recreate the object on the receiver:

```
// Creates a picture segment from data types
// Used by the server application
public PicturePackage(string name, int id, int segmentNumber,
                      int numberOfSegments, byte[] segmentBuffer)
{
   this.name = name;
   this.id = id;
   this.segmentNumber = segmentNumber;
   this.numberOfSegments = numberOfSegments;
   this.segmentBuffer = segmentBuffer;
}

// Creates a picture segment from XML code
// Used by the client application
public PicturePackage(XmlDocument xml)
{
   XmlNode rootNode = xml.SelectSingleNode("PicturePackage");
   id = int.Parse(rootNode.Attributes["Number"].Value);

   XmlNode nodeName = rootNode.SelectSingleNode("Name");
   this.name = nodeName.InnerXml;

   XmlNode nodeData = rootNode.SelectSingleNode("Data");
   numberOfSegments = int.Parse(nodeData.Attributes[
                                "LastSegmentNumber"].Value);
```

```
          segmentNumber = int.Parse(nodeData.Attributes[
                               "SegmentNumber"].Value);
          int size = int.Parse(nodeData.Attributes["Size"].Value);
          segmentBuffer = Convert.FromBase64String(nodeData.InnerText);
   }
```

The only other item in this class is the GetXml() method, which converts the picture segment into an XmlDocument object with the help of classes from the System.Xml namespace. The XML representation is returned as a string:

```
// Return XML code representing a picture segment
public string GetXml()
{
    XmlDocument doc = new XmlDocument();

    // Root element <PicturePackage>
    XmlElement picturePackage = doc.CreateElement("PicturePackage");

    // <PicturePackage Number="number"></PicturePackage>
    XmlAttribute pictureNumber = doc.CreateAttribute("Number");
    pictureNumber.Value = id.ToString();
    picturePackage.Attributes.Append(pictureNumber);

    // <Name>pictureName</Name>
    XmlElement pictureName = doc.CreateElement("Name");
    pictureName.InnerText = name;
    picturePackage.AppendChild(pictureName);

    // <Data SegmentNumber="" Size=""> (base-64 encoded fragment)
    XmlElement data = doc.CreateElement("Data");
    XmlAttribute numberAttr = doc.CreateAttribute("SegmentNumber");
    numberAttr.Value = segmentNumber.ToString();
    data.Attributes.Append(numberAttr);

    XmlAttribute lastNumberAttr =
            doc.CreateAttribute("LastSegmentNumber");
    lastNumberAttr.Value = numberOfSegments.ToString();
    data.Attributes.Append(lastNumberAttr);

    data.InnerText = Convert.ToBase64String(segmentBuffer);
    XmlAttribute sizeAttr = doc.CreateAttribute("Size");
    sizeAttr.Value = segmentBuffer.Length.ToString();
    data.Attributes.Append(sizeAttr);

    picturePackage.AppendChild(data);

    doc.AppendChild(picturePackage);

    return doc.InnerXml;
    }
  }
}
```

More detailed information about XML and the .NET classes that work with it can be found in the Wrox book Professional XML for .NET Developers *(ISBN 1-86100-531-8).*

Picture Packager

The `PicturePackager` class is a utility class consisting of static methods only. It is used by both sender and receiver. The `GetPicturePackages()` method splits up an image into multiple packages in the form of an array of `PicturePackage` objects where every segment of the picture is represented by a single `PicturePackage` object:

```
using System;
using System.Drawing;
using System.Drawing.Imaging;
using System.IO;

namespace Wrox.Networking.Multicast
{

    public class PicturePackager
    {

        protected PicturePackager()
        {
        }

        // Return picture segments for a complete picture
        public static PicturePackage[] GetPicturePackages(string name,
                                                          int id,
                                                          Image picture)
        {
            return GetPicturePackages(name, id, picture, 4000);
        }

        // Return picture segments for a complete picture
        public static PicturePackage[] GetPicturePackages(string name, int id,
                                                          Image picture,
                                                          int segmentSize)
        {
            // Save the picture in a byte array
            MemoryStream stream = new MemoryStream();
            picture.Save(stream, ImageFormat.Jpeg);

            // Calculate the number of segments to split the picture
            int numberSegments = (int)stream.Position / segmentSize + 1;

            PicturePackage[] packages = new PicturePackage[numberSegments];

            // Create the picture segments
            int sourceIndex = 0;
            for (int i=0; i < numberSegments; i++)
            {
                // Calculate the size of the segment buffer
                int bytesToCopy = (int)stream.Position - sourceIndex;
                if (bytesToCopy > segmentSize)
                    bytesToCopy = segmentSize;
```

```
            byte[] segmentBuffer = new byte[bytesToCopy];
            Array.Copy(stream.GetBuffer(), sourceIndex, segmentBuffer,
                    0, bytesToCopy);

            packages[i] = new PicturePackage(name, id, i + 1,
                                        numberSegments, segmentBuffer);

            sourceIndex += bytesToCopy;
        }

        return packages;
    }
```

The receiver uses the inverse `GetPicture()` method that takes all `PicturePackage` objects for a single picture and returns the complete image object:

```
        // Returns a complete picture from the segments passed in
        public static Image GetPicture(PicturePackage[] packages)
        {
            int fullSizeNeeded = 0;
            int numberPackages = packages[0].NumberOfSegments;
            int pictureId = packages[0].Id;

            // Calculate the size of the picture data and check for consistent
            //   picture IDs
            for (int i=0; i < numberPackages; i++)
            {
                fullSizeNeeded += packages[i].SegmentBuffer.Length;
                if (packages[i].Id != pictureId)
                    throw new ArgumentException(
                        "Inconsistent picture ids passed", "packages");
            }

            // Merge the segments to a binary array
            byte[] buffer = new byte[fullSizeNeeded];
            int destinationIndex = 0;
            for (int i = 0; i < numberPackages; i++)
            {
                int length = packages[i].SegmentBuffer.Length;
                Array.Copy(packages[i].SegmentBuffer, 0, buffer,
                        destinationIndex, length);
                destinationIndex += length;
            }

            // Create the image from the binary data
            MemoryStream stream = new MemoryStream(buffer);
            Image image = Image.FromStream(stream);

            return image;
        }
    }
}
```

The System.Drawing *and* System.Xml *assemblies must be referenced by the* PicturePackager *assembly.*

Picture Show Server

Now we've got the assembly to split and merge pictures, we can start on the implementation of the server application. The server project is PictureShowServer, and its main form class is PictureServerForm, contained in the file PictureShowServer.cs shown here:

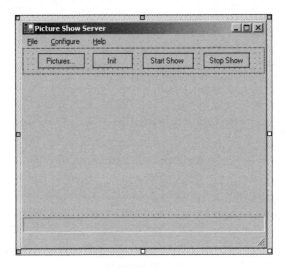

The controls on this dialog are listed in the following table:

Control Type	Name	Comments
MainMenu	mainMenu	The menu has the main entries File, Configure, and Help. The File menu has the submenus Init, Start, Stop, and Exit. The Configure menu allows configuration of the Multicast Session, the Show Timings, and Pictures. The Help menu just offers an About option.
Button	buttonPictures	The Pictures... button will allow the user to configure the pictures that should be presented.
Button	buttonInit	The Init button will publish the multicast address and port number to clients using a TCP socket.
Button	buttonStart	The Start button starts sending the pictures to the multicast group address.
Button	buttonStop	The Stop button stops the picture show prematurely.
PictureBox	pictureBox	The picture box will show the picture that is currently being transferred to clients.

Control Type	Name	Comments
ProgressBar	progressBar	The progress bar indicates how many pictures of the show have been transferred.
StatusBar	statusBar	The status bar shows information about what's currently going on.
ImageList	imageList	The image list holds all images that make up the show.

The `PictureServerForm` class contains the `Main()` method, and there are three other dialog classes, and the `InfoServer` class.

The other three dialogs, `ConfigurePicturesDialog`, `MulticastConfigurationDialog`, and `ConfigureShowDialog`, are used to configure application settings. The `ConfigurePicturesDialog` dialog allows us to select image files from the server's file system to make up the picture show. `MulticastConfigurationDialog` sets up the multicast address and port number, and the interface where the pictures should be sent to in case the server system has multiple network cards. `ConfigureShowDialog` allows the time between pictures to be specified.

The other class, `InfoServer.cs`, starts its own thread that acts as an answering server for a client application. This thread returns information about the group address and port number to clients.

Let's have a look at the code for the start up class for the application, which is called `PictureServerForm` and resides in the `PictureShowServer.cs` source file. Firstly, we'll see the namespaces and fields that the class will require for the methods covered in subsequent sections:

```
using System;
using System.Drawing;
using System.Windows.Forms;
using System.Net;
using System.Net.Sockets;
using System.Text;
using System.IO;
using System.Xml;
using System.Threading;

namespace Wrox.Networking.Multicast
{
    public class PictureServerForm : System.Windows.Forms.Form
    {
        private string[] fileNames;      // Array of picture filenames
        private object filesLock = new object();  // Lock to synchronize
                                                  //  access to filenames

        private UnicodeEncoding encoding = new UnicodeEncoding();

        // Multicast group address, port, and endpoint
        private IPAddress groupAddress = IPAddress.Parse("231.4.5.11");
        private int groupPort = 8765;
        private IPEndPoint groupEP;
        private UdpClient udpClient;
```

```
        private Thread senderThread;       // Thread to send pictures

        private Image currentImage;        // Current image sent

        private int pictureIntervalSeconds = 3; // Time between sending
                                                 // pictures
    //...
```

Opening Files

One of the first actions the picture show server application must do is configure the pictures that are to be presented. `OnConfigurePictures()` is the handler for the **Configure | Pictures** menu item and the click event of the **Pictures...** button:

```
        private void OnConfigurePictures(object sender, System.EventArgs e)
        {
            ConfigurePicturesDialog dialog = new ConfigurePicturesDialog();
            if (dialog.ShowDialog() == DialogResult.OK)
            {
                lock (filesLock)
                {
                    fileNames = dialog.FileNames;
                    progressBar.Maximum = filenames.Length;
                }
            }
        }
```

This dialog opens a configure pictures dialog, which offers a preview of the pictures in a `ListView` with a `LargeIcon` view:

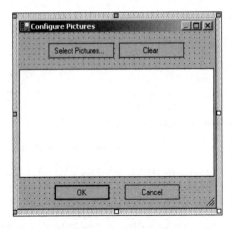

The controls used on this Form are detailed in the next table:

Control Type	Name	Comments
Button OpenFileDialog	buttonSelect openFileDialog	The Select Pictures... button displays the openFileDialog so the user can select the pictures for the show.
Button	buttonClear	The Clear button removes all selected images.
Button Button	buttonOK buttonCancel	The OK or Cancel buttons close the dialog. If OK is clicked, the selected files are sent to the main form, and if Cancel is clicked, all file selections are ignored.
ImageList ListView	imageList listViewPictures	The ImageList Windows Forms component collects all selected images for display in the listViewPictures list view showing a preview for the user.

OnFileOpen() is the handler for the Click event of the Select Pictures... button. It is where we create Image objects from the files selected by OpenFileDialog for adding to the ImageList associated with the ListView:

```
private void OnFileOpen(object sender, System.EventArgs e)
{
    if (openFileDialog.ShowDialog() == DialogResult.OK)
    {
        fileNames = openFileDialog.FileNames;

        int imageIndex = 0;
        foreach (string fileName in fileNames)
        {
            using (Image image = Image.FromFile(fileName))
            {
                imageList.Images.Add(image);

                listViewPictures.Items.Add(fileName, imageIndex++);
            }
        }
    }
}
```

Configuring Multicasting

Another configuration dialog of the server application allows configuring of the multicast address and multicast port number:

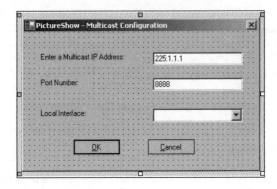

This dialog also allows us to select the local interface that should be used for sending multicast messages. This can be useful if the system has multiple network cards, or is connected both to a dial-up network and a local network.

The combo box listing the local interfaces is filled at form startup. First we call Dns.GetHostName() to retrieve the hostname of the local host, and then Dns.GetHostByName() to get an IPHostEntry object containing all the IP addresses of the local host. If the host has multiple IP addresses, the string "Any" is added to the combo box to allow the user to send multicast messages across all network interfaces. If there is only one network interface, the combo box is disabled, as it will not be possible to select a different interface.

Here is the constructor in MulticastConfigurationDialog.cs

```
public MulticastConfigurationDialog()
{
    //
    // Required for Windows Form Designer support
    //
    InitializeComponent();

    string hostname = Dns.GetHostName();
    IPHostEntry entry = Dns.GetHostByName(hostname);
    IPAddress[] addresses = entry.AddressList;

    foreach (IPAddress address in addresses)
    {
        comboBoxLocalInterface.Items.Add(address.ToString());
    }
    comboBoxLocalInterface.SelectedIndex = 0;

    if (addresses.Length > 1)
    {
        comboBoxLocalInterface.Items.Add("Any");
    }
    else
    {
        comboBoxLocalInterface.Enabled = false;
    }
}
```

Another interesting aspect of this class is the validation of the multicast address. The text box `textBoxIPAddress` has the handler `OnValidateMulticastAddress()` assigned to the event `Validating`. The handler checks that the IP address entered is in the valid range of multicast addresses:

```
private void OnValidateMulticastAddress(object sender,
                       System.ComponentModel.CancelEventArgs e)
{
    try
    {
        IPAddress address = IPAddress.Parse(textBoxIPAddress.Text);

        string[] segments = textBoxIPAddress.Text.Split('.');
        int network = int.Parse(segments[0]);

        // Check address falls in correct range
        if ((network < 224) || (network > 239))
            throw new FormatException("Multicast addresses have the" +
                                "range 224.x.x.x to 239.x.x.x");

        // Check address is not a reserved class D
        if ((network == 224) && (int.Parse(segments[1]) == 0)
            && (int.Parse(segments[2]) == 0))
            throw new FormatException("The Local Network Control Block" +
                    "cannot be used for multicasting groups");
    }
    catch (FormatException ex)
    {
        MessageBox.Show(ex.Message);
        e.Cancel = true;
    }
}
```

We now return to the events in the main `PictureServerForm` class in the file `PictureShowServer.cs`. When the Init button is pressed on the main dialog, we want the listening server to start up so that it can send the group address and port number to requesting clients. We do this by creating an `InfoServer` object with the IP address and the port number, and then invoke `Start()`. This method starts a new thread to handle client requests, as we will see next. `OnInit()` finishes by calling some helper methods that enable the Start button, and disable the Init button:

```
// PictureShowServer.cs

    private void OnInit(object sender, System.EventArgs e)
    {
        InfoServer info = new InfoServer(groupAddress, groupPort);
        info.Start();

        UIEnableStart(true);
        UIEnableInit(false);
    }
```

The `InfoServer` class does all the work of responding to client requests by sending the multicast group address and port number to the clients in a separate thread. The class constructor initializes the `InfoServer` object with the group address and the group port. The `Start()` method (invoked by the `OnInit()` in the `PictureShowServer` class) creates the new thread. The main method of the newly created thread, `InfoMain()`, sets up a TCP stream socket where we simply place the multicast address and the port number separated by a colon (`:`) for sending to the client as soon as one connects to the server:

```csharp
// InfoServer.cs

using System;
using System.Net;
using System.Net.Sockets;
using System.Text;
using System.Threading;

namespace Wrox.Networking.Multicast
{
    public class InfoServer
    {
        private IPAddress groupAddress;
        private int groupPort;
        private UnicodeEncoding encoding = new UnicodeEncoding();

        public InfoServer(IPAddress groupAddress, int groupPort)
        {
            this.groupAddress = groupAddress;
            this.groupPort = groupPort;
        }

        public void Start()
        {
            // Create a new listener thread
            Thread infoThread = new Thread(new ThreadStart(InfoMain));
            infoThread.IsBackground = true;
            infoThread.Start();
        }

        protected void InfoMain()
        {
            string configuration = groupAddress.Address.ToString() + ":" +
                                    groupPort.ToString();

            // Create a TCP streaming socket that listens to client requests
            Socket infoSocket = new Socket(AddressFamily.InterNetwork,
                                           SocketType.Stream,
                                           ProtocolType.Tcp);

            try
            {
                infoSocket.Bind(new IPEndPoint(IPAddress.Any, 8777));
                infoSocket.Listen(5);
```

```
            while (true)
            {
                // Send multicast configuration information to clients
                Socket clientConnection = infoSocket.Accept();
                clientConnection.Send(encoding.GetBytes(configuration));
                clientConnection.Shutdown(SocketShutdown.Both);
                clientConnection.Close();
            }
        }
        finally
        {
            infoSocket.Shutdown(SocketShutdown.Both);
            infoSocket.Close();
        }
    }
}
```

Chapter 4 delved into stream sockets in more detail.

The UIEnableStart() helper method enables or disables the Start button to prevent the user pressing the wrong button. This method is called in the method OnInit(), and, as you would expect, is very similar to UIEnableInit:

```
// PictureShowServer.cs

    private void UIEnableStart(bool flag)
    {
        if (flag)
        {
            buttonStart.Enabled = true;
            buttonStart.BackColor = Color.SpringGreen;
            miFileStart.Enabled = true;
        }
        else
        {
            buttonStart.Enabled = false;
            buttonStart.BackColor = Color.LightGray;
            miFileStart.Enabled = false;
        }
    }
```

Sending Pictures

OnStart() is the method that handles the Click event of the Start button, and is where the sending thread is initialized and started. The start method of this thread is SendPictures(), which we look at next.

```
// PictureShowServer.cs

    private void OnStart(object sender, System.EventArgs e)
    {
        if (fileNames == null)
```

```
        {
            MessageBox.Show("Select pictures before starting the show!");
            return;
        }

        // Initialize picture sending thread
        senderThread = new Thread(new ThreadStart(SendPictures));
        senderThread.Name = "Sender";
        senderThread.Priority = ThreadPriority.BelowNormal;
        senderThread.Start();

        UIEnableStart(false);
        UIEnableStop(true);
    }
```

The list of filenames that we receive from the **Configure Pictures** dialog is used by the
`SendPictures()` method of the sending thread. Here we load a file from the array `fileNames` to
create a new `Image` object that is passed to the `SendPicture()` method. Then the progress bar is
updated with the help of a delegate to reflect the ongoing progress. When building the multicast chat
application, we discussed issues relating to the use of Windows controls in multiple threads, and now we
have to use the `Invoke()` method again:

```
// PictureShowServer.cs

    private void SendPictures()
    {
        InitializeNetwork();

        lock (filesLock)
        {
            int pictureNumber = 1;
            foreach (string fileName in fileNames)
            {
                currentImage = Image.FromFile(filename);
                Invoke(new MethodInvoker(SetPictureBoxImage);

                SendPicture(image, fileName, pictureNumber);
                Invoke(new MethodInvokerInt(IncrementProgressBar),
                                    new object[] {1});

                Thread.Sleep(pictureIntervalSeconds);
                pictureNumber++;
            }
        }
        Invoke(new MethodInvoker(ResetProgress));
        Invoke(new MethodInvokerBoolean(UIEnableStart),
                new object[] {true});
        Invoke(new MethodInvokerBoolean(UIEnableStop),
                new object[] {false});
    }
```

We've already discussed the `MethodInvoker` delegate in the `System.Windows.Forms` namespace when we used it in the multicast chat application. The `MethodInvoker` delegate allows us to call methods that take no arguments. Now we also need methods that take an `int`, a `string`, or a `bool` argument to set specific values and enable or disable certain user interface elements. The delegates for these purposes are placed at the top of the `PictureShowServer.cs` file:

```
namespace Wrox.Networking.Multicast
{
    public delegate void MethodInvokerInt(int x);
    public delegate void MethodInvokerString(string s);
    public delegate void MethodInvokerBoolean(bool flag);
    //...
```

The `SendPicture()` method splits up a single picture image using the `PicturePackager` utility class. Every individual picture package is converted to a byte array with an `Encoding` object of type `UnicodeEncoding`. This byte array is then sent to the multicast group address by the `Send()` method of `UdpClient`:

```
// PictureShowServer.cs

    private void SendPicture(Image image, string name, int index)
    {
        string message = "Sending picture " + name;
        Invoke(new MethodInvokerString(SetStatusBar),
                                new Object[] {message});

        PicturePackage[] packages =
            PicturePackager.GetPicturePackages(name, index, image, 1024);

        // Send all segments of a single picture to the group
        foreach (PicturePackage package in packages)
        {
            byte[] data = encoding.GetBytes(package.GetXml());
            int sendBytes = udpClient.Send(data, data.Length);
            if (sendBytes < 0)
                MessageBox.Show("Error sending");

            Thread.Sleep(300);
        }

        message = "Picture " + name + " sent";
        Invoke(new MethodInvokerString(SetStatusBar),
            new object[] { message });
    }
```

Picture Show Client

The multicast picture show client has a simple user interface consisting of a menu, a picture box, and a status bar on a form. The status bar has three panels showing not only status messages but also the multicast address and port numbers. The File menu entry has Start, Stop, and Exit submenus:

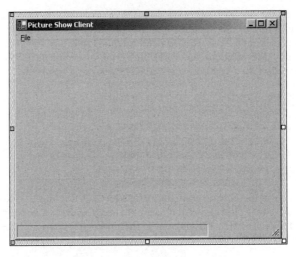

The components on this form are described in the following table:

Control Type	Name	Comments
MainMenu	mainMenu	The main menu has a single **File** menu entry with **Start**, **Stop**, and **Exit** submenus.
PictureBox	pictureBox	The picture box displays a picture as soon as all fragments that make it up have been received.
StatusBar	statusBar	The status bar is split into three panels with the Panels property. The first panel (statusBarPanelMain) shows normal status text, the second and the third (statusBarPanelAddress and statusBarPanelPort) display the group address and port number.

The form class is PictureClientForm in the file PictureShowClient.cs. It houses the methods GetMulticastConfiguration() (to request the multicast group information from the server) OnStart() (to join the multicast group), and Listener() (to start a new thread). It also contains the method DisplayPicture(), which is called for each picture in the show, and OnStop(), which terminates the listening thread.

Let's start with the namespaces and private fields that the client PictureClientForm class requires:

```
// PictureShowClient.cs

using System;
using System.Drawing;
using System.Collections;
using System.Windows.Forms;
using System.Collections.Specialized;
using System.Net;
```

```
using System.Net.Sockets;
using System.Threading;
using System.Text;
using System.Configuration;

namespace Wrox.Networking.Multicast
{
  public delegate void MethodInvokerInt(int i);
  public delegate void MethodInvokerString(string s);

  public class PictureClientForm : System.Windows.Forms.Form
  {
    private IPAddress groupAddress;   // Multicast group address
    private int groupPort;            // Multicast group port
    private int ttl;
    private UdpClient udpClient;      // Client socket for receiving
    private string serverName;        // Hostname of the server
    private int serverInfoPort;       // Port for group information

    private bool done = false;        // Flag to end receiving thread

    private UnicodeEncoding encoding = new UnicodeEncoding();

    // Array of all pictures received
    private SortedList pictureArray = new SortedList();
```

Receiving the Multicast Group Address

As in the multicast chat application, we use a configuration file for setting up the client picture show application. In this case, it is used to configure the name and address of the server so clients can connect to the TCP socket that returns the multicast address and port number:

```xml
<?xml version="1.0" encoding="utf-8" ?>
<configuration>
  <appSettings>
    <add key="ServerName" value="localhost" />
    <add key="ServerPort" value="7777" />
    <add key="TTL" value="32" />
  </appSettings>
</configuration>
```

The values in this configuration file are read by the `PictureClientForm` form class constructor, which also invokes the `GetMulticastConfiguration()` method:

```csharp
// PictureShowClient.cs

    public PictureClientForm()
    {
        //
        // Required for Windows Form Designer support
        //
        InitializeComponent();
```

```
        try
        {
            // Read the application configuration file
            NameValueCollection configuration =
                    ConfigurationSettings.AppSettings;
            serverName = configuration["ServerName"];
            serverInfoPort = int.Parse(configuration["ServerPort"]);
            ttl = int.Parse(configuration["TTL"]);
        }
        catch
        {
            MessageBox.Show("Check the configuration file");
        }

        GetMulticastConfiguration();
    }
```

We connect to the server in the `GetMulticastConfiguration()` method. After connecting, we can call `Receive()`, as the server immediately starts to send once a connection is received. The byte array received is converted to a string using an object of the `UnicodeEncoding` class. The string contains the multicast address and the port number separated by a colon (`:`), so we split the string and set the member variables `groupAddress` and `groupPort`.

As mentioned above, the status bar has two additional panels, `statusBarPanelAddress` and `statusBarPanelPort`, where the multicast address and multicast port number are displayed:

```
// PictureShowClient.cs

    private void GetMulticastConfiguration()
    {
        Socket socket = new Socket(AddressFamily.InterNetwork,
                                SocketType.Stream, ProtocolType.Tcp);
        try
        {
            // Get the multicast configuration info from the server
            IPHostEntry server = Dns.GetHostByName(serverName);
            socket.Connect(new IPEndPoint(server.AddressList[0],
                            serverInfoPort));
            byte[] buffer = new byte[512];
            int receivedBytes = socket.Receive(buffer);
            if (receivedBytes < 0)
            {
                MessageBox.Show("Error receiving");
                return;
            }
            socket.Shutdown(SocketShutdown.Both);

            string config = encoding.GetString(buffer);
            string[] multicastAddress = config.Split(':');
            groupAddress = new IPAddress(long.Parse(multicastAddress[0]));
            groupPort = int.Parse(multicastAddress[1]);
```

```
          statusBarPanelAddress.Text = groupAddress.ToString();
          statusBarPanelPort.Text = groupPort.ToString();
      }
      catch (SocketException ex)
      {
          if (ex.ErrorCode == 10061)
          {
              MessageBox.Show(this, "No server can be found on "
                          + serverName + ", at port " + serverInfoPort,
                          "Error Picture Show", MessageBoxButtons.OK,
                          MessageBoxIcon.Error);
          }
          else
          {
              MessageBox.Show(this, ex.Message, "Error Picture Show",
                          MessageBoxButtons.OK, MessageBoxIcon.Error);
          }
      }
      finally
      {
          socket.Close();
      }
  }
```

Joining the Multicast Group

Once we have the multicast address and port number, we can join the multicast group. The constructor of the UdpClient class creates a socket listening to the port of the group multicast, and then we join the multicast group by calling JoinMulticastGroup().

The task of receiving the messages and packaging the pictures together belongs to the newly created listener thread that invokes the Listener() method:

```
// PictureShowClient.cs

    private void OnStart(object sender, System.EventArgs e)
    {
        udpClient = new UdpClient(groupPort);
        try
        {
            udpClient.JoinMulticastGroup(groupAddress, ttl);
        }
        catch (Exception ex)
        {
            MessageBox.Show(ex.Message);
        }

        Thread t1 = new Thread(new ThreadStart(Listener));
        t1.Name = "Listener";
        t1.IsBackground = true;
        t1.Start();
    }
```

Receiving the Multicast Picture Data

The listener thread waits in the Receive() method of the UdpClient object until data is received. The byte array received is converted to a string with the encoding object, and in turn a PicturePackage object is initialized, passing in the XML string that is returned from the encoding object.

We have to merge all the picture fragments of a single picture received together to create full images for the client. This is done using the pictureArray member variable of type SortedList. The key of the sorted list is the picture ID; the value is an array of PicturePackage objects that make up a complete picture.

We then check whether the pictureArray already contains an array of PicturePackages for the received picture. If it does, the fragment is added to the array; if not, we allocate a new array of PicturePackages.

After updating the status bar with information about the picture fragment, we invoke the DisplayPicture() method if we have already received all the fragments of a picture:

```
// PictureShowClient.cs

    private void Listener()
    {
        while (!done)
        {
            // Receive a picture segment from the multicast group
            IPEndPoint ep = null;
            byte[] data = udpClient.Receive(ref ep);

            PicturePackage package = new PicturePackage(
                                encoding.GetString(data));

            PicturePackage[] packages;
            if (pictureArray.ContainsKey(package.Id))
            {
                packages = (PicturePackage[])pictureArray[package.Id];
                packages[package.SegmentNumber - 1] = package;
            }
            else
            {
                packages = new PicturePackage[package.NumberOfSegments];
                packages[package.SegmentNumber - 1] = package;
                pictureArray.Add(package.Id, packages);
            }

            string message = "Received picture " + package.Id + " Segment "
                        + package.SegmentNumber;
            Invoke(new MethodInvokerString(SetStatusBar),
                                    new object[] {message});

            // Check if all segments of a picture are received
            int segmentCount = 0;
            for (int i = 0; i < package.NumberOfSegments; i++)
            {
                if (packages[i] != null)
                segmentCount++;
```

```
        }

        // All segments are received, so draw the picture
        if (segmentCount == package.NumberOfSegments)
        {
            this.Invoke(new MethodInvokerInt(DisplayPicture),
                    new object[] {package.Id});
        }
    }
}
```

All we have to do in `DisplayPicture()` is recreate the picture with the help of the `PicturePackager` utility class. The picture is displayed in the picture box on the form. Because the picture fragments are no longer needed, we can now free some memory by removing the item representing the `PicturePackage` array of the sorted list collection:

```
private void DisplayPicture(int id)
{
    PicturePackage[] packages = (PicturePackage[])pictureArray[id];

    Image picture = PicturePackager.GetPicture(packages);

    pictureArray.Remove(id);

    pictureBox.Image = picture;
}
```

Starting the Picture Show

Now we can start the server and client picture show applications. We first need to select the pictures using the **Select Pictures...** button on the server interface. The picture below shows the Configure Pictures dialog after some pictures have been selected:

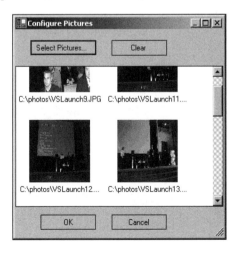

Pressing the Init button on the main dialog starts the InfoServer thread, listening for client requests. Before starting this thread, the multicast addresses can be changed, but the defaults should be enough to get going. Once the InfoServer thread is underway, clients can join the session by selecting File | Start from their menus.

The screenshot below shows the server application in action:

The client application details picture segments as they are received in the status bar, to the right of the multicast group address and port number:

Summary

In this chapter, we've looked at the architecture and issues of multicasting, and seen how multicasting can be implemented with .NET classes.

Multicasting is a pretty young technology, and it has a bright future. I expect many issues, such as security and reliability, will be resolved by the standards fairly soon. For multicasting to be truly viable across the Internet, one or two improvements are required.

However, multicasting already has many useful applications, and its usage is set to grow a great deal in the coming years. Using multicasting to send data in a one-to-many scenario, or for many-to-many group applications, considerably reduces the network load when compared to unicasting.

After discussing the architecture of multicasting, we implemented two multicast applications. The first was a chat application in a many-to-many scenario; the second was a picture server in a one-to-many scenario sending large data to the multicast group. These demonstrated how easy the built-in multicast methods of the UdpClient class make multicasting in .NET.

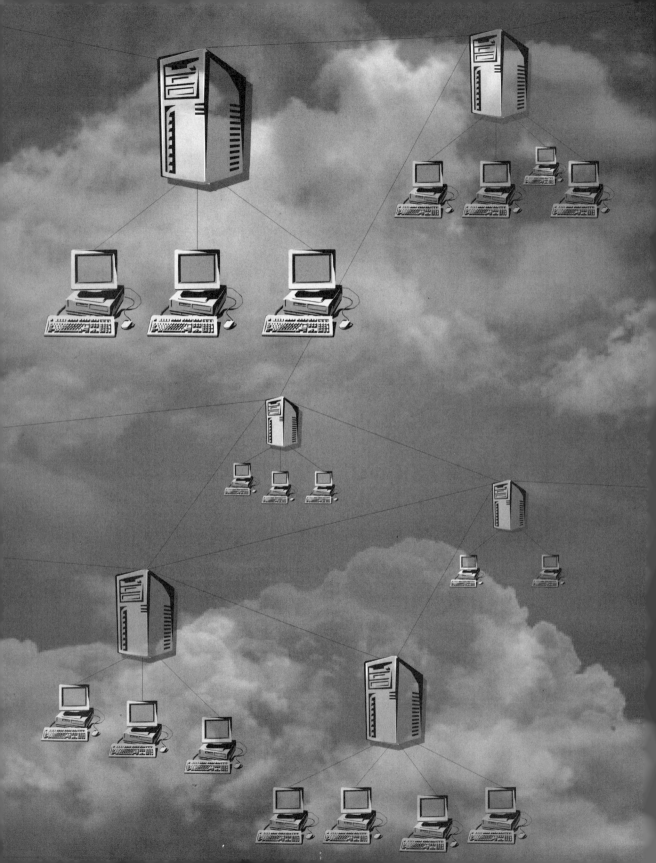

8

HTTP

In the previous chapter, we saw how the classes in the `System.Net` namespace help us to provide a complete solution for writing networked applications in managed code. In this chapter, we shall see how .NET exposes a robust implementation of the HTTP protocol. The HTTP protocol's importance as an application protocol is significant, since a large share of web traffic today uses this protocol. The .NET classes support most of the HTTP 1.1 protocol features. The advanced features include pipelining, chunking, authentication, pre-authentication, encryption, proxy support, server-certificate validation, connection management, and HTTP extensions. .NET also provides support for creating applications that use Internet protocols to send and receive data.

This chapter looks at:

- ❑ An overview of the HTTP protocol – HTTP headers, and the format of HTTP requests and responses.

- ❑ HTTP in .NET – using the `HttpWebResponse`/`HttpWebRequest`, `WebClient`, `ServicePoint`, and `ServicePointManager` classes

- ❑ Reading and writing cookies in .NET

- ❑ Creating an HTTP server with ASP.NET support

- ❑ Using the HTTP transport channel with .NET Remoting

Overview of the HTTP Protocol

With the advent of the World Wide Web, there has been a massive increase in the usage of the Internet since 1990. This was made possible with the advent of HyperText Transport Protocol (HTTP). Tim Berners-Lee first implemented the HTTP protocol in 1990–91 at CERN, the European Center for High-Energy Physics in Geneva, Switzerland.

HTTP is a lightweight application-level protocol that sits on top of TCP, and it is of course known chiefly as the transport channel of the World Wide Web, and local intranets. However, it is a generic protocol that is used for many other tasks as well as hypertext, such as for name servers and distributed object management systems through its request methods, error codes, and headers. HTTP messages are in a MIME-like format, and contain meta data about the message (such as the type of content it contains and its length), and information about the request and response, such as the method used to send the request.

There are two essential components on which the Web depends – the TCP/IP network protocol and HTTP. Almost everything that happens on the Web happens over HTTP, and the HTTP protocol is mainly used for exchanging documents (such as web pages) in the World Wide Web.

HTTP is a client-server protocol through which two systems communicate, usually over a TCP/IP connection. An HTTP server is a program that listens on a port on the machine for incoming HTTP requests.

An HTTP client opens a connection to the server through a socket, sends a request message for a particular document, and waits for a reply from the server. The server sends a response message containing a success or error code, headers containing information about the response, and (if the request was successful) the requested document. The general format of an HTTP message is the same for both requests and responses:

```
start-line
message-header(s)

[message-body]
```

There may be any number of headers, each on a separate line (that is, each one is preceded by a carriage return and line feed character). The message body is optional, but, if present, is separated from the headers by two CRLF sequences.

HTTP uses both persistent connections and non-persistent connections. Non-persistent connections are the default mode for HTTP version 1.0, whereas persistent connections are the default mode for HTTP version 1.1. A connection is said to be non-persistent if each of the TCP connections is closed immediately after the server sends the requested object to the client. This means that the connection is used for exactly one request and one response, and it does not persist for other requests.

With persistent connections, the server leaves the TCP connection open after sending the response, and hence subsequent requests and responses between the same client and server can be sent over the same connection. The server closes the connection only when it isn't used for a certain time.

Let's look briefly at a sample request from an HTTP client (such as a web browser) and the response from the web server (we'll look at the individual parts of these in more detail shortly). The following message is a request for the page http://www.dotnetforce.com/default.aspx, sent from the IE 6 browser:

```
GET /default.aspx HTTP/1.1
Connection: Keep-Alive
User-Agent: Mozilla/4.0 (compatible; MSIE 6.0; Windows NT 5.1; .NET CLR 1.0.3705)
Host: www.dotnetforce.com
Accept: image/gif, image/x-xbitmap, image/jpeg, image/pjpeg, */*
<CRLF><CRLF>
```

The first line specifies the HTTP method to use, the relative address of the document to retrieve, and the HTTP protocol version to use. This is followed by a set of headers containing information about the request. In this case, the request doesn't include a message body, so the request ends with two CRLF sequences.

The response from an IIS 5 web server to this request might look like this:

```
HTTP/1.1 200 OK
Server: Microsoft-IIS/5.0
Date: Thu, 08 Aug 2002 19:07:29 GMT
Content-Type: text/html
Accept-Ranges: bytes
Last-Modified: Tue, 22 May 2001 11:19:22 GMT
ETag: "7e9623db1e2c01:a3d"
Content-Length: 2499

<html>
   <!-- HTML content here -->
</html>
```

Here, the first line contains the HTTP version, a status code and message, followed by the message headers, a blank line, and the message body. The message body typically consists of the content of the requested document (or content generated by an ASP.NET page or a server-side script).

HTTP Headers

As we've seen, an HTTP message consists of a start line, followed by a set of headers, an empty line and some data. The start line specifies the action required of the server, or the type of data being returned, or a status code.

HTTP headers can be divided into three broad categories: headers that are sent in the request; those that are sent in the response; and those that may be sent with either. Request headers specify the capabilities of the client, such as the type of documents that the client can handle, while response headers provide information about the document returned.

Request Headers

The most important HTTP headers that can be included in the request but not the response include the following:

❑   Accept is a list of MIME types that the client accepts, in the format type/subtype. Each item in this list should be separated by commas:

```
Accept: text/html, image/gif, */*
```

/ indicates that files of all types will be accepted and handled by the client. If the file type requested can't be handled by the client, an HTTP 406 "Not acceptable" error will be returned.

❏ From indicates the Internet e-mail address of the user account under which the requesting client is running:

```
From: response@dotnetforce.com
```

❏ Referer allows the client to specify the address (URI) of the resource from which the requested URI is obtained. This allows a server to generate lists of back-links to resources for interest, logging, optimized caching, etc. It also allows obsolete or mistyped links to be traced for maintenance:

```
Referer: http://www.dotnetforce.com/Default.aspx
```

❏ The User-Agent header is a string that identifies the client application (typically a browser), as well as the platform it's running on. The general format is: software/version library/version, but this isn't invariable. The string for IE 6 is:

```
User-Agent: Mozilla/4.0 (compatible; MSIE 6.0; Windows NT 5.1; .NET CLR
1.0.3705)
```

This information can be used for statistical purposes, to trace protocol violations, and for automated recognition of the client. This allows a response to be tailored to avoid particular client limitations, such as the inability to support HTML tables.

Response Headers

The response headers include:

❏ Content-Type is used to indicate the media type of the data that is sent to the recipient or, in the case of the HEAD method, the media type that would have been sent had the request been a GET:

```
Content-Type: text/html
```

❏ Expires is the date after which the information in the document ceases to be valid. Caching clients, including proxies, must not cache this copy of the resource beyond the date given, unless its status has been updated by a later check of the origin server:

```
Expires: Fri, 09 Aug 2002 16:00:00 GMT
```

❏ The Location header defines the exact location of another resource to which the client is to be redirected. If the value is a full URL, the server returns a "redirect" to the client to retrieve the specified object directly:

```
Location: http://www.dotnetforce.com/WS/Default.aspx
```

If a reference to another file has to be made on the server, a partial URL has to be specified:

```
Location: /Tutorial/HTTP/index.html
```

❏ Server contains information about the software used by the origin server to handle the request:

```
Server: Microsoft-IIS/5.0
```

General Headers

A few headers can be included in either the response or request, for example:

❑ Date is used to set the date and time at which the message was originated:

```
Date: Tue, 06 Aug 2002 18:12:31 GMT
```

❑ In HTTP/1.0, we could use the Connection header in the request to indicate that we wanted to keep the connection alive after the response has been sent. This is now the default behavior, so in HTTP/1.1 we can use the Connection header to indicate that we *don't* want a persistent connection:

```
Connection: close
```

HTTP Requests

Each client makes a request and the server responds to that request. Every request and response has three parts – namely the request or response line, a header section, and the entity body (any content sent with the message, such as an HTML page to display in the browser, or form data to send to the server). The client contacts the server at a designated port number (the default is 80), and requests a document from the server by specifying an HTTP command called a method, followed by the document address and an HTTP version number. The client also sends the optional header information to the server in order to inform the server of its configuration and the document formats that it accepts. The header information is given in a line, along with header name and value. The client sends a blank line to end the header. After this, the client sends additional data. This could be form data sent to the server using the POST method, or a file to upload with the PUT method.

Client requests are divided into three sections. The first line of a message should always contain an HTTP command called a method, followed by a URI which identifies the file or resource that the client queries, and the HTTP version number:

```
GET /default.aspx HTTP/1.1
```

Let's examine each of these sections now. A **method** is an HTTP command that begins the first line of a client request. The method informs the server of the purpose of the client request. There are seven methods defined for HTTP – GET, HEAD, POST, OPTIONS, PUT, DELETE, and TRACE, but HTTP servers can also implement extension methods that aren't defined by the HTTP protocol. Note that method names are case-sensitive, so for example get won't be recognized as a valid method.

The GET method is used to request information that is located at a specified URI on the server. It is the method commonly used by browsers to retrieve documents for viewing. The result of a GET request is generated in different ways. It could be a file accessible by the server, the output of a program, or the output from a hardware device, and so on.

When a client uses the GET method in its request, the server sends a response containing a status line, headers, and the requested data. If the server cannot process the request due to an error or lack of authorization, the server sends a textual explanation in the data portion of the response.

The entity-body portion of a GET request is always empty. The file or program that the client requests is identified by its full path name on the server. Any additional information, such as form values, that the client needs to send to the server is appended to the URL as a query string:

```
GET /default.aspx?name=Vinod HTTP/1.1
```

The HEAD method is functionally similar to the GET method, except that the server does not send anything in the data portion of the reply. The HEAD method requests only the header information on a file or resource. The HTTP server should send the same header information for a HEAD request as it would for a GET request. This method is used when the client needs information about the document, but doesn't need to retrieve it.

The POST method allows data to be sent to the server in a client request. The data is sent to a data-handling program that the server has access to. The POST method can be used for many applications, such as providing inputs to network services, command-line interface programs, and so on. The data is sent to the server in the entity-body section of the client's request. After the server has processed the POST request and headers, it passes the entity-body to the program specified by the URI.

The OPTIONS method requests information about the HTTP support on the web server. OPTIONS can be used with a URL to retrieve information about a specific document, or with the wildcard * to retrieve information about the server's capabilities in general. This information is returned in the response headers; the following response contains the information returned from a request for options for the postinfo.html page on an IIS 5 server (OPTIONS/postinfo.html HTTP/1.1):

```
HTTP/1.1 200 OK
Server: Microsoft-IIS/5.0
Date: Fri, 09 Aug 2002 18:52:18 GMT
MS-Author-Via: DAV
Content-Length: 0
Accept-Ranges: bytes
DASL: <DAV:sql>
DAV: 1, 2
Public: OPTIONS, TRACE, GET, HEAD, DELETE, PUT, POST, COPY, MOVE, MKCOL, PROPFIND,
PROPPATCH, LOCK, UNLOCK, SEARCH
Allow: OPTIONS, TRACE, GET, HEAD, COPY, PROPFIND, SEARCH, LOCK, UNLOCK
Cache-Control: private
<CRLF><CRLF>
```

The Allow header indicates which HTTP methods are permitted for this particular document, while the Public header specifies all of the methods supported by the server. For example, the response above shows that DELETE is supported by the server, but not permitted for postinfo.html.

The response also indicates the server's support for DAV (Distributed Authoring and Versioning) and DASL (DAV Searching and Locating).

> *DAV is a standard that extends HTTP/1.1 by providing a new set of methods to allow us to manage resources on a web server, such as setting and retrieving properties of the resources, and moving and copying files. DASL defines extensions to allow us to search DAV servers. DAV is defined in RFC 2518 (http://www.ietf.org/rfc/rfc2518.txt).*

The DELETE method requests the named file to be deleted from the server, and the PUT method requests that the document included as the request body be uploaded to the server and made available with the specified URI. Finally, the TRACE method is used for debugging the request/response chain; the server should return the entire request message in the response body.

After the request method comes the URI specifying the file we want to retrieve, post data to, etc. This may be an absolute URI, such as http://www.wrox.com/default.aspx, or a path relative to the document root directory of the server, such as /default.aspx (the relative path *must* be prefixed by a forward slash). It is the responsibility of the server to map these URIs to file-system paths such as C:\inetpub\wwwroot\default.aspx.

The last component of a request line is the HTTP version number, which is used to specify the version of the HTTP specification used. Usually this will be either HTTP/1.1 or HTTP/1.0 (although there is an older version, HTTP/0.9).

HTTP Responses

The server's response to a client request is again divided into three parts. The first line is the server response line, which contains the HTTP version number, a number indicating the status of the request, and a short phrase describing the status. Then comes the header information, followed by an empty line and the entity body (which may be empty, for example if responding to a HEAD or OPTIONS request).

The HTTP version indicates the version of HTTP that the server uses to respond. The status code is a three-digit number that indicates the server's result of the client's request. The description following the status code is just a human-readable description of the status code. There are a number of predefined status codes, but the server can define additional codes. Some of the most common predefined status codes are:

Code	Description
200	OK – the request was received and processed
301	The resource has been moved permanently
302	The resource has temporarily been moved
400	Bad request – the request message was not correctly formatted
401	Unauthorized – the user doesn't have rights to access the requested document
402	Payment required to access the resource
408	The request timed out
500	Internal server error – an error prevented the HTTP server processing the request

After the status line, the server sends header information to the client about itself and the requested document. A blank line (that is, two consecutive CRLF sequences) ends the header.

If the client requested data, and the request is successful, the requested data will be sent as the entity body after the response headers. This data could be a copy of the requested file, or it could be content generated dynamically, for example by an ASP.NET page or by a server-side script. If the client's request is not fulfilled, additional data may be provided explaining why the server could not fulfill the request.

In HTTP 1.0, after the server has finished sending the requested data, it disconnects from the client and the transaction is over unless a `Connection: Keep-Alive` header is sent. However, in HTTP 1.1, the default is that the server should maintain the connection and allow the client to make additional requests, even if the `Connection` header isn't sent. If we don't want this behavior, we need to send a `Connection: close` header to specify that the connection should be closed after the response has been sent.

HTTP in .NET

Although we can implement the HTTP protocol manually using the standard Sockets or TCP classes, .NET provides a number of classes (mostly in the `System.Net` namespace) that are designed to facilitate communication with an HTTP server. These implement the generic request/response model, along with some of the additional properties that provide a greater level of control over the HTTP-specific features, such as access to the HTTP protocol in an object model for property-level control over headers, authentication, pre-authentication, encryption, proxy support, pipelining, and connection management:

Class	Namespace	Inherits From	Description
HttpWebRequest	System.Net	WebRequest	Represents an HTTP request
HttpWebResponse	System.Net	WebResponse	Represents an HTTP response
WebClient	System.Net	Component	Provides easy-to-use methods for sending files or data to a URI, and receiving data from a URI
Uri	System	MarshalByRef Object	Represents a URI, allowing easy access to the component parts of the URI, such as the hostname and absolute path
UriBuilder	System	Object	Utility class for creating and modifying Uri objects
ServicePoint	System.Net	Object	Handles connections to a given URI
ServicePoint Manager	System.Net	Object	Manager class for managing ServicePoint objects

HttpWebRequest and HttpWebResponse

The .NET Framework provides two basic classes for simplifying HTTP access: `HttpWebRequest` and `HttpWebResponse`. These classes handle most of the functionality provided through the HTTP protocol in a straightforward manner. They derive from the abstract `WebRequest` and `WebResponse` classes that we looked at in Chapter 3.

To see how these classes work, let's look at an example of using them to retrieve a web page from the Internet:

```
using System;
using System.Net;
using System.IO;
using System.Text;

class SimpleWebRequest
{
    public static void Main()
    {
        string query = "http://www.wrox.com";
        HttpWebRequest req = (HttpWebRequest)HttpWebRequest.Create(query);
        HttpWebResponse resp = (HttpWebResponse)req.GetResponse();
        StreamReader sr = new StreamReader(resp.GetResponseStream,
                                           Encoding.ASCII);
        Console.WriteLine(sr.ReadToEnd());
        resp.Close();
        sr.Close();
    }
}
```

In order to create an `HttpWebRequest` object, we need to call the static `WebRequest.Create()` method (also inherited by the `HttpWebRequest` class). This method examines the format of the URI passed in, and returns a `WebRequest` object representing an HTTP request or a file system request as appropriate. Since the same method is used to create both HTTP and file system requests, the object returned is of type `WebRequest`, and must be cast to `HttpWebRequest` or `FileWebRequest`. The `Create()` method parses the URL and passes the resolved URL into the request object. The request portion structures the outbound HTTP request and also handles the configuration of the HTTP headers.

Once we have the request object, we can call its `GetResponse()` method. This sends the request to the server, and returns a `WebResponse` object (again, we need to cast this to `HttpWebResponse`). This object represents an HTTP response message, and contains the HTTP header information such as `ContentType`, `ContentLength`, `StatusCode`, and `Cookies`, and the first part of the data, which is buffered internally until read from the stream itself. The `HttpWebResponse` object's properties are set with this data.

Next, a stream is returned using the `GetResponseStream()` method. The stream points at the actual binary HTTP response from the web server (the entity body of the response message). A stream provides a lot of flexibility in handling how data is retrieved from the web server. To retrieve the actual data and read the rest of the result document from the web server, the stream has to be read. Here we use `StreamReader` object to return a string from the data. The encoding type is set to `ASCII` (although a more robust solution would check the `Content-Encoding` header and use the encoding specified there). The encoding is important because, if the data is transferred as a byte stream without the encoding, it results in invalid character translations for any extended characters.

The above sample uses the `StreamReader` object's `ReadToEnd()` method to retrieve the entire data from the web server as a string. However, the data could also be read in parts using the `StreamReader`'s `Read()` method. See Chapter 2 for more information about reading data from streams.

Setting and Reading the HTTP Headers

Both the `HttpWebRequest` and `HttpWebResponse` classes have a `Headers` property that returns a `WebHeaderCollection` object containing information about the headers for the HTTP message. We can add headers to an HTTP request by calling either the `Add()` method or the `Set()` method of this object:

```
HttpWebRequest req = (HttpWebRequest)WebRequest.Create(
                                        "http://localhost:81");
req.Headers.Add("Accept-Language: en-us");
// This is exactly equivalent
// req.Headers.Set("Accept-Language", "en-us");
```

As the above example shows, the `Add()` method takes a single string parameter representing the entire header field, whereas the `Set()` method takes two string values – the name of the header, and the value we want to set it to. Both these methods can be used equally for standard and custom HTTP headers. However, the `HttpWebRequest` class also has a number of public properties that allow us to set a request header without accessing the `Headers` property:

Property	Data Type	HTTP Header
Accept	string	Accept
Connection	string	Connection
ContentLength	long	Content-Length
ContentType	string	Content-Type
Expect	string	Expect
IfModifiedSince	DateTime	If-Modified-Since
Referer	string	Referer
TransferEncoding	string	Transfer-Encoding
UserAgent	string	User-Agent

For example, to set the `User-Agent` header to `"User-Agent: SimpleHttpClient"`, we would use:

```
req.UserAgent = "SimpleHttpClient";
```

Notice that where a property exists to set a header, this *must* be used. For example, if we attempt to set the `User-Agent` header using:

```
req.Headers.Add("User-Agent: SimpleHttpClient");
```

a run-time exception will be thrown.

The `HttpWebResponse` object also contains a number of public properties (all read-only), which allow us to access the value of selected HTTP headers:

Property	Type	HTTP Header
ContentEncoding	string	Content-Encoding
ContentLength	long	Content-Length
ContentType	string	Content-Type
LastModified	DateTime	Last-Modified
Server	string	Server

Each individual header field can also be accessed as a name/value pair within the WebHeaderCollection. The names of the headers are the keys to the collection, and the header values the associated values. We can therefore access the value of a header using the indexer of the collection with the name of the header. The following code writes all the headers in the response to the console window:

```
foreach (string header in resp.Headers)
    Console.WriteLine("{0}: {1}", header, resp.Headers[header]);
```

Currency Converter Application

We have seen how to get the contents from the Web using the HttpWebRequest and HttpWebResponse objects, so now let's look at a sample application that uses these objects to convert one currency to another using live currency rates from the http://finance.yahoo.com web site:

```
using System;
using System.IO;
using System.Net;
using System.Text;

class CurrencyConverter
{
    static void Main()
    {
        HttpWebRequest req;
        HttpWebResponse resp;
        StreamReader sr;

        char[] separator = { ',' };

        string result;
        string fullPath;
        string currencyFrom = "USD";    // US Dollar
        string currencyTo = "INR";      // Indian Rupee
        double amount = 100d;

        Console.WriteLine("Currency Converter");
        Console.WriteLine("Currency From : {0}", currencyFrom);
        Console.WriteLine("Currency To : {0}", currencyTo);
        Console.WriteLine("Amount : {0}", amount);
```

```
            // Build the URL that returns the quote
            fullPath = "http://finance.yahoo.com/d/quotes.csv?s=" + currencyFrom +
                    currencyTo + "=X&f=s1l1d1t1c1ohgv&e=.csv";
            try
            {
                req = (HttpWebRequest)WebRequest.Create(fullPath);
                resp = (HttpWebResponse)req.GetResponse();
                sr = new StreamReader(resp.GetResponseStream(), Encoding.ASCII);
                result = sr.ReadLine();
                resp.Close();
                sr.Close();
                string[] temp = result.Split(separator);

                if(temp.Length > 1)
                {
                    // Only show the relevant portions
                    double rate = Convert.ToDouble(temp[1]);
                    double convert = amount * rate;
                    Console.WriteLine("{0} {1}(s) = {2} {3}(s)", amount,
                                    currencyFrom, convert, currencyTo);
                }
                else
                {
                    Console.WriteLine("Error in getting currency rates " +
                                    "from website.");
                }
            }
            catch(Exception e)
            {
                Console.WriteLine("Exception occurred");
            }
        }
    }
```

We retrieve the live currency rates by building a URL pointing to the finance.yahoo.com web site, including a query string that specifies the currencies we want to convert to and from as three-character strings (in this example, USD for US Dollars, and INR for Indian Rupees), together with some more cryptic information required by Yahoo's server. We use the HttpWebRequest object to send this request to the server, and use the HttpWebResponse object to access the returned document. This is a comma-separated values (CSV) file, the second value of which is the current exchange rate. This is the only value we're interested in, so we convert it to a double and store it in the rate variable. We then use this variable to calculate the value of the converted currency:

Notice that this example might not work correctly in some countries, where the period (.) is used as a thousands separator rather than a decimal point. A work-around to this would be to replace the decimal point with a comma before calling `Convert.ToDouble()` *on the value read from the CSV file:*

```
double rate = Convert.ToDouble(temp[1].Replace(".", ","));
```

A more robust solution would be to check the `CurrencyDecimalSeparator` *property of the* `NumberFormatInfo` *object for the current culture.*

Posting Data

This Currency Converter application retrieves data using an HTTP GET request. If we want to post data to the server, the HTTP POST method is used. POST data refers to the process of taking data and sending it to the web server as a part of the request payload. A POST operation not only sends data to the server, but also retrieves a response from the server indicating success or failure, and possibly other content such as a web page.

```csharp
using System;
using System.IO;
using System.Net;
using System.Text;
using System.Web;

class PostData
{
    static void Main()
    {
        string SiteURL="http://www.dotnetforce.com/postsample.asp";
        StreamWriter sw = null;

        // Preparing the data to post
        string postData = "Posted=" + HttpUtility.UrlEncode("True") +
                          "&X=" + HttpUtility.UrlEncode("Value");

        HttpWebRequest req = (HttpWebRequest)WebRequest.Create(SiteURL);
        req.Method = "POST";
        req.ContentLength = postData.Length;
        req.ContentType = "application/x-www-form-urlencoded";
```

```
        sw = new StreamWriter(req.GetRequestStream());

        // Encoding the data
        byte[] sendBuffer = Encoding.ASCII.GetBytes(postData);

        // Posting the data
        sw.Write(postData);
        sw.Close();

        HttpWebResponse resp = (HttpWebResponse)req.GetResponse();
        StreamReader srData = new StreamReader(resp.GetResponseStream(),
                                    Encoding.ASCII);

        // Reading the output stream
        string outHtml = srData.ReadToEnd();
        Console.WriteLine(outHtml);

        // Close and clean up the StreamReader
        resp.Close();
        srData.Close();
    }
}
```

Posted data needs to be encoded properly before sending to the server. Data posted to a web page can have one of two different MIME types – `application/x-www-form-urlencoded` (as in this example), or `multipart/form-data`. In the former case, the data is encoded in the same way as for a query string – the data has to be encoded in the buffer into key value pairs, and we have to use URL encoding for the values. The static `UrlEncode()` method of the `System.Web.HttpUtility` class can be used for encoding the data. The `multipart/form-data` type allows us to upload files from the client via an HTML form. As the name suggests, the data is divided into sections, which can contain binary or character data, or standard URL-encoded form data.

> *Note that URL encoding should only be used when we post data to a web page. It's not needed for any other content – we can post the data directly.*

The posted data has to be encoded and saved to a byte array using the static `Encoding.ASCII` object with the `GetBytes()` method, which returns a byte array. After setting the `ContentLength` property, which helps the remote server to handle the size of the data stream, the post data is written to the server using a `StreamWriter` object. This object writes to the output stream returned from the `GetRequestStream()` method of our `HttpWebRequest` object. Once we've sent the data, we use a `StreamReader` object to read the response returned from the server.

Up to now, we have just been looking at the basic use of `HttpWebRequest` and `HttpWebResponse` objects. However, to build a typical application that uses HTTP, we need to make use of some more advanced features, such as `KeepAlive`, `ConnectionLimit`, Connection Groups, etc. Now let's see the way to use these properties, and we will also have a look at a few other advanced features of HTTP.

HTTP Chunking

One of the features added to HTTP in version 1.1 is **chunking**. Chunking refers to the process of sending a message body in multiple fragments, rather than in one go. Each fragment must be prefixed by its size if the connection is persistent, and the header does not include a `Content-Length` field. Otherwise, there would be no way for the recipient to know when the message body has been completely sent and the connection is free for the next transaction.

Chunked transfer coding may be used by both requests and responses, although it is more commonly seen in the latter. It is used mainly when an application needs to send or receive data whose exact size is not known at the time when the download/upload begins. This is most commonly found when the data in question is created dynamically based on other application or server logic. To send chunked data, the `SendChunked` property of the `HttpWebRequest` should be set to `true`:

```
using System;
using System.IO;
using System.Net;
using System.Text;

class ChunkingExample
{
    static void Main()
    {
        string query = "http://localhost/postsample.aspx";
        StreamWriter sw = null;
        string postData = "Posted=true&X=Value";

        HttpWebRequest req = (HttpWebRequest)HttpWebRequest.Create(query);

        // Setting the request method
        req.Method = "POST";

        // Setting the Content-Type header
        req.ContentType = "application/x-www-form-urlencoded";

        // Setting the Content-Length header
        req.ContentLength = postData.Length;

        // Setting the SendChunked property
        req.SendChunked = true;

        // Posting the data
        sw = new StreamWriter(req.GetRequestStream());
        sw.Write(postData);
        sw.Close();

        HttpWebResponse resp = (HttpWebResponse)req.GetResponse();

        StreamReader sr = new StreamReader(resp.GetResponseStream());

        // Reading the output stream
        string outHtml = sr.ReadToEnd();
        Console.WriteLine(outHtml);
        resp.Close();
        sr.Close();
    }
}
```

HTTP Pipelining

One of the most important features of HTTP 1.1 is **pipelining**. This feature allows the .NET classes to send simultaneous multiple HTTP requests to a back-end server over a persistent connection without waiting for a response from the server before the next request is sent. Thus, by enabling pipelining, an application requesting multiple resources from a server doesn't get blocked waiting for one particular resource, which may take longer to send than the others. This can therefore increase the performance of the application. The figure below demonstrates the use of pipelining in comparison to the traditional request/response behavior of HTTP. Pipelining is enabled by default in .NET, but it can be disabled by setting the `Pipelined` property of the `HttpWebRequest` to `false`. We might do this if it's important that we get the response to each request before sending the next request.

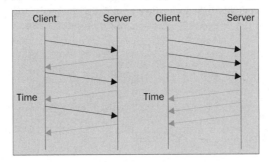

HTTP Keep-Alive

Persistent connections (or keep-alive connections) were introduced in HTTP/1.0 to allow a client using HTTP to conserve network resources and behave in a more efficient manner by keeping an existing TCP connection to the server alive and reusing that connection, rather than closing it and creating a new one for each request.

The `Connection` header controls connection persistence. By default, all HTTP/1.1 connections are considered persistent, unless a request or response includes a `Connection: close` header. When a server or client receives a message with this header, it closes the connection as soon as the transaction is complete.

By default, the `KeepAlive` property of an `HttpWebRequest` object is set to `true`, causing a persistent connection to be created with the server, provided that the server supports this behavior. If you are accessing a back-end server from a middle-tier ASP.NET application, you should be aware that the connection to the back-end server stays open until the server times out the connection.

If `KeepAlive` is set to `true`, the connection won't be closed until the timeout duration elapses with no new request made, or the server explicitly terminates the connection. In most cases, both the client and the server are permitted to close the connection by sending a `Connection: close` header in the request/response.

HTTP Connection Management

Connection management is an important feature for achieving maximum scalability and performance in a networked application. This is achieved by limiting the number of outbound sockets established and making use of advanced HTTP features such as persistent connections to optimize client-server interaction. .NET manages connections through the `ServicePoint` and `ServicePointManager` classes.

The `ServicePoint` class in the `System.Net` namespace manages connections to an Internet resource on the basis of the host information that is passed in the resource's URI. The initial connection to the resource determines the information that has to be maintained by the `ServicePoint`, which in turn is shared by all the subsequent requests to that resource.

A `ServicePoint` object represents a connection to a URI with a particular protocol identifier (such as http://) and hostname (such as www.dotnetforce.com). If two or more requests are made to access resources with the same protocol and host details, the same connection will be used for both requests. For example, if we make a request for http://www.dotnetforce.com/default.aspx, and then make a second request for http://www.dotnetforce.com/SiteContent.aspx?Type=1, the same connection will be used both times, as they share the same host details and protocol identifier.

We instantiate a `ServicePoint` using the `FindServicePoint()` static method of the `ServicePointManager` class. This takes as a parameter a `Uri` object representing the Internet resource this service point will be used to connect to, or either a `Uri` object or a URL in string format, together with an `IWebProxy` object. We'll look at issues with web proxies shortly. For example:

```
// Get a Uri object to point to http://www.dotnetforce.com
Uri siteURL = new Uri("http://www.dotnetforce.com");

// Call FindServicePoint() to get a ServicePoint object for this URI
ServicePoint spSite = ServicePointManager.FindServicePoint(siteURL);
```

Connection Timeout

When an instance of a `ServicePoint` is created, it maintains the connection to an Internet resource specified until the connection times out. We can change this timeout value for an individual `ServicePoint` object by setting the `MaxIdleTime` property. The default value of `MaxIdleTime` is set by the `ServicePointManager.MaxServicePointIdleTime` property. We can also find out how long has elapsed since the last connection was made to the service point through the `IdleSince` property:

```
// Get the date and time of the connection since it was last connected
DateTime idleTime = spSite.IdleSince;

// Setting the MaxIdleTime in Milliseconds
spSite.MaxIdleTime = 5000;
```

> The default `MaxIdleTime` value is 900,000 milliseconds (15 minutes).

We can also set the `MaxIdleTime` to `Timeout.Infinite` (in the `System.Threading` namespace) to indicate that the `ServicePoint` should never timeout (although the connection can of course be terminated by the server):

```
spSite.MaxIdleTime = Timeout.Infinite;
```

Connection Limit

The default maximum number of connections permitted from an application using the `HttpWebRequest` class to a given server is two. This number can be increased or decreased depending on the actual conditions under which the application is running. The code below sets the client's maximum number of connections to four:

```
Uri SiteURL = new Uri("http://www.dotnetforce.com");
ServicePoint spSite = ServicePointManager.FindServicePoint(SiteURL);

spSite.ConnectionLimit = 4;
```

The maximum number of connections that are to be used depends on the criteria on which the application runs. As a result, it's better to get a baseline measurement of the application's throughput with the default setting, and then change the default, and check how the performance is affected. For example, assuming that the default is two, we might try changing it to four.

> It is recommended in the HTTP/1.1 specification that a client application should have no more than two simultaneous open connections to a server.

Generally, the number of concurrent connections shouldn't be too high, as there is a fine balance between the benefits of the application having multiple connections, and the overhead of creating a new connection. At some point, an application that creates a lot of connections will actually perform slower than an application wisely using fewer connections.

The WebClient Class

In most web applications, uploading and downloading data is a day-to-day task. Before .NET, we had to either buy a third-party component or use the WinSock API to do this, which was a tedious job. The .NET Framework class library has just the component for this. Residing in the `System.Net` namespace, the `WebClient` class exposes three methods for downloading data from a remote resource, and four methods for uploading raw data or files to a remote resource. `WebClient` relies on the `WebRequest` class to provide access to Internet resources, so the `WebClient` class can use any registered pluggable protocol. In general, this class is a great way for accomplishing HTTP, HTTPS, and file protocol communications. In this section, we will see how to upload and download data using these methods.

The `WebClient` class can be instantiated directly as shown below:

```
WebClient client = new WebClient();
```

The DownloadData() Method

The `DownloadData()` method takes a string value representing a URL address as an argument, and returns a byte array of data from the specified address:

```
using System;
using System.Net;
using System.Text;
```

```
class WebTest
{
   static void Main()
   {
      WebClient client = new WebClient();
      byte[] urlData = client.DownloadData("http://www.dotnetforce.com");
      string data = Encoding.ASCII.GetString(urlData);
      Console.WriteLine(data);
   }
}
```

The DownloadFile() Method

The DownloadFile() method takes a URL address and a filename as parameters. The file will be downloaded to a local drive. The code sample downloads an image file from a remote location to the local hard disk:

```
using System;
using System.Net;
using System.IO;

class DownloadFile
{
   static void Main(string[] args)
   {
      string siteURL = "http://www.dotnetforce.com/images/logo11.gif";
      string fileName = "C:\\ASP.gif";

      // Create a new WebClient instance.
      WebClient client = new WebClient();

      // Concatenate the domain with the Web resource filename.
      Console.WriteLine("Downloading File \"{0}\" from \"{1}\" .......\n\n",
                        fileName, siteURL);

      // Download the Web resource and save it into the
      // current filesystem folder.
      client.DownloadFile(siteURL,fileName);

      Console.WriteLine("Successfully Downloaded File \"{0}\" from \"{1}\"",
                        fileName, siteURL);
      Console.WriteLine("\nDownloaded file saved in the following " +
                        "file system folder:\n\t" + fileName);
   }
}
```

The OpenRead() Method

The OpenRead() method is similar to the DownloadData() method; the only difference is that it returns a Stream object that enables us to read the data from the target URL. Using this method, the data can be retrieved in parts with the help of the Stream object's Read() and ReadBlock() methods. This allows us to give the status of the download to the user.

The sample below uses the OpenRead() method to read the data from the remote location:

```csharp
using System;
using System.IO;
using System.Net;

class OpenRead
{
    static void Main(string[] args)
    {
        string siteURL = "http://www.rediff.com";

        // Create a new WebClient instance.
        WebClient client = new WebClient();

        // Concatenate the domain with the Web resource filename.
        Console.WriteLine("Start Downloading Data From \"{0}\" .......\n\n",
                    siteURL);

        // Download the web resource from the RemoteURL.
        Stream stmData = client.OpenRead(siteURL);
        StreamReader srData = new StreamReader(stmData);

        // Create file
        FileInfo fiData = new FileInfo("C:\\Default.htm");
        StreamWriter st = fiData.CreateText();
        Console.WriteLine("Writing to the file...");

        // Write to file
        st.WriteLine(srData.ReadToEnd());

        st.Close();
        stmData.Close();
    }
}
```

The OpenWrite() Method

The `OpenWrite()` method is used to send data to the specified URL. This can be done using the POST method, or through another supported method (such as a DAV method). `OpenWrite()` takes a string address parameter and the name of the HTTP method to use, and returns a stream that we can write to in order to place data into the specified URL.

The code below uploads a file from the hard disk to the remote location (supposing that we have the necessary permissions on the server). First we create a `WebClient` object that points to the Internet resource (such as an ASP.NET page) where we want to post the data. Next, we convert the string data we want to post into a byte array, and write this to the stream returned from our call to the `WebClient`'s `OpenWrite()` method. Since we specified "POST" as the second parameter of `OpenWrite()`, this has the effect of posting the data to the specified page:

```
using System;
using System.IO;
using System.Net;
using System.Text;

class OpenWrite
{
    static void Main(string[] args)
    {
        string siteURL = "http://localhost/postsample.aspx";

        // Create a new WebClient instance.
        string uploadData = "Posted=True&X=Value";

        // Apply ASCII encoding to obtain an array of bytes .
        byte[] uploadArray = Encoding.ASCII.GetBytes(uploadData);

        // Create a new WebClient instance.
        WebClient client = new WebClient();
        Console.WriteLine("Uploading data to {0}...", siteURL);

        Stream stmUpload = client.OpenWrite(siteURL, "POST");
        stmUpload.Write(uploadArray, 0, uploadArray.Length);

        // Close the stream and release resources.
        stmUpload.Close();
        Console.WriteLine("Successfully posted the data.");
    }
}
```

The UploadData() Method

The `UploadData()` method sends data in the form of a byte array to the server without encoding it. This method takes the URL and optionally also the upload method ("POST", "GET", etc.) as parameters.

The sample application uploads a string using the POST method with `UploadData()`:

```
using System;
using System.Net;
using System.IO;
using System.Text;

class UploadData
{
    static void Main(string[] args)
    {
        string siteURL;
        siteURL = "http://localhost/postsample.aspx";
        WebClient client = new WebClient();
        client.Credentials = System.Net.CredentialCache.DefaultCredentials ;
        string uploadString = "Hello Force..";

        // Adding the HTTP Content-Type Header
        client.Headers.Add("Content-Type",
                        "application/x-www-form-urlencoded");

        // Apply ASCII Encoding to obtain the string as a byte array.
        byte[] sendData = Encoding.ASCII.GetBytes(uploadString);
        Console.WriteLine("Uploading to {0} ...", siteURL);

        // Upload the string using the POST method.
        byte[] recData = client.UploadData(siteURL, "POST", sendData);

        // Display the response.
        Console.WriteLine("\nResponse received was {0}",
                        Encoding.ASCII.GetString(recData));
    }
}
```

The UploadFile() Method

UploadFile() is similar to the UploadData() method. This method uploads a file (for example, from the local hard drive). The UploadFile() method accepts a URL, filename, and optionally the HTTP method to use as parameters. This method uploads the specified file to the specified location and optionally returns the response of the target URL as a byte array.

The sample below uploads a file from the local disk to the remote location using the UploadFile() method. Notice that we specify the account details using a NetworkCredential object, as the server may not allow anonymous uploads. We use the PUT HTTP method, which is specifically intended for uploading files to an HTTP server. The remote server response is sent in a byte array, which has to be transformed into a string. We use the static ASCII property of the Encoding class in the System.Text namespace for this task. This returns an ASCIIEncoding object, which has a GetString() method that accepts the byte array as a parameter. The byte array is translated to a string, which is written to the console:

```
using System;
using System.Net;
using System.IO;
using System.Text;
```

```
class UploadFile
{
    static void Main(string[] args)
    {
        string siteURL="http://localhost/images/http.txt";
        string remoteResponse;

        // Create a new WebClient instance.
        WebClient client = new WebClient();

        NetworkCredential cred = new NetworkCredential("username",
                                            "password", "domain");

        string fileName = "C:\\http.txt";
        Console.WriteLine("Uploading {0} to {1} ...", fileName, siteURL);

        // File Uploaded using PUT method
        byte[] responseArray = client.UploadFile(siteURL, "PUT", fileName);

        //Response from the Target URL
        remoteResponse = Encoding.ASCII.GetString(responseArray);
        Console.WriteLine(remoteResponse);
    }
}
```

Notice that the uploaded file will be sent as `multipart/form-data`, and will contain meta data as well as the actual file data, so it will need to be trimmed on the server side. For example, if our original file contains the text:

```
Imagine some text about the HTTP protocol here...
```

this will be sent to the server in the format:

```
----------------------8c410e41d7c7730
Content-Disposition: form-data; name="file"; filename="HTTP.txt"
Content-Type: application/octet-stream

Imagine some text about the HTTP protocol here...
----------------------8c410e41d7c7730
```

The first and last lines (the boundaries for the content) can be discovered from the `boundary` token in the `Content-Type` header of the request.

The UploadValues() Method

The `UploadValues()` method enables us to upload a name/value pair collection to an Internet resource. This method is useful when one needs to emulate a `POST` request from an HTML form and retrieve the response. With this method, values are passed to the remote target using the `NameValueCollection` of the `System.Collections.Specialized` namespace. Optionally, we can also specify the method for sending the value. The method can be `POST`, `GET`, or any other supported method.

The sample code below gets the search result information from the web page `SiteContent.aspx`. The values `Type` and `Keyword` are passed to this page using the `UploadValues()` method:

```
using System.Net;
using System.IO;
using System.Text;
using System.Collections.Specialized;

class UploadValues
{
    static void Main(string[] args)
    {
        string siteURL = "http://localhost/Force/SiteContent.aspx";
        string remoteResponse;

        // Create a new WebClient instance.
        WebClient client = new WebClient();
        NameValueCollection appendURL = new NameValueCollection();

        // Add the NameValueCollection
        appendURL.Add("Type", "14");
        appendURL.Add("Keyword", "WebService");
        Console.WriteLine("Uploading the Value pair");

        // Upload the NameValueCollection using POST method
        byte[] responseArray = client.UploadValues(siteURL, "POST",
                                                   appendURL);
        remoteResponse = Encoding.ASCII.GetString(responseArray);
        Console.WriteLine(remoteResponse);
    }
}
```

Authentication

The HTTP protocol provides for some simple security measures, such as credential-based access control. The .NET classes support a variety of client authentication mechanisms, including digest, basic, Kerberos, NTLM, and custom. To obtain this functionality, we can use the `CredentialCache` class or the `NetworkCredential` class (both in the `System.Net` namespace). Both of these classes implement the `ICredentials` interface, so it's often possible to use either class.

A `NetworkCredential` object stores a single set of credentials for logging on to a network or Internet resource, and contains information about the username and password for the user account it represents, and (for Windows-based authentication systems) the domain to which the user account belongs. The `CredentialCache` class can store multiple sets of authentication credentials; the default set of credentials for the application can be set or retrieved by calling the `DefaultCredentials` static property of the `CredentialCache` class.

Authentication is achieved by setting the `Credentials` object of the `HttpWebRequest` or `WebClient` class before making a request. In the case of digest and basic authentication, a username and password are specified. For NTLM or Kerberos, Windows security is used and the `Credential` object can either be set to a username, password, and domain combination, or the system defaults can be requested. The best way of understanding this is by looking at the code we would use to authenticate ourselves to an Internet resource that requires a login.

We'll cover authentication and authorization in more detail in Chapter 11, so we'll keep this discussion very simple.

Basic Authentication

To make a request to an Internet site using basic authentication, we should specify the username and password for accessing it. We do this by creating a new `NetworkCredential` object, passing in the username and password as strings, and setting the `Credentials` property of the `HttpWebRequest` or of the `WebClient` object to point to this. For example, using the `HttpWebRequest` class to make the request:

```
string query = "http://www.rediff.com/";
WebRequest request = (HttpWebRequest)WebRequest.Create(query);

request.Credentials = new NetworkCredential("Username", "Password");
HttpWebResponse response = (HttpWebResponse)request.GetResponse();

StreamReader reader = new StreamReader(response.GetResponseStream(),
                                       Encoding.ASCII);

Console.WriteLine(reader.ReadToEnd());
response.Close();
reader.Close();
```

Similarly, for a `WebClient` object we would specify:

```
WebClient client = new WebClient();
client.Credentials  = new NetworkCredential("Username", "Password");
```

NTLM Authentication

The code below makes a request to a secured internal site using NTLM authentication. In this case, we're using the application's default credentials, so we set the `HttpWebRequest` object's Credentials property to `CredentialCache.DefaultCredentials`.

```
using System;
using System.Net;
using System.IO;
using System.Text;

class Credential
{
    static void Main(string[] args)
    {
        string query= "http://www.rediff.com/";
        WebRequest request = (HttpWebRequest)WebRequest.Create(query);
        request.Credentials = CredentialCache.DefaultCredentials;
        HttpWebResponse response = (HttpWebResponse)request.GetResponse();
        StreamReader reader = new StreamReader(response.GetResponseStream(),
                                               Encoding.ASCII);
        Console.WriteLine(reader.ReadToEnd());
        response.Close();
        reader.Close();
    }
}
```

Similarly, for the `WebClient` class we should specify:

```
WebClient objWeb = new WebClient();
objWeb.Credentials = CredentialCache.DefaultCredentials;
```

If we wanted to use a different Windows user account to log on, we could create a new `NetworkCredential` object, specifying the account's domain as well as the username and password:

```
request.Credentials = new NetworkCredential("Username", "Password",
                                            "Domain");
```

We can add credentials to a `CredentialCache` by calling its `Add()` method. This allows us to associate a particular set of credentials with a specific URI. The `Add()` method takes three parameters – a `Uri` object representing the URI prefix for which this set of credentials is to be used, a string specifying the type of authentication, and a `NetworkCredential` object representing the user account to be used for this URI:

```
CredentialCache myCreds = new CredentialCache();
NetworkCredential localCred = new NetworkCredential("Username", "Password",
                                                    "Domain");

Uri localUri = new Uri("http://localhost");
myCreds.Add(localUri, "NTLM", localCred);

HttpWebRequest req = (HttpWebRequest)WebRequest.Create(
                                  "http://localhost/postinfo.html");
req.Credentials = myCreds;
```

When we set the `HttpWebRequest`'s `Credentials` property to point to our new `CredentialCache` object, the objects in the cache are checked to find the set of credentials that is associated with the URI we want to access. The first set of credentials that matches both the URI and the authentication type required by the resource will be used to log on to the resource.

Proxy Support

HTTP proxy support in the .NET classes can be controlled on a per-request basis, or it can be set once globally for the lifetime of the application.

To set the default proxy for all web requests, we use the `GlobalProxySelection` class:

```
GlobalProxySelection.Select = new WebProxy("proxyserver", 80);
```

The `GlobalProxySelection` stores the default proxy settings that will be used to access remote resources beyond the local network. The default proxy settings are taken from the application's configuration file. However, these settings can be overridden for individual requests. We can also disable proxy support by setting the `Proxy` property of the `HttpWebRequest` object to the return value of the `GlobalProxySelection`'s static `GetEmptyWebProxy()` method.

Alternatively, to set the proxy server for a specific web request, we can create a `WebProxy` object using the URI of the proxy server and the port on which it is running. Other overloads take the URI of the proxy, a Boolean value indicating whether or not the proxy is to be bypassed for local addresses, a string array of other URIs for which the proxy shouldn't be used, and an `ICredentials` object that is used to authenticate against the proxy server.

```
using System;
using System.Net;
using System.IO;
using System.Text;
class Proxy
{
    static void Main(string[] args)
    {
        WebProxy myProxy = new WebProxy("proxyserver", 80);
        myProxy.BypassProxyOnLocal = true;
        string query= "http://www.dotnetforce.com/";
        HttpWebRequest request = (HttpWebRequest)HttpWebRequest.Create(query);
        request.Proxy = myProxy;
    }
}
```

Reading and Writing Cookies

The HTTP protocol is stateless, so in principle HTTP servers respond to each client's request without relating that request to previous or subsequent requests. To maintain state between the client and the server, we need to track the user's session programmatically, recording information about which resources the user accessed, and keeping track of any information entered by the user. Session tracking allows us to maintain a relationship between two successive requests made to a server on the Internet. There are many ways to maintain state over a session, such as <hidden> HTML form fields, cookies, and URL query strings. However, cookies are perhaps the most widely used means of maintaining the state of an application.

Cookies work by storing tokens on the client; this means the client is responsible for managing the cookies created. Normally, the browser manages all of this (although a few browsers don't support cookies, and users can disable cookie support), but when the application front-end isn't a browser, we need to perform tracking manually, and manage the session state ourselves.

Whenever the server assigns a cookie for one request, the client must retain it and send it back to the server on its next request. The `HttpWebRequest` and `HttpWebResponse` objects provide the container to hold cookies, both for sending and receiving, but they don't automatically persist them, so it becomes our responsibility to store a cookie and send it back to the server on its next request.

To manage the cookies, we use the `CookieCollection` class in the `System.Net` namespace; this class provides a mechanism for handling multiple cookies.

Writing Cookies on the Client

To demonstrate the use of cookies in .NET, we will build a sample application that will create a cookie, and then we will build an ASP.NET test page to check that the cookie has been created. For this we will need to create an IIS virtual directory named CookieSample.

The code below (WriteCookie.cs) sets a cookie called MyName with the value "Vinod" using the Cookie object, and sends it to the server as part of an HTTP request. Notice that the Cookie object is only an in-memory representation of the cookie – it doesn't save any data to disk on the client. When we create the cookie, we also set the path (the URIs on the server to which the cookie will be sent) and domain name for which the cookie is valid. Once we have a Cookie object, we can also set its Expires property to specify when the cookie will expire (and no longer be sent to the server). Once we have set these properties, the cookie is added into the request's CookieContainer. The CookieContainer is a collection of cookie collections that enables us to store cookies for multiple sites. Each cookie added to the CookieContainer is added to an internal cookie collection associated with a particular URI.

```csharp
using System;
using System.Net;
using System.IO;
using System.Text;

class WriteCookie
{
    static void Main(string[] args)
    {
        CookieCollection cookies = new CookieCollection();

        // Creating the cookie
        Cookie cookie = new Cookie("MyName", "Vinod", "/", "localhost");
        string query = "http://localhost/CookieSample/CookiesText.aspx";
        HttpWebRequest request = (HttpWebRequest)WebRequest.Create(query);
        request.CookieContainer = new CookieContainer();
        request.CookieContainer.Add(cookie);

        HttpWebResponse response = (HttpWebResponse)request.GetResponse();
        StreamReader reader = new StreamReader(response.GetResponseStream(),
                                               Encoding.ASCII);

        Console.WriteLine(reader.ReadToEnd());
        reader.Close();
        response.Close();
    }
}
```

To test this code, we'll create a very simple ASP.NET page named CookiesTest.aspx. This page should be saved in the root of the CookieSample virtual directory, and just gets the value of the cookie that we added in WriteCookie.cs. This is written to the response stream:

```csharp
<%@ Page language="C#" %>
<%
HttpCookie cookie = Request.Cookies["MyName"];
if (cookie != null)
    Response.Write("Value for cookie MyName: " + cookie.Value);
else
    Response.Write("Cookie not set");
%>
```

Now we compile and execute the `WriteCookie.cs` code. The program makes a request to `CookiesTest.aspx`, and the response is displayed in the console. The screenshot below shows the output of the content of this page when we execute the program. As we can see, the value of the cookie `MyName` has been retrieved by the ASP.NET page:

Reading Cookies on the Client

Reading the cookie is as simple as writing the cookie using the .NET Framework's `System.Net` namespace. To test this, we'll again use a very simple ASP.NET page, `WriteCookie.aspx`. This file is again placed in the root of the `CookieSample` virtual directory, and simply creates a new cookie and sends it to the client:

```
<%@ Page language="C#" %>
<%
string username = "Vinod";

HttpCookie cookie = new HttpCookie("username", username);
Response.Cookies.Add(cookie);
Response.Write("Hello, " + username);
%>
```

If we request this page from the client, we can access the `username` cookie through the `Cookies` property of the `HttpWebResponse` class:

```
string query = "http://localhost/CookieSample/WriteCookie.aspx";
HttpWebRequest req = (HttpWebRequest)WebRequest.Create(query);
HttpWebResponse resp = (HttpWebResponse)req.GetResponse();
Console.WriteLine("Value of Cookie MyName :" +
                  resp.Cookies["MyName"].Value);
```

The cookie value can be retrieved once the request headers have been received after the call to `GetResponse()`.

Note that the `Cookies` collection of the `HttpWebResponse` object will only be populated if the `CookieContainer` of the corresponding `HttpWebRequest` was set. Otherwise, we need to read the cookie from the `Headers` collection. Cookies are sent in the `Set-Cookie` header in a format similar to the following:

```
Set-Cookie: FirstName=Vinod; path=/,LastName=Kumar; path=/
```

We can therefore find the value of a cookie by finding the name of the cookie in the header, calculating the positions of the next equals sign and the next semi-colon, and retrieving the substring between these two characters:

```
string cookie = response.Headers["Set-Cookie"];
if (cookie != null)
{
    int start = cookie.IndexOf("FirstName");
    int equals = cookie.IndexOf('=', start);
    int end = cookie.IndexOf(';', equals);

    if (equals != -1 && end != -1)
    {
        string value = cookie.Substring(equals + 1, end - equals - 1);
    }
}
```

Maintaining State with Cookies

The easiest way to maintain state on the client is to store cookies sent from the server in a `CookieCollection`. Let's see how this works by making two consecutive requests. First, we'll call `WriteCookie.aspx`, where the `MyName` cookie is set with the value "Vinod". Once we receive the response for this request, we'll save the cookies in the response into a `CookieCollection`. Next, we'll create a new `HttpWebRequest` object, and add our `CookieCollection` object to its `CookieContainer`. Then we send the request to our `CookiesTest.aspx` page, which reads the value of the `MyName` cookie and writes it to the response stream:

```
using System;
using System.Net;
using System.IO;
using System.Text;

class CookiePersist
{
    static void Main()
    {
        // Make the first request (to WriteCookie.aspx)
        string query = "http://localhost/CookieSample/WriteCookie.aspx";
        HttpWebRequest request = (HttpWebRequest)WebRequest.Create(query);

        // Set the request's CookieContainer, or we won't be able to
        // read the cookies in the response header.
        request.CookieContainer = new CookieContainer();

        // Send the request and get the response
        HttpWebResponse response = (HttpWebResponse)request.GetResponse();

        // Save the response cookies in a CookieCollection object
        CookieCollection cookies = response.Cookies;

        // Display the response body in the console window
        StreamReader reader = new StreamReader(response.GetResponseStream());
        Console.WriteLine(reader.ReadToEnd());
```

```
        reader.Close();
        response.Close();

        // Make the second request (to CookiesTest.aspx)
        HttpWebRequest nextRequest = (HttpWebRequest)WebRequest.Create(
                        "http://localhost/CookieSample/CookiesTest.aspx");

        // Add our saved CookieCollection to the request's CookieContainer
        nextRequest.CookieContainer = new CookieContainer();
        nextRequest.CookieContainer.Add(cookies);

        // Send the request, and print out the response
        HttpWebResponse nextResponse = (HttpWebResponse)
                                            nextRequest.GetResponse();
        reader = new StreamReader(nextResponse.GetResponseStream());
        Console.WriteLine(reader.ReadToEnd());
        reader.Close();
        nextResponse.Close();
    }
}
```

When you run this program, you should see that the value set for the `MyName` cookie in `WriteCookie.aspx` has been passed to the `CookiesText.aspx` page:

An HTTP Server with ASP.NET Support

One of the coolest features of ASP.NET is its ability to run outside of IIS. Specifically, it supports a hosting framework (within the `System.Web.Hosting` namespace) that enables us to create our own web server with ASP.NET support. In this section of the chapter, we will build an HTTP server that can process ASP.NET pages. We will call this server `WroxServer`.

The Server Configuration Files

Before we start to write any code, let's look at the XML files that will store the configuration information for our server. There are three of these files:

❑   `HostInfo.xml`

❑   `Default.xml`

❑   `Mime.xml`

The `HostInfo.xml` file will store hosting information for the server – the virtual path and the port number. We use 8001 as the port, but we could choose any free port:

```
<HostLocation>
    <VDir>C:\\WroxServer</VDir>
    <Port>8001</Port>
</HostLocation>
```

The `Default.xml` file stores the default document names. These are the documents that the server will look for in a virtual directory if the browser request only specifies a directory, rather than an actual document. A default document could be the home page for a directory, or an index page listing the documents in that directory.

```
<Document>
    <File>default.htm</File>
    <File>default.aspx</File>
    <File>Index.htm</File>
    <File>Home.aspx</File>
</Document>
```

`Mime.xml` contains information on the different MIME types supported by the server, and the file extensions associated with each type. This information will allow the server to set the `Content-Type` header correctly for each file type:

```
<Mime>
    <Values>
        <Ext>.htm</Ext>
        <Type>text/html</Type>
    </Values>
    <Values>
        <Ext>.html</Ext>
        <Type>text/html</Type>
    </Values>
    <Values>
        <Ext>.aspx</Ext>
        <Type>text/html</Type>
    </Values>
    <Values>
        <Ext>.gif</Ext>
        <Type>image/gif</Type>
    </Values>
    <Values>
        <Ext>.jpg</Ext>
        <Type>image/jpg</Type>
    </Values>
</Mime>
```

We're storing all the information in XML format for easy retrieval, but we could also use text files, the Registry, and so on, to store the information.

Coding the Server

Now let's see how our HTTP server works. The client initiates an HTTP request by opening a TCP/IP socket to the web server port (8001 for our server), and sending an ASCII request such as the following:

```
GET /Server.html HTTP/1.1
Accept: image/gif, image/x-xbitmap, image/jpeg, image/pjpeg, application/vnd.ms-
powerpoint, application/vnd.ms-excel, application/msword, */*
Accept-Language: en-us
Accept-Encoding: gzip, deflate
User-Agent: Mozilla/4.0 (compatible; MSIE 6.0; Windows NT 5.0; .NET CLR 1.0.2914)
Host: localhost:8001
Connection: Keep-Alive
```

After receiving this request, the server writes a copy of the requested resource to the socket, where it is read by the client; it then closes the connection. Once the connection is closed, the server doesn't remember anything about this request.

Let's start by creating a new Visual C# Console Application project called `HttpServer` in Visual Studio .NET. This project contains three classes – `WroxServer`, where we implement the HTTP server, and `Host` and `ASPXHosting`, which we will use to process any ASP.NET pages requested. Add a reference to `System.Web.dll` to the project.

The WroxServer Class

We start by importing the namespaces required for the application and defining the `HttpServer` namespace. The first class in this namespace is the `WroxServer` class. This class has two fields – a public enumeration that we will use to specify which piece of configuration we want to retrieve from the `HostInfo.xml` file, and the `TcpListener` that will listen for requests from clients.

In the constructor for the `WroxServer` class, we simply start the `TcpListener` on the port read from the `HostInfo.xml` configuration file. We then create a new thread and call the `StartListen()` method on this thread. This method will accept any requests from clients.

```
using System;
using System.IO;
using System.Net;
using System.Net.Sockets;
using System.Text;
using System.Threading ;
using System.Web;
using System.Web.Hosting ;
using System.Xml;

namespace HttpServer
{
    class WroxServer : MarshalByRefObject
    {
        // enum for HostInfo
        public enum HostInfo { VirtualDirectory, Port }
        private TcpListener myListener;
```

```
            // The constructor which makes the TcpListener start listening on the
            // given port. It also calls a Thread on the method StartListen().
            public WroxServer()
            {
                try
                {
                    // Start listing on the given port
                    myListener = new TcpListener(Int32.Parse(GetHostingInfo(
                                        HttpServer.WroxServer.HostInfo.Port)));
                    myListener.Start();
                    Console.WriteLine("Web Server Running... Press ^C to Stop...");

                    // Start the thread which calls the method 'StartListen'
                    Thread thread = new Thread(new ThreadStart(StartListen));
                    thread.Start();
                }
                catch (NullReferenceException)
                {
                    // Don't even ask me why they throw this exception
                    // when this happens
                    Console.WriteLine("Accept failed. Another process might be " +
                                                        "bound to port " +
                                HttpServer.WroxServer.HostInfo.Port.ToString());
                }
            }
```

Reading from the Configuration Files

We get the port information from the HostInfo.xml in the GetHostingInfo() method. This method takes a HostInfo value as an argument, and returns either the virtual directory or the port number, depending upon the argument:

```
            public string GetHostingInfo(HostInfo InfoType)
            {
                string retVal = "";
                string xPath = "";
                try
                {
                    // Set the XPath expression to find the VDir or Port node,
                    // depending on the argument passed into the method
                    if (InfoType.Equals(HostInfo.VirtualDirectory))
                        xPath = "HostLocation/VDir";
                    else if (InfoType.Equals(HostInfo.Port))
                        xPath = "HostLocation/Port";
                    else
                        return "";

                    // Load the XML file
                    XmlDataDocument xDHost = new XmlDataDocument();
                    xDHost.Load("data\\HostInfo.xml");

                    // Select the appropriate node
                    XmlNode node = xDHost.SelectSingleNode(xPath);
```

```
            // Get the text value of the element
            retVal = node.InnerText.Trim();
        }
        catch(XmlException  eXML)
        {
            Console.WriteLine("An ConfigFile Exception Occurred : " +
                                            eXML.ToString());
        }


        return retVal;
    }
```

The GetTheDefaultFileName() method retrieves the default filename from the default.xml file, if the user hasn't provided a filename. This method takes the directory path as input, and looks for the file in the directory provided. If one of the default files is found, it returns the filename; otherwise it returns an empty string:

```
    public string GetTheDefaultFileName(string sLocalDirectory)
    {
        string sLine = "";
        try
        {
            // Load the XML document
            XmlDataDocument xDFile = new XmlDataDocument();
            xDFile.Load("data\\Default.xml");

            // Select all the <File> elements
            XmlNodeList fileNodes = xDFile.SelectNodes("Document/File");

            // Iterate through the selected nodes, until we find one of the
            // default files
            foreach(XmlNode node in fileNodes)
            {
                if (File.Exists(sLocalDirectory + node.InnerText.Trim()))
                {
                    sLine = node.InnerText.Trim();
                    break;
                }
            }
        }
        catch(XmlException  eXML)
        {
            Console.WriteLine("A ConfigFile Exception Occurred : " +
                                            eXML.ToString());
        }

        // Return the filename if a default file exists,
        // or an empty string otherwise
        if (File.Exists(sLocalDirectory + sLine))
            return sLine;
        else
            return "";
    }
```

The next method, `GetMimeType()`, is used to identify the MIME type, using the extension of the file requested by the user. This method takes the filename as an input argument, and checks the file extension with the MIME information in the `Mime.xml` file. It returns the corresponding MIME type:

```
public string GetMimeType(string sRequestedFile)
{
    string sMimeType = "";
    string sFileExt = "";
    string sMimeExt = "";

    // Convert to lowercase
    sRequestedFile = sRequestedFile.ToLower();
    int iStartPos = sRequestedFile.IndexOf(".");
    sFileExt = sRequestedFile.Substring(iStartPos);
    try
    {
        // Load the Mime.xml file to find out the Mime Type
        XmlDataDocument xDMime = new XmlDataDocument();
        xDMime.Load("data\\Mime.xml");

        // Select the <Type> element that has an <Ext> sibling
        // with the same value as the extension for our file
        string xPath = "Mime/Values/Type[../Ext='" + sFileExt +"']";
        XmlNode mimeNode = xDMime.SelectSingleNode(xPath);

        if (mimeNode != null)
        {
            sMimeType = mimeNode.InnerText.Trim();

            // Get the value of the previous <Ext> element
            sMimeExt = mimeNode.PreviousSibling.InnerText.Trim();
        }
    }
    catch (Exception e)
    {
        Console.WriteLine("An Exception Occurred : " + e.ToString());
    }

    if (sMimeExt == sFileExt)
        return sMimeType;
    else
        return "";
}
```

Sending Data to the Client

That finishes our set of methods for reading our configuration files. The next method we'll look at, `WriteHeader()`, is used to build and send the HTTP header information to the browser. This method takes as parameters the information used to build the headers, such as the HTTP version, the content type, and the content length. It also takes a `Socket` as a reference parameter. When we've built the header, we send it to the client using this socket:

```
public void WriteHeader(string sHttpVersion, string sMIMEHeader,
                        int iTotalBytes, string sStatusCode,
                        ref Socket mySocket)
{
    string sBuffer = "";

    // If Mime type is not provided set default to text/html
    if (sMIMEHeader.Length == 0)
        sMIMEHeader = "text/html";

    sBuffer = sBuffer + sHttpVersion + sStatusCode + "\r\n";
    sBuffer = sBuffer + "Server: WroxServer\r\n";
    sBuffer = sBuffer + "Content-Type: " + sMIMEHeader + "\r\n";
    sBuffer = sBuffer + "Accept-Ranges: bytes\r\n";
    sBuffer = sBuffer + "Content-Length: " + iTotalBytes + "\r\n\r\n";

    byte[] bSendData = Encoding.ASCII.GetBytes(sBuffer);
    SendToBrowser(bSendData, ref mySocket);
    Console.WriteLine("Total Bytes : " + iTotalBytes.ToString());
}
```

The `SendToBrowser()` method is an overloaded method that sends the information to the client. This method takes as arguments either a string or a byte array, and the socket reference. The HTML code generated after the ASP.NET file is processed using the `ASPXHosting` class is passed as a string argument and converted to a byte array using the `System.Text.Encoding` class; this is then passed to the other overload of `SendToBrowser()`:

```
public void SendToBrowser(string data, ref Socket socket)
{
    SendToBrowser(Encoding.ASCII.GetBytes(data), ref socket);
}
```

The other overload of `SendToBrowser()` simply sends the byte data to the client calling the `Send()` method of the `Socket` that is passed in. If this returns -1, we know that an error has occurred:

```
public void SendToBrowser(Byte[] bSendData, ref Socket socket)
{
    int iNumByte = 0;
    try
    {
        if (socket.Connected)
        {
            if ((iNumByte = socket.Send(
                            bSendData, bSendData.Length,0)) == -1)
                Console.WriteLine("Socket error: cannot send packet");
            else
                Console.WriteLine("No. of bytes sent {0}", iNumByte);
        }
        else
            Console.WriteLine("Connection Dropped....");
    }
    catch (Exception  e)
```

```
            {
                Console.WriteLine("Error Occurred : {0} ", e );
            }
    }
}
```

Accepting Connections

The methods that we have seen so far are the building blocks of the application. Now let's see the method `StartListen()`. This is the key method that accepts the connection established between the client and server, processes the request from the client, and sends a response to it depending upon the request:

```
public void StartListen()
{
    int iStartPos = 0;
    string sRequest;
    string sDirName;
    string sRequestedFile;
    string sErrorMessage;
    string sLocalDir;

    // Get the virtualDir info
    string sWebServerRoot = GetHostingInfo(
                    HttpServer.WroxServer.HostInfo.VirtualDirectory);
    string sPhysicalFilePath = "";
    string sFormattedMessage = "";
    string sResponse = "";

    while(true)
    {
        // Accept a new connection
        Socket socket = myListener.AcceptSocket();
        Console.WriteLine("Socket Type " + socket.SocketType);
        if(socket.Connected)
        {
            Console.WriteLine("\nClient Connected!!\n" +
                            "====================\nCLient IP {0}\n",
                            socket.RemoteEndPoint);

            // Make a byte array and receive data from the client
            byte[] bReceive = new byte[1024];
            int i = socket.Receive(bReceive, bReceive.Length, 0);

            // Convert Byte to string
            string sBuffer = Encoding.ASCII.GetString(bReceive);

            // Let's just make sure we are using HTTP,
            // that's about all I care about
            iStartPos = sBuffer.IndexOf("HTTP", 1);

            // Get the HTTP text and version, e.g. "HTTP/1.1"
            string sHttpVersion = sBuffer.Substring(iStartPos, 8);

            sRequest = sBuffer.Substring(0, iStartPos - 1);
```

```
                    // Replace backslash with forward slash, if any
                    sRequest.Replace("\\","/");

                    // If a filename is not supplied, add a forward slash to
                    // indicate that it is a directory, and then we will look
                    // for the default filename...
                    if ((sRequest.IndexOf(".") < 1) && (!sRequest.EndsWith("/")))
                        sRequest = sRequest + "/";

                    // Extract the requested file name
                    iStartPos = sRequest.LastIndexOf("/") + 1;
                    sRequestedFile = sRequest.Substring(iStartPos);

                    // Extract the directory name
                    sDirName = sRequest.Substring(sRequest.IndexOf("/"),
                                           sRequest.LastIndexOf("/") - 3);

                    // Identify the physical directory
                    if (sDirName == "/")
                        sLocalDir = sWebServerRoot;
                    else
                    {
                        // Get the virtual directory
                        sDirName =sDirName.Replace(@"/",@"\");
                        sLocalDir = sWebServerRoot + sDirName;
                    }

                Console.WriteLine("Directory Requested : " + sLocalDir);
```

The above code is more-or-less self-explanatory. As mentioned, it accepts the connection and receives the request, and converts it into a string from a byte array. It then looks for the request type, extracts the HTTP version, file, and directory information, and also gets the virtual directory information from the HostInfo.xml file using the GetHostingInfo() method.

If no file is specified, and a default file can't be found, we send an HTTP 404 Not Found error to the browser:

```
                    // Identify the filename. If the filename is not supplied,
                    // look in the default file list
                    if (sRequestedFile.Length == 0)
                    {
                        // Get the default filename
                        sRequestedFile = GetTheDefaultFileName(sLocalDir);
                        if (sRequestedFile == "")
                        {
                            sErrorMessage = "<H2>Error!! No Default File Name " +
                                         "Specified</H2>";
                            WriteHeader(sHttpVersion, "", sErrorMessage.Length,
                                      " 404 Not Found", ref socket);
                            SendToBrowser(sErrorMessage, ref socket);
                            socket.Close();
                            return;
                        }
                    }
                }
```

Similarly, the code below gets the MIME type from the XML file Mime.xml using the GetMimeType() method, and then checks for the file extension. If the file extension is .aspx, then an instance of the ASPXHosting class will be created and the HTML output will be passed as an argument to the SendToBrowser() method (along with the Socket reference). This is generated by the CreateHost() method, which takes the ASP.NET file name as argument.

If the requested file is not an .aspx file, the file is read using the BinaryReader() and sent to the browser using the SendToBrowser() method. In both cases, the SendHeader() method is called before the SendToBrowser() method. After sending the data to the client, the connection is closed:

```
        else
        {
            int iTotBytes=0;
            sResponse = "";
            FileStream fs = new FileStream(sPhysicalFilePath,
                FileMode.Open, FileAccess.Read, FileShare.Read);

            // Create a reader that can read bytes
            // from the FileStream
            BinaryReader reader = new BinaryReader(fs);
            byte[] bytes = new byte[fs.Length];
            int read;
            while ((read = reader.Read(
                                bytes, 0, bytes.Length)) != 0)
            {
                // Read from the file and write the data
                // to the network
                sResponse = sResponse + Encoding.ASCII.GetString(
                                                bytes, 0, read);
                iTotBytes = iTotBytes + read;
            }
            reader.Close();
            fs.Close();
            WriteHeader(sHttpVersion,  sMimeType, iTotBytes,
                        " 200 OK", ref socket);
            SendToBrowser(bytes, ref socket);
        }
    }
    socket.Close();
    }
    }
}
```

Finally, we need the Main() method to start the server running:

```
    static void Main()
    {
        WroxServer server = new WroxServer();
    }
```

Now's let see the Host and ASPXHosting classes that will process any ASP.NET files requested.

Hosting ASP.NET Applications Outside IIS

As mentioned earlier, one of the more interesting features of ASP.NET is its ability to run outside IIS. Specifically, it supports a hosting framework (within the System.Web.Hosting namespace) that enables us to run it on top of other web servers. For this we use the SimpleWorkerRequest and ApplicationHost classes. The latter has a static method called CreateApplicationHost(), which we use to create an instance of our Host class in the application domain used to host ASP.NET. This class allows us to marshal method calls between our web server's AppDomain and the ASP.NET AppDomain.

The SimpleWorkerRequest class is a simple predefined implementation of the HttpWorkerRequest abstract class, which provides methods and enumerations used by ASP.NET to process requests. We need to pass an HttpWorkerRequest object into the ProcessRequest() method of the HttpRuntime class (in the System.Web namespace) to process the ASP.NET page, so using SimpleWorkerRequest avoids the necessity of creating our own implementation:

```
using System;
using System.IO;
using System.Web;
using System.Web.Hosting;
using System.Xml;

public class Host : MarshalByRefObject
{
    public string HandleRequest(string fileName)
    {
        StringWriter wr = new StringWriter();
        Console.WriteLine("The output from the {0} file", fileName);

        // Create a Worker to execute the aspx file
        HttpWorkerRequest worker = new SimpleWorkerRequest(fileName, "" , wr);

        // Execute the page
        HttpRuntime.ProcessRequest(worker);
        return wr.ToString();
    }
}

public class ASPXHosting
{
    public enum HostInfo{VirtualDirectory, Port}
    public  string CreateHost(string fileName)
    {
        Host myHost = (Host)ApplicationHost.CreateApplicationHost(
                            typeof(Host), "/", GetHostingInfo(
                            ASPXHosting.HostInfo.VirtualDirectory));
        return myHost.HandleRequest(fileName);
    }

    public string GetHostingInfo(HostInfo InfoType)
    {
```

```
        // As in the WroxServer class -
        // we won't repeat the code here
    }
}
```

To test this code, install the assembly produced into the global assembly cache – if you need a refresher on how to do this, take a look at Chapter 8 of "Professional C# 2nd Edition", (Wrox Press, ISBN 1-86100-704-3).

Now, let's execute an ASP.NET page named `WroxServerSample.aspx`. This page is placed in the root directory of the web server. Since we use 8001 as our port, we call the file by specifying the URL as http://localhost:8001/WroxServerSample.aspx. This file simply has a `Label` Web Control that contains some information:

```
<%@ Page language="c#" %>
<!DOCTYPE HTML PUBLIC "-//W3C//DTD HTML 4.0 Transitional//EN" >
<html>
    <head>
        <title>WroxServerSample</title>
    </head>
    <body MS_POSITIONING="GridLayout">
        <form id="WroxServerSample" method="post" runat="server">
            <asp:Label id="Label1" runat="server" ForeColor="#C00000"
                        Font-Bold="True" Font-Names="verdana">
WroxServerSample.aspx page Processed using Wrox Server</asp:Label>
        </form>
    </body>
</html>
```

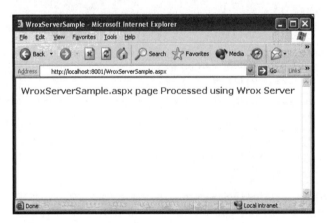

The above figure shows the output of the `WroxServerSample.aspx` file in a web browser.

This example demonstrates the power of the .NET classes and its simple and straightforward support for most HTTP/1.1 features.

HTTP and .NET Remoting

In Chapter 5, we introduced the basic concepts of .NET Remoting, and saw how we can use this with the TCP channel. The .NET Remoting Framework uses channels to connect applications together. The two channels that are currently available in the .NET Framework are the TcpChannel and the HttpChannel. The TCP channel should generally be used if the message is to be sent over the local network, as it has better performance, whereas if the message is to be sent over the Internet, HTTP is generally the better choice, as TCP connections won't usually be permitted over a firewall. By default, messages sent over the HTTP channel are formatted using SOAP. This is good for interoperability, but has poorer performance than the binary channel used by default with TCP.

As with the TCP channel, we need to register the HTTP channel with channel services before we can use it in our applications:

```
public class LoadHttpChannel
{
    HttpChannel httpChannel;
    public void LoadChannel()
    {
        httpChannel =  new HttpChannel();

        // Register the HTTP Channel
        ChannelServices.RegisterChannel(httpChannel);
    }
}
```

Building a Simple Remoting Application

Since using Remoting with the HTTP channel is conceptually very similar to the TCP channel we covered in Chapter 5, we won't rehash the theory, but we'll go straight on to look at a short example application.

First we need to define the class that we will instantiate remotely. We'll keep this as simple as possible, and just define one method that writes a string passed in as a parameter to the console. This class will need to exist both on the client and on the remote server, as Remoting uses reflection to call methods on the remote object.

```
// WroxLog.cs
using System;

namespace WroxLog
{
    public class RemotingSample : MarshalByRefObject
    {
        public void RemoteLog(string value)
        {
            Console.WriteLine(value);
        }
    }
}
```

Compile this into a DLL using the command csc /t:library WroxLog.cs.

To make a class accessible remotely, we should derive it from MarshalByRefObject. If an object is **Marshaled By Reference (MBR)**, a reference to the object is passed from one AppDomain to another. In contrast, if an object is marshaled by value, a copy of the complete state of the object is passed to the target AppDomain. The remote application uses the object's meta data to create a "proxy" for the original object. We can make method calls against this proxy, which will then be marshaled to the real object.

Now let's create a simple server application that listens to the requests:

```
// RemoteServer.cs
using System;
using WroxLog;
using System.Runtime.Remoting;
using System.Runtime.Remoting.Channels;
using System.Runtime.Remoting.Channels.Http ;

namespace RemoteServer
{
    class RemotingServer
    {
        public static void Main()
        {
            ChannelServices.RegisterChannel(new HttpChannel(8000));

            RemotingConfiguration.RegisterWellKnownServiceType(
                                    typeof(RemotingSample), "WroxLog",
                                    WellKnownObjectMode.Singleton);

            Console.WriteLine("Log Server Listening on endpoints:\r\n" +
                            "\thttp://localhost:8000/WroxLog\r\n");
            Console.WriteLine("Press enter to stop the server...");
            Console.ReadLine();
        }
    }
}
```

This should be compiled into a console application, referencing our WroxLog.dll assembly:

```
csc RemoteServer.cs /r:WroxLog.dll
```

In the code above, we register the HTTP channel to use as the transport mechanism, and to listen on port 8000. After registering the channel, we register the object that will actually be instantiated on the remote server, using the RegisterWellKnownServiceType method. This method tells the Remoting infrastructure where to find the remote object. It takes as parameters the object type, URI, and WellKnownObjectMode as arguments for locating the object. Here we use Singleton as the WellKnownObjectMode, which means that the same object instance will be used for each of the incoming messages.

When the call arrives at the server, the .NET Framework extracts the URI from the message, examines the Remoting tables to locate the reference for the object that matches the URI, and then instantiates the object if necessary, forwarding the method call to the object. If the object is registered as `SingleCall`, it won't be reused after the method call is completed, but left for the Garbage Collector to destroy, so a new instance of the object is created for each method call. The remote object itself is not instantiated by the registration process. This happens only when a client attempts to call a method on the object or activates the object from the client side.

The client code to access this server application is shown below:

```
// RemoteClient.cs
using System;
using System.Runtime.Remoting;
using WroxLog;

namespace RemotingClient
{
   class Client
   {
      static void Main()
      {
         RemotingSample httpWroxLog = (RemotingSample)Activator.GetObject(
                  typeof(RemotingSample), "http://localhost:8000/WroxLog");
         httpWroxLog.RemoteLog("Client : Hello..Server");
      }
   }
}
```

Again, this should be compiled into a console application referencing our `WroxLog.dll` assembly:

csc RemoteClient.cs /r:WroxLog.dll

In the code, the `RemotingSample` object is created using the server-activation model, by calling the `Activator.GetObject()` method. Server-activated objects are objects whose lifetimes are directly controlled by the server. The server application domain creates these objects only when the client makes a method call on the object, not when the client first instantiates the object using the new keyword or `Activator.GetObject()` (similar to late binding); this saves a network round trip solely for the purpose of instantiating the object. Only a proxy is created in the client application domain when a client requests an instance of a server-activated type.

The following screenshot displays the output on the server side when we start the server and then run the client application:

Summary

This chapter has covered HTTP programming in detail. The first step in Internet programming is to have a good knowledge of how HTTP works, so we started the chapter by giving an overview of the HTTP protocol, before looking at the support for HTTP programming in .NET. This chapter basically concentrated on:

❑ An overview of HTTP – the basics of HTTP, its properties and features, and HTTP requests and responses

❑ Using the .NET methods and classes to work with the HTTP protocol

❑ Reading and writing cookies in .NET

❑ Creating an HTTP server and client in .NET, and hosting ASP.NET apps outside IIS

❑ Using the HTTP channel with .NET Remoting

9

E-Mail Protocols

Back in Chapter 1, we touched on the various protocols that exist for sending and receiving e-mails across the network. E-mail protocols are broad in the sense that they don't only pertain to .NET. Ever since the rise of Internet messaging, e-mail has been a cornerstone of electronic communication. I'm sure almost everyone reading this book has had some prior experience sending e-mails within a programming language, so we aren't really covering some new and exciting technology that .NET brings to the table. What is exciting is how easy and seamless .NET makes network programming, especially with regard to using the various e-mail protocols to send and retrieve e-mails, and to perform various tasks that may have been convoluted or difficult in the past. In this chapter, we are going to give a high-level overview of the various e-mail protocols and how they are accessed and used in a .NET environment. Particular examples will be given in C#, and discussion will follow.

E-mail in a Nutshell

It's quite easy to think of e-mail like ordinary mail that you may send out. The big difference is that no stamps are needed! Well, that and the fact that e-mail sending is almost instantaneous, and the postal service is usually very slow. There are various advantages to sending e-mail, though. E-mail can be sent to many recipients at once, as well as forwarded on and on very easily. However, in both cases we know that there is a starting point and an endpoint to a communication session. There is also a delivery mechanism that transfers the mail from one point to another along its mail route until it reaches its final destination. In the most generic sense, there are two components interacting in this scenario:

- ❑ Message Transfer Agent (MTA)
- ❑ User Agent (E-mail client)

In our real-world snail mail example, the Transfer Agent may be a postal or carrier company such as the USPS (United States Postal Service), FedEx, or UPS. The sender and receiver are quite obvious. In the electronic world, the place of the Transfer Agent is taken by the implementation of the SMTP (Simple Mail Transfer Protocol), which is responsible for directing e-mail from the starting point (sender) to the endpoint (receiver), bouncing the e-mail across various machines on the Internet. Keep in mind that this method stems from roots in TCP/IP, and is the most prevalent messaging topology used today. However, there are a number of other systems and standards that have been used for messaging in the past.

How does E-Mail Work?

When we think about how e-mails are actually sent across the Internet, we must first realize that the Internet is nothing more than hundreds of thousands of computers that are networked together, using the same standard protocols for communication. How does that fit into our e-mail situation? Endpoints are simply mailboxes or message stores on e-mail servers (although you could also view the sender and receivers as the starting and endpoints, and the message stores as holding places for the messages until they are received by a client program). A mail server is simply the machine (or virtual machine) that handles sending and receiving messages, and communicates with other machines in the process of handling e-mails.

A common scenario in a company may be to have employees using a Microsoft Outlook mail client that connects to the company's mail server (which may be running Exchange). All e-mail messages that come in and go out of that company are handled by the mail server. It acts as both the endpoint and starting point for any e-mails sent out over the Internet:

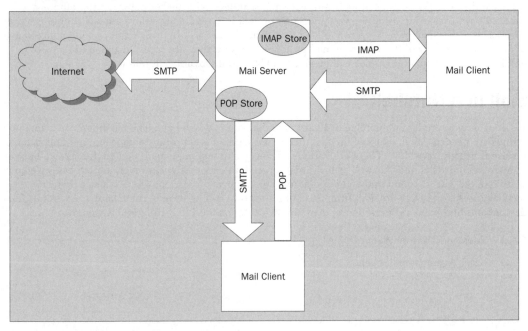

This is a simplified situation, as many companies have multiple servers to handle e-mail communications.

Notice that the mail clients (such as Outlook) communicate with the mail server using SMTP, and that the mail server also communicates with other machines over the Internet using SMTP. POP3 (Post Office Protocol) and IMAP (Internet Message Access Protocol) are also depicted in the diagram; these protocols only allow mail clients to access and retrieve e-mail. To send mail, e-mail clients use SMTP.

E-Mail Protocols

As this scenario shows, the three main topics for e-mail programming are SMTP, POP3, and IMAP. This is not to say that they are the only topics, just the ones that are most important to us developers when we are writing our applications that send and retrieve e-mail messages. This is because these are the standard protocols for sending and retrieving e-mail. We must keep in mind that these aren't the only ones, but the most commonly used and accepted methods. Other messaging standards such as X.400 exist as an alternative to TCP/IP related messaging. For more information about the X.400 protocol, see http://www.itu.int/ and http://www.alvestrand.no/x400/.

Internet mail is largely defined by a number of standards and recommendations made by companies and individuals close to Internet technology research and design. These standards are endorsed by the IMC or Internet Mail Consortium (http://www.imc.org/) and the IETF or Internet Engineering Task Force (http://www.ietf.org). The current set of Internet mail standards is composed of many related RFCs (Request For Comments), recommendations, and statements on common practices. Not all standards are fully endorsed or full IETF standards documents, but are considered stable and are used throughout the industry for developing e-mail software.

There are many RFCs available on the IMC web site (http://www.imc.org/rfcs.html). These documents are detailed and speak in much greater depth about every aspect of e-mail handling. For our purposes we are going to touch on a few of these RFCs within our discussion of various topics in this chapter. In particular, we will look at RFC 2821, which defines the SMTP protocol, and RFC 2822, which defines what an e-mail message should look like. For more information about these RFCs, take a look at the IMC web site.

SMTP

Simple Mail Transfer Protocol, or SMTP, is outlined in RFC 2821, and defines the interaction between mail servers that are transporting e-mails. It's good to note that SMTP for the most part uses TCP as a transport protocol (see RFC 1090 for SMTP over X.25). In essence, an SMTP session consists of a conversation between two machines that are trying to hand off or pass along an e-mail message. A simplified view of this is shown in the following figure:

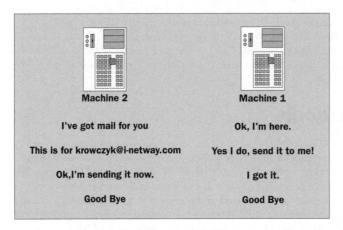

As you can see, an SMTP session can be summed up in a simple communication between two computers in which the e-mail is relayed along. At this point, the e-mail will have bounced around the Internet to finally reach Machine 2 that is the mail handler for i-netway.com. If for instance, there was no user at this e-mail address (the address was invalid) or the mail handler didn't have any way to deliver the message, the machine would have replied that the e-mail was undeliverable.

Another View of an SMTP Session

Another way to look at an SMTP e-mail session would be to take a look at a Telnet connection to an actual e-mail server. Most ISPs disable this sort of access, as it allows for hackers and the like to easily spoof e-mails, which is not a good thing! This sample is only meant to show an example of the conversation between an SMTP e-mail server and a client. If someone at Wrox were trying to send me an e-mail via Telnet, the conversation would look something like this:

```
open i-netway.com 25
Trying. . . Connected to i-netway.com
220 I-NETWAY.COM - Server ESMTP (PMDF v4.3-10 #2381)

helo wrox.com
250 I-NETWAY.COM OK, WROX.COM.

mail from:<editor@wrox.com>
250 Address Ok.

rcpt to:<krowczyk@i-netway.com>
250 krowczyk@i-netway.com OK.

data
354 Enter mail, end with a single ".".
SUBJECT:E-mail Chapter
Andy, thanks for the chapter!
.
250 OK.

//by quitting, the message is sent
quit
221 Bye received. Goodbye.
```

See Chapter 1 for a brief discussion of using the Microsoft Telnet client.

As you can see, the session begins with the Telnet command to open a connection to the `i-netway.com` e-mail server. This is followed by a few different SMTP commands that are needed to send the e-mail message, and the responses from the SMTP server. We looked at the most common SMTP commands in Chapter 5, where we built a simple SMTP client, but now let's look at the complete list.

SMTP Command Summary

Here is a quick summary of the various SMTP commands that are available. For more detailed explanations, please read RFC 2821.

Command Summary	Description
HELLO (**HELO**)	Identifies the SMTP client to the SMTP server.
MAIL (**MAIL**)	Initiates a mail transaction to deliver an e-mail to one or more mailboxes.
RECIPIENT (**RCPT**)	Identifies the recipient to whom the mail data is to be sent. If the data is to be sent to more than one recipient, multiple RCPT commands can be used.
DATA (**DATA**)	Marks the start of the mail data. The data following the DATA command is appended to the mail buffer. The mail data may contain any of the 128 ASCII character codes. The end of the data is marked by the sequence <CRLF>.<CRLF>.
SEND (**SEND**)	Initiates a mail transaction to deliver an e-mail to one or more terminals. **Here it is important to note that 'terminal' refers to a user's terminal screen. Because most clients are not terminal clients nowadays, the** SEND, SOML, **and** SAML **commands are for the most part obsolete. They are included here for the sake of completeness, because they are part of the RFC.**
SEND or MAIL (**SOML**)	Initiates a mail transaction to deliver an e-mail to one or more terminals or mailboxes. The e-mail is delivered to the terminal of each recipient if that recipient is active on the host and accepting terminal messages, or else to the recipient's mailbox.
SEND and MAIL (**SAML**)	Initiates a mail transaction to deliver an e-mail to one or more terminals or mailboxes. The e-mail is delivered to the terminal of each recipient if that recipient is active on the host and accepting terminal messages, and to every recipient's mailbox.
RESET (**RSET**)	Aborts the current mail transaction. All data will be discarded, and all buffers cleared. The receiver must send an OK reply.
VERIFY (**VRFY**)	Asks the receiver to confirm that the following argument is a valid username. If it is, the full name of the user (if known) and the fully specified mailbox are returned.

Table continued on following page

Command Summary	Description
EXPAND (**EXPN**)	Asks the receiver to confirm that the following argument is a mailing list, and if so, to return the names of the members of that list. The full names of the users (if known) and the fully specified mailboxes are returned in a multi-line reply. This command is similar to the VRFY command, but is used for multiple recipients.
HELP (**HELP**)	Asks the receiver to send helpful information to the sender. The command can take an argument (such as a command name) and return more specific information as a response.
NOOP (**NOOP**)	This command has no effect, except that the receiver should send an OK reply. No operation takes place, and no other commands or data should be affected.
QUIT (**QUIT**)	On receiving a QUIT command, the receiver must send an OK reply, and then close the connection to the sender.
TURN (**TURN**)	On receiving a TURN command, the receiver must either (1) send an OK reply and take on the role of the SMTP client; or (2) send a refusal reply and retain the role of the SMTP server. This command is deprecated because of security concerns. Poor authentication implementations would allow a client machine to take on the role of the SMTP server and divert e-mail messages.

Reply Codes

If you look back at the example of sending an e-mail using SMTP through Telnet, you will see that the server sends back a reply code for each SMTP command. Actually, the reply codes sent back by the server provide us with much information about the status of the current e-mail transaction. Let's take a look at a typical reply code and see what information it contains:

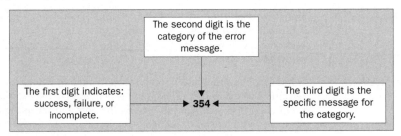

Since the first two digits of the SMTP reply code are the most important to us, let's look at what they indicate. Please note that the first digit only gives the status of the command. The subsequent digits give us greater detail as to what the success or error was caused by.

❑   **First Digit**

   1   indicates preliminary acceptance of the command, pending confirmation

   2   indicates successful completion of the command

3   indicates intermediate acceptance of the command, pending further information

4   indicates temporary negative status

5   indicates failure

❑ **Second Digit**

0   syntax

1   connection

5   mail

To see how this works, let's go over a few of the most common reply codes that we might receive back from an SMTP transaction call. The error or status messages given may differ from SMTP server to SMTP server, but the reply code means the same thing in each case. The status message is really just a human-readable description of what went wrong.

Reply Code	Message
500	Syntax error, command unrecognized
501	Syntax error in parameters or arguments
502	Command not implemented
503	Bad sequence of commands
220	<domain> Service ready
221	<domain> Service closing transmission channel
421	<domain> Service not available, closing transmission channel
250	Requested mail action OK, completed
354	Start mail input, end with <CRLF>.<CRLF>
550	Requested action not taken, mailbox unavailable
553	Requested action not taken, mailbox name not allowed
554	Transaction failed

RFC 2821 defines all of the reply codes available, and the numeric codes are definitive. This means that you can't define new codes as you see fit! However, since we are talking about an agreed standard protocol, the response codes should be predefined and set in stone.

A Typical E-Mail Message

Before we start talking about accessing e-mails with POP3 and IMAP, let's first briefly touch on the content and structure of a mail message as it relates to the other important standards document that we spoke about earlier. RFC 2822 describes the content of what an e-mail message should look like. Think of it as sort of a "schema" or outline of a typical mail message. The following is a typical mail message:

353

```
Received: from MAILCLUSTER [111.111.111.111] by mail.brinkster.com with ESMTP
(SMTPD32-6.05) id AF1F18B600FA; Fri, 28 Jun 2002 05:40:47 -0400
Received: by MAILCLUSTER with Internet Mail Service (5.5.2653.19)
id <NZPCN64X>; Fri, 28 Jun 2002 10:39:30 +0100
Message-ID: <E12F1784B51ED5119EA900D0B74D69240EFEAF87@MAILCLUSTER>
From: Wrox Press <wrox@wrox.com>
To: "'Andrew Krowczyk'" <krowczyk@i-netway.com>
Subject: C# Networking Chapter
Date: Fri, 28 Jun 2002 10:39:28 +0100
Importance: high
X-Priority: 1
MIME-Version: 1.0
X-Mailer: Internet Mail Service (5.5.2653.19)
Content-Type: text/plain
X-RCPT-TO: <krowczyk@i-netway.com>
X-UIDL: 323073316
Status: U

Andy, thanks for the work you've done!

-Wrox Press
```

This typical e-mail structure consists of both message headers and message text. Some information is required for the message to conform to the e-mail standards while some information is optional and can be included or excluded depending on many factors.

Required Information

There are a few headers that are generally required in all e-mails:

❑ **FROM**: The agent (person, system, or process) that created the message. This should be a single authenticated machine address generated by the sending agent. As you would imagine, this tells us who/what is sending us the e-mail message.

❑ **DATE**: The date the message was sent. The only optional parts of the date specification are the day of the week and the seconds. The timezone may be given in usual denotations such as CST, EDT, GMT. The timezone is preferred as a numeric offset from the GMT. In the message above, you will see +0100 to denote the GMT offset.

❑ **One Recipient Address**: At least one recipient address must be used, which can be either **To**, **Cc**, or **Bcc**.

Some Optional Information

There are also other headers and information that may be optional and not required in every message. A few of these are listed below:

❑ **REPLY-TO**: The reply-to header is often used to designate the preferred e-mail address for responses to be sent to. This is often used by list mail and other processes to correctly identify the return e-mail address location.

❑ **SENDER**: Why would the sender be optional? This is really the same thing as the required FROM field listed above. This field is intended for use when the sender of the e-mail is not the author of the e-mail, or is one of a group of authors. This shouldn't be used if it's identical to the FROM field. The SENDER field must be present if it's different from the FROM field.

An example of the SENDER field usage would be.

```
FROM: "Joe Someone" <joe@someone.com>
SENDER: INFO-SAMPLE Discussion <INFO-SAMPLE@SOMEDOMAIN.COM>
TO: Multiple recipients of list INFO-SAMPLE Discussion <INFO-
SAMPLE@SOMEDOMAIN.COM>
```

Received Headers

One of the most important parts of an e-mail message is the data that is transmitted in the received headers of the mail message. This provides debugging information, as well as a good look at where the e-mail came from and how it got from point A to point B.

Our sample above contains the following received lines:

```
Received: from MAILCLUSTER [111.111.111.111] by mail.brinkster.com with ESMTP
(SMTPD32-6.05) id AF1F18B600FA; Fri, 28 Jun 2002 05:40:47 -0400
Received: by MAILCLUSTER with Internet Mail Service (5.5.2653.19)
id <NZPCN64X>; Fri, 28 Jun 2002 10:39:30 +0100
```

The received lines tell us many things:

❑   They are the postmaster's primary debugging tool. By reading the header, we can find out much information about where the mail came from and how it got to the final destination.

❑   They tell which systems have touched or tampered with the mail.

❑   Each MTA (Mail Transfer Agent) that relays a message attaches its own Received header line.

❑   RFC 2882 requires that MTAs add their own received line when they handle the mail, and they are prohibited by the RFC from touching the received lines put in by other mailers.

❑   The received headers show us the path, hop by hop, that the mail took from the sender to the receiver.

An example of how the messages can be traced via the received lines in the headers is shown in the diagram below:

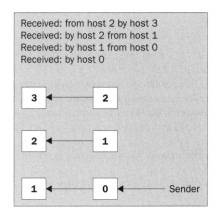

Viewing Headers in Outlook

Since the headers contain so much information, it's worth seeing quickly how to view header information from Microsoft Outlook. First, right-click on the message that you wish to view the header information for, and select Options. The Internet headers for the message are displayed at the bottom of the resulting dialog:

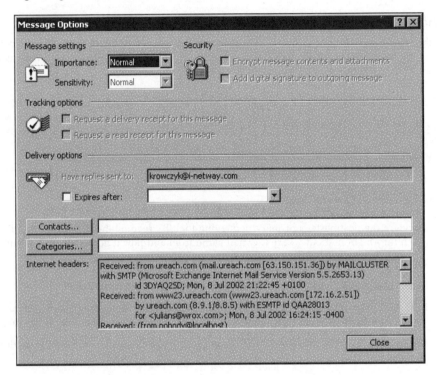

Note that Internet headers might not be displayed for e-mails that are sent internally on the same network.

What About MIME?

Now that we've seen the basics of an e-mail message and looked at a high-level overview of the e-mail protocol, we come to the question, "What about attachments?" E-mail was originally a text-only messaging system using just ASCII characters. But that quickly changed into the need to "attach" binary files of different types to the e-mail messages and have the attachments transferred along with the ASCII text messages. So, to address this need, MIME (Multi-purpose Internet Mail Extensions) was developed; MIME defines extensions to the SMTP protocol to support binary attachments of arbitrary format.

When we look at what MIME is composed of, we find that it really encompasses two main functions:

❑   MIME encodes binary data so that it can be passed over the Internet. There are two points to notice here:

❑ We must remember that the Internet is a 7-bit ASCII world.

❑ 8-bit extensions don't work, as there are issues with line length and file formatting.

❑ MIME attaches a label or tag to the encoded data so that the content can be determined and interpreted at the end point of the message. For example, this is a movie file, or a Microsoft Excel document.

MIME uses a new encoding scheme that is called BASE64. It also adds new SMTP headers that describe the attached document. The idea is actually quite simple – we are just encoding the binary data into a different bit data representation and then piggybacking that data with the e-mail itself as an attached bit of data. Once the endpoint e-mail client receives the message, the new headers tell it that there is an attached document (or attached documents) embedded within the e-mail message, and the client can properly decode and display the document. The RFCs that define MIME and its composition are RFC 2045 through RFC 2049.

MIME Headers

When we take a look at the headers that must be used when MIME is used to attach a bit of information we will find that there are a few different fields that are available for use. Let's look first at the required field:

Required Fields	Description
MIME-Version	This field indicates which version of MIME is being used (currently 1.0).

Now the optional fields:

Optional Fields	Description
Content-type	This field describes what format this part of the message is in, such as text, message, application, multipart, image, audio, among others. The default type is ASCII text. A few common content types include: **text/plain** **text/html** **application/binary** **application/postscript** **image/gif** **image/jpeg**

Table continued on following page

Optional Fields	Description
Content-transfer_encoding	This header tells how to decode the message. There are a few different encoding schemes that may be used.

Base64. This encoding is used to encode binary data in 7-bit ASCII data.

7-bit. No encoding, case insensitive.

8-bit. No encoding.

binary. No encoding.

x-**token** proprietary encoding designation. The x designates that this is a non-standard status encoding scheme. This simply means that the content is not encoded with a standardized coding scheme, which in most cases is bad, as it doesn't fall into interoperability guidelines. |
Content-ID	ID field that allows one body to make reference to another. Similar to Message-ID (unique identifier in the e-mail message structure). Generally this field is optional.
Content-description	A textual description about the encoded data. For example, an image content type might contain "a picture of the moon".
Content-disposition	Field used to tell the e-mail client if the content should be displayed "inline" with the message or as an "attachment" to the message. There is a parameter called Filename that is a suggestion for a name if the encoded data is detached from the mail message.

Now let's take a quick look at a typical mail message that includes a MIME attachment:

```
From: krowczyk@i-netway.com (Andrew Krowczyk)
Subject: Sample message with Word Document Attachment
To: mailto:editor@wrox.com
MIME-version: 1.0
Content-type: MULTIPART/MIXED; BOUNDARY="Boundary_[ID_nf991kyavAuSo/HeKKQ]"—
Boundary_[ID_nf991kyavAuSo/HeKKQ]
Content-type: text/plain; charset=us-ascii

Hi, please see the attached Word Document.
-Andy—Boundary_[ID_nf991kyavAuSo/HeKKQ]
Date: Fri, 3 Jul 2002 16:43:34 -0700
Content-type: application/mac-binhex40; name=sample_worddoc.doc
Content-disposition: attachment; filename=sample_worddoc.doc

<Word Document etc. . . below here>
PGh0bWw+DQo8aGVhZD4NCjx0aXRsZT6q967mpcC/y7hgrKGwyjwvdGl0bGU+DQo8bWV0YSBodHRw
LWVxdWl2PSJDb250ZW50LVR5cGUiIGNvbnRlbnQ9InRleHQvaHRtbDsgY2hhcnNldD1iaWc1Ij4N
CjxsaW5rIHJlbD0ic3R5bGVzaGVldCIgaHJlZj0iaHR0cDovL3d3dy5aW5nLmNvbS50dy9wbS5j
c3MiIHR5cGU9InRleHQvY3NzIj4NCjwvaGVhZD4NCjxzY3JpcHQgbGFuZ3VhZ2U9Ikphdmcm3Jp
cHQiPg0KZnVuY3Rpb24gZ290b3VybChaX1eXBlKSB7DQogdmFyIHB3Xdpbmdvdy5vcGVuKCdo
```

As you can see, the MIME sections and headers define the message boundaries and the binary content. For brevity, I've left out the actual binary encoding of the document. It would look like a bunch of garbled data in ASCII characters.

For the most part, I've covered only a few topics on MIME attachments. This was only to give a brief high-level overview of how attachments are included in SMTP e-mail messages. Later in the chapter, we'll look at an example of sending e-mails that include attachments from a .NET application. Hopefully, this overview of MIME will help you to understand what our .NET code is causing to happen behind the scenes when we send e-mail messages. Now we've seen what happens when we send an e-mail, we'll look at the protocols and methods for retrieving e-mail messages.

Retrieving Client-Server E-Mail

When we think about and look at how e-mail messages are retrieved from mail server message stores, we generally think of it as a client-server relationship. We use an e-mail client, such as Microsoft Outlook, Lotus Notes, or other such mail packages to retrieve messages from a central mail server mailbox. There are also web based e-mail services such as Hotmail that follow along the same lines. There are generally three models of e-mail handling:

- **Offline (POP3 model)**

    - Client connects to the mail server and pulls or retrieves e-mail down to the client.

    - In this instance, all the mail is stored on the client machine, not the server. Usually e-mail is deleted from the server once it's retrieved, although some mail clients give the ability to "leave messages on the server".

- **Online (Original IMAP model)**

    - The client application connects to the server for every transaction.

    - Everything is stored on the server.

- **Disconnected (Later IMAP model)**

    - Client and server share the storage of messages.

    - The server is always correct, and the client application must "synchronize" the list of messages with the server.

One of the most important points to note is that POP and IMAP only *get* the mail messages from the server's mailbox. As with all e-mail transactions, sending mail requires the use of SMTP. In the next few sections, we'll talk in a little more depth about the POP and IMAP protocols for retrieving e-mails. After that, we'll delve into the code required in .NET to perform all the actions we've discussed so far.

POP3

There are actually a few versions of the POP protocol that have been around. The POP2 and POP3 standards are not even compatible from a protocol standpoint. But since the huge majority of POP clients are POP3, we'll restrict our discussion to that protocol.

So what does POP3 allow us to do? As we've already learned, POP3 only allows a client to retrieve mail from a mail server. This protocol allows us to write nice-looking GUI (Graphical User Interface) applications that will present e-mail in a way that's easy to read and manage. For reference, POP3 is outlined in further detail in RFC 1939.

In the POP3 world, the mail exists on the mail server when it's received by the system. It just sits there, waiting to be picked up by a mail client. Once we connect to the mail server with a client mail program, the POP3 client copies the mail from the server to the local machine's hard drive. This method locks us into reading the mail on the client machine. Why would this make a difference? Depending on the situation, POP3 access might not be ideal. For instance, suppose we have a mail account that we read both at work and at home. Let's suppose that we have Microsoft Outlook installed on both the office and home machines. If we connect at the office and Outlook downloads four new mail messages, those messages will generally be removed from the server and transported to the local hard drive on the office machine. This means that we've lost access to those messages from our home machine. Because POP3 moves the messages from the server to your client machine, sharing a POP3 e-mail system between multiple machines can be troublesome.

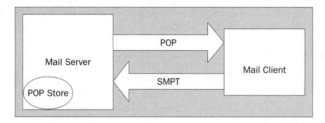

POP3 Via Telnet

The only reason that I'm going to cover this is to quickly show the steps or procedures that allow us to access a typical POP3 mailbox on a mail server. The internal methods used in the .NET C# System.Web.Mail namespace would do something very similar to this while retrieving messages using the POP3 protocol. Although most of this is abstracted away by the .NET runtime components, it's interesting to see what happens behind the scenes.

```
open mail.someserver.com 110
Trying. . . Connected to MAIL.SOMESERVER.COM

+OK test.someserver.COM MultiNet POP3 Server Process v4.0(1) at Fri 20-Jun-2002
3:21PM-CST
user krowczyk                                    //designate user
+OK User Name (krowczyk) ok. Password, please.

pass thisismypassword                            //enter password
+OK 3 messages in folder INBOX (V4.0)

list 2                                           //list gives message size
+OK 2 7124                                       //in bytes

stat                                             //stat gives total message
+OK 3 14749                                      //size in bytes

quit
+OK POP# MultiNet test.somewhere.COM Server exiting (3 INBOX messages left)

Connection closed by Foreign Host
```

POP Commands

A typical POP session consists of a client connecting to the POP3 server on TCP port 110 (the default). Once the client is connected, the POP3 server sends back a connection-greeting message that acknowledges the connection and starts the POP3 session. Commands are then issued and responded to by the client and server until the connection has been closed and the session ends.

According to the RFC, POP3 commands consist of a keyword optionally followed by arguments. Some of the specifics for commands are as follows:

- Commands are terminated by a CRLF sequence
- Keywords are separated by a SPACE character
- Keywords are three or four characters long
- Each argument may be up to 40 characters in length
- Responses may be up to 512 characters in length
- +OK designates a positive response
- -ERR designates a negative response or error condition

Required Commands	Description
USER [name]	Username sent to the server.
PASS [password]	The password.
QUIT	Terminates or ends the current session.
DELE [msg]	Deletes mail from the server.
RSET	Undoes any changes made during the current session.
STAT	Returns the number of messages on the server.
RETR [msg]	Retrieves the content of a message.
LIST [msg]	Returns information about the message in parameter. Such as size in bytes. If no parameter is given, a list with all messages and their sizes is returned.
NOOP	Does nothing but cause the server to respond with a positive response.

Optional Commands	Description
TOP [msg] [n]	The server sends the headers of the message, the blank line separating the headers from the body, and then the number of lines of the indicated message's body. [msg] is the message number desired. [n] specifies the top n lines to be retrieved.

Table continued on following page

Optional Commands	Description
UIDL [*msg*]	If an argument is given, the server issues a positive response with a line containing information about the specified message. Called a "unique id listing" for the message selected. The unique-id of a message is an arbitrary server-determined string, consisting of one to 70 characters in the range 0x21 to 0x7E, which uniquely identifies a message within a maildrop.
APOP [*mailbox*] [*digest*]	A string identifying a mailbox and an MD5 digest string. The MD5 algorithm takes a message of arbitrary length as an input, and produces a 128-bit fingerprint message digest of the input. Typically used within RSA cryptography and such.

The POP3 protocol gives us basic functionality for retrieving messages from our mail server. It serves its purpose very well, and is pretty much the standard that the majority of mail servers and clients use.

IMAP

IMAP gives us everything that POP3 doesn't. It provides capability for on-line, off-line, or disconnected modes of operation. It allows us to control folders on both the client machine as well as the server. It also provides enhanced authentication (POP3 authentication is relatively weak). And it allows the use of multiple mail servers that can work together with the same mail client.

Let's take a brief look at how an IMAP client and server might interact:

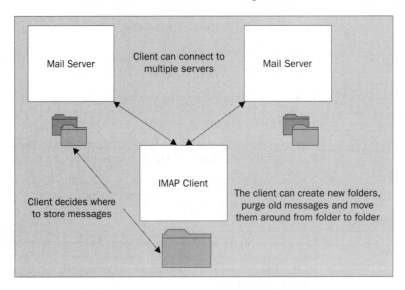

IMAP4 is outlined and documented in RFC 2060. Some of IMAP's features include:

Server-side Mailbox Manipulation

- ❏ Ability to add messages to a remote mailbox
- ❏ Support for and notification of simultaneous updates in shared mailboxes
- ❏ New mail notification

Multiple Mailbox Support

- ❏ Remote folder management: list/create/delete/rename
- ❏ Support for folder hierarchies
- ❏ Access to message types other than e-mail, such as NetNews

Online Performance Optimization

- ❏ Provision for determining message structure without downloading the entire message
- ❏ Selected retrieval of MIME body parts
- ❏ Server-based search and retrieval to minimize data transfer

Perfect for Roaming Power Users

- ❏ Shared folders overcome limitations of POP3 access on more than one machine
- ❏ Performance optimization helps with slow mail server connections

Although IMAP gives us much more advanced functionality than POP3, you'll find that many of the e-mail users and clients in the world are using POP3 servers for mail retrieval. IMAP is often much more complex to implement than POP3. For offline processing mode, POP3 and IMAP have almost equivalent possibilities, but for online or disconnected processing mode, IMAP is clearly superior. However, because of POP3's inherent simplicity, we'll slant our discussion in this chapter to cover the POP3 implementation in more detail.

.NET and E-Mails

Now that we've had an overview of mail protocols, we can get to the most interesting bits of information. Once you understand the way the SMTP, POP3, and IMAP protocols work, the code being presented here should be very easy to follow.

We'll start by looking at how to send e-mails using the .NET `System.Web.Mail` namespace, which allows us to send e-mail and attachments using SMTP. We'll also develop some sample applications that implement the SMTP and NNTP (the Network News Transport Protocol, which is used for newsgroup access and is very similar to SMTP).

SMTP

In your past life (when you programmed without .NET), you may have used CDONTS to send e-mails within your applications. This was commonly done from within both ASP and Visual Basic. There were often third-party ActiveX components that took the place of CDONTS and made sending e-mails a bit easier than dealing with Microsoft's confusing objects. In .NET, Microsoft has wrapped all the SMTP e-mail functionality up and rolled it directly into the .NET Framework under the `System.Web.Mail` namespace. Using the classes within this namespace, we can easily construct and send mail, with attachments if desired, using the SMTP service built into IIS.

Using the `System.Web.Mail` namespace actually allows us to send messages using the CDOSYS (Collaboration Data Objects for Windows 2000) message component. In fact, .NET simply wraps the functionality of the underlying messaging components. This allows the e-mail messages to be delivered either through the SMTP mail service built into Windows 2000 or through an arbitrary SMTP server.

It's been my experience in the past that third-party components often provide the deep and managed functionality that my applications have needed. In particular, if you need a component that contains more functionality than the `System.Web.Mail` namespace, you can take a look at the following components:

❑ EasyMail.NET (http://www.quicksoft.com). This also provides a very nice parsing library and IMAP capabilities.

❑ aspNetEmail (http://www.aspnetemail.com)

❑ Smtp.NET (http://www.exclamationsoft.com/exclamationsoft/smtp.net/default.asp)

System.Web.Mail Namespace

The `System.Web.Mail` namespace contains three classes and three enumerations:

Class	Description
MailAttachment	Represents the attachments of an e-mail.
MailMessage	Represents the e-mail message itself.
SmtpMail	Responsible for sending a MailMessage via SMTP.

Enumeration	Description
MailEncoding	Specifies the encoding of the message – Base64 or UUEncode.
MailFormat	Specifies the format of the message. Either HTML or Text.
MailPriority	Specifies the priority of the message. High, Medium, or Low

Sending a message using this namespace requires us first to construct a MailMessage object to represent the e-mail. Once we've set the properties of this object and populated it with the details of the e-mail message, we send it using the SmtpMail class

You are most likely to use these various properties when initializing the MailMessage object:

MailMessage Class Properties	Description
Attachments	The list of attachments (MailAttachment objects) that are transmitted with the e-mail.
Bcc	A semicolon-delimited list of e-mail addresses that receive a Blind Carbon Copy (Bcc) copy of the e-mail.
Body	The body of the e-mail.
BodyFormat	Specifies the MailFormat of the e-mail. This can be either MailFormat.Text or MailFormat.Html.
Cc	A semicolon-delimited list of e-mail addresses that receive a Carbon Copy (Cc) of the e-mail.
From	The e-mail address of the sender.
Priority	Specifies the MailPriority of the e-mail.
Subject	The subject of the e-mail.
To	The e-mail address of the recipient.
UrlContentBase	Gets or sets the Content-Base HTTP header. The URL base of all relative URLs used in an HTML body.
UrlContentLocation	Gets or sets the Content-Location HTTP header for the e-mail message.
Headers	Read-only property that consists of the list of custom headers to be transmitted with the message.

Constructing a MailMessage Object

The first step in constructing a MailMessage object is to set a reference to the System.Web.dll assembly, since the System.Web and System.Web.Mail namespaces aren't available until the reference is set:

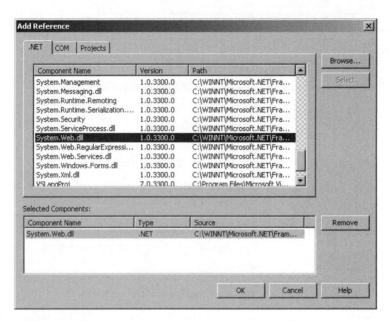

After we have added the reference to `System.Web.dll`, we can include it in a `using` statement, and instantiate our `MailMessage` object:

```
using System.Web.Mail;

// Create a mail message object
MailMessage email = new MailMessage();
```

Next, we'll set up a few properties of the e-mail:

```
// Set message parameters
email.From = "someone@someone.com";
email.To = "krowczyk@i-netway.com";
email.Subject = "Test message using SmtpMail";
email.BodyFormat = MailFormat.Text;
email.Body = "This is just a test message";
```

Adding an Attachment

Adding an attachment is as easy as creating one or more `MailAttachment` objects and adding them to the `Attachments` list of the `MailMessage` object. Here's a quick look at the members of the `MailAttachment` class:

MailAttachment Class Properties	Description
Encoding	Type of encoding for the e-mail attachment. This can be either `MailEncoding.Base64` or `MailEncoding.UUEncode`.
Filename	Name of the attachment file.

Now let's add an attachment. We do this by calling the `Add()` method of the `Attachments` collection, passing in the path of the file that we want to attach to the mail, and the `MailEncoding` to use:

```
email.Attachments.Add(new MailAttachment(@"c:\testfile.txt",
                                         MailEncoding.Base64));
```

We can add any number of attachments to the e-mail message in this way by continuing to add `MailAttachment` objects to the `Attachments` list of the `MailMessage`.

An SmtpMail Object

To send an e-mail message that you've composed, you need to call a method of the `SmtpMail` object. The interesting thing to note is that there is only one really important method of the `SmtpMail` class – the static `Send()` method. This method sends off the mail message to the SMTP server. It can take a `MailMessage` object as a parameter, or it can take four strings that specify the sender, recipient, subject, and body of the e-mail.

The `SmtpMail` class also has one public property:

SmtpMail Class Properties	Description
SmtpServer	This is the server to which the SMTP mail should be sent. If this property is not set, the `SmtpMail` object defaults to sending the mail to the Windows SMTP service for delivery.

Please note that you must have the SMTP service installed on your machine before this code will work when not specifying an SMTP server. To install the IIS SMTP service, select Control Panel | Add Remove Programs | Add Remove Windows Components | Internet Information Services | SMTP Service.

```
// Send the e-mail using the SmtpMail object
SmtpMail.Send(email);

//or also like this - without a mail message object
string from = "from@somewhere.com";
string to = "to@somewhere.com";
string subject = "test";
string body = "test message";

SmtpMail.Send (from, to, subject, body);
```

If we don't set the `SmtpServer` property, the e-mail will be sent via the Windows SMTP service. To set the `SmtpServer` property we can just use the following code:

```
// For example, here we want to set the SMTP server field before sending the mail
// message
SmtpMail.SmtpServer = "mail.testserver.com";

// Now send message as we did before
SmtpMail.Send(email);
```

The previous code snippets have shown the various parts of sending e-mail using the SMTP capabilities of .NET. Now we'll look at a sample application that ties it all together.

SMTP Mailer Application

Our finished sample SMTP mail application will be a simple .NET Windows Form application that allows us to set various properties of an e-mail and send it using a designated SMTP server. The following screenshot depicts the end result of the code we're going to cover. The form has five single-line text boxes, where the user can enter the name of the SMTP server to use, the e-mail addresses of the sender and recipient, the subject of the mail, and the path to any attachment to send with the mail. There is also a multi-line text box, where the body of the mail can be typed:

This code is available in the chapter download materials. There is really no magic to writing this sort of simple application. We basically just create a form with appropriate text boxes and enter some code in the Click event handler for the Send button that uses the SMTP mail capabilities we've been looking at to send the mail on its way.

Important Code

As before, we need to add a reference to the System.Web.dll assembly, and a using directive to point to the System.Web.Mail namespace. Apart from the standard Windows code (generated by Visual Studio .NET), we only need to add the code behind the Send button. This is very similar to the code we've already seen:

```
private void button1_Click(object sender, System.EventArgs e)
{
    // Create mail message
    MailMessage email = new MailMessage();

    // Set message parameters
    email.From = txtFrom.Text;
    email.To = txtRecipient.Text;
```

```
            email.Subject = txtSubject.Text;
            email.BodyFormat = System.Web.Mail.MailFormat.Text;
            email.Body = txtMessage.Text;

            // Add attachment
            email.Attachments.Add(new MailAttachment(txtAttachment.Text,
                                            MailEncoding.Base64));

            // Set SMTP server
            SmtpMail.SmtpServer = txtSmtpServer.Text;

            // Now send message
            SmtpMail.Send(email);
        }
```

Check out the download materials for the full sample application.

POP3

If you've had any experience with .NET mail programming or development, you will probably know that .NET doesn't provide inherent support for retrieving mail from POP3 and IMAP mailboxes. Although we've already covered the SMTP component of the .NET Framework that merrily allows us to send SMTP e-mails and so on, what we haven't said yet is that the `System.Web.Mail` namespace is basically just a wrapper for the CDOSYS component. This unmanaged component is really used underneath to send the e-mails.

So how do we retrieve mails using .NET? We could try using CDO to retrieve mails, but that will only work for Microsoft Exchange Servers, and not all the mail servers out there in the world are based on Microsoft Exchange! What we really want to do, seeing that this is a networking book, is to code our own POP3 e-mail class that uses the POP3 protocol to retrieve e-mails. We'll use some of the networking namespaces that exist in .NET to accomplish this goal.

Creating a POP3 C# Class

Our first task in creating a class that handles POP3 messages is to determine what exactly a message consists of. First create a new C# Windows Application project called `POPMail`.

Let's start off by creating a class that represents the core of a POP3 e-mail message, so add a new class to the project called `POP3EmailMessage`:

```
public class POP3EmailMessage
{
    // Define public members
    public long msgNumber;
    public long msgSize;
    public bool msgReceived;
    public string msgContent;
}
```

This class contains a message number, the size of the message (in bytes), a flag indicating whether or not the message has been received from the server, and a string containing the actual content of the e-mail message. If you remember in our protocol discussion, these fields are common within a typical e-mail message and are used/shown when retrieving a message. For example, we need an index (msgNumber) to the message that we want to deal with when listing out or retrieving from the POP3 server.

System.Net.Sockets.TcpClient

As we've seen in the last few chapters, the .NET Framework presents us with a rich base of classes to deal with low-level networking needs. In our case, we want to harness the TcpClient class, because we will make remote connections to the mail server using the TCP protocol. We will therefore create a class that is derived from the System.Net.Sockets.TcpClient namespace:

```
// Define the POP3 class
public class POP3 : System.Net.Sockets.TcpClient
{
```

Connecting to a Server

There are a few things that this class must be able to do, the first of which is connect to the POP3 server passing in a username and password.

Remember our Telnet session back in our discussion about the POP3 protocol to draw similarities to what we are doing here.

So, let's start by writing a ConnectPOP() method. This takes three parameters – the name of the server to connect to, and the username and password of the mailbox we want to access. Note that it will call some methods that are presented later in the chapter:

```
public void ConnectPOP(string sServerName, string sUserName, string sPassword)
{
    // Message and the server resulting response
    string sMessage;
    string sResult;

    // Call the connect method of the TcpClient class
    // Remember default port for server is 110
    Connect(sServerName, 110);

    // Get result back
    sResult = Response();

    // Check response to make sure it's +OK
    if (sResult.Substring(0,3) != "+OK")
        throw new POPException(sResult);

    // Got past connect, send username
    sMessage = "USER " + sUserName + "\r\n";

    // Write() sends data to the Tcp Connection
    Write(sMessage);
    sResult = Response();
```

```
    // Check response
    if (sResult.Substring(0,3) != "+OK")
    {
        throw new POPException(sResult);
    }

    // Now follow up with sending password in same manner
    sMessage = "PASS " + sPassword + "\r\n";
    Write(sMessage);
    sResult = Response();
    if (sResult.Substring(0,3) != "+OK")
        throw new POPException(sResult);
}
```

I've put comments in the above code to help with its readability. We connect to the POP3 server and send the username and password using the `Connect()` method of the `TcpClient` class, and our methods `Write()` and `Response()`. As we saw in the POP3 Telnet session that we discussed earlier, the POP3 server should send back a +OK response if we were successful, and a -ERR message when a failure occurs. If this happens, we throw an exception using the message sent back from the server.

When You Connect, You Must Disconnect

Since we're talking about connecting, we may as well also show the disconnect method now. To disconnect from the server, we simply need to issue the QUIT command. That makes our `DisconnectPOP()` method really quite simple:

```
public void DisconnectPOP()
{
    string sMessage;
    string sResult;

    sMessage = "QUIT\r\n";
    Write(sMessage);

    sResult = Response();
    if (sResult.Substring(0,3) != "+OK")
        throw new POPException(sResult);
}
```

So far, we have a way to connect to the POP3 server, as well as a way to disconnect from it. The typical POP3 session will consist of a call to `ConnectPOP()`, commands to get e-mails and so on, and then a call to `DisconnectPOP()`.

Getting a List of Messages

We can get a list of messages on the POP3 inbox simply by issuing a LIST command to the server. The `ListMessages()` method shows how we can do this.

> Note that using the **ArrayList** requires us to import the **System.Collections** namespace.

```
public ArrayList ListMessages()
{
    // Same sort of thing as in ConnectPOP and DisconnectPOP
    string sMessage;
    string sResult;
    ArrayList returnValue = new ArrayList();
    sMessage = "LIST\r\n";
    Write(sMessage);

    sResult = Response();
    if (sResult.Substring(0, 3) != "+OK")
        throw new POPException(sResult);

    while (true)
    {
        sResult = Response();
        if (sResult == ".\r\n")
        {
            return returnValue;
        }
        else
        {
            POP3EmailMessage oMailMessage = new POP3EmailMessage();

            // Define a separator
            char[] sep = { ' ' };

            // Use the split method to break out array of data
            string[] values = sResult.Split(sep);

            // Put data into oMailMessage object
            oMailMessage.msgNumber = Int32.Parse(values[0]);
            oMailMessage.msgSize = Int32.Parse(values[1]);
            oMailMessage.msgReceived = false;
            returnValue.Add(oMailMessage);
            continue;
        }
    }
}
```

As we saw in the Telnet example, sending a LIST command to the POP3 server will cause the server to send back multiple lines of text. Each line represents an e-mail message that contains a message number and a number of bytes that the e-mail message contains. It's key to note that this method only returns an array of message objects that have very minimal data in them. The way that we receive more information and the message content is by creating a mirror of the RETR command that retrieves the actual message.

Retrieving a Specific Message

To retrieve a full message from the POP3 server, we need to issue the RETR command with the msgNumber of the message that we want to retrieve. This follows the same procedure as we described before:

```
public POP3EmailMessage RetrieveMessage(POP3EmailMessage msgRETR)
{
    string sMessage;
    string sResult;

    // Create new instance of object and set new values
    POP3EmailMessage oMailMessage = new POP3EmailMessage ();
    oMailMessage.msgSize = msgRETR.msgSize;
    oMailMessage.msgNumber = msgRETR.msgNumber;

    // Call the RETR command to get the appropriate message
    sMessage = "RETR " + msgRETR.msgNumber + "\r\n";
    Write(sMessage);
    sResult = Response();
    if (sResult.Substring(0, 3) != "+OK")
        throw new POPException (sResult);

    // Set the received flag equal to true since we got the message
    oMailMessage.msgReceived = true;

    // Now loop to get the message text until we hit the "." end point
    while (true)
    {
        sResult = Response();
        if (sResult == ".\r\n")
            break;
        else
            oMailMessage.msgContent = sResult;
    }

    return oMailMessage;
}
```

Deleting a Message

Since the POP3 protocol states that a message isn't deleted from the server when the message is retrieved, we need to call the DELE command explicitly to remove the message from the server. Writing that method is also quite simple:

```
public void DeleteMessage(POP3EmailMessage msgDELE)
{
    string sMessage;
    string sResult;

    sMessage = "DELE " + msgDELE.msgNumber + "\r\n";
    Write(sMessage);
    sResult = Response();
    if (sResult.Substring(0, 3) != "+OK")
        throw new POPException(sResult);
}
```

373

The Write() Method

The write method takes a message as input and writes it out to the TCP network stream. This will in effect send our command to the POP3 server we are connected to. Since C# string data types cannot be directly buffered to the network stream, we must use the ASCIIEncoding class of the System.Text namespace to get the byte representation of the string data. Once this is done, we just write that out to the network stream:

```
private void Write(string sMessage)
{
    // Used for Data Encoding
    System.Text.ASCIIEncoding oEncodedData = new System.Text.ASCIIEncoding() ;

    // Now grab the message into a buffer for sending to the TCP network stream
    byte[] WriteBuffer = new byte[1024] ;
    WriteBuffer = oEncodedData.GetBytes(sMessage) ;

    // Take the buffer and output it to the TCP stream
    NetworkStream NetStream = GetStream();
    NetStream.Write(WriteBuffer, 0, WriteBuffer.Length);
}
```

The Response( ) Method

The flip side of the Write() method described above is the Response() method. This method allows us to read data back from the POP3 server connection. This is used throughout the class to grab the result codes sent back from the server in response to commands that we've sent with each Write(). Again, we need to use the ASCIIEncoding class to get the string representation of the bytes being received across the network stream.

This code sample should be quite self-explanatory:

```
private string Response()
{
    System.Text.ASCIIEncoding oEncodedData = new System.Text.ASCIIEncoding();
    byte []ServerBuffer = new Byte[1024];
    NetworkStream NetStream = GetStream();
    int count = 0;

    // Here we read from the server network stream and place data into
    // the buffer (to later decode and return)
    while (true)
    {
      byte []buff = new Byte[2];
      int bytes = NetStream.Read( buff, 0, 1 );

      if (bytes == 1)
      {
          ServerBuffer[count] = buff[0];
          count++;

          if (buff[0] == '\n')
          {
```

```
            break;
        }
    }
    else
    {
        break;
    }
}


// Return the decoded ASCII string value
string ReturnValue = oEncodedData.GetString(ServerBuffer, 0, count );
return ReturnValue;
}
```

PopException Class

This class simply encapsulates an application exception that we may throw in our code:

```
namespace POPMailException
{
    public class POPException : System.ApplicationException
    {
        public POPException(string str) : base(str)
        {
        }
    }
}
```

A Quick Console Application Sample

The full sample application given here can be found in this book's download from www.wrox.com. The sample application adds a GUI front end to the POP3 class that we just wrote, but the basic use of this class can be seen by taking a look at the Main() method of the console application listed below. This method steps through the items needed to instantiate the class and retrieve the message numbers and message text:

```
static void Main(string[] args)
{
    try
    {
        POP3 oPOP = new POP3();
        oPOP.ConnectPOP("mail.someserver.com", "username", "password");
        ArrayList MessageList = oPOP.ListMessages();
        foreach (POP3EmailMessage POPMsg in MessageList)
        {
            POP3EmailMessage POPMsgContent = oPOP.RetrieveMessage(POPMsg);
            System.Console.WriteLine("Message {0}: {1}",
            POPMsgContent.msgNumber, POPMsgContent.msgContent);
        }
        oPOP.DisconnectPOP();
    }
    catch ( POPException e )
    {
```

375

```
        System.Console.WriteLine(e.ToString());
    }
    catch ( System.Exception e)
    {
        System.Console.WriteLine(e.ToString());
    }
}
}
```

The image below is a screenshot of the sample PopMail application that I've written. It uses the POP3 class above to list the e-mails in my mailbox. The user can then retrieve the message text by inserting the number of the message to display. The entire message is then retrieved from the mailbox:

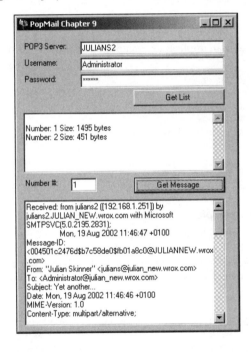

Expanding on this Class

There are many ways in which this class could be improved and expanded upon. You may want to expand the POP3EmailMessage class to include much more functionality. Individual properties that describe the headers, subject, message, and so on. I made the class simple to use and tried to follow the same sort of design as you would see via logging into a Telnet session with the POP3 server, as this stays more true to the design of the POP3 protocol and is useful for our understanding in a networking frame of mind.

There are also many popular third-party components that encapsulate this functionality very nicely. But what fun would buying one of those be?

NNTP

NNTP is commonly used to access the content of newsgroups on the Internet. The protocol is defined in RFC 977, and has been around for a while. We'll briefly cover a class that encapsulates access to NNTP newsgroups and servers, which is based upon and quite similar to the POP3 class that we described earlier. Why is it similar? Firstly, it's a basic TCP network stream-based protocol, much like SMTP and other e-mail related protocols. We haven't really touched much on NNTP up until this point in a protocol discussion, since this chapter is really targeted towards the topic of .NET and e-mail access. Therefore, if you'd like to read further information about the NNTP protocol, I'd advise reading RFC 977 located at http://www.ietf.org/rfc/rfc0977.txt?number=977 for further information. For ease of reading the code, I will list the common commands and responses that may be used against an NNTP server. These are very similar to the POP3 items listed in our previous examples.

NNTP Commands

The most common commands issued to an NNTP newsgroup server are listed in the following table:

NNTP Commands	Description
ARTICLE	Displays the header, a blank line, then the body text of the current or specified article.
GROUP	Will return the article numbers of the first and last articles in the group, and an estimate of the number of articles on file in the group.
LAST	The internally maintained "current article pointer" is set to the previous article in the current newsgroup.
LIST	Returns a list of valid newsgroups and associated information.
NEWSGROUPS	A list of newsgroups created since a specified date and time will be listed in a similar format to the LIST command.
NEWNEWS	A list of message IDs of articles posted or received in the specified newsgroup since the date specified.
NEXT	The internally maintained "current article pointer" is advanced to the next article in the current newsgroup. If no more articles remain in the current group, an error message is returned and the article remains selected.
POST	If posting is allowed, the article is posted to the server.
QUIT	Closes the connection with the server.

NNTP Responses

The most common responses received back from an NNTP newsgroup server are listed below. These are not specific messages, but a listing of the meaning of different digits that compose the NNTP response. For more complete response listings, please view the RFC.

NNTP Responses	Description
1xx	Informative message
2xx	Command OK
3xx	Command OK so far, send the rest of it
4xx	Command was correct, but couldn't be performed for some reason
5xx	Command unimplemented, or incorrect, or a serious program error occurred
x0x	Connection, setup, and miscellaneous messages
x1x	Newsgroup selection
x2x	Article selection
x3x	Distribution functions
x4x	Posting
x8x	Nonstandard (private implementation) extensions
x9x	Debugging output

Some common response codes include:

Common Messages	Description
100	Help text
190 through 199	Debug output
200	Server ready – posting allowed
201	Server ready – no posting allowed
400	Service discontinued
500	Command not recognized
501	Command syntax error
502	Access restriction or permission denied
503	Program fault – command not performed

You'll see more specific responses and commands as we discuss the NNTP code class below.

Creating an NNTP Class in C#

This explanation of the class will follow the same sort of presentation as the POP3 class. We will derive the NNTP class from the same System.Net.Sockets.TcpClient class. First we import the necessary namespaces:

```
using System;
using System.Net.Sockets;
using NNTPServerException;      // Our own exception class implementation
using System.Collections;
```

Inheriting from the TCP Client Class

As in the POP3 client, inheriting from the `TcpClient` gives us a wealth of functionality that we don't need to implement ourselves, such as the network transfer layers responsible for connecting to the server and allowing us to send data across the network stream.

```
public class NNTP : System.Net.Sockets.TcpClient
```

Connecting to the Server

Our `ConnectNNTP()` method simply calls the `TcpClient`'s `Connect()` method, passing in the server name as well as the standard port number (119) for the NNTP server connection:

```
public void ConnectNNTP(string sServer)
{
   string sResult;

   // Connect to the server on the default port #119
   Connect(sServer, 119);
   sResult = Response();

   // In this case, a response code of 200 is an OK response
   if (sResult.Substring(0, 3) != "200")
      throw new NNTPException(sResult);
}
```

Disconnecting from the Server

Again, if we write a connect function, we must write a disconnect function. This simply sends the QUIT command to the NNTP server:

```
public void DisconnectNNTP()
{
   string sMessage;
   string sResult;

   // Send the QUIT command
   sMessage = "QUIT\r\n";

   Write(sMessage);
   sResult = Response();

   // We expect a code of 205 acknowledging the quit
   if (sResult.Substring( 0, 3) != "205")
      throw new NNTPException(sResult);
}
```

Getting the Newsgroups

As you might imagine, calling GetNewsGroupListing() in our class will use the LIST command to return all of the groups that are available on the NNTP server. This may be a lot, depending on the server!

```
public ArrayList GetNewsGroupListing()
{
    string sMessage;
    string sResult;

    // Create an array for the return values
    ArrayList ReturnValue = new ArrayList();

    sMessage = "LIST\r\n";
    Write(sMessage);

    // Check the response, if OK continue
    sResult = Response();
    if (sResult.Substring(0, 3) != "215")
        throw new NNTPException(sResult);

    // While there are more results, loop and append to output array list
    while (true)
    {
        sResult = Response();
        if (sResult == ".\r\n" || sResult == ".\n")
        {
            return ReturnValue;
        }
        else
        {
            char[] separator = { ' ' };
            string[] values = sResult.Split(separator);
            ReturnValue.Add(values[0]);
            continue;
        }
    }
}
```

Getting News from a Group

To get the news from a specific newsgroup that is listed on the NNTP server, we simply need to create a method that calls the GROUP command, passing in the name of the newsgroup for which we want to retrieve the messages:

```
public ArrayList GetNews(string sNewsGroup)
{
    string sMessage;
    string sResult;
    ArrayList ReturnValue = new ArrayList();
    sMessage = "GROUP " + sNewsGroup + "\r\n";

    // Write the message to the server
    Write(sMessage);
```

```
      sResult = Response();

      // Check for successful operation
      if (sResult.Substring(0, 3) != "211")
         throw new NNTPException(sResult);

      char[] separator = { ' ' };
      string[] values = sResult.Split(separator);

      // For beginning and end
      long begin = Int32.Parse(values[2]);
      long end = Int32.Parse(values[3]);

      if (begin + 100 < end && end > 100)
         begin = end - 100;

      for (long i = begin; i<end; i++)
      {
         sMessage = "ARTICLE " + i + "\r\n";
         Write(sMessage);
         sResult = Response();

         if (sResult.Substring( 0, 3) == "423")
            continue;

         if (sResult.Substring( 0, 3) != "220")
            throw new NNTPException(sResult);

         string sArticle = "";
         while (true)
         {
            sResult = Response();
            if (sResult == ".\r\n")
               break;

            if (sResult == ".\n")
               break;

            if (sArticle.Length < 1024)
               sArticle += sResult;
         }
         ReturnValue.Add(sArticle);
      }
      return ReturnValue;
   }
```

Posting to a Group

Posting to a newsgroup is also an easy task. It consists of simply calling the POST command with the name of the newsgroup, followed by the headers and the body of the message we want to post:

```
public void PostMessage(string sNewsGroup, string sSubject, string sFrom,
                        string sContent)
{
    string sMessage;
    string sResult;
    sMessage = "POST " + sNewsGroup + "\r\n";

    Write(sMessage);
    sResult = Response();

    if (sResult.Substring( 0, 3) != "340")
        throw new NNTPException(sResult);

    // Build message
    sMessage = "From: " + sFrom + "\r\n"
            + "Newsgroups: " + sNewsGroup + "\r\n"
            + "Subject: " + sSubject + "\r\n\r\n"
            + sContent + "\r\n.\r\n";

    Write(sMessage);
    sResult = Response();

    if (sResult.Substring( 0, 3) != "240")
        throw new NNTPException(sResult);
}
```

The Write() Method

Again, due to the encoding/decoding that must take place to allow the C# string type to be transported in bytes over the network stream, we need to come up with our own method that writes the data in a memory buffer to the server:

```
private void Write(string sMessage)
{
    System.Text.ASCIIEncoding oEncode = new System.Text.ASCIIEncoding() ;
    byte[] WriteBuffer = new byte[1024];
    WriteBuffer = oEncode.GetBytes(sMessage);
    NetworkStream oNetworkStream = GetStream();

    oNetworkStream.Write(WriteBuffer, 0, WriteBuffer.Length);
}
```

The Response() Method

We also need to transform the data coming back from the server to an appropriate string format for our class representation:

```
private string Response()
{
    System.Text.ASCIIEncoding oEncode = new System.Text.ASCIIEncoding();
    byte []ServerBuffer = new byte[1024];
    NetworkStream oNetworkStream = GetStream();
    int count = 0;
    while (true)
```

```
   {
      byte []LocalBuffer = new Byte[2];
      int bytes = oNetworkStream.Read(LocalBuffer, 0, 1);
      if (bytes == 1)
      {
         ServerBuffer[count] = LocalBuffer[0];
         count++;
         if (LocalBuffer[0] == '\n')
            break;
      }
      else
         break;

      string ReturnValue = oEncode.GetString(ServerBuffer, 0, count);
      return ReturnValue;
   }
}
```

NNTPException Class

Again, we define our own exception class for NNTP errors:

```
namespace NNTPServerException
{
   public class NNTPException : System.ApplicationException
   {
      public NNTPException(string str) : base(str)
      {
      }
   }
}
```

Sample Class Use

Using the above class is quite straightforward, as you can see from the code below (again, the `Main()` method for a simple console application). This takes you through the use of the different methods in the class:

```
static void Main(string[] args)
{
   try
   {
      // Create NNTP object
      NNTP oNNTP = new NNTP();

      // Connect to a server
      oNNTP.ConnectNNTP("news.testserver.com");

      // Get a list of newsgroups for the server
      ArrayList NewsGroupList = oNNTP.GetNewsGroupListing();
      foreach (string NewsGroupEntry in NewsGroupList)
         System.Console.WriteLine("Newsgroup :{0}", NewsGroupEntry);

      // Now let's get the news for an article called "this article"
      NewsGroupList = oNNTP.GetNews("msnews.microsoft.com");
```

```
        foreach (string sArticle in NewsGroupList)
           System.Console.WriteLine("{0}", sArticle);

        oNNTP.PostMessage("test", "test", "test@test.com (Test User)",
                          "test");
        oNNTP.DisconnectNNTP();
    }
    catch (NNTPException e)
    {
        System.Console.WriteLine(e.ToString());
    }
    catch (System.Exception)
    {
        System.Console.WriteLine("Unhandled Exception");
    }
}
```

I've also included a sample NNTP application in the code download for this chapter. It works much like the POPMail sample that we saw earlier. It follows the basic structure of the POPMail sample, but instead uses our NNTP class to retrieve posting from newsgroups:

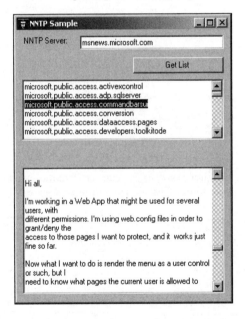

Expanding the NNTP Class

As with any bit of code, there is always room for improvement. The same improvements could be made for the NNTP class as for the POP3 class. Creating a better object representation of the NNTP message would be a place to start, as well as adding behind the scenes implementations of message retrieval and navigation. That would avoid any client applications that you may write having to explicitly work at the protocol level to work with the newsgroups.

Summary

That just about concludes our talk about e-mail protocols. As you can clearly see, there is much more to learn and dive into, and we've only touched the surface of fully understanding every nook and cranny of the RFCs and the protocols themselves. Just to recap, in this chapter we covered the basics of the SMTP, POP3, IMAP, and NNTP protocols and saw how those protocols worked together in sending and receiving e-mail messages over the Internet. We also took a deeper look and presented sample code to send e-mails via the .NET Framework's in-built classes for sending e-mails via SMTP, as well as developing some grassroots protocol implementation classes for POP3 and SMTP.

Although I would have liked to dive deeper into topics such as the IMAP and MIME protocols, those are such deep and complex protocols that they would be hard to cover within the constraints of this chapter. However, there are third-party tools that allow you to use these protocols in .NET. Unfortunately, there is no easy way to implement this functionality ourselves, so for production use, one of the third-party controls would probably be more economical than developing our own implementation. It's not as easy as POP3 and NNTP.

10

Cryptography in .NET

Every year computer crime increases dramatically, and it is always a challenge to keep up with the hackers. The `System.Security.Cryptography` namespace of the .NET Framework provides programmatic access to the variety of cryptographic services that we can incorporate into our applications to encrypt and decrypt data, ensure data integrity, and handle digital signatures and certificates. In this chapter, we'll explore the `System.Security.Cryptography` namespace so that we can utilize the cryptographic services in our applications.

Let's not waste a minute and dive into the exciting world of cryptography!

History of Cryptography

Cryptography is the art and science of secret writing (encrypting and decrypting information). The term cryptography is originally derived from the two Greek words "*kryptos*" and "*graph*", meaning hidden and writing. Much of cryptography is math-oriented and uses patterns and algorithms to encrypt messages and other forms of communication. Cryptography is a branch of mathematics, and is a combination of **cryptology** and **cryptanalysis** studies.

> **Cryptology** *is the science of coding and decoding secret messages, which is concerned with "breaking" cryptosystems, or deciphering messages without prior detailed knowledge of the cryptosystem.* **Cryptanalysis** *is the flip-side of cryptography: it is the science of cracking codes, decoding secrets, violating authentication schemes, and in general, breaking cryptographic protocols.*

Historically, the use of cryptography dates back to 1900 BC when a scribe in Egypt first used a derivation of the standard hieroglyphics of the day to communicate. Fast-forward thousands of years, and in the late 1970s, **Dr. Horst Feistel** of IBM Research Laboratory creates the precursor of the famous DES (Data Encryption Standard) algorithm. Until 1998, the US Government had tough restrictions preventing US companies exporting cryptographic software; that restriction was eased in 1998.

What is Cryptography?

Cryptography is all about converting plain text or clear text into cipher text through a process known as encryption. The cipher text is converted back to plain text or clear text by the opposite process called decryption:

The mathematical cryptography algorithm that performs the encryption and decryption transformations is also called a cipher and the encrypted text is called the cipher text.

Let's look at a simple example. Let's build a simple ASP.NET page.

```
<html>
<script language="C#" runat="server">
    public void Page_Load(Object sender, EventArgs E)
    {
        lblHello.Text = "Some information!";
    }
</script>

<body style="font: 10pt verdana" bgcolor="ffffcc">
    <form runat="server">
        <h3>Hacking!</h3>
        <asp:Label id="lblHello" Text="Default text" runat="server" />
    </form>
</body>
</html>
```

All this ASPX page does is to display "Some Information!" in a label server control in the Page_Load() event. Pretty simple, isn't it? Let's see what the page looks like in IE 6:

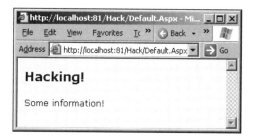

Let's use a tool called `TCPTrace.exe`, which is a network-sniffing tool. Microsoft also ships a similar tool called Network Monitor with the Windows Server products.

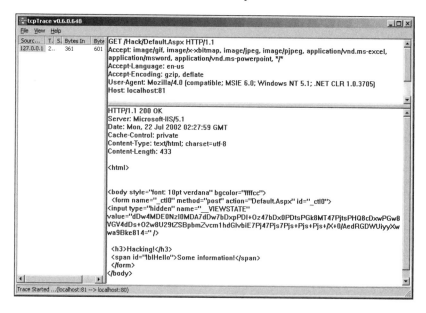

The TCPTrace.EXE tool can be downloaded from www.PocketSOAP.com

My web server (IIS 5.0) is running on port 80 and in order to sniff the packets sent to my web server, we've to change the port on the TCPTrace utility to 81 and the TCPTrace utility will forward all the requests received at port 81 to port 80 (to the web server). When accessing the site from IE use port 81. For example, if you're accessing your localhost then you've to access it like this: http://localhost:81/

As you can see, anyone who has access to a simple network-sniffing tool can read the information that we've transmitted over the public network. So how do you prevent this information leak? Cryptography plays a major role in the network safety.

Why Use Cryptography?

If your computer is connected to or transmits information over an electronic network your data is visible to everyone and is available for hackers. Today, more and more companies are doing business online and this increases the security risk for the companies online business as well as the customers and partners that interact with the company. To address these problems, each and every company must take strong steps to protect their online business as well as their customers and partners.

When used properly, cryptography addresses the following problems:

❑ **Confidentiality** – confidentiality assures that your information is protected.

❑ **Authentication** – authentication assures that you know who is accessing your private network.

❑ **Integrity** – integrity assures that information is not being tampered with during transit.

❑ **Non-repudiation** – non-repudiation assures that the sender can't deny sending the message.

Cryptography provides all the services to address the security and privacy concerns of transmitting sensitive data over a public network.

Concepts of Cryptography

A cryptography algorithm is a mathematical function that transforms the readable plain text message into unreadable text garbage, and reverses the process to produce readable text from an encrypted message. All cryptographic algorithms are based on two simple principles:

❑ **Substitution** – the concept of substitution is based on simply replacing every character in the message with another one. For example, when using the **Caesar cipher**, for a given letter in the message, shift to the right (in the alphabet) by three. That is, an "a" becomes "d", "b" becomes "e", and so on. This can be generalized to work for any number n not greater than 25 (assuming a 26 letter alphabet). In this cipher, the number n is the "key".

There are many varieties of the substitution ciphers available, including mono-alphabetic substitution ciphers, poly-alphabetic substitution ciphers, and perfect substitution ciphers.

❑ **Transposition** – the concept of transposition is based on scrambling the characters that are in the message. Some common forms of transposition algorithm involve writing the message into a table row-by-row and reading them column-by-column. Some of the transposition algorithms such as **Triple-DES** perform this process three times to create the cipher text.

The math formula of cryptography is simple. When you pass the plain text message into the encryption function, the function should provide the CipherMessage, and when you pass the CipherMessage into the decryption function, it should return the original message:

```
Encryption(Message) = CipherMessage
```

And:

```
Decryption(CipherMessage) = Message
```

In the same way, the following formula should also be true:

```
Decryption(Encryption(Message)) = Message
```

In the simple encryption/decryption algorithms, the algorithm is well known, and anyone who knows the algorithm should be able to decrypt the CipherMessage. Therefore, to provide more security for the algorithms, a key is added.

> *We need a key to lock and unlock a lock. In the same way, a cipher is a math algorithm and a key is a sequence of bytes that is used to encrypt and decrypt the information. If we don't have the key, we can't unlock the lock. In the same way, if we lose the key we can't decrypt the encrypted data. The keys come in different sizes based on the cryptography algorithms. For example, the DES algorithm is based on 56 bits and the RC2 algorithm is based on 128 bits.*

In order to encrypt or decrypt the message we have to pass the appropriate key into the function:

```
Encryption(Message, Key) = CipherMessage
```

And:

```
Decryption(CipherMessage, Key) = Message
```

In the same way, the following formula should also be true:

```
Decryption(Encryption(Message, Key), Key) = Message
```

Cryptographic Algorithms

Cryptographic algorithms can be divided into three types:

- ❑ **Symmetric algorithms** – in symmetric cryptographic algorithms, the same key is used for encrypting and decrypting the message.

- ❑ **Asymmetric algorithms** – in asymmetric cryptography algorithms, different keys are used for encrypting and decrypting the messages. The asymmetric cryptography algorithms are also known as public key infrastructure (or PKI).

- ❑ **Hashing or Message Digest algorithms** – in hash cryptographic algorithms, the original text is transformed into a fixed-length cipher text. The hash algorithms also perform one-way encryption meaning the hashed cipher text can't be decrypted to its original clear text version. The fixed length of the cipher text changes based on the algorithm from 128 to 256 bits.

Symmetric Algorithms

When encrypting and decrypting the information, the same key is used for the encrypting and decrypting process in symmetric algorithms, as shown in the following figure:

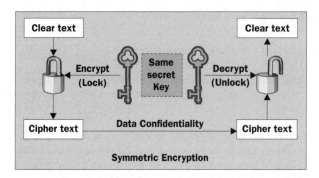

With this method, the data can be transmitted in an insecure network and the receiver can decrypt the information using the same cryptography algorithm used by the sender. Of course, the key that is used to encrypt and decrypt should be kept secret if you want this method to work for you. Another problem with this approach is distributing the key to the other end where it needs to be encrypted or decrypted.

> *For more information about the key sizes, read the paper "Selecting Cryptographic Key Sizes" at www.Cryptosavvy.com/Cryptosizes.pdf.*

Some of the common symmetric encryption algorithms are:

- ❏ **DES** – the Data Encryption Standard was adopted by the US Government in 1977, and by ANSI in 1981. DES follows 56-bit key for encryption and decryption. DES is a very famous algorithm but due to its small key length support, its use is very limited in today's world.

- ❏ **Triple-DES** – Triple-DES (or 3DES) is a very secure algorithm when compared with DES, since Triple-DES encrypts the message three times using the DES algorithm with different keys. The total key length of Triple-DES is 168 bits.

- ❏ **Blowfish** – Blowfish is a fast, compact, and simple encryption algorithm invented by the famous author Bruce Schneier, who is the author of the celebrated book "*Applied Cryptography*" (John Wiley & Sons, ISBN 0471128457). This algorithm allows a variable key length up to 448 bits.

- ❏ **IDEA** – the International Data Encryption Algorithm (IDEA) was developed by James L. Massey and Xuejia Lai in Switzerland. Widespread use of this algorithm was hindered by several patent problems.

- ❏ **RC2, RC4, RC5** – the RC2 and RC4 algorithms were originally developed by Ronald Rivest for RSA Security. Both RC2 and RC4 allow key lengths between 1 and 2,048 bits. On the other hand, RC5 allows a user-defined key length, data block size, and number of encryption rounds.

- ❏ **Rijndael (AES)** – this algorithm was originally developed by Joan Daemen and Vincent Rijmen. Rijndael is a fast and compact algorithm that supports keys of 128, 192, and 256 bits in length.

> **The .NET Framework supports DES, Triple-DES, RC2 and Rijndael symmetric encryption algorithms.**

Symmetric key algorithms are much faster than PKI algorithms, so they are the preferred choice for encrypting and decrypting large blocks of data. Also, they're also very easy to implement. The main disadvantage of symmetric encryption is that we need to protect the keys, and it is a challenge to exchange the keys between the encryption source and the decryption destination. The security of the algorithms is also related to the length of the key: the longer the key, the slimmer the probability of the information being decrypted. The possibility of information being decrypted is also based on the complexity of the key that you've chosen. The more complex the key, the slimmer the probability of the information being decrypted.

Asymmetric Algorithms

With asymmetric algorithms, one key encrypts the message and the other key decrypts the information as shown in the following figure:

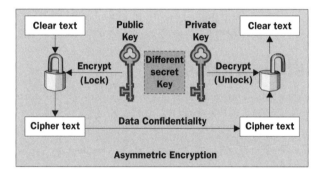

Both the keys are different but they're related to each other. Therefore, we can publish the public key without worrying about the possibility of our encryption being compromised. This encryption is also called **public-key encryption**, or **Public Key Infrastructure** (PKI), since the public key is available publicly without compromising the integrity and security of the key or message. The decryption key is normally called the private key or secret key.

Public-key cryptography and related standards and techniques underlie security features of many products, including signed and encrypted e-mail, form signing, object signing, single sign-on, and the most popular Secure Sockets Layer (SSL)/TLS protocol.

As shown in the figure above, the public key can be freely distributed, but only you will be able to read a message encrypted using this key. When someone sends an encrypted message to you, they encrypt the message with your public key, and upon receiving the encrypted data you can decrypt it with the corresponding private key. The message encrypted with the public key can be decrypted only with the corresponding private key.

> The PKI systems also use key exchange methods such as "Diffie-Hellman key exchange". The Diffie-Hellman key exchange is not an algorithm – it is a method that allows us to develop secure key exchange between two parties. The other methods are Digital Signature Standard (or DSS) and Elliptic Curve Cryptosystems.

The other way is to download the public key from an online repository. For example, if you get a client certificate from Thawte, you've an option to add your public key to the online repository. When someone wants to send something very secure all they've to do is to get the public key from you or from the online repository and sign the information with your public key and send it to you. When you receive the message, you decrypt it with your private key. This is one of the most common ways of exchanging the key.

Compared with symmetric-key encryption, public-key encryption requires more computation and is therefore not always appropriate for large amounts of data.

The .NET Framework supports two asymmetric algorithms:

❑   **DSA/DSS** – Digital Signature Standard (DSS) was developed by the National Security Agency. DSS is based on the Digital Signature Algorithm (DSA), and it supports any key length.

❑   **RSA** – RSA is a well-known public key algorithm developed by Ronald Rivest, Adi Shamir, and Leonard Adleman, and supports variable key length based on the implementation.

Message Digest Algorithms

Message Digest Algorithms (also known as MAC or hash algorithms) transform a variable-size input and return a fixed-size string as shown in the following figure:

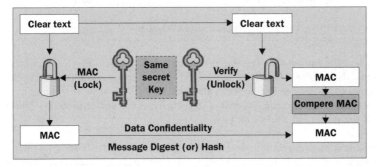

The hash algorithms are also called one-way hash, since the hashed string can't be converted back to the original state – once the original clear text value has been hashed, it is not possible to get the original hashed value from the MAC.

When we hash a clear text message with a hash algorithm, it uses a key to produce the hash value. Once the hash value is generated, we can send the clear text and the hash to the other end, where the clear text value can be hashed with the same key and algorithm – the generated hash value can then be compared with the one supplied by the other end. If the values match, we can be sure that the message has not been altered in transit.

> ASP.NET's Forms authentication module supports the one-way hash algorithms MD5 or SHA3 to authenticate the usernames/passwords stored in the `config.web` file. The same functionality can also be extended by storing the hashed passwords in the database using the `HashPasswordForStoringInConfigFile` method of the `FormsAuthentication` class available in the `System.Web.Security` namespace. For more information, have a look at *"Professional ASP.NET Security"* (Wrox Press, ISBN: 1-86100-620-9).

Some of the common MAC functions are MD2, MD4, MD5, SHA, SHA-1, SHA-256, SHA-384, and SHA-512. The .NET Framework supports the following hash functions:

❑ HMACSHA-1

❑ MACTripleDES

❑ MD-5

❑ SHA-1

❑ SHA-256

❑ SHA-384

❑ SHA-512

A Hash Message Authentication Code (or HMAC) function is a technique for verifying the integrity of a message transmitted between two parties that agree on a shared key.

Digital Signatures

Although encryption and decryption address a few problems, there are two important problems they don't address:

❑ Tampering

❑ Impersonation

Digital signatures use the one-way hashing functions for tamper detection and related authentication problems. Since the value of the hash is unique for the hashed data, any change in the data, even deleting or altering a single character, results in a different value. Moreover, the content of the hashed data cannot, for all practical purposes, be deduced from the hash. This therefore becomes the best way to detect tampering.

In public key encryption, it's possible to use the private key for encryption and the public key for decryption. Since this could create problems when encrypting sensitive information, we can digitally sign any data, instead of encrypting the data itself. Signing the data creates a one-way hash of the data, which can then be encrypted using the private key. The encrypted hash, along with other information, such as the hashing algorithm, is known as a digital signature. The following figure shows a simplified view of the way a digital signature can be used to validate the integrity of signed data:

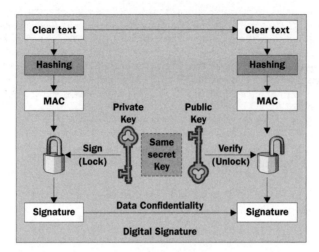

If you look at the above figure, the sender sends the clear text (or encrypted) message with the Digital Signature. The Digital Signature is computed based on the clear text message and the clear text message is hashed using a hashing algorithm such as MD5 and the hashed value will be signed by the private key. At the other end, we'll receive the clear text message (or encrypted) with the digital signature. Then we'll compute a hash value for the clear text and compare it with the Digital Signature. If the Digital Signature verification process was successful then, we're assured that the data has not been tampered with in transit.

Cryptography Terminology

Before diving into the world of crypto coding, we need to understand some cryptographic terminology.

Block Ciphers and Stream Ciphers

Cryptographic ciphers handle data in two formats:

❑ Block ciphers

❑ Stream ciphers

Block ciphers are traditionally the most popular ones. A block cipher transforms a fixed-length block of plain text data into a block of cipher text data of the same length and then repeats the process until the entire message has been processed. This transformation takes place under the action of a user-provided secret key. Decryption is performed by applying the reverse transformation to the cipher text block using the same secret key. The fixed length is called the block size, and for many block ciphers, the block size is 64 bits. Typically, symmetric algorithms are based on the block cipher format. For example, the DES and RC2 algorithms use 8 bytes, 3DES uses 16 bytes, and Rijndael uses 32 bytes as input. Using this scale each algorithm splits the input into the blocks and performs the transformation.

More recent symmetric encryption algorithms are based on stream ciphers. Every stream cipher generates a **keystream** and encryption is provided by combining the keystream with the plain text (usually with the bitwise XOR operator). Stream ciphers can be designed to be exceptionally fast, much faster in fact than any block cipher. While block ciphers operate on large blocks of data, stream ciphers typically operate on smaller units of plain text, usually bits. The encryption of any particular plain text with a block cipher will result in the same cipher text when the same key is used. With a stream cipher, the transformation of these smaller plain text units will vary, depending on when they are encountered during the encryption process.

Padding

Block ciphers deal with blocks of bits (usually 64 bits), and the last remaining bits may not fit in a block. For example, suppose we have 136 bits of information that we are trying to encrypt using a block cipher that takes 64 bits (or 8 bytes) at a time to encrypt. The following figure shows how the 136-bits input is split into 64-bit blocks for the padding process.

In the process of encryption, the first two blocks will contain 128 bits, and the remaining eight bits will not fit in the block cipher's buffer. To address the incomplete block, padding is needed. A padding scheme will define how the last incomplete block of data will be handled in the process of encryption. The padding will be addressed in the process of decryption by removing all the padded characters and restoring the original text.

> *PKCS#5 (or Public Key Cryptography Standard) is one of the most famous padding schemas and it was published by RSA Security, Inc. For more information, please visit the RSA web site at http://www.rsa.com/rsalabs/pubs/PKCS/.*

The .NET Framework handles padding using the `PaddingMode` enumeration. The `PaddingMode` enumeration supports three values:

❑ `None`

❑ `PKCS7`

❑ `Zeros`

As the name suggests, when we use `None`, no padding is done. When `PKCS7` is used, the remaining number of blocks will be filled with the remaining number of bits. For example, if six bits are free in a given byte, the last six bits will be padded with the value six. If four bits are free, the last four bits will be padded with the value four:

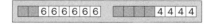

When `PaddingMode.Zeros` is used, the remaining bytes will be filled with the value zero:

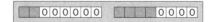

Modes

The mode of a cipher determines how blocks of plain text will be encrypted into blocks of cipher text, and decrypted back. The `CipherMode` enumeration defines the block cipher mode to be used when performing the encryption or decryption process. You can specify the mode using the `Mode` property of many of the cipher algorithms. The .NET Framework supports CBC, CFB, CTS, ECB, and OFB modes.

When using ECB (or Electronic Code Book) mode, each block of plain text is encrypted to a block of cipher text. The main drawback to ECB mode is that the same plain text will always encrypt to the same cipher text when the same key is used.

The CBC (or Cipher Block Chaining) mode overcomes the drawbacks of ECB mode. When using CBC mode, each block of plain text is combined with the previous block's cipher text (using an `XOR` operation), which produces encrypted blocks of cipher text:

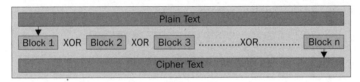

Since there is no previous cipher text block when starting the process, an initialization vector (or IV) is used for the first block of plain text.

The CFB (or Cipher Feedback) mode allows a block cipher to act like a stream cipher by processing the small increment of plain text into cipher text instead of processing it block by block. CFB mode also uses an IV to process the initial plain text.

The CTS (or Cipher Text Stealing) mode is a very versatile mode, which behaves pretty much like CBC mode. The CTS mode handles any length of plain text and produces cipher text that matches the length of the plain text.

The OFB (or Output Feedback) mode works pretty much like CFB mode; the only difference is the way that the internal buffer (shift register) is handled.

The System.Security.Cryptography Namespace

The `System.Security.Cryptography` namespace provides a simple way to implement security in your .NET application using the cryptography classes. Some of the cryptography classes are pure .NET managed code, and some of them are wrappers for the unmanaged **Microsoft Crypto API**. You can find out if the cryptography class is a managed or unmanaged code by looking at the class name. All the unmanaged providers end with the suffix `CryptoServiceProvider`, and all managed providers end with the `Managed` suffix. For example, if you look at the hashing classes such as `MD5CryptoServiceProvider`, `SHA1Managed`, and `SHA256Managed`, you can figure out that `SHA1Managed` and `SHA256Managed` are pure .NET managed implementations of the SHA algorithm.

The Crypto API is Microsoft's API for accessing cryptographic functions built in to the Windows platform. Microsoft recently released CAPICOM, an ActiveX wrapper around the Crypto API to simplify Crypto API programming in Visual Basic 6, but it implements only a subset of the API.

Note that the .NET Framework supports the use of strong key lengths in all encryption algorithms. However, for encryption algorithms that are implemented on top of Crypto API, you need to install a High Encryption Pack to upgrade your version of Windows:

- ❑ For Windows 2000 users, Service Pack 2 includes the High Encryption Pack. It can also be obtained from the following URL:
  http://www.microsoft.com/windows2000/downloads/recommended/encryption/.

- ❑ For Windows NT 4.0 users, Service Pack 6a includes the High Encryption Pack; this can be downloaded from:
  http://www.microsoft.com/ntserver/nts/downloads/recommended/SP6/allSP6.asp.

- ❑ For Windows ME, Windows 98, and Windows 95 users, Internet Explorer 5.5 includes the High Encryption Pack, or you can download it from:
  http://www.microsoft.com/windows/ie/download/128bit/default.asp.

Cryptography Class Hierarchy

The `System.Security.Cryptography` namespace provides three top-level classes, `SymmetricAlgorithm`, `AsymmetricAlgorithm`, and `HashAlgorithm`, representing the three main areas of cryptography as shown below:

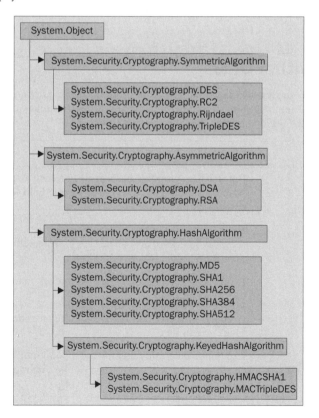

This model also brings the flexibility of extending the namespace. For example, the `System.Security.Cryptography` namespace doesn't currently support the **Blowfish** symmetric algorithm. If we wanted to add this algorithm to this namespace, all we would have to do is to derive our Blowfish algorithm class from the `SymmetricAlgorithm` class, and we'd get most of the standard functionality for free. The next advantage is that all the algorithm provider classes are inherited from their algorithm implementation classes. For example, the SHA1 hashing algorithm provider (the `SHA1Managed` class) is derived from the `SHA1` hash algorithms implementation (the `SHA1` class).

Hashing with .NET

The `System.Security.Cryptography` namespace in the .NET Framework provides several interfaces, known as **Cryptographic Service Providers** (CSPs), which implement a variety of hashing algorithms and make hashing simple and straightforward.

As we saw earlier, the .NET Framework implements several well-known, secure hash algorithms, including Message Digest 5 (or MD5) and Secure Hash Algorithm (or SHA). The MD5 provider generates 128-bit hash values, and the SHA provider can generate 160-bit, 256-bit, 384-bit, and 512-bit hash values. The `ComputeHash()` method of both the MD5 and SHA CSPs accepts a byte array or a `Stream` object, and returns a hash value.

> *The .NET Framework also implements a key-based hash, which is often used to generate digital signatures.*

The HashAlgorithm Class

All the hash algorithm classes are inherited from the `HashAlgorithm` abstract class. The `HashAlgorithm` class exposes some common methods and properties that can be used across all the hashing algorithms. The following table discusses a few of them:

Class Member	Description
Hash HashValue	Returns the computed hash value in a byte array. Hash is a public property and HashValue is a protected field – both return a byte array.
HashSize HashSizeValue	Returns the size of the hash in bits. HashSize is a public property and HashSizeValue is a protected field – both return an integer value.
InputBlockSize	A public property that returns an integer representing the input block size in bits.
OutputBlockSize	A public property that returns an integer representing the output block size in bits.
ComputeHash()	Computes the hash value for the given input byte array or Stream. ComputeHash() is a public method that returns the output in a byte array or Stream object.

Class Member	Description
Create()	Creates an instance of the hash algorithm that is currently in use. For example, if you are using an MD5 hash algorithm then it'll create an object type of that algorithm. Create() is a static method.
TransformBlock()	Generates the hash value for a given range of the input byte array and copies the result into another byte array. TransformBlock() is a public method that returns a byte array.
TransformFinalBlock()	Generates the hash value for a given range and returns a byte array. TransformFinalBlock() is a public method that returns a byte array.
State	Returns the state of the hash computation. This property will contain a zero before the computations and a non-zero value after a successful hash computation. State is a protected field that returns an integer value representing the current state of the hash value computation.

Let's see a simple example to compute an MD5 hash. This method takes a byte array (clear text) and returns a byte array (hash value):

```
byte[] ComputeMD5(byte [] input)
{
    MD5CryptoServiceProvider md5Provider = new MD5CryptoServiceProvider();
    return md5Provider.ComputeHash(input);
}
```

As you can see, the MD5 provider is very easy to use. All we have to do is create a new object of the type MD5CryptoServiceProvider and pass the byte array to the ComputeHash() method, which returns a byte array. The same technique can be used for all the hash algorithms available in the .NET Framework. Let's write a simple Windows application to hash a string using multiple hash algorithms. Here is the application in action:

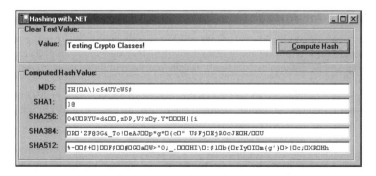

The implementation of the application is quite simple. We accept a string from the user and hash it using different hash algorithms. Here is the code for the **Compute Hash** button's Click event handler:

```
private void btnCompute_Click(object sender, System.EventArgs e)
{
    if (txtHash.Text.Trim() != "")
    {
        // Generate bytes for the input string
        byte[] inputData = ASCIIEncoding.ASCII.GetBytes(txtHash.Text);

        // Display the hash value in textbox
        txtMD5.Text = ASCIIEncoding.ASCII.GetString(new
                              MD5CryptoServiceProvider().ComputeHash(inputData));

        txtSHA1.Text = ASCIIEncoding.ASCII.GetString(new
                                      SHA1Managed().ComputeHash(inputData));

        txtSHA256.Text = ASCIIEncoding.ASCII.GetString(new
                                      SHA256Managed().ComputeHash(inputData));

        txtSHA384.Text = ASCIIEncoding.ASCII.GetString(new
                                      SHA384Managed().ComputeHash(inputData));

        txtSHA512.Text = ASCIIEncoding.ASCII.GetString(new
                                      SHA512Managed().ComputeHash(inputData));
    }
}
```

First, we call the GetBytes() method of the ASCIIEncoding class to convert the string variable into a byte array. Then, we create a new object for each algorithm, and pass the input byte array to the ComputeHash() method. Then, we call the GetString() method of the ASCIIEncoding class again to convert the byte array into a string. Quite simple, isn't it – don't forget to add using directives for the System.Text namespace and System.Security.Cryptography namespaces to run this code.

> If you're dealing with non-ASCII strings, you can use the **UnicodeEncoding** class in the **System.Text** namespace.

Using Hash Values for Authentication

Hashing techniques are very useful when it comes to authenticating users. We're going to see a simple authentication method for a Windows application using the MD5 algorithm. The username and the password supplied by the user will be authenticated against, for the purposes of illustration, an Access database.

Let's create an Access database called WroxDBAuth.mdb with a single table called Tbl_MA_Users. The table is going to store the user ID, e-mail address, password, first name, and last name, as shown below:

Field Name	Data Type	
UserID	Number	
Email	Text	Length - 100
Pwd	Text	Length - 192
FirstName	Text	Length - 50
LastName	Text	Length - 50

Tbl_MA_Users : Table

The e-mail address will be the login name for the users, and the password is stored in the database in the MD5 hash format.

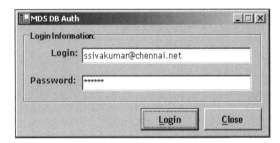

This assures the users that their password can't be hacked. For example, the user's password "MyPass" is stored in the database as "{?•H!8•XJ~•N"H•S" in MD5 hash format. Let's build a simple authentication screen to authenticate users against the Access database:

Here is the code for the Login button:

```
private void btnLogin_Click(object sender, System.EventArgs e)
{
    if (txtEmail.Text.Trim() != "" && txtPwd.Text.Trim() != "")
        authenticateUser();
}
```

First, we check that something was entered in the username and the password text boxes. If something was entered, we call the authenticateUser() method. In the authenticateUser() method, we're connecting to the Access database and querying the table that matches the login name entered by the users.

```
private bool authenticateUser()
{
    bool bRtnValue = false;
    string strConn = "PROVIDER=Microsoft.Jet.OLEDB.4.0;" +
                     "DATA SOURCE=c:\\DB\\WroxDBAuth.mdb;";
    OleDbConnection Conn = new OleDbConnection(strConn) ;
    Conn.Open();

    String strSQL = "SELECT Pwd FROM Tbl_MA_Users WHERE Email = '" +
                                            txtEmail.Text + "'";
    OleDbCommand Cmd = new OleDbCommand(strSQL,Conn);

    //Create a datareader, connection object
    OleDbDataReader Dr = Cmd.ExecuteReader(
                             System.Data.CommandBehavior.CloseConnection);

    //Get the first row and check the password.
    if (Dr.Read())
    {
```

Next, we pass the clear text password entered by the user into the `GenerateMD5Hash()` method, which returns the hashed string. If the current hashed password stored in the database and the hash generated by the `GenerateMD5Hash()` method are the same, we display the message **Password was successful!**; otherwise we displaying the message **Invalid password**:

```
        if (Dr["Pwd"].ToString() == GenerateMD5Hash(txtPwd.Text))
        {
            MessageBox.Show(this,"Password was successful!");
            bRtnValue = true;
        }
        else
        {
            MessageBox.Show(this,"Invalid password.");
        }
    }
    else
    {
        MessageBox.Show(this,"Login name not found.");
    }

    Dr.Close();

    return bRtnValue;
}
```

The `GenerateMD5Hash()` method is very simple. First, we convert the input string into a byte array using the `ASCIIEncoding` class. Next, we create a new object of type `MD5CryptoServiceProvider` and call its `ComputeHash()` method to generate the hash value. Then, we convert the hash value into a string and send it back to the caller:

```
string GenerateMD5Hash(string input)
{
    // Generate bytes for the input string
    byte[] inputData = ASCIIEncoding.ASCII.GetBytes(input);

    // Compute the MD5 hash
    MD5 md5Provider = new MD5CryptoServiceProvider();
    byte[] hashResult = md5Provider.ComputeHash(inputData);

    return ASCIIEncoding.ASCII.GetString(hashResult);
}
```

This is a simple procedure to implement, and it gives us an excellent security model for applications. In this example, we've used the MD5 algorithm. In the same way, we could use any of the other hash algorithms such as SHA1 to implement the application.

> **The only problem with this approach is that if the user wants his or her password e-mailed back to him or her, we won't be able to do it, since we can't convert the hash value back to clear text. However, we can always reset the password and send the new password back to the user.**

Keyed Hash Values

The keyed hash or HMAC (Hash Message Authentication Code) algorithms are very similar to the hash algorithms, except that they generate the hash values based on a key. The HMAC algorithms are useful in the same way as the hash algorithms. For example, an HMAC value can be used to verify the integrity of a message transmitted between two parties that agree on a shared secret key. This is similar to the symmetric algorithm.

HMAC combines the original message with the key to compute a hash value. The sender computes the HMAC of the clear text and sends the HMAC with the clear text. The recipient recalculates the HMAC using the clear text and the sender's copy of the key. If the computed HMAC matches with the one sent from the other end, then the recipient knows that the original message has not been modified, since the message digest hasn't changed. In this way, the receiver can test the authenticity of the transmission. HMACs are commonly used as digital signatures.

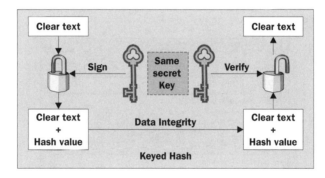

The .NET Framework supports the `HMACSHA1` and `MACTripleDES` algorithms. The `HMACSHA1` algorithm computes keyed hash values using the SHA1 algorithm, and the `MACTripleDES` algorithm computes it based on the Triple-DES algorithm. We're going to see a simple example on how to use the HMAC classes. We'll build a Windows application that shows the HMAC value for the given clear text value and key.

First, we convert the input string and the key into byte arrays. Then we create an object of type `HMACSHA1` and pass this object into a `CryptoStream` object. Then, we use the standard stream operations to read the input array and close the stream. The `Hash` property of the `HMACSHA1` object returns the HMAC value. The same process is repeated for the `MACTripleDES` algorithm:

```
void ProcessKeyedHash(string input, string key)
{
    try
    {
        // Generate bytes for the input string
        byte[] inputData = ASCIIEncoding.ASCII.GetBytes(input);
        byte[] keyBytes = new byte[16];
        keyBytes = ASCIIEncoding.ASCII.GetBytes(key);

        // Compute HMACSHA1
        HMACSHA1 hmac = new HMACSHA1(keyBytes);
        CryptoStream cs = new CryptoStream(Stream.Null, hmac,
                                CryptoStreamMode.Write);
```

```
        cs.Write(inputData, 0, inputData.Length);
        cs.Close();

        txtHMACSHA1.Text = ASCIIEncoding.ASCII.GetString(hmac.Hash);

        // Compute the MACTripleDES
        MACTripleDES macTripleDES = new MACTripleDES(keyBytes);
        txtMACTripleDES.Text = ASCIIEncoding.ASCII.GetString(
                                      macTripleDES.ComputeHash(inputData));
    }
    catch (Exception e)
    {
        MessageBox.Show(this, e.ToString());
    }
}
```

Here is the application in action:

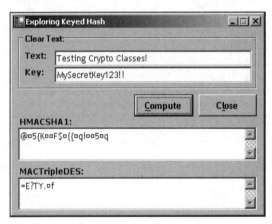

The only difference between these two algorithms is that the HMACSHA1 algorithm accepts keys of any size, and produces a hash value that is 20 bytes long. On the other hand, the MACTripleDES algorithm uses key lengths of 8, 16, or 24 bytes, and produces a hash value eight bytes long. If the key length is different from the requirement then an exception is thrown.

Symmetric Transformation with .NET

The System.Security.Cryptography namespace supports the DES, Triple-DES, RC2, and Rijndael symmetric algorithms. In this list, only the Rijndael algorithm is a managed implementation; the other algorithms use their counterparts in the Microsoft Crypto API.

The SymmetricAlgorithm Class

All the symmetric algorithm classes are inherited from the SymmetricAlgorithm class. The SymmetricAlgorithm class exposes some common methods and properties that can be used across all the hashing algorithms. The following table discusses a few of them:

Class Member	Description
Key KeyValue	Specifies the secret key for the symmetric algorithm. Key is a public property and KeyValue is a protected field – both return a byte array.
KeySize KeySizeValue	Specifies the size of the secret key in bits. KeySize is a public property and the KeySizeValue is a protected field – both return an integer value representing the length of the key in bits.
LegalKeySizes LegalKeySizesValue	Specifies the valid key sizes in bytes for the current symmetric algorithm. LegalKeySizes is a public property and LegalKeySizesValue is a protected field – both return a KeySizes array.
IV IVValue	Specifies the initialization vector for the symmetric algorithm. IV is a public property and IVValue is a protected field – both return a byte array.
BlockSize BlockSizeValue	Specifies the block size in bits for the current symmetric algorithm. BlockSize is a public property and BlockSizeValue is a protected field – both return an integer.
LegalBlockSizes LegalBlockSizesValue	Specifies the valid block size supported by the current symmetric algorithm. LegalBlockSizes is a public property and LegalBlockSizesValue is a protected field – both return a KeySizes array.
Mode ModeValue	Specifies the mode of symmetric operation used by the current algorithm. Mode is a public property and ModeValue is a protected field – both return a CipherMode.
Padding PaddingValue	Specifies the padding mode used by the current symmetric algorithm. Padding is a public property and PaddingValue is a protected field – both return a PaddingMode.
CreateEncryptor()	The CreateEncryptor() method creates a symmetric encryption object using the key and the initialization vector specified. CreateEncryptor() is a public method and returns an ICryptoTransform interface.
CreateDecryptor()	The CreateDecryptor() method creates a symmetric decryption object using the key and the initialization vector specified. CreateDecryptor() is a public method and returns an ICryptoTransform interface.
GenerateKey()	The GenerateKey() method generates a random key for the symmetric algorithm and overrides the value stored in the Key property. GenerateKey() is a public method and returns a random key in a byte array.

Table continued on following page

Class Member	Description
GenerateIV()	The GenerateIV() method generates a random initialization vector for the symmetric algorithm and overrides the value stored in the IV property. GenerateIV() is a public method and returns a random vector in a byte array
ValidKeySize()	Indicates whether the specified key size is valid for the current symmetric algorithm. ValidKeySizes() is a public method and returns an integer.

Let's start out by exploring the symmetric algorithms using the DES algorithm. Since symmetric algorithms tend to be faster than asymmetric ones, symmetric algorithms are good candidates for bulk encryption/decryption operations such as encrypting and decrypting entire files. We'll write a Windows application that will encrypt and decrypt files using the DES algorithm.

The user interface will provide options for locating a file using the Windows Common Dialog controls. There will be options provided to encrypt and decrypt a file with a secret key.

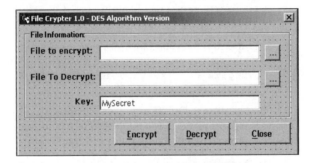

The Encrypt button will add a .enc extension to the source file when generating the encrypted destination file. Here is what the code looks like for the Encrypt button.

```
private void button1_Click(object sender, System.EventArgs e)
{
    if (encryptData(encFile.Text, encFile.Text + ".enc" , txtKey.Text) == true)
        MessageBox.Show(this, "Done!", "Encryption Status", MessageBoxButtons.OK,
                    MessageBoxIcon.Information);
    else
        MessageBox.Show(this, "The encryption process failed!", "Fatal Error",
                    MessageBoxButtons.OK, MessageBoxIcon.Stop);
}
```

The Encrypt button event calls the encryptData() method, passing in the source filename, destination filename, and the secret key for the encryption operation. Let's take look at the encryptData() method.

First, we create an object type of `DESCryptoServiceProvider` and assign the secret key supplied by the user to the `Key` property. Then we call the `GenerateIV()` method to generate an initialization vector for the encryption operation. Next, we create the DES encryption object by calling the `CreateEncryptor()` method of the `DESCryptoServiceProvider` class. After that, we instantiate two `FileStream` objects, one in read mode (the source file), and the other in write mode (the destination file) to encrypt the file:

```
// The encryptData method will encrypt the given file using the DES algorithm
public bool encryptData(string sourceFile, string destinationFile,
                        string cryptoKey)
{
   try
   {
      // Create the DES Service Provider object and assign the key and vector
      DESCryptoServiceProvider DESProvider = new DESCryptoServiceProvider();
      DESProvider.Key = ASCIIEncoding.ASCII.GetBytes(cryptoKey);
      DESProvider.GenerateIV();
      ICryptoTransform DESEncrypt = DESProvider.CreateEncryptor();

      // Open the source and destination file using the file stream object
      FileStream inFileStream = new FileStream(sourceFile,
                                     FileMode.Open, FileAccess.Read);
      FileStream outFileStream = new FileStream(destinationFile, FileMode.Create,
                                     FileAccess.Write);
```

The initialization vector (or IV) is always used to initialize the first block of plain text for encryption. We've already talked about this in the Modes *section.*

Once we've created these objects, we need a `CryptoStream` object to which we write the encrypted file. We pass the DES encryption object and the output file stream into the `CryptoStream`'s constructor. Then we read the content of the input file and write it back into the `CryptoStream`. Then, we close all the stream objects and return `true`:

```
      // Create a CrytoStream class and write the encrypted out
      CryptoStream cryptoStream = new CryptoStream(outFileStream, DESEncrypt,
                                         CryptoStreamMode.Write);

      // Declare the byte array of the length of the input file
      byte[] bytearrayinput = new byte[inFileStream.Length - 1];

      // Read the input file stream in to the byte array and write
      // it back in the CryptoStream
      inFileStream.Read(bytearrayinput, 0, bytearrayinput.Length);
      cryptoStream.Write(bytearrayinput, 0, bytearrayinput.Length);

      // Close the stream handlers
      cryptoStream.Close();
      inFileStream.Close();
      outFileStream.Close();
      return true;
   }
   catch (Exception e)
```

```
        {
            MessageBox.Show(this, e.ToString(), "Encryption Error",
                            MessageBoxButtons.OK, MessageBoxIcon.Stop);
            return false;
        }
    }
```

The decryption process does the opposite of the encryption process. Let's look at the **Decrypt** button code. First, we retrieve the original filename from the selected one by removing the .enc extension from the filename. Then we call the decryptData() method with the source, destination, and the secret key.

```
    private void button2_Click(object sender, System.EventArgs e)
    {
        string decFileName = decFile.Text.Replace(".enc", "");
        if (decryptData(decFile.Text, decFileName, txtKey.Text) == true)
            MessageBox.Show(this, "Done!", "Decryption Status", MessageBoxButtons.OK,
                            MessageBoxIcon.Information);
        else
            MessageBox.Show(this, "The decryption process failed!", "Fatal Error",
                            MessageBoxButtons.OK, MessageBoxIcon.Stop);
    }
```

The decryptData() method works in a very similar way to encryptData(). We create an object of type DESCryptoServiceProvider and assign the key to it. Then, we generate a new VI and create a new DES decryption object by calling the CreateDecryptor() method. Next, we read the source file into the CrytoStream and transform the content into a new file. Finally, we close the stream objects and return true:

```
    // The decryptData method will decrypt the given file using the DES algorithm
    public bool decryptData(string sourceFile, string destinationFile,
                            string cryptoKey)
    {
        try
        {
            // Create the DES Service Provider object and assign the key and vector
            DESCryptoServiceProvider DESProvider = new DESCryptoServiceProvider();
            DESProvider.Key = ASCIIEncoding.ASCII.GetBytes(cryptoKey);
            DESProvider.GenerateIV();

            FileStream DecryptedFile = new FileStream(sourceFile, FileMode.Open,
                                                       FileAccess.Read);
            ICryptoTransform desDecrypt = DESProvider.CreateDecryptor();

            CryptoStream cryptostreamDecr = new CryptoStream(DecryptedFile, desDecrypt,
                                                             CryptoStreamMode.Read);
            StreamWriter DecryptedOutput = new StreamWriter(destinationFile);
            DecryptedOutput.Write(new StreamReader(cryptostreamDecr).ReadToEnd());
            DecryptedOutput.Flush();
            DecryptedOutput.Close();
            return true;
        }
```

```
    catch (Exception e)
    {
       MessageBox.Show(this, e.ToString(), "Decryption Error",
                      MessageBoxButtons.OK, MessageBoxIcon.Stop);
       return false;
    }
 }
```

Using Other Symmetric Algorithms

Since all the symmetric algorithms are derived from the `SymmetricAlgorithm` class, it is very easy to implement the encryption/decryption process with the previous code base. For example, if you want to use the RC2, Triple-DES, or Rijndael algorithm, all you've to do is replace the following declaration in the `encryptData()` and `decryptData()` methods with the appropriate declarations shown below:

❑ **DES**

```
DESCryptoServiceProvider DESProvider = new DESCryptoServiceProvider();
```

❑ **RC2**

```
RC2CryptoServiceProvider RC2Provider = new RC2CryptoServiceProvider();
```

❑ **Triple-DES**

```
TripleDESCryptoServiceProvider tDESProvider = new
                             TripleDESCryptoServiceProvider();
```

❑ **Rijndael**

```
RijndaelManaged RijndaelProvider = new RijndaelManaged();
```

If you make this change, our file encrypter/decrypter application will work fine.

The success of the symmetric encryption and decryption process is based on the key value. If you don't supply a proper key length to the algorithm, then a `CryptographicException` will be raised. The key sizes supported by the algorithm can be fetched by accessing the `LegalKeySizes` property. This property returns an array of `KeySizes` objects. The `KeySizes` class has three integer public properties – `MaxSize`, `MinSize`, and `SkipSize`. The `MaxSize` and `MinSize` properties specify the maximum key size (in bits) and the minimum key size (in bits) respectively. The `SkipSize` returns the interval between the valid key sizes in bits.

The following table lists the key sizes supported by the major algorithms:

Algorithm	Key Size
DES	64 bits or 8 bytes
RC2	128 bits or 16 bytes
Triple-DES	192 bits or 24 bytes
Rijndael	256 bits or 32 bytes

The strength of the encryption is also based on the key. The larger the key, the better the encryption. Thus the likelihood of a hacker being able to decrypt the data with a brute-force attack is decreased. However, there is one more constraint that we should remember – the bigger the key, the more time required for the encryption and decryption process.

Asymmetric Transformation with .NET

As we discussed earlier in the chapter, asymmetric algorithms are based on the concept of public and private keys (PKI). The System.Security.Cryptography namespace supports two asymmetric algorithms: RSA and DSA.

The AsymmetricAlgorithm Class

Both the RSA and DSA algorithms inherit from the base class AsymmetricAlgorithm. The AsymmetricAlgorithm class exposes some common methods and properties that can be used across all the hashing algorithms:

Class Member	Description
KeySize KeySizeValue	Specifies the size of the key modules in bits. KeySize is a public property and KeySizeValue is a protected field – both return an integer value representing the length of the key in bits.
LegalKeySizes LegalKeySizesValue	Specifies a valid key size in bytes for the current asymmetric algorithm. LegalKeySizes is a public property and LegalKeySizesValue is a protected field – both return a KeySizes array.
KeyExchangeAlgorithm	Specifies the key exchange algorithm used when communicating between two ends and the way the public key and private key will be exchanged. This is a public property that returns a string representing the name of the key exchange algorithm used.
SignatureAlgorithm	Specifies the name of the algorithm used to sign the current object. This is a public property that returns a string representing the name of the signature algorithm used.
FromXmlString()	Reconstructs an Asymmetric object from an XML file. This is a public method that takes a string as input.
ToXmlString()	Returns an XML representation of the current algorithm object. This is a public method that returns a string.

As we've already discussed, many of the cryptography algorithms are implemented on top of the Crypto API library. The .NET Framework wraps the Crypto API library with sets of managed classes, called Cryptographic Service Providers (or CSPs). The `CspParameters` class is used to send values to and receive values from the unmanaged Crypto API.

The Cryptographic Service Providers are plug-ins for the Crypto API. These plug-ins are encryption engines that perform the encryption/decryption process.

The CSP operation is based on an enumeration value called `CspProviderFlags`. The `CspProviderFlags` enumeration supports two values: `UseDefaultKeyContainer` and `UseMachineKeyStore`. If the `UseDefaultKeyContainer` option is specified, the key information is read from the default key container. If the `UseMachineKeyStore` option is specified, the key information is read from the computer's key container.

CSPs maintain a database to store public/private key pairs. Some CSPs maintain their key container in the Registry, whereas others maintain it in other locations, such as in Smart Cards or encrypted, hidden files.

Using the RSA Algorithm

The RSA algorithm is implemented in the `RSACryptoServiceProvider` class, which inherits from the `RSA` class. The `RSA` class inherits from the `AsymmetricAlgorithm` class. The RSA algorithm allows us to encrypt, decrypt, sign data with a digital signature, and verify the signature. We'll look at these one by one in this section.

Let's start with a simple encryption/decryption approach. Since the RSA algorithm is an asymmetric algorithm, it is slower than its symmetric counterpart. Therefore, the RSA algorithm is best for small amounts of message encryption. Accordingly, we'll build a Windows application that will encrypt and decrypt the message entered by the user using PKI technology.

Whenever you create a new default constructor instance of the `RSACryptoServiceProvider` class, it automatically creates a new set of public/private key information, ready to use. We can also store the PKI values into XML files. This demonstration will be our first example. Let's build a UI as shown below.

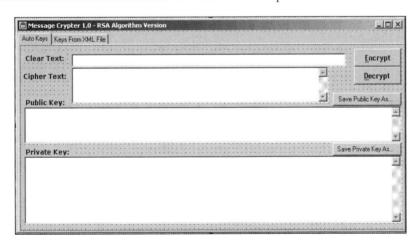

This UI allows us to see the clear text as well as the encrypted cipher text. Our code will also show the public key and the private key used in this process and we'll have an option to store the public and private keys in different XML files.

Since we're going to use the RSA auto generated public/private keys, we declare a class level static object.

```
static RSACryptoServiceProvider objRSAProvider;
```

Here is the code for the **Encrypt** button:

```
if (txtClearText.Text.Trim() != "")
{
    // Initialize the RSA Cryptography Service Provider (CSP)
    rsaProvider = new RSACryptoServiceProvider();

    UTF8Encoding utf8 = new UTF8Encoding();
    byte[] clearText = utf8.GetBytes(txtClearText.Text.Trim());

    // Encrypting the data received
    txtCipherText.Text = Convert.ToBase64String(rsaProvider.Encrypt(clearText,
                                                 false));

    // Show the private key
    txtPrvKey.Text = rsaProvider.ToXmlString(true);

    // Show the public Key
    txtPubKey.Text = rsaProvider.ToXmlString(false);
}
```

We create a new object type of RSACryptoServiceProvider. Then we transform the user-entered message into a byte array using the UTF8Encoding class. Then we call the Encrypt() method of the RSACryptoServiceProvider class, pass the input byte array and a second parameter of false.

> *The second parameter in the Encrypt() method deals with the mode of operation. If you are running Windows 2000 OS with SP2 or higher then you can set this parameter to true, which will use the OAEP padding method. When set to false it'll use PKCS version 1.5.*

The Encrypt() method returns an encrypted byte array. We're using the ToBase64String() method of the Convert class to convert the byte array into a string for display in the textbox. We also display the private/public key generated by the RSA algorithm in two text boxes using the ToXmlString() method of the RSACryptoServiceProvider class. ToXmlString() takes a Boolean as input and if the value is false, it generates the public key value as an XML string; if the value is true, it generates the private key.

Here is the code for our **Decrypt** button. This method just calls the Decrypt() method of the RSACryptoServiceProvider object:

```
private void btnDecrypt_Click(object sender, System.EventArgs e)
{
    if (txtCipherText.Text.Trim() != "")
```

```
    {
        //Convert the input string into a byte array
        byte[] bCipherText =
            Convert.FromBase64String(txtCipherText.Text.Trim());

        //Decrypt the data and convert it back to a string
        string strValue =
            ASCIIEncoding.ASCII.GetString(objRSAProvider.Decrypt(
            bCipherText, false));

        //Display the decrypted string in a MessageBox
        MessageBox.Show(this, strValue , "Decrypted value",
        MessageBoxButtons.OK,MessageBoxIcon.Information);
    }
}
```

Now let's look at saving the public/private key into an XML file. We display the SaveFile common dialog box to get the desired filename from the user. Then we load the XML data into an XmlDocument object and call its Save() method to save the data to disk:

```
private void btnSave_Click(object sender, System.EventArgs e)
{
    SaveFileDialog saveFileDialog1 = new SaveFileDialog();

    saveFileDialog1.Filter = "XML files (*.xml)|*.xml|All files (*.*)|*.*"  ;
    saveFileDialog1.FilterIndex = 2 ;
    saveFileDialog1.RestoreDirectory = true ;

    if(saveFileDialog1.ShowDialog() == DialogResult.OK)
    {
        // Write the content to an XML file
        XmlDocument xmlDoc = new XmlDocument();
        xmlDoc.LoadXml(this.txtPubKey.Text);

        // Save the document to a file.
        xmlDoc.Save(saveFileDialog1.OpenFile());
    }
}
```

Here is the application in action:

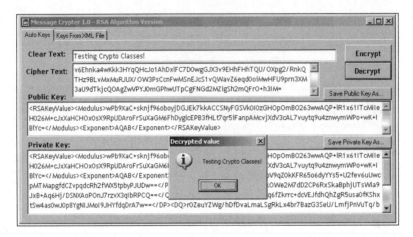

As you can see, the clear text, encrypted cipher text, and the decrypted clear text is shown on the screen with the public and private key information.

Loading the Public and Private Keys

In the previous example, we saw how to encrypt and decrypt data using the auto-generated public and private keys. We also saw how to save the keys into an XML file. However, if you want to reuse previously created or saved keys, you can do this by initializing the class with a populated `CspParameters` object. Let's see an example of this. Create a UI like the previous one, but this time we'll load the public and private keys from the XML files:

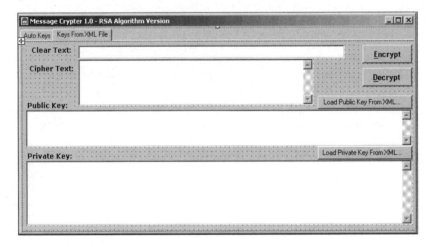

Here is the code to load a key from XML. First, we display an `OpenFile` dialog to get the filename from the user. Then, we load the file into an `XmlTextReader` object and display the key information in the appropriate text box:

```
private void btnLoadPub_Click(object sender, System.EventArgs e)
{
    // Show the open file dialog
    openFileDialog1.Title = "Select the Public Key file";
    openFileDialog1.Filter = "XML Files (*.xml)|*.xml";

    if(openFileDialog1.ShowDialog() == DialogResult.OK)
    {
        string fileName = openFileDialog1.FileName;
        btnEncrypt1.Enabled = true;

        // Load the document
        XmlTextReader xmlReader = new XmlTextReader(fileName);
        xmlReader.WhitespaceHandling = WhitespaceHandling.None;
        xmlReader.Read();

        // Assign the public key to the textbox
        txtPubKey1.Text = xmlReader.ReadOuterXml();
    }
}
```

Now let's look at the code behind the **Encrypt** button. First, we create an object of the `CspParameters` class and set the flag to use the machine store to look for the PKI keys. Then we give the key container the name `WroxRSAStore`.

```
private void btnEncrypt1_Click(object sender, System.EventArgs e)
{
    if (txtClearText1.Text.Trim() != "")
    {
        try
        {
            CspParameters cspParam = new CspParameters();
            cspParam.Flags = CspProviderFlags.UseMachineKeyStore;
            cspParam.KeyContainerName = "WroxRSAStore";
            cspParam.ProviderName = "MS Strong Cryptographic Provider";

            // CryptoAPI constant -> PROV_RSA_FULL = 1
            // This provider type supports both digital
            // signatures and data encryption, and is considered
            // general purpose. The RSA public-key algorithm
            // is used for all public-key operations.
            cspParam.ProviderType = 1;
```

Once we've initialized the parameters for the CSP, we create a new object of type `RSACryptoServiceProvider` using our `CspParameters` object. Then, we assign the public key by calling the `FromXmlString()` method. After that, we perform our usual process of converting the string into a byte array and passing the byte array into the `Encrypt()` method and converting the byte array back to a string:

```
// Initializing the RSA Cryptography Service Provider (CSP)
RSACryptoServiceProvider rsaProvider1 = new
                        RSACryptoServiceProvider(cspParam);
```

417

```
            // Load the public key
            rsaProvider1.FromXmlString(txtPubKey1.Text);

            UTF8Encoding utf8 = new UTF8Encoding();
            byte[] clearText = utf8.GetBytes(txtClearText1.Text);

            // Convert encrypted text to base64
            txtCipherText1.Text = Convert.ToBase64String(
                                    rsaProvider1.Encrypt(clearText, false));
        }
        catch (Exception e)
        {
            MessageBox.Show(this, e.ToString());
        }
    }
}
```

The decryption method is again very simple – we just create an RSA CSP object and assign the private key to it. We then decrypt the message using the `Decrypt()` method:

```
private void btnDecrypt1_Click(object sender, System.EventArgs e)
{
    if (txtClearText1.Text.Trim() != "")
    {
        // Initialize the RSA Cryptography Service Provider (CSP)
        RSACryptoServiceProvider rsaProvider1 = new RSACryptoServiceProvider();

        // Load the private key
        rsaProvider1.FromXmlString(this.txtPriKey1.Text);

        // Encrypt the data received
        MessageBox.Show(this, ASCIIEncoding.ASCII.GetString(
                    rsaProvider1.Decrypt(Convert.FromBase64String(
                    txtCipherText1.Text.Trim()), false)), "Decrypted value",
                    MessageBoxButtons.OK, MessageBoxIcon.Information);
    }
}
```

Here is the application in action:

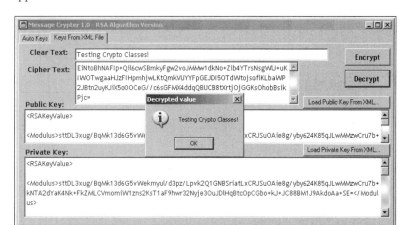

There is one limitation of the RSA algorithm that you should know – the Encrypt() *method can only encrypt up to 16 bytes if the High Encryption pack is installed. Otherwise, it can only encrypt 5 bytes.*

Reading an X509 Certificate

A certificate is like a "voucher" that contains information about the person holding the voucher, such as who authorized the certificate, its public keys, and its expiration information. Certificates are signed by a certifying authority (or CA), such as VeriSign or Thawte. The Microsoft Certificate Server also allows us to create "self-signed" certificates. However, they may not be trusted by the rest of the world, since this is not issued by a well-known CA, but they are very useful in an intranet scenario.

Server certificates are used to identify the trustworthiness of the server, and client certificates to identify a client to the server. A CA issues both client and server certificates after verifying the identity. For example, when the client is requesting a web resource, it can also send a client certificate along with the request. The server can then determine who the client is and authorize or deny them.

Thawte provides the client certificate free of charge but VeriSign charges a fee for it.

Client certificates are usually installed on web clients such as browsers and e-mail clients. You can view all the client certificates installed in IE by clicking on Tools | Internet Options... and selecting the Content tab in the dialog box. Click on the Certificates... button here. As you can see, I have two client certificates installed in IE 6:

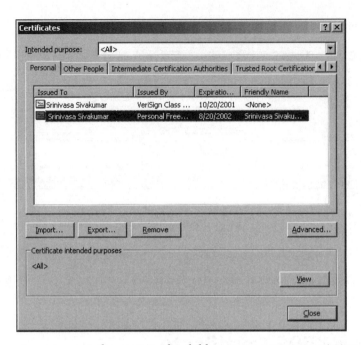

The `Cryptography` namespace also contains the child namespace `X509Certificates`. This contains just three classes used to represent and manage Authenticode X509 v.3 certificates. The `X509Certificate` class exposes the static methods `CreateFromCertFile()` and `CreateFromSignedFile()` to create an instance of the certificate.

The `CreateFromCertFile()` method reads the content of the X509 certificate from a certificate file and the `CreateFromSignedFile()` method reads the content of the X509 certificate from a Digitally Signed file. We will use the `CreateFromCertFile()` method to read the contents of the X509 client certificate:

```
private void btnView_Click(object sender, System.EventArgs e)
{
    // Read the client certificate from the file
    // into the object variable of the type X509Certificate
    X509Certificate clientCert =
                        X509Certificate.CreateFromCertFile("C:\\test.cer");

    StringBuilder sb = new StringBuilder();

    sb.Append("Issuer Name: " + clientCert.GetIssuerName() + "\n");
    sb.Append("Public Key String: " + clientCert.GetPublicKeyString() + "\n");
    sb.Append("Key Algorithm: " + clientCert.GetKeyAlgorithm().ToString() + "\n");
    sb.Append("Serial Number: " + clientCert.GetSerialNumberString() + "\n");
    sb.Append("Effective Date: " +
            clientCert.GetEffectiveDateString().ToString() + "\n");
    sb.Append("Expiration Date: " +
            clientCert.GetExpirationDateString().ToString() + "\n");
    MessageBox.Show(this, sb.ToString());
}
```

We've declared an object of type X509Certificate, and we've used the CreateFromCertFile() method to read the certificate content into the object. Then we've read the main properties of the certificate and displayed it to a message box:

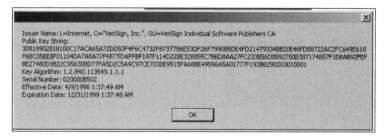

Cryptography and Network Programming

So far in this chapter we've learnt all about cryptography – now it's time to use some of the techniques in network programming. Remember the simple UDP chat utility that we wrote in Chapter 6? The UDP chat application is very simple. It takes the local and remote port numbers and the IP address and passes the information back and forth.

Here is the code before adding any cryptography algorithms. The Send() method here gets the datagram, converts it into a byte array, and sends the data using the Send() method of the UdpClient class. The Receiver() method here also works in the same way.

```
private static void Send(string datagram)
{
    // Create UdpClient
    UdpClient sender = new UdpClient();

    // Create IPEndPoint with details of remote host
    IPEndPoint endPoint = new IPEndPoint(remoteIPAddress, remotePort);

    try
    {
        // Convert data to byte array
        byte[] bytes = Encoding.ASCII.GetBytes(datagram);

        // Send data
        sender.Send(bytes, bytes.Length, endPoint);
    }
    catch (Exception e)
    {
        Console.WriteLine(e.ToString());
    }
    finally
    {
        // Close connection
        sender.Close();
    }
}
```

```
public static void Receiver()
{
    // Create a UdpClient for reading incoming data.
    UdpClient receivingUdpClient = new UdpClient(localPort);

    // IPEndPoint with remote host information
    IPEndPoint RemoteIpEndPoint = null;

    try
    {
        Console.WriteLine(
                "-----------*******Ready for chat!!!*******-----------");

        while(true)
        {
            // Wait for datagram
            byte[] receiveBytes = receivingUdpClient.Receive(
                                                ref RemoteIpEndPoint);

            // Convert and display data
            string returnData = Encoding.ASCII.GetString(receiveBytes);
            Console.WriteLine("-" + returnData.ToString());
        }
    }
    catch (Exception e)
    {
        Console.WriteLine(e.ToString ());
    }
}
```

Let's use the Rijndael symmetric algorithm to send secure information between two chat clients. The `Rijndael` algorithm is a symmetric algorithm and it is best for bulk data transfer. This is the main reason that I've chosen this algorithm. We're going to add `encryptData()` and `decryptData()` methods to this class to take care of the secure communication process. When we're sending information to the remote socket we'll call the `encryptData()` method to encrypt the data, and then we'll pass the encrypted byte array to the other end. When we receive the encrypted byte array on the other end, we'll call the `decryptData()` method to decrypt the byte array.

As you can see, our design is very simple. To support the symmetric algorithms, we've added two private class level members that store the shared key and vector.

```
private static IPAddress remoteIPAddress;
private static int remotePort;
private static int localPort;
private static UTF8Encoding Utf8Encod;
private static string CryptoKey = "!i~6ox1i@]t2K'y$";
private static string CryptoVI =  "!~x7Oq{6+q1@#VI$";
```

The `encryptData()` method takes a string as input and returns a byte array.

```
static byte[] encryptData(string theDataGram)
{
    byte[] bCipherText = null;
    try
    {
```

We create a new object type of `RijndaelManaged`, and assign the shared key and vector. Then we create an `ICryptoTransform` object using the `CreateEncryptor()` method.

```
// Create the Rijndael Service Provider object and assign the
// key and vector to it
RijndaelManaged RijndaelProvider = new RijndaelManaged();
RijndaelProvider.Key = Utf8Encod.GetBytes(CryptoKey);
RijndaelProvider.IV = Utf8Encod.GetBytes(CryptoVI);

ICryptoTransform RijndaelEncrypt = RijndaelProvider.CreateEncryptor();
```

Now, we convert the datagram into a byte array using the `UTF8Encoding` class. Then we declare a `MemoryStream` object and use a `CryptoStream` object to perform the cryptographic transformation – you may recall that we had a fleeting look at the `CryptoStream` class in Chapter 2.

```
// Convert string to byte array
byte[] bClearText = Utf8Encod.GetBytes(theDataGram);
MemoryStream Mstm = new MemoryStream();

//Create Crypto Stream that transforms a stream using the encryption
CryptoStream Cstm = new CryptoStream(Mstm, RijndaelEncrypt,
                                     CryptoStreamMode.Write);

//Write out encrypted content into MemoryStream
Cstm.Write(bClearText, 0, bClearText.Length);
Ctms.FlushFinalBlock();
```

We create the byte array back from the `MemoryStream` and return the byte array to the caller.

```
//Get the output
bCipherText = Mstm.ToArray();

//Close the stream handlers
Cstm.Close();
Mstm.Close();
    }
    catch (Exception e)
    {
        Console.WriteLine(e.ToString ());
    }
    return bCipherText;
}
```

The `decryptData()` method, which does the decryption process, is similar to the `encryptData()` method. The `decryptData()` method takes a byte array as input and returns a string as output.

```
static string decryptData(byte[] bCipherText)
{
    string sEncoded ="";

    try
    {
        // Create the RijndaelManaged Service Provider object and assign
        // the key and vector to it
        RijndaelManaged RijndaelProvider = new RijndaelManaged();
        RijndaelProvider.Key = Utf8Encod.GetBytes(strCryptoKey);
        RijndaelProvider.IV = Utf8Encod.GetBytes(strCryptoVI);

        ICryptoTransform RijndaelDecrypt= RijndaelProvider.CreateDecryptor();

        //Create a MemoryStream with the input
        MemoryStream Mstm = new MemoryStream(bCipherText, 0, bCipherText.Length);

        //Create Crypto Stream that transforms a stream using the decryption
        CryptoStream Cstm = new CryptoStream(Mstm, RijndaelDecrypt,
                                             CryptoStreamMode.Read);

        // read out the result from the Crypto Stream
        StreamReader Sr = new StreamReader(Cstm);
        sEncoded = Sr.ReadToEnd();

        Sr.Close();
        Cstm.Close();
        Mstm.Close();
    }
    catch (Exception e)
    {
        Console.WriteLine(e.ToString ());
    }

    return sEncoded;
}
```

Let's call the `encryptData()` and `decryptData()` methods in the proper places in the chat application. The `Send()` method calls the `encryptData` method, with the string entered by the user, and sends the result via the `Send()` method of the `UdpClient`. The `Receiver()` method passes the received byte array into the `decryptData()` method and displays the decrypted message.

```
private static void Send(string datagram)
{
    ...
    try
    {
        // Convert string to byte array
        //byte[] bClearText = Utf8Encod.GetBytes(datagram);
```

```
        // Encrypting the data recived
        byte[] bytes = encryptData(datagram);

        // Send data
        sender.Send(bytes, bytes.Length, endPoint);
    }
    ...
}

public static void Receiver()
{
    ...
    while(true)
    {
        // Wait for datagram
        byte[] receiveBytes = receivingUdpClient.Receive(ref RemoteIpEndPoint);

        //Decrypt the incoming byte array
        string returnData = decryptData(receiveBytes);

        Console.WriteLine("-" + returnData.ToString());
    }
    ...
}
```

We can also implement this with an asymmetric algorithm such as RSA – let's see an example of this. We'll just rewrite the encryptData() and decryptData() methods using the RSA algorithm. The rest of the implementation will remain the same.

Before writing the encryptData() and decryptData() methods we've to store the public key and the private key in private class level variables.

```
private static IPAddress remoteIPAddress;
private static int remotePort;
private static int localPort;
private static UTF8Encoding Utf8Encod;
```

```
private static string PubKey =
"<RSAKeyValue><Modulus>sttDL3xug/BqMk13d6G5vWekmyul/d3pz/Lpvk2Q1GNBSriatLxCRJSuOAi
e8g/yby624K85qJLwMMzwCru7b+kNTA2dYaK4Nk+FkZMLCVmomiW1zns2KsT1aF9hwr32Nyje3OuJDlHqB
tcOpCGbo+kJ+JC88BM1J9AkdoAa+SE=</Modulus><Exponent>AQAB</Exponent></RSAKeyValue>";
```

```
private static string PriKey =
"<RSAKeyValue><Modulus>sttDL3xug/BqMk13d6G5vWekmyul/d3pz/Lpvk2Q1GNBSriatLxCRJSuOAi
e8g/yby624K85qJLwMMzwCru7b+kNTA2dYaK4Nk+FkZMLCVmomiW1zns2KsT1aF9hwr32Nyje3OuJDlHqB
tcOpCGbo+kJ+JC88BM1J9AkdoAa+SE=</Modulus><Exponent>AQAB</Exponent><P>3BoisxTvnh8Xt
g/02fTGtr/k8OXUOiEfKwAKzWje36v8zkTfIc4EzdZbRskJywq1NMo9U1EHM3DUv+Ya/KGPzQ==</P><Q>
0AcCph/CdQeB2/M+q3BS1zimr9Chw9zaHk1x8MBCHdRB9c26VcS0AmKW+G4VzjWJjI6cK8j/GQjhnRn7Ub
BypQ==</Q><DP>bikCjwD+gPRs6KmJ0gCp6FOY4V0WYFWthNcLkQ1Y5zfsWsyrpP649tC/dGkwZpggY6CJ
GwcmBIAHa1hez2yJTQ==</DP><DQ>Uzva1Xkzpvuf+89xrcq9YQArwYDqmKGPLDy0cC2cxq6czarI+XRAy
guEeFYjp2RIatLMrcA4QV4KV3+DzQWaeQ==</DQ><InverseQ>eriVG9Kp3CQ/J9PpfMlemC7tPIs6m//L
yhKD7J5zLGIzz+71C5QjVi2dRwtvjGJaexOTi+TRIv2fT/LhWmsCDQ==</InverseQ><D>sjfHZ47OtIuf
1gXY8AznfnLC05eXrDIuo/YBsY2qredFDQaLqWIZiiq4ur7kWoFHakAbHCGeC3p2+bmLyrYr2nm8Ogj0c1
NUneE8ASoKWfnbcWxW377Oeogj16frPUoAgwU1gFURdTxozgNLThVtNItrc3Doa5eJ+U7pRSz2edE=</D>
</RSAKeyValue>";
```

Here is how the `encryptData()` and `decryptData()` methods look. In the `encryptData()` method we create a new `CspParameters` object, and use the object to create a new RSA algorithm object. Next, we assign the public key from the private class member. Then, we call the `Encrypt()` method of the RSA object.

```
static byte[] encryptData(string strDataGram)
{
    CspParameters theCspParam = new CspParameters();
    theCspParam.Flags = CspProviderFlags.UseMachineKeyStore;
    theCspParam.KeyContainerName = "WroxRSAStore";

    // Initializing the RSA Cryptography Service Provider (CSP)
    RSACryptoServiceProvider theRSAProvider = new
                                RSACryptoServiceProvider(objCspParam);

    //Set the Load the public key
    theRSAProvider.FromXmlString(PubKey);

    // Convert string to byte array
    byte[] bClearText = Utf8Encod.GetBytes(strDataGram);

    // Encrypting the data received
    byte[] bytes = theRSAProvider.Encrypt(bClearText, false);
    theRSAProvider.Clear();

    return bytes;
}
```

The `decryptData()` method does pretty much the same thing. It creates a new RSA object and assigns the private key from the class member. Then it calls the `Decrypt()` method and sends the string back to the caller.

```
static string decryptData(byte[] bCipherText)
{
    // Initializing the RSA Cryptography Service Provider (CSP)
    RSACryptoServiceProvider theRSAProvider = new RSACryptoServiceProvider();

    //Load the private key
    theRSAProvider.FromXmlString(PriKey);

    // Encrypting the data received
    string strRtnData = Utf8Encod.GetString(theRSAProvider.Decrypt(bCipherText,
                                                        false));
    theRSAProvider.Clear();

    return strRtnData;
}
```

This implementation of the `encryptData()` and `decryptData()` methods can be replaced with the previous example and the code will work fine. The only thing that we've to be careful about in this example is the size limitations of the `Encrypt()` method – we talked about these limitations earlier.

Summary

In this chapter, we've covered lot of ground, starting with a very brief history of cryptography. We went into why we need to use cryptography, and gave a hacking example that shows how the transmitted information is visible to the whole world.

Then, we introduced the different types of cryptographic algorithms, such as symmetric algorithms, asymmetric algorithms, and hash algorithms, before looking in detail at how each of these types works. Next, we introduced the basic concepts of cryptography, such as block ciphers and stream ciphers, padding, and mode.

After the introduction to cryptography in general, we dived into the specifics of using cryptography in .NET. We learnt about the `System.Security.Cryptography` namespace, including the cryptography class hierarchy, before walking through examples demonstrating the use of hashing, symmetric, and asymmetric algorithms in .NET. Then, we covered RSA encryption extensively, and touched on accessing X509 certificates from .NET. Finally, we saw some examples of how to use cryptography in network programming using the Rijndael and RSA algorithms.

11

Authentication Protocols

Authentication has become a major issue for any application developer who expects code to run across a network, or across the Internet. Making sure that users are who they say they are, and verifying machine identities on demand, is all part of an application's security module. Developers of Windows applications should conform to the Windows-specific security procedures implemented by Microsoft, in addition to any additional security measures to be imposed by the application.

Windows 4.0 NT and Windows 2000 focused on authentication as a major issue because of the weak security implemented in earlier versions of Windows NT and the Windows 9X family of operating systems. Rather than invent a new authentication system from scratch, Microsoft examined the existing authentication methods and embraced them, especially the use of Kerberos with Windows 2000.

In this chapter, you'll see what the authentication protocols involved in Microsoft's networking schemes are, how they work, and how they apply to the various versions of Windows.

Authentication Protocols

In this section we'll look at the major authentication protocols used by Windows and .NET. These include:

- ❑ LANMAN (Microsoft's LAN Manager)
- ❑ NTLM (Windows NT LAN Manager)
- ❑ Kerberos

Before looking at these authentication protocols, though, we should quickly mention the Secure Sockets Layer (SSL), a protocol used for sending encrypted data. SSL has been through several iterations since its introduction (by Netscape), and has been incorporated into the Transport Layer Security (TLS) protocol developed by the Internet Engineering Task Force (IETF). Since SSL and TLS are used to send authentication information over the Internet, you should have an overview of how they work.

SSL is a protocol that sits between the application layer and the underlying TCP layer. The SSL layer is responsible for providing encryption, authentication, and data integrity information, using a different algorithm for each task. Because SSL is trying to hide these complexities from the user (and the developer), actually employing SSL is remarkably simple. If your computer has the software for encryption enabled, you can simply change the `http` component in the URL to `https`, which invokes the SSL components in a browser. When using `https` an encrypted connection is established to the target URL.

NTLM

Microsoft's Windows NT LAN Manager Authentication (NTLM) is a one-time password, challenge–response authentication system. This type of authentication system goes back many years and has been used for many different purposes. In its simplest form, a challenge–response authentication system displays a challenge (also called a nonce), which is usually a number or string. A response is created based on the challenge, and once accepted the authentication is complete. This is usually a one-time authentication, performed at the start of the session, and valid until the session ends.

Early challenge–response authentication systems used manual lookups: the computer would display a challenge and the user would look up the reply from a book or software tool (called a password token), sending the reply back to the computer. This process was quickly automated, such as when a client attempts to access a server resource. The server generates and sends the challenge, which the client software processes to determine the reply based on algorithms and then after the server has acknowledged the response is correct, the client is authenticated.

These challenge–response authentication systems have a few major advantages. Since the challenge can be generated randomly every time one is needed, there is no need to store challenge and response pairs in a file or algorithm, which would be accessible to hackers or reverse-engineering attacks. With this system, reuse of a challenge and corresponding password is also extremely unlikely, thus preventing hacking using repeated codes. Also, there is no need to maintain synchronization between the client and the server. Whenever the client contacts the server, the random challenge is generated and the correct response calculated. The primary disadvantage of the challenge-response authentication system is that the client has to generate a proper response to the challenge, which means either involving the user in a lookup operation or employing an algorithm on the client. To prevent unwanted attacks, the client algorithm is usually a one-way system that does not allow generation of challenges, only responses.

Many current challenge–response authentication systems adhere to standards adopted by the American Bankers Association (the standard is called X9.9) and the US Government (called FIPS 113). Both systems use DES as a one-way hash function. When the server sends the challenge, it is encrypted using DES and a secret key embedded in the hardware or software. Internal algorithms then create the password response, valid one-time only. By publishing the standards, software developers can not only decide whether the challenge–response authentication systems are secure enough for use, but can more easily implement them by following the standards.

When Microsoft was developing its LAN Manager product, it needed an authentication system that would allow not only the (then new) Windows NT operating system but also older PCs running DOS and Windows to participate in client-server transactions securely. LAN Manager used a challenge-response authentication system for this reason. With the addition of a small piece of software, a client could communicate with the server in a manner much more secure than otherwise possible. NTLM was used for all NT products through Windows NT 4, but Windows 2000 also added the option of using Kerberos authentication, a more secure option than NTLM.

A challenge–response authentication system was ideal for the early requirements of LAN Manager. Since the sharing of resources was an integral part of Microsoft's vision for Windows PCs and Windows NT servers, a way of verifying legal access to resources like printers, files, and external peripherals was necessary. Ideally, the new authentication system had to be relatively fast, require nothing more than the addition of some compatible software on the client, and it had to be secure. With such a product, Microsoft could compete with the resource sharing and inherent security that the UNIX world offered, but within the familiar Windows environment.

Microsoft handled the network authentication by using a protocol that could be transmitted in existing SMB (Server Message Block) messages, already used for resource sharing. The client software package required contained all the complex algorithms for generating the authentication tokens, using the new protocol, and embedding that content in SMB messages. Challenge–response authentication was necessary to prevent password sniffing on the network (wherein a hacker watches for passwords in network messages, and simply reuses them for their own purpose). Because challenge–response authentication systems use one-time passwords, intercepting a password would not gain a hacker any advantage. Further, Microsoft made sure that all user login passwords on the server were encrypted in an attempt to prevent reverse-engineering of the challenge and response tokens, as well as to secure the basic login information.

Naturally, weaknesses with any challenge–response authentication system are inevitable. In Microsoft's case, the major problem with the NTLM system was not with the challenge–response authentication system itself, but with the way passwords were stored on the server. As it turns out, the password encryption used by Windows NT was relatively weak and could be cracked quite easily (you'll see why in the next section). With Windows 2000, the password encryption system was beefed up considerably. Furthermore, the use of the Registry on most Windows versions caused problems.

The Registry is a data file maintained by Windows for information about the hardware, installed software, the user, the system security, and many other aspects of the machine. One area of the Registry is the Security Accounts Manager (SAM), which has entries inside it for every user allowed to access the system or to share resources. Naturally, Microsoft did its best to restrict access to the SAM and its contents, but the relatively weak encryption led to hackers accessing the information. Attacks on the SAM itself even became part of regular life with the Samba project, which was designed to allow non-Windows operating systems to share resources with Windows machines, and vice versa. As part of the sharing from a Linux client to a Windows server, for example, the server's SAM had to be fooled into thinking it was a Windows machine at the other end and the authentication messages coming in were correct. This inevitably meant the SAM had to be compromised, and many hackers used Samba toolsets to crack Windows NT Server Registries.

LANMAN Encryption

The LAN Manager (LANMAN for short) was the predecessor to NTLM, and hence worth looking at so the evolution of NTLM and Kerberos can be seen. The process that is performed by the LANMAN software is easily explained in terms of hashing the user's password.

When a client attempts to access a server resource, the user's password is first converted to a 14-character string. (If the password is longer than 14 characters, the extra characters are dropped; if the password is shorter than 14 characters, additional characters are added to pad the length to 14 characters.) All the characters are then converted to uppercase, since case independence was required for the LAN Manager system (DOS and early Windows systems were not case dependent). The client software then splits the 14-character password into two 7-character strings. (Windows NT did not break the 14-character string into two, but treated the string as one entity.) Each of the two 7-character strings is then used as the key to encrypt a 64-bit constant using DES. These two encrypted strings are then concatenated into one string, which is then the encrypted password that is saved in the SAM. (When a client logs in, the password they type is encrypted using this process and compared to the encrypted string in the SAM; the SAM's encrypted string is never decrypted.)

As mentioned earlier, the encryption process used by LANMAN is not as strong as most users assumed it would be. The reason is easily seen with a few calculations. Because LANMAN uses a 14-character single-case password, there are 26^{14} combinations possible (assuming only alphabetic characters in the password). This requires 65 bits to represent. That's formidable, but the LANMAN practice of dividing the password into two 7-character strings compromised the security. Instead of cracking a 65 bit key, a hacker only has to crack two 32 bit keys (26^7 twice, resulting in 32 bits). While a 32-bit key is still strong, it can easily be attacked with repetitive scripts.

But the problem is made even simpler for a hacker because of two factors: LANMAN's use of concatenated strings and LANMAN's lax password length requirement. Because LANMAN used two 7-character strings, each string could be attacked separately. If the second string could be cracked first, it could often give a clue as to the first string using dictionary searches. For example, if the second string was decrypted to "tion" followed by three nulls (from the padding to 14-character strings), all dictionary words with seven letters before "tion" could be searched and tested quickly. Of course, the same applied if the first string could be cracked, leaving the second string easily tested (assuming regular dictionary words were used in the password). The second advantage for a hacker arises because LANMAN did not force passwords of any particular length. Most user's passwords average six or seven characters. With LANMAN's scheme, the extra characters were padded to 14 with nulls, and cracking encrypted null strings is easy (which is why the second 7-character string was usually attacked before the first). So, instead of having to worry about 32-bit keys, if only half the strings are actual characters you can see the process would progress much faster.

Windows NT Encryption

LANMAN's password encryption system was reasonably effective, but also prone to hacking. Windows NT tried to improve on the LANMAN scheme in a number of ways by implementing the Windows logon protocol (which appeared as part of the package for Windows 9X client platforms). The Windows logon protocol intercepts all challenges and generates the responses automatically, using the user's password as the key for the token generation.

When a user logs in, Windows encrypts the password into a 128-bit key (which is maintained in encrypted form until the user logs off, with Windows discarding the clear text password). The Windows logon protocol works by having a server generate a 64-bit (eight byte) challenge when a request to log on or use a resource is initiated. The client receives the 64-bit challenge and uses the user's 128-bit encrypted password as a key to three separate 56-bit DES encryptions of the challenge. The three 56-bit encrypted strings are then concatenated into one larger 168-bit string. Adding hyphens between the substrings results in a 24-byte response for the challenge.

The primary weakness of this challenge–response authentication system is the use of the encrypted passwords. If a hacker can obtain the password from the Registry or through interception of network traffic containing the encrypted password, they can use that encrypted password to determine a response to a challenge. (The user's real password doesn't matter, because Windows logon uses the encrypted password only.) Once the encrypted password is in a hacker's control, a machine can be set up to masquerade as a valid client, and using the encrypted password it can respond properly to a server's challenge. A brute-force hack attack can be performed looking for the user's plaintext password, but this is much more time-consuming and less likely to succeed than with LANMAN's challenge-response authentication scheme. A hacker is given a better chance if a number of successful challenge-response messages can be intercepted, allowing analysis of the responses and potentially leading to better guesses at the plaintext password.

NTLM Authentication

As security concerns increased in the 1990s, Microsoft responded by increasing security measures in each subsequent release of LANMAN and Windows NT. Windows NT 4 provides three different authentication systems, referred to as "local", "domain", and "remote" by Microsoft. Both domain and remote systems use challenge–response authentication and are usually collectively treated as NTLM.

The security improvements started with the user's password itself. Instead of using only uppercase characters, Windows NT 4 supported Unicode, allowing many more characters in the password with case sensitivity. While the 14-character limit was still used in Windows NT 4, the extra allowable Unicode characters meant that 28 bytes (14 two-byte characters; Unicode requires two bytes to represent all possible characters) now made up the password string. Further, Microsoft abandoned DES in favor of the commercially available Message Digest #4 (MD4), which is inherently more complex. Windows NT 4 uses MD4 and the 28-byte password to create a 128-bit encrypted password, which is used internally. (This is frequently called the "NTLM hash".)

Unfortunately, because of backwards compatibility requirements, some compromises in the design of the Windows NT 4 were imposed. Instead of using only the NTLM hash, two encrypted passwords are actually used: the NTLM hash and the older LANMAN hash. Either could be used for the challenge-response authentication process, as the client can generate responses to both challenges. Obviously, it was easier to crack the older LANMAN hash, so hackers focused on that instead of the harder NTLM hash. Cracking the LANMAN hash still gave them the same access to the Windows NT 4 servers and resources.

To try and patch the security hole, Microsoft released a patch to Windows NT 4 that added encryption to the SAM entries. Called a "system key", the new encryption system was used to encrypt the SAM database, but the key had to be provided every time the SAM was required. This was no problem while the machine was turned on (and the system administrator had supplied the key once), but every reboot required the key to be retrieved. Microsoft allowed the administrator to input the key each time the system rebooted, but this required a physical presence whenever the machine boots (a problem with remote systems). The patch did allow the key to be placed on a diskette, read when the system booted. However, the floppy had to be available on reboot, which again was a problem for remote systems. The alternative was to place the key in the Registry itself, allowing automatic booting and decryption of the SAM. The downside is obvious: anyone could snag a copy of the Registry and obtain the key.

Kerberos

NTLM and other challenge–response authentication systems work by having the client machine talk directly to the server, authenticating itself on the server. This works well in certain architectures, but isn't very efficient when you have many different machines that want to talk to each other at intervals without becoming overly burdened by playing a role as a server. In this case, a third machine that can authenticate both machines that need to talk together is a better model, allowing many different machines to employ a single authentication server. This is the principle of Key Distribution Centers, which led to the development of Kerberos.

Kerberos authentication is used in Windows 2000, and can be added to other operating systems. Kerberos is a key-based system, offering strong authentication capabilities. Before looking at Kerberos specifically, we should look at key-based authentication in general, and how Kerberos came to be.

Key Distribution Centers

Encryption keys are a necessary part of any encryption algorithm. The problem with encryption keys is that someone or something has to have them, and make them available as needed (with proper authorization processes to ensure the request is valid). Static encryption keys are obviously less secure than keys that change at intervals. Changing keys frequently reduces the chances of someone obtaining a key and using it for future access. To provide dynamic keys, available on demand, the banking industry developed key distribution centers (KDCs) in the 1980s. KDCs were machines that provided keys on request, to any authorized user.

The main advantages of KDCs were they could be used by any number of sites, they did not require the physical distribution of keys to many locations, and they provided constantly changing keys. Each machine has a unique master key which it uses both as an authentication key with the KDC and as a means of encrypting temporary key information passed between the machine and the KDC, as well as to other machines that need to use the same temporary key.

The figure below shows the KDC process:

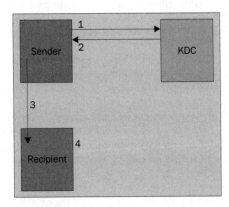

1. Whenever two machines want to communicate with each other, one obtains a random, temporary encryption key from the KDC using its master key to authenticate itself as well as to encrypt the traffic between that machine and the KDC.

2. The server sends back two temporary encryption keys, one encrypted with the master key from the originating machine and one encrypted with the master key of the other machine. These messages from the KDCs containing the temporary keys are called "tickets".

3. The machine that started the process sends the ticket with the other machine's copy of the temporary key (which is encrypted with the other machine's master key) to the other machine.

4. The receiving machine decrypts the ticket using its master key, and the two machines can then communicate using the temporary key for encryption. After the session terminates, the key is useless and a new, different key has to be obtained from the KDC for the next session. Because the KDC sends two tickets, one encrypted with each machine's master key, the KDC has to maintain a master database of all the master keys. No other machine ever gets the master key of another machine.

There is one main problem with the process: the machine that starts the process has no way of knowing if the ticket for machine B really is for that machine, or whether it is for another machine masquerading as machine B. Also, there is no ability to control access on the user level to the KDC and other machines using the KDC. To solve this problem, a protocol called Needham-Schroeder was developed to incorporate a challenge–response authentication system into KDC – the figure below illustrates this protocol:

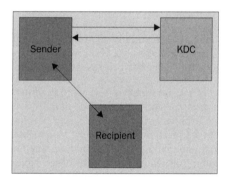

In this protocol, the following happens:

1. The initiating machine sends a request to the KDC which includes its own master key (to authenticate the initiating machine), the user ID of the user initiating the process, the destination machine's identification, and a randomly generated challenge.

2. The KDC then returns the temporary key ticket for both the initiating and receiving machines, and the challenge, encrypted with the initiating machine's master key.

3. The initiating machine decrypts the message and verifies the challenge as well as the destination machine's identification (to prevent masquerading), and then forwards the destination's temporary key and the challenge nonce to that machine.

4. The destination machine uses its master key to decrypt the message from the KDC and has the temporary key for the session. The destination machine also has the initiating user's ID in the message, which can be used to generate a challenge message, encrypted with the temporary key, and sends this back to the initiating user.

5. Upon receipt, the user's software decrypts the nonce, subtracts one from it, and encrypts it again using the temporary key for retransmission to the destination.

6. Finally, the destination machine decrypts the response, checks that one has been deducted (which would not be possible without the temporary key), and assumes all is well. The user is (in theory) verified, both machines have the temporary key, and masquerading is (again in theory) thwarted.

The theory falls apart when a hacker intercepts one of the messages flying back and forth between the destination and recipient machines. With a little brute-force attack, it is possible that a hacker could decrypt the session key. By obtaining the session key, any machine could then use the same key to continue a conversation with the destination machine even after the initiating machine terminates the session. To prevent this from occurring, timestamps were proposed in the protocols, either in addition to, or replacing, the nonce.

Kerberos KDC

Kerberos was originally developed at MIT and included the Needham-Schroeder protocol as well as the time-stamp ideas proposed by Denning and Sacco. Kerberos went through four iterations until it was finally released as Kerberos v4 in 1989. The next release, Kerberos 5, is the release used today.

The Kerberos KDC is made up of several different servers that all perform different functions. An "Authentication Server" uses a protocol similar to the Needham-Schroeder protocol to issue tickets. For a machine to be granted a ticket from an authentication server, a request known as a "KRB_AS_REQ" (Kerberos Authentication Server Request) message is sent. This message includes the name of the initiating machine, the user name, the name of the destination machine, a nonce, and a validity timespan indicating when the temporary key is to be considered valid and when it expires. The authentication server generates a random temporary key and returns it in a "KRB_AS_REP" (Kerberos Authentication Server Reply) message that includes the destination machine's ticket as well.

Next, the initiating machine constructs a "KRB_AS_REQ" message to the destination machine. This contains the encrypted ticket from the authentication server, as well as the initiating user name and a timestamp. The user name and timestamp are encrypted with the temporary key. When the destination machine receives the message, it decrypts the ticket from the authentication server and uses the temporary key contained therein to decrypt the user name and timestamp from the initiating machine. The user name in the authentication server's ticket and the user name in the message from the initiating machine must match, and the timestamp should be recent (usually around five minutes).

Kerberos goes on to address another problem with keys: storing the master key. Master keys are maintained on the KDC and used on each machine that wants to use the KDC. This means the master key resides somewhere on the machines, vulnerable to snooping by others. The obvious solution is to obtain the master key from users when they log on or need to use Kerberos, and then lose the key as quickly as possible to prevent interception. Since prompting the user for the key every time it was needed is not good from a user's point of view, another way of handling the master key is needed. The solution is to create a temporary key right away from the master key, then discard the master key. The temporary key (called a "session key") is then used for all interactions with the KDC.

To handle the session keys, another server is employed by Kerberos. This is called the "ticket-granting server" and it accepts "ticket-granting tickets". When a user logs into a machine, the master key is used to contact the authentication server, which issues a ticket-granting ticket back using the master key for encryption. After decrypting the reply, the master key is discarded. Then, the ticket-granting ticket is used to connect to the ticket-granting server for every service the machine needs access to. Any time the user needs a new service, the temporary ticket is used with the ticket-granting server, until the user logs off at which point the temporary ticket is invalid.

The process for these ticket-granting tickets is a variation on the Kerberos messages you just saw. When the user sends the request to the authentication server he or she receives back the temporary session key in a ticket-granting ticket format. To connect to the ticket-granting server, a new message called the "KRB_TGS_REQ" (Kerberos Ticket-Granting Server Request) is used. This contains the user name and timestamp, the ticket-granting ticket, a validity period, a nonce, and the destination name. The ticket-granting server decrypts the message, extracts the temporary key, decrypts the ticketing key with that temporary key, and checks the validity component. The ticket-granting server then creates a session key that is sent back to the initiating machine along with a copy encrypted for the destination machine in a "KRB_TGS_REP" message.

The focus so far has been authenticating the user. Kerberos includes routines to authenticate machines, as well. The Kerberos protocols you've seen so far do not maintain a unique key on each machine, so authentication is on the user level. This is good, because access to resources is usually on a user, not a machine, basis. It also allows users to log on from any machine and complete their tasks. The approach does have its flaws, though, especially in locations where individual PCs or workstations are assigned to single users. Local files on those machines will be specific to the machine, so there's no authentication to provide verification that the user of a particular machine is allowed to access those files. To restrict access to local resources, preauthentication (or local authentication, to use Windows NT terms) is required.

Preauthentication was added to Kerberos 5 to permit authentication of users or machines sending requests to a KDC, instead of relying on the KDC to authenticate the source. With preauthentication, a workstation will request the user's master key (password) before making any attempt to connect with the KDC. (This is different from before, where the KDC can send a reply to a request before asking for the master key.) With preauthentication, the initial request to the KDC is slightly different as the master key can be used to encrypt the request, which includes a timestamp. The server receives these requests and checks its internal database to see if preauthentication is required. If so, the KDC uses the master key to decrypt the request, checks the timestamp for currency, then completes the request.

Kerberos 5 also added two other capabilities: forwardable and proxiable tickets. A forwardable ticket means that a workstation can request a ticket-granting ticket tied to another network (called "realms" in Kerberos terminology). Proxiable tickets allow a workstation to request tickets valid on machines on another network. Kerberos can authenticate users on other networks, by having KDC communicate with KDC using so-called referral tickets.

Windows 2000 and Kerberos

Windows 2000 replaced the NTLM authentication methods with Kerberos methods. All requests for files and directories on remote machines under Windows 2000 involve tickets. When you log on to a Windows 2000 server or workstation, a ticket-granting ticket is obtained from the server, which stores all the master keys in the Active Directory.

There are some differences between Kerberos and Windows 2000's implementation, although Microsoft claims complete interoperability according to the Kerberos standards. This is important to allow non-Windows machines to integrate with Windows 2000 machines. (Windows 2000 includes backwards-compatible support for both LANMAN and NTLM protocols, but these give up the advantages of the Kerberos protocols.) Windows 2000 treats each machine as an individual entity, storing master keys for that machine (as well as any logged-in users' master keys) on the system.

The way Windows 2000 institutes Kerberos in addition to the usual Windows logon is with a three-step process:

1. The process starts with the Winlogon window collecting the user's login and password, which it passes to the Local Security Authority (LSA).

2. The LSA converts the password into a Kerberos master key, then passes the user name and hashed master key to the Security Support Provider (SSP).

3. The SSP communicates with the Kerberos servers and tries to get a ticket-granting ticket from a server using preauthenticated messages created by the user's master key. (If there is no Kerberos server available, the SSP defaults to the NTLM protocol.)

.NET Security and Windows

Microsoft considered security an essential component of the .NET Framework and included a complex security mechanism. For most applications, the security available in the .NET Framework is overkill: most developers will find the simpler embedded routines are all they really need.

The .NET Framework's security is composed of the following namespaces:

❑ `System.Security` – the embedded security structure for .NET

❑ `System.Security.Cryptography` – includes three separate namespaces, providing cryptographic and authentication services

❑ `System.Security.Permissions` – classes to control access to resources

❑ `System.Security.Policy` – code groups and membership conditions used by CLR to enforce security policy

❑ `System.Security.Principal` – classes representing a program's security context

Of these namespaces, the four that are not part of `System.Security.Cryptography` are the most widely used by developers. Before we look at the use of the namespaces, though, we should see how the .NET security apparatus interacts with the Windows security features discussed earlier in this chapter.

When a .NET application tries to access a resource such as a file or directory, the CLR checks the security policy in place on the executing computer. Windows NT allows security policies to be implemented on a user-by-user basis (with each user's permissions and rights specified in detail as to allowed or disallowed actions), or on a machine-by-machine basis. The .NET Framework uses a security policy called Code Access Security (CAS), which is a hierarchical extensible model, composed of "code groups". Code groups can be set up by many criteria such as site names, publisher or developer names, network zone names, and so on. There are many different criteria that can be established for code groups and each code group has a set of permissions associated with it. The allowable code group criteria are:

- ❑ Application directory – the home directory of the application

- ❑ Cryptographic hash – the hash used in the encryption

- ❑ Custom – an application-defined condition

- ❑ File – file access

- ❑ Net – network identification for the application's home network

- ❑ Software publisher – publisher's Authenticode signature

- ❑ Strong name – the .NET strong name

- ❑ URL – URL of the code

- ❑ Web site – web site of the code

- ❑ Zone – zone of the code

.NET Resource Security

Microsoft designed the .NET Framework security to work with the existing security features of Microsoft's Windows operating systems, especially Windows 2000 and Windows NT. The Common Language Runtime of .NET applications works with Windows NT's users and groups to provide controlled access to resources. Any applications written to .NET standards can specify the types of access they require, and then it is up to the operating system's security policy to decide whether to grant those permissions. For access to resources, there are a number of classes involved, all derived from the `System.Security.CodeAccessPermission` base class. The subclasses, usually called "code access permission classes" are:

Class	Description
DirectoryServicesPermission	Gives access to `System.DirectoryServices` classes
DnsPermission	Gives access to DNS
EnvironmentPermission	Gives access to environment variables
EventLogPermission	Gives access to the Event log
FileDialogPermission	Gives access to files selected in the File Open dialog
FileIOPermission	Gives access to files in read, write, and append modes
IsolatedStorageFilepermission	Gives access to virtual file systems
IsolatedStoragePermission	Gives access to storage allocated to specific users
MessageQueuePermission	Gives access to Messaging Service
OleDbPermission	Gives access to databases using OLE DB

Table continued on following page

Class	Description
PerformanceCounterPermission	Gives access to performance counters
PrintingPermission	Gives access to printers
ReflectionPermission	Gives access to run time type information
RegistryPermission	Gives access to the Registry
SecurityPermission	Gives access to execute code, and set permissions and rights
ServiceControllerPermission	Gives access to Windows services
SocketPermission	Gives access to sockets
SqlClientPermission	Gives access to SQL databases
UIPermission	Gives access to UI features (dialogs, clipboard, etc.)
WebPermission	Gives access to web connections

The `System.Security.CodeAccessPermission` base class also includes several methods that are used to implement security. The methods are:

Method	Description
Assert()	Asserts that the code can access the resource
Copy()	Creates a copy of the object
Demand()	Determines whether all callers have been granted permission
Deny()	Denies access to callers higher in the stack
FromXml()	Reconstructs a permission object from XML code
Intersect()	Creates a permission from the intersection of two other permission objects
IsSubsetOf()	Determines whether one permission object is a subset of another object
PermitOnly()	Restricts permissions to callers higher in the stack
RevertAll()	Static – revokes all permission overrides
RevertAssert()	Static – revokes each Assert
RevertDeny()	Static – revokes each Deny
RevertPermitOnly()	Static – revokes each PermitOnly
ToString()	Converts the permission object to a string
ToXml()	Converts the permission object to XML
Union()	Creates a permission from the union of two other permission objects

The Assert(), Demand(), and Deny() methods are used to implement run-time checking of permissions in code. To handle combinations of two permissions, you can use either the Intersect() or Union() methods. Here's a simple example of code showing these methods in use to allow access to the directory c:\Networking\Authentication\codetemp:

```
using System;
using System.Security;
using System.Security.Permissions;

public class FileIOPDemo
{
    public static void Main(String[] args)
    {
        FileIOPermission myPerm = new
                    FileIOPermission(FileIOPermissionAccess.AllAccess,
                            @"c:\Networking\Authentication\codetemp");
        SecurityElement mySec = myPerm.ToXml();
        Console.WriteLine(mySec.ToString());
    }
}
```

The FileIOPermission object is used to create an object with all access to the target directory, and the ToXml() call is used to return the SecurityElement, which is converted to a string and written out to the console.

In your code, you can use the System.Security.CodeAccessPermission methods to request access to a resource. The permissions that are controlled by FileIOPermissionAccess are:

❑   AllAccess – full access to file or directory

❑   Append – append permission for file or directory

❑   NoAccess – no access to file or directory

❑   PathDiscovery – information about the path

❑   Read – read access to file or directory

❑   Write – write access to file or directory

These permissions can be used as flags to a FileIOPermissionAccess variable. For example, you can write code to gain read access to the file c:\codetemp\data.dat like this:

```
using System;
using System.Security;
using System.Security.Permissions;

public class FileIOPDemo2
{
    public static void Main(String[] args)
    {
        FileIOPermissionAccess myPermsAcc  = FileIOPermissionAccess.Read;
        FileIOPermission myPerm = new FileIOPermission(myPermsAcc,
```

```
                                    @"c:\Networking\Authentication\data.dat ");
      try
      {
          myPerm.Demand();
      }
      catch (SecurityException res)
      {
          Console.WriteLine("Sorry, no access.");
      }
   }
}
```

Code similar to this is used for the `Deny()` and `Assert()` methods. To deny access to a resource to prevent overwriting (or for some other reason), you can override default permissions to deny access such as this code that prevents access to the file `c:\codetemp\data.dat`:

```
PermissionSet myPerm = new PermissionSet(PermissionState.None);

myPerm.AddPermission(new FileIOPermission(FileIOPermissionAccess.AllAccess,
                        @"c:\Networking\Authentication\data.dat ");;

myPerm.Deny();
```

To remove the `Deny` permission you can use static the `RevertDeny()` method:

```
CodeAccessPermission.RevertDeny()
```

A second set of classes derived from the `System.Security.CodeAccessPermission` base class is the "identity permission classes". These classes involve characteristics of an application such as its digital signatures, storage location, and more. When executing, the CLR uses these characteristics to grant identity permissions. The classes involved in identity permissions are:

❑ `PublisherIdentityPermission` – the publisher's digital signature

❑ `SiteIdentityPermission` – the site containing the application

❑ `StrongNameIdentityPermission` – the strong name (see below)

❑ `URLIdentityPermission` – the originating URL

❑ `ZoneIdentityPermission` – the originating security zone

Normally, the application name, version number, and some additional information defining the local machine are enough to identify applications, but this can be insufficient for security purposes. The concept of a strong name was introduced to include all this basic information as well as a public encryption key and a digital signature. Because the process of creating a strong key uses checksums, tampering with the contents of the application will be detectable. Also, the use of the private key ensures that masquerading as a particular machine is avoided.

In your applications you can use the `System.Security.Permissions` namespace with classes and objects from `System.Net`. For example, if you want to check access permissions to a file, the `FileIOPermission` class has to be called for every access performed (not just the first one). Any failure of a call will result in a `SecurityException` being thrown.

.NET Role-based Security

Role-based security determines whether a user executing a .NET application has a particular role and can also help determine the user's identity. All of .NET's role-based security is contained in the `PrincipalPermission` class. You can use this class by creating an object from the class and calling its `Demand()` method. If users and roles don't match those contained in the object, a `SecurityException` is generated and the `Demand()` method fails.

You can also perform declarative security checks by adding attributes that provide the uses and roles for the application. A failure to match the user executing the code will cause an application failure.

System.Net.IAuthenticationModule

The `System.Net.IAuthenticationModule` is used to set the properties and method use to handle client authentication in .NET applications. The property `System.Net.IAuthenticationModule.AuthenticationType` is a case-insensitive string that indicates the protocol implemented by the module. These string values are reserved for use by modules implementing the indicated protocols:

- ❑ `Basic` – basic authentication (defined by IETF RFC 2617)
- ❑ `Digest` – digest authentication (defined by IETF RFC 2617)
- ❑ `Kerberos` – Kerberos authentication (defined by IETF RFC 1510)

A second property is `IAuthenticationModule.CanPreAuthenticate`, which indicates whether pre-authentication is possible or not for the code.

The two methods in `System.Net.IAuthenticationModule` are:

- ❑ `IAuthenticationModule.Authenticate()` – returns an instance of the `Authorization` class that provides a response to an authentication challenge
- ❑ `IAuthenticationModule.PreAuthenticate()` – returns an instance of the `Authorization` class containing client authentication information

Anything that implements `System.Net.IAuthenticationModule` is called an authentication module. Each authentication module registered with the authentication manager is required to have a unique `System.Net.IAuthenticationModule.AuthenticationType`. An authentication module is registered with the authentication manager by calling the `System.Net.AuthenticationManager.Register()` method, passing your authentication module. If the authentication manager receives an authentication request, registered authentication modules are given the opportunity to handle the authentication in their own `System.Net.IAuthenticationModule.Authenticate()` method. The authentication manager searches for an authentication module by invoking the `System.Net.IAuthenticationModule.Authenticate()` or `System.Net.IAuthenticationModule.PreAuthenticate()` method of each registered module, in the order it was registered. Once a module returns an `Authorization` instance (which indicates it can handle the authentication) the authentication manager terminates the search.

443

If a client wishes to avoid waiting for the server to request authentication, it can request pre-authentication information with a request using the
`System.Net.IAuthenticationModule.CanPreAuthenticate` property of a registered module. If this module returns a value of `true` the modules are given the opportunity to provide the pre-authentication information.

Impersonation

One final aspect we should consider is impersonation (which is disabled by default). Impersonation is a useful trick when you don't want to code a lot of authentication code into a .NET application, simply letting Windows perform all the tasks for you. On the other hand, if you need to write a specific authentication table yourself, you do not need impersonation.

Impersonation is when a .NET application executes using the client's authenticated identity. Before you do a double take and decide this is what normally happens, a quick explanation is useful. For example, when a user requesting an ASP.NET page is authenticated by IIS, IIS passes the "local machine" identity back to the application. In a normal configuration, the "local machine" identity has full access to all directories and files, leaving authorization for access to other mechanisms (such as URL authorization). With impersonation turned on, the .NET application takes on the actual user's identity instead of the one passed back by IIS. For example, if the user "tparker" tries to access a resource, IIS will normally authenticate the user and pass back "local machine" as the identity to use in the .NET application. With impersonation turned on, the identity "tparker" is used instead. The advantage to this technique is that when impersonating a specific user, ACLs can be used to restrict access (which isn't possible with "local machine" since it normally has full access).

Another way of thinking of impersonation is this: with impersonation turned off and a user properly authenticated by IIS, when an ASP.NET application tries to access a directory, Windows thinks that the "local machine" user is trying to access the directory and grants access on that basis. With impersonation turned on, the .NET application is treated as though it is the user, so Windows thinks the user is trying to access the resource and the ACLs can be checked normally for permission. (The exception to using the impersonated identity is for configuration information: even when impersonating a user, an application will use the "local machine" identity to read configuration files otherwise the application could lock up.)

In ASP.NET to turn on impersonation you add a new line to the `web.config` file using the identity tag:

```
<configuration>
   <system.web>
      <identity impersonate="true" />
   </system.web>
</configuration>
```

A slight twist is that you can tell ASP.NET applications to always use a specific user identity when impersonating. To do this, you need to specify the user name and password (used for authentication) on the identity line:

```
<configuration>
   <system.web>
      <identity impersonate="true" username="tparker" password="secret" />
   </system.web>
</configuration>
```

Why bother with impersonating a single user? The reason is simply because it can save a lot of time setting ACLs on a web site for each user or group.

Summary

In this chapter you've seen the way Windows can handle authentication of users, as well as authorizations to access resources. We looked at:

- ❑   LANMAN (Microsoft's LAN Manager)
- ❑   NTLM (Windows NT LAN Manager)
- ❑   Kerberos.

We looked at .NET resource and role-based security, and took a glimpse at `System.Net.IAuthenticationModule`.

Index

A Guide to the Index

The index is arranged hierarchically, in alphabetical order, with symbols preceding the letter A. Most second-level entries and many third-level entries also occur as first-level entries. This is to ensure that users will find the information they require however they choose to search for it.

P